# Love.Life.™

A Handbook for Being Well Loved,
Happy & Healthy

Lisa A. Lundy

www.LisaALundy.com

Copyright © 2020 by Lisa A. Lundy

First Printing
Published by Lisa A. Lundy
All rights reserved. No part of this book may be reprinted or reproduced in any manner whatsoever without written permission.
For information contact: Lisa A. Lundy,
19 Colonnade Way, Suite 117, MB# 227, State College, PA 16803

# CONTENTS

| | |
|---|---|
| *Important Note to Readers* | vii |
| *Acknowledgments* | ix |
| **INTRODUCTION** | 1 |
| Love.Life. | 7 |
| **OBSTACLES & ROADBLOCKS TO BEING WELL LOVED** | 12 |
| Why Are You Not Well Loved | 12 |
| **LOVE & HAPPINESS** | 19 |
| Living Life with Your Whole Heart | 19 |
| Level Up Your Happiness | 24 |
| Love & Miracles – How to Get More Love & Miracles in Your Life | 28 |
| How to Generate Your Own Happiness & Why It's THE Skill to Learn this Year | 36 |
| LOVE Involves Trust: Why It's Time to Deal with Your Trust Issues | 40 |
| The Power & Magic of Vulnerability: Top 10 Ways You Can Start Increasing Your Ability to be Vulnerable | 49 |
| LOVE in the Midst of Chaos – And, Yes I love you! | 59 |
| The Miracles of Gratitude | 65 |
| The Road to Happiness Starts Here | 71 |
| September Theme: Building a Base for Happiness | 74 |
| October Theme: Healing Your Heart | 78 |
| **PERSONAL GROWTH & DEVELOPMENT** | 87 |
| Road Map for Creating a Life that YOU LOVE | 87 |
| What Tripping Over the Truth Looks Like in Real Life- Ker splat | 92 |
| Top 45 Ways that Personal Growth & Development Will Help You Have a Life You Love | 96 |
| Top 45 Reasons Why Growth & Development Will Help You Have a Life You Love | 99 |

| | |
|---|---|
| Self-Mastery, Self-Motivation, & Self-Care: The Holy Grail of Happiness & Joy | 107 |
| August Theme: Awake & Aware | 115 |
| **EMPOWERING PRACTICES, SKILLS, HABITS, ATTITUDES & BELIEFS** | 122 |
| LOVE the TIME of YOUR Life | 122 |
| The LOVE and POWER of Completion | 129 |
| The Sheer Joy and Magic of Integrity | 135 |
| 10 Ways to Get Yourself Motivated for a Happier Life | 139 |
| Top 35 Ways that Making a List Will Help You Have a Life You LOVE | 144 |
| Top 35 Ways Making A List Will Benefit You | 148 |
| 21 Reasons Why Making Friends Will Help You LOVE Your Life & 17 Ways to Make New Friends | 155 |
| Here's How to Have the Best New Year of Your Life | 162 |
| How Hobbies Can Help You Love Your Life and the Top 23 Reasons You Should Hobby Up Now | 169 |
| Self-Motivation: The Nuts & Bolts of Leveling Up with a Reward System | 174 |
| Do You Have these 8 Things That Will Help You Flourish in Life Regardless of What Happens? Hint: It's not too late to get them! | 180 |
| Feel Better Now with Self-Care | 188 |
| Pandemic Sleeping Tips | 196 |
| The Healing Nature of Self-Compassion | 203 |
| The Healing Nature of Assertiveness | 211 |
| **NUTRITION, HEALTH & GENERAL WELLNESS** | 220 |
| 8 Ways to Improve Your Health & Look Younger | 220 |
| The Ultimate Consumer Guide to Nutrition, Why It Matters & How It Could Save or Change your Life | 226 |
| Stress Kills Your Brain Cells – Here's 19 Strategies to Prevent that and help you To Be Happy & Healthy | 235 |
| **DEALING WITH EMOTIONS & PROBLEMS** | 246 |
| Top 17 Benefits to High Emotional Intelligence and the 29 Traits of People Who Have It | 246 |

| | |
|---|---|
| Dealing with Overwhelm: How to Put an End to Feeling Overwhelmed with Life Once and For All Plus 29 Tips to Help You in the Meantime | 257 |
| How to Be Happy When You Are Suffering or Life is Bad | 270 |
| Dealing with Depression – 43 Tips to Help You Stave Off Depression | 279 |
| Worry & Fear Hurt Your Health: 15 Tips to Overpower Fear & Worry & Start Taking Risks | 289 |
| Is Low Self-Esteem Stealing Love, Joy & Happiness from Your Life? Top 29 Tips For Boosting Self-Esteem Like a Boss | 301 |
| Deep Dive into Emotional Pain and How to Use It to Your Advantage | 310 |
| Here's How to Ditch Loneliness and Isolation for Good | 323 |
| How Anger Can Help You Heal | 331 |
| Healing from Dysfunctional & Toxic Families and People | 343 |
| CORONAVIRUS & PANDEMIC | 354 |
| The Juicy Good Parts of the Coronavirus PLUS the Top 52 Things You Can Do to Make This a Good Thing In Your Life Now | 354 |
| Disaster Relief: How to "Flip the Switch" on Your Emotions and Feel Better Now! | 366 |
| The ONE Coronavirus Article That Could Change Your Life for the Better FOREVER | 376 |
| 19 Potential GIFTS of the Pandemic & the Top 29 Tips to Help You Get Through It | 386 |
| The Coronavirus Tipping Point: Which Way Will You Tip? | 394 |
| The Do's and Don'ts of Handling Challenging Times | 399 |
| Getting Unstuck – Pandemic Style | 405 |
| MISCELLANEOUS | 416 |
| Why It IS Okay to be Mad at God and What to Do If You Are Mad at HIM | 416 |
| FORCED Home Schooling: Short Cuts to Better Results | 420 |

| | |
|---|---|
| A Glimpse into My Observations of the World at Age 22 | 428 |
| Call to Action | 441 |
| *About Lisa Lundy: B.S., D.T.M.* | 443 |
| *Blog Posts – Title – Date – Content* | 445 |
| *Notes* | 449 |

# IMPORTANT NOTE TO READERS

The author of this book is not a medical physician, a medical practitioner or a therapist. Readers should seek personal medical evaluations and advice from qualified, licensed health care professionals. The author and publisher of this book recommend that you consult with your primary health care provider for any and all medical advice. The author and publisher of this book disclaim any liability directly or indirectly arising from the use of this book and any suggestions contained in this book.

### Suicide Warning/Mental Health Waiver

If you have any thoughts of suicide or harming yourself or others please call the National Suicide Prevention Lifeline at 1-800-273-8255 or call 911 immediately. Please call someone, tell someone or post it on social media and ask for help right now! We have more people suffering from depression, anxiety, and negative emotions than ever before, which means that you are in good company. I am asking that you take a specific action if you are feeling suicidal or that harming yourself because your life matters more than you realize and because there is help available to you.

# ACKNOWLEDGMENTS

*To my three living children: Luke, Noah & Anne for giving me the gift of being your Mom,
and to Christina – deeply loved and missed;
To my family and friends who have loved me and helped me become the person I am;
To past managers, co-workers and neighbors for your love and support;
To Ron DiCerbo, Esquire and George McAndrews, Esquire at McAndrews Held & Malloy
For their generosity and support since 2004;
To George McAndrews, Esquire for saving the field of chiropractic through your Heroic legal efforts and tenacity.*

*This book is dedicated to each person on the planet
that you may be well loved in your life,
learn how to be happy and
develop the skills and abilities
to be very functional in life no matter
what challenges you face.
Love.Life.* ™

# INTRODUCTION

It is my greatest hope that you already feel well loved, yet I am deeply aware that it is the one thing that many people don't feel – as though they have been well loved, which breaks my heart. I made a YouTube video called "Be Well Loved" and after I made that video I realized that this is the one thing that is missing for many people of all ages in life. It is the one thing that a majority of people would say is absent from their life – feeling as though they have been well loved in their life. I hope that you will make this your number one goal in life. You have this one life to live. How are you living it? What do you want from life? I am suggesting firmly that being well loved should be your primary goal in life because it is so miraculous.

Even if you don't feel well loved right now, you can still have that in your life. It's not too late regardless of your current age or status in life. The reality is that you can change your life so that you ARE well loved. Just because you might not feel well loved in this given moment in time, that does not dictate your future. You have the option of saying how your future will go. You can create your future. You can take the actions necessary to be well loved. You can learn the skills, habits, practices and attitudes that will allow you to be well loved. This book will show you the path and access to a life where you are well loved if you are open to that if you are willing to look inward at yourself and make the necessary changes.

In the next chapter I discuss the obstacles that block people from love and being well loved. There are so many things that stop people from being well loved and they can all be remedied. You are not stuck in this life without love or being well loved. Love is worth it. Love is the best thing ever and you want to have that in your life. And I am not just speaking about romantic love. I am talking about being loved by many people and knowing that you are loved, feeling that you are loved. Knowing deep in your heart that you are well loved. This is what is possible for you out of the contents of my book coupled with you doing the work involved.

Let me digress for a moment to address trying to be perfect or perfectionism. I am not a fan of trying to be perfect or perfectionism in any form. It is my opinion that perfectionism is exhausting. I am a huge proponent of being authentic and real. To that end, this book is the compilation of my blog posts – unedited. What that means is that for a small percentage of you who are grammar aficionados or who otherwise demand perfection in writing, this book might be irritating for you. Sometime ago, I did have someone edit one of my blog posts for grammar and sentence structure and what I ended up with was not authentic or real in any capacity and in a few instances changed the intention of my point, so I powerfully chose not to continue with that process.

What I learned from the chapters in my first book, *The Super Allergy Girl™ Allergy & Celiac Cookbook*, was that the vast majority of people loved the way that I wrote because for them, the readers, it felt like I was talking to them. In many ways, that is exactly how I write, which is not how grammar and sentence structure works in a professional sense. Prior to the publication of this book I faced a choice as to whether or not to have each and every word and sentence scrutinized and "made perfect" in a grammar and sentence construction form. I have chosen not to do that and I beg your forgiveness if you are one of those people who demands that level of perfection. I have chosen to write just as if I were speaking to you because I am speaking to you and hopefully in a way to motivate you to seize the day and your life and begin living it in a way that gives you great love and happiness.

It is my greatest desire for you and for everyone to be well loved, happy, healthy and fully functional in life. This book deals with the habits, practices, attitudes and beliefs and skills that it takes to be happy, very functional in life and to be well loved. You have to be able to trust people if you want to be deeply connected to people. You have to be able to let love in and give love. You have to be able to heal from past wounds, hurts, traumas and other difficulties to be freed up and happy.

My promise to you is that if you actually engage in the steps I have outlined in this book, which includes taking on new habits and practices, learning new skills and having empowering attitudes and beliefs that you will:

- Become much happier
- Become significantly healthier
- Become able to deal with your emotions and control them better
- Become much more functional in life
- Be better able to handle hardships in life
- Be less stressed
- Have more friends
- Have more social connections
- Be freed up from anxiety and depression
- Feel in control of your life
- Be able to be your authentic and real self without apology
- Be able to be a better friend, co-worker, sibling, parent, aunt, uncle, etc.
- Be clearer in your thinking

I am completely confident that if you are willing to do the work – to grow yourself and develop yourself – that you can absolutely obtain those promises listed above. Read them again. Wouldn't you like to have all of that in your life? Of course, you would want that if you believed that it was possible. I am telling you from all of the work that I have done in coaching people over many decades that it is definitely possible.

Simply reading this book is not going to be enough. You are going to have to take steps and get into action to change your life, which means learning new skills, attitudes, habits and practices. It might mean ditching some habits or attitudes or beliefs that simply are not serving you. It means that you open your eyes and your heart to what is stopping you from having an amazing life. Right now. Why would you wait?

Well, let me be frank with you – there are people who are more committed to suffering and having a bad life (or being the victim). Yes, there are those kinds of people and they will not change their attitudes, beliefs, or the way that they live life. They are simply unwilling to change. There are more people in my experience who are willing to change and who do actually want a better life for themselves. They just don't know how to get there. This book is for those people who are willing to do something to have a better life. It is not for people who just want to whine and complain about how terrible their life is.

Even if you have experienced tremendous hardship and/or suffering up to this point, it is not too late to get on the road to growth and development. Growth and development is amazing. Please join me because I want you to be well loved. And that starts with you.

I am going to leave you with something that I wrote back in college for a senior send-off when I was about 22 years old. I probably wouldn't even have this now except that my Mom could see the wisdom in this and saved it for me.

*Love.Life.*

## If I Could Give You Anything, I'd give you...

1. The gift of being able to say *"I'm sorry"* even when it's NOT your fault.
2. The ability to live life to the fullest – no holds barred!
3. The gift of optimism – or looking at life on the bright side.
4. The knowledge that with God, you are never alone in this world.
5. The ability to pick good friends and enjoy their friendship.
6. The gift of being able to say *"I was wrong."*
7. The wisdom to know when to stay and fight and when to cut your losses and leave.
8. The comfort of knowing that in the worst of times, better days are ahead.
9. The gift of being able to make mistakes in life, and the even bigger gift of being able to admit it when you do make a mistake.
10. The gift of enjoying the little things in life like sunshine on a spring day or the bright smile of a total stranger.
11. The ability to laugh at yourself.
12. The gift of compassion for other people and their suffering.
13. The ability to treat all human beings with dignity and respect no matter what their sex, race, religion, age, or disability.
14. The gift of appreciating how hard your parents worked to provide for you regardless of how well or how poorly they did.
15. The gift of always being able to play and have fun in life.
16. The belief that whenever there is a WILL, there is a WAY.
17. The capacity to push yourself to your outermost limits.
18. The gift of self-control.
19. The knowledge that where ever you go, the Lord is with you always.
20. The gift of many interests and hobbies that give you joy.
21. The realization that the best things in life are free...a smile, a hug, or a complement on a job well done.

22. The ability to express yourself freely.
23. The gift of knowing that no matter how big your problems are, somebody out there is worse off and has bigger problems than you do. (If you doubt this one, just read the newspapers for one week.)
24. The knowledge that no amount of money can bring you happiness.
25. The ability to appreciate good advice when it is given.
26. The ability to recognize evil when it presents itself.
27. The wisdom of knowing that no matter what you do there will always be at least one person who doesn't like you.
28. The belief that you can attain any goal that you set for yourself.
29. The ability to see yourself as other people see you.
30. The gift of enjoying being a parent if you choose to become one.
31. The wisdom not to let fears run your life.
32. The ability to find lasting happiness from God and from within yourself and not from life's circumstances.
33. A healthy respect for life.
34. The skill of time management for that skill provides infinite freedom.
35. The ability to recognize negative thoughts when you have them, AND to replace them with more empowering, positive thoughts.
36. The wisdom and ability to learn from other people's mistakes.
37. The ability to cry when you feel like it.
38. The gift of strong convictions.
39. The knowledge that if you work hard and are willing to persevere, you can attain any dream you can envision.
40. The ability to keep your promises and your word.

© 1983 Lisa A. Lundy

**Love.Life.**

September 4, 2019

I chose the name of my blog to be Love.Life. with intentionality. First and foremost, I LOVE the word Love and everything about Love. I love so many people, groups, organizations, places and things. I am a fan of love and doing all things with great love. Love is the most natural expression of who I am in the world. To me love IS what life is about. For me, Love is what makes life meaningful, colorful and joyful. It is one of my favorite things – loving people, loving moments with people, feeling love, giving love, receiving love. Just love. The point of my blog is to help my readers get back to love, to help you love more, feel love, have love and in particular love your life.

Consider the feelings and emotions that love carries with it – feeling loved, cared for, safe, happy, peaceful, contented, hopeful, joyous, excited, and so much more. There are tons of love songs and songs about love, books on love, movies about love stories, it is a very pervasive subject in our society. What's not to like about love? Well, the downside of opening your heart to love is being rejected, not being treated well, failing in relationships, getting hurt or your heart broken to name a few of the top risks. Love even in platonic friendships can be risky because even friends can use or exploit you. To be able to love and love freely and deeply carries risk with it. That is a fact of life.

When children are very young, unless they are neglected, abandoned, or treated badly, they are just full of love, openness, curiosity and wonder. As children grow up long before adulthood, they most often experience some hurt, embarrassment, shame, and rejection and as a result they begin to shut down or close off their heart. To be an adult and have your heart wide open, to live life full of curiosity and wonder, to risk failing, to give love openly despite the inherent risks is a lovely way to live life. It is a powerful way to live life. It is how I live my life. Is it how you are living your life?

We have all been hurt in life. Some of us more than others. Many of us have experienced serious trauma, betrayals, exploitation, and worse. And that leaves many people jaded, with trust issues, and more than a little wary of other people. There is a lot of sadness, loneliness, and isolation in our world today. Bad things happen to people. Life is messy. Life is hard. Life can be excruciatingly painful. And then there's your reaction to life.

By the Grace of God, and I do mean that literally not figuratively, I have not only survived deep difficulties and traumas, but I have come out the other side with my heart intact, able to feel love, be loving, and still have my childlike wonder and excitement about life. While I simply am not able to discuss all of the difficulties and traumas in a public forum, suffice to say that I was told that I would be scarred for life and that I would not come out of it "okay".

Hence, I promptly went into psychotherapy to figure out what the damage was, if I had any therapy issues, and get tested for PTSD (Post Traumatic Stress Disorder), Dissociative Disorder (or something like that), etc. Imagine my surprise, no shock, when the therapist said early on that I was "the polar opposite of a person who walks through the doors of the practice for therapy". I was very surprised to learn that my religious beliefs were one of my strongest coping mechanisms! I didn't know that religion or a strong belief in God could be a way to cope with life. I was released from therapy in short order after the PTSD and Dissociative testing came back negative and it was determined that while I am still in a trauma, that I have the skills and abilities to deal with it. It is a miracle that I have not only survived the difficulties, but have come out a better person because of it. It is a testament to God and God's Love for me that I have made it through so many hardships and can be happy, loving, and full of energy and a zest for living.

I make no bones about the fact that I am a better person for what I have been through AND I would never wish it on anyone else. Like flowing water softens a sharp rock, going through periods of suffering can make you more loving, more compassionate, more generous, more understanding. The operative word here is CAN.

For many people weathering life's difficulties does not make them become better people. It hardens them or makes them suspicious or jaded. I want to take you on a journey of love and healing where you can heal yourself from your past and whatever happened to you and open yourself to love and having love in your life.

If you believe that you can move from point A, which we will call tolerating life or getting through the day, to point B, which we will call engaged and loving your life, then you will be able to take the actions and make the changes to move yourself from point A to point B. Equally as important if you believe that you cannot change your life – you will not be able to. I am speaking about your belief system and what your beliefs are. The beliefs that you have in either your conscious, subconscious or unconscious mind are running your life whether you realize it or not. How your mind works, in particular the conscious, subconscious and unconscious mind will be the subject of a future post because that is too much ground to cover in this post. The bottom line is you can only get what you believe you can have or what you believe that you deserve.

For some of you, particularly if you have low self-esteem (another topic of a future blog post), to begin to say or think that you deserve to have love, to be loved, or to have a life that you love is a leap that you might not be able or willing to take. And, I am asking you to do that anyway. Religion is all about faith! Faith is defined as either complete trust or confidence in someone or something or strong belief in God or in the doctrine of a religion, based on spiritual apprehension rather than proof. I am asking you to be open to changing your life for the better because that is why I am here. That is what my blog is for. It's for you.

And quite frankly, it's your life. If you are happy with it the way it is, then you don't need to do a thing. And even if you are unhappy with your life, you can go on being unhappy with your life. It is, after all, your life. It is my assertion that we either grow and develop through a trauma, bad event, accident, health issue, natural disaster, or other unplanned situation OR we grow and develop by choice. Sometimes it happens both ways. In either case, in this instance I am asking you to take on your own growth and development in an intentional manner for the purpose of ramping up your life to have more love, more fun, more freedom and all the benefits that Love has to offer.

So, here's how it is going to go – or at least this is the plan at this moment in time. I will be taking you on a journey about love and life with the stated intention to help you move to a point where your life is full of love and you love your life. On a weekly basis I will be posting blogs on a wide variety of topics that all relate in some way to loving life. My blog posts will cover a wide variety of topics including self-awareness, emotional quotient, empowerment and time management techniques, books that I love, a good bit on health because it is difficult to love your life if you don't feel well, and so much more (more details in the About Me post). I know it can be scary, uncomfortable, and disconcerting to begin this process, but I promise you that it is going to be well worth it. I would assert that there is nothing more valuable that you could be using your free time or your energy for.

A few points worth mentioning. I am not into perfectionism at all. Therefore, there will be typos, grammatical errors, improper sentence construction, and likely some points that do not come across well or cause confusion. And you are welcome to point out all of my imperfections in the comment section. I will not be upset. There will be homework assignments in some posts for those of you who are committed and dedicated to having your life go a different way than the trajectory that it is presently on. And they will not be hard assignments, but the ones that I feel are necessary for you to create love, happiness, joy and contentment in your life. For you to love life. I request that you post any questions or just comments on this blog in the comment section because that is the best way for you to get a response.

I want you to join me on a delicious and FUN ride of self-discovery where you take back your power and create a life that you love. A life where you can feel the full complement of emotions and know how to feel all of what life has to offer both the good stuff and the not so happy stuff. It is powerful to be able to grieve sadness. Being able to grieve a loss is part of the process that allows you to get complete and create something new. And grieving is not something that we in society is very good at or something that we talk about much. And sometimes we in society are just not so good at expressing love either.

Point of order: If you happen to know some of the hardships that I have faced in the last few decades, please do not include that in your comments as there are very serious reasons why I am not addressing some things that have happened to me.

Thank you for visiting my blog! Hopefully you will be able to sign up to receive any new posts by email. I leave you with my love for you even though I might not know you. I leave you with my most heartfelt desire that you have a life that you love. I hope you will play with me in creating something new for yourself!

# OBSTACLES & ROADBLOCKS TO BEING WELL LOVED

## Why Are You Not Well Loved

There are so many obstacles that prevent people from being well loved. Here is my list from my Love.Life. Podcast titled "Be Well Loved."

1. Dysfunctional families, which is 70-96% of American families
2. Wounds from people, events, situations
3. Abuse of any kind
4. Traumas
5. Trust issues
6. Disempowering attitudes & beliefs (I can't win; I don't deserve it; etc.)
7. Low self-esteem
8. Low emotional abilities
9. Self-sabotage
10. Self-loathing
11. Being a negative thinker
12. Cognitive distortions (like emotional reasoning)

13. Self-defeating prophecy (the opposite of the self-fulfilling prophecy)
14. Poor role models or no role models
15. Belief that you don't deserve to be loved
16. Negative experiences with love or friendship
17. Overthinking or catastrophizing
18. Unrealistic expectations of others
19. Not being able to be vulnerable
20. Being afraid including fear of rejections, fear of failure, etc.
21. Perfectionist tendencies or being too demanding
22. False reality or distorted perceptions of self or others
23. Lack of self-awareness

From the above list I have broken the issues or obstacles stopping you from having love and being well loved into four categories and addressed each category with what is required to bring love into your life so you can be well loved, as discussed in my first podcast.

**1. Wounds:** Healing is necessary.

Wounds often come from dysfunctional families where love was missing or parents played favorites or there were other things going on that cause pain and hurt. Wounds come from abuse of any kind and traumas. You can also be wounded by a bad experience or from just living life. Wounds in and of themselves can lead a person to take on a disempowering attitude or belief. For example, after a bad experience you could say to yourself: I'm never going to do that again. Or I would rather be alone than risk that again. Wounds can leave you with low self-esteem, a very harsh inner critic (lacking self-compassion), self-loathing and a host of other things that will cut you off from love and life. Wounds can also lead to bad habits or practices that really don't help you. There is nothing wrong with wounds it's just that they usually take you out of the game of life. Healing is the medicine for wounds. Much of what I have included in this book is on healing and how to heal.

**2. Low emotional abilities:** Growing your emotional abilities or your emotional intelligence is required.

Low emotional abilities are often found in dysfunctional families and quite frankly it is one of the number one problems in the world. People just don't know how to identify, manage and process their own emotions. Low emotional abilities can show up as trust issues, low self-esteem, fears, using emotional reasoning (a cognitive distortion), not being able to be vulnerable, and having misperceptions of others intentions or actions to name a few of the top ways it might look. To have a very functional and happy life you want to be able to identify, manage and process your emotions. You want to have high emotional intelligence because that is truly a superpower. To give you an idea of the type of superpower having high emotional intelligence really is I have included in this chapter a list of the 29 personality traits of people who have high emotional intelligence. That is what you want. Trust me.

**3. Personality traits or habits:** Change is required.

There are certain personality traits and habits that the majority of people just don't like. If you have these personality traits it acts as a repellant causing people to want to run away from you. I am very serious. These personality traits or habits are the ones that you will want to change. Examples of personality traits or habits that stop you from being well loved include: being a know-it-all, being self-centered, being an attention seeker, being arrogant, judgmental, or overly opinionated, being a negative thinker, catastrophizing, overthinking, being a perfectionist or too demanding of others, not taking care of yourself and not developing self-compassion (inner critic is too harsh). Many people who have these personality traits can't recognize them in themselves because they are not self-aware. Self-awareness is a hallmark of having high emotional intelligence, which is lacking in people who cannot accurately assess themselves. All is not lost if you have one or more of these traits because we know from science and neuroplasticity of the brain that people can change, which I discussed briefly in my YouTube video titled "You Can Teach an Old Dog New Tricks". You can change. That is an absolute fact.

**4. Attitudes and beliefs:** Change is required.

Some of the people who are not well loved fall into this situation because they have developed disempowering attitudes or beliefs that stop them from love and life, cut them off from being connected to others, and prevent them from being able to be their authentic and real self. Disempowering attitudes and beliefs can really be stealth in that they are not always on the surface of your consciousness. Sometimes you have to dig to see what is running the show. Regardless, this is definitely an area that prevents people from being well loved, from being happy, and from being highly functional in life.

## GROWTH & DEVELOPMENT = ACCESS to LOVE

The access to love is growth and development, which means growing new skills, abilities, habits, practices, attitudes and beliefs. It means change. And it doesn't have to be hard. It can be fun. I am a fan of making life fun.

From my November 29, 2019 Blog post on the top 45 Ways Personal Growth & Development will help you have a life you love… (a few of the 45)

1. You will be happier.
2. You will get freed up from so many things.
3. You will have less anxiety.
4. It builds self-esteem and confidence.
5. It will help you in every area of your life.
6. It will help you be more authentic and real.
7. It will help you when life is hard.
8. It can be very fun.
9. It makes you more relatable and likeable.
10. It will help you grow your emotional abilities, which is like a superpower.
11. People won't be so annoying anymore.
12. It is good for your brain.
13. It builds character.

14. It is a very high return on your investment of time or energy (the best ROI).
15. It will help you appreciate yourself and others.

Another way to look at it is through the lens of the **benefits to having high emotional intelligence or growing your emotional abilitie**s:

1. Helpful for depressing situations (broader perspective on handling challenges and problems)
2. Helps create better and more rewarding relationships with people
3. Helps you deal with stress more efficiently
4. Helps reduce anxiety
5. Helps diffuse conflict
6. Allows you to empathize with others
7. Provides calmness and clarity of mind
8. Allows for better communication
9. Helps build resilience
10. Increases confidence
11. Increases creativity
12. Builds integrity
13. Helps you manage change better
14. Highly correlated with top work performance, promotions and higher pay
15. Links strongly to love and spirituality
16. Makes for more effective leaders and managers
17. Increases performance and productivity

**29 Traits of People with High Emotional Intelligence:**

1. They are change agents. (think growth and development)
2. They are aware of their strengths and weaknesses. (self-aware)
3. They are empathetic.
4. They are not perfectionists.

5. They are balanced and healthy. (sleep and outside, non-work interests)
6. They are curious. (an inborn sense of wonder and curiosity)
7. They are gracious and thankful.
8. They are focused. (not easily distracted)
9. They are self-motivated.
10. They do not dwell on the past.
11. They focus on the positive.
12. They set boundaries.
13. They are great at managing their own emotions.
14. They are creative and deep thinkers. (NOT over-thinkers)
15. They are hard to offend.
16. They know when to say no.
17. They can distinguish between wants and needs.
18. They can determine the moods and energy of a group.
19. They think about feelings both their own and others.
20. They ask others for their perspective.
21. They pause or know when to pause.
22. They ask why.
23. They are open to criticism.
24. They apologize.
25. They forgive.
26. They have an expansive emotional vocabulary.
27. They respond rather than react.
28. They show up as their authentic selves.
29. They handle difficulties better.

Yes, you are going to have to make some changes in your life if you want to be well loved. I suggest that you keep the lists of benefits from this chapter handy and use it as motivation. You are going to want a reward system, which I discuss in the chapter on Empowering Practices, Skills, Habits, Attitudes & Beliefs (Self-Motivation: The Nuts & Bolts of Leveling Up with a Reward System). A personal reward system can help you stay motivated and keep moving forward and I highly recommend them.

Here is the good news: this is not that difficult. Maybe you are overwhelmed at the idea of this, in which case I would suggest that you look at my post on Dealing with Overwhelm in the Chapter on Dealing with Emotions and Problems. Overwhelm is a construct. You might not understand what I mean by a construct, but you will if you read that post. You can actually deal with overwhelm to put it to bed instead of having it show up in your life over and over again.

Make this a fun journey. I am a huge fan of making life fun. Why not? Life is hard. You want to have as much happiness and fun in life as you can because there are enough parts of life that are just hard not matter what you do. It's time to tackle the obstacles that are holding you back from a life filled with love where you are well loved.

# LOVE & HAPPINESS

**Living Life with Your Whole Heart**

September 4, 2019

The point and purpose of my blog is to enable you, my beloved readers, to **Love Life** – to LOVE YOUR LIFE. So, what is living life with your whole heart and why does it matter? When I say living life with your whole heart that encompasses a multitude of things. Is your heart open to people? Is your heart open to life? Is your heart open to love? Can you trust others? Are you engaged in life? Can you be vulnerable with other people? Have you dealt with past hurts and betrayal or other trauma? Are you jaded? How authentic can you be with people? Are you really happy? Do you feel a lot of joy in your life? Do you have good or great health? Are you doing what you want to be doing or biding your time until X, Y, or Z happens? Are you living a life that you love? Another way to look at living life with your whole heart would be getting your act together because to LOVE LIFE requires some level of that.

I want to engage with you on the process of getting from where you are right now to a point where you are happy and engaged and loving life! Even if you feel like your life sucks big time, you will be able to change your life regardless of your circumstances. I know this first hand. Over the course of the coming year I will be blogging about a wide variety of topics that are critical to loving life. I will be giving homework assignments to you and the most courageous of you, the readers who are most committed to having a better life, will actually do the work I am suggesting and reap significant benefits. My promise to you is that if you stay with me (meaning read my blog posts) and do the work required, the homework, that in a year your life will look and feel very different. I have coached enough people at this stage of my life and have done enough significant training and development on myself to know for sure that anyone can do what is necessary to love life and have a life that they love.

While it might seem scary to some of you especially if you have had difficulties, the benefits to taking on your life are enormous! They are so huge! Let me list for you what I feel are the top benefits of living life with your whole heart!

**Benefits of Living Life with Your Whole Heart:**

You will feel, have or be…

1. Happy
2. Peaceful
3. Powerful
4. Energetic or energized
5. LOVE -feeling it, giving it, receiving it
6. Joy
7. FUN
8. Contentment
9. Freedom
10. Compassion
11. Empathy
12. Forgiveness

13. Passion/Passionate
14. Assertive
15. Focused
16. Clear headed
17. Courageous
18. Improved health
19. Contributing to others/Making a difference in the world
20. Generosity
21. Relationships flourish
22. Doing things you always wanted to do

What this means if you get the benefits from living life with your whole heart, you will then be experiencing LESS anxiety, fear, resentment, anger, frustration, jealousy, envy, regret, loneliness, boredom, restlessness, and tiredness. While I have been deeply betrayed, lied to, exploited and used, I can still trust people. I can still be vulnerable and open with others. I am fully engaged in life. I am living my life with an open heart. I am doing what I love and I am extremely happy.

I am choosing to live my life in this deliberate fashion because I am fully aware that I can handle it if someone lies to me, if someone tries to use or exploit me, or otherwise engages in behaviors that are unacceptable to me. That I choose to be and can be trusting, vulnerable and authentic allows me to connect with others on a very deep and intimate level. Yes, being trusting, vulnerable and authentic also exposes me to possibly being used, disappointed, or betrayed or even getting my heart broken, but you don't get the joys of life, the joys of love, the joys of deep connection without being able to trust, be vulnerable, share yourself and be real. For me, the delicious moments in life that I treasure are being with people- really being with people in our state of brokenness and humanity. Not having to be perfect. Being able to laugh at myself and laugh with others. To me this is the meaning and point to life other than using your life to make a difference for others – to contribute to others in a meaningful way.

To reach this state in life, to be blessed enough to have arrived at this point means that I have done an extraordinary amount of work on myself to grow and develop. Growth and development, in my humble opinion, are the keys to a rich and fulfilling life and much of the focus of my Love.Life. blog. The old saying in psychotherapy goes that "we are all works in progress" and the caveat should be "except that some people are closed off or asleep at the wheel". Where are YOU in your growth and development? For some of you reading this, you might be thinking what the heck is she talking about? I am talking about your self-awareness. How aware of yourself are you? What is your emotional quotient or emotional intelligence? This process of being self-aware or knowing what areas you have to work is something that we will begin with and cover in the ensuing weeks and months.

Emotional quotient (EQ) or emotional intelligence (EI), two interchangeable terms, will be the focus of an entire blog post soon enough because understanding that will be immensely helpful to you in creating a powerful life that you love! It will be helpful to you in your self-assessment. It will be helpful to you in relating to other people. It's just one of my favorite subjects. Okay. I do have a lot of favorite subjects. Understanding yourself and how you are put together is exceptionally powerful in life because it is a path to feeling freed up, feeling powerful, and not taking things that happen to you so personally – or not personally at all even when it IS personal!

There is a dichotomy to life or the contrast of life that I feel is very powerful and helpful. I have put together in the two columns below some of the major points to the contrast of life to provide a visual to what I am saying. To be able to live life with your whole heart you have to be able to deal with all of the aspects of life – not just the good stuff. I have included emotional states as well as character traits and skills and abilities in this contrast.

**The Contrast of Life**

| | |
|---|---|
| Excited | Bored, restless |
| Purposeful | Aimless |
| Clear | Confused |
| Fun | Stoic, serious |
| Empathy | Lack of empathy |
| Humility | Arrogance |
| Open | Guarded, closed |
| Compassion | Judgement |
| Powerful | Powerless |
| Generous | Selfish |
| Direct | Indirect, passive-aggressive |
| Love | Hate, Loss |
| Peaceful | Discontented, angry, resentful |
| Organized | Unorganized |
| Nurturing | Controlling, cold |
| Forgiveness | Resentment, holding grudges |
| Honest | Dishonest |
| Joy | Sadness |
| Self-care | Self-sabotage |
| Healthy | Unhealthy |
| Plays fair | Cheats |
| Supports others | Undermines others |
| Happy for others | Jealous, envious |
| Full of energy | Lethargic, tired |
| Managing life | Overwhelmed |
| Vulnerable | Closed off, guarded |
| Inspires others | Critical, brings others down |
| Authentic, real | Inauthentic, fake |
| Naïve, Innocent, child-like | Jaded, hardened to life |
| Happy | Unhappy, grief, loss |
| High Emotional Quotient or intelligence | Low emotional quotient or intelligence |
| Physically healthy | Physically unhealthy or struggling with health |
| In control of life | The victim of life or the circumstances |
| Courage | Cowardly |
| Confidence | Low-self-esteem, lacking confidence |

You could use the contrast of life as a tool for your own self-assessment. Where are you in these areas of life? Where can you go to work on yourself to improve? To be able to live life fully and live life with your whole heart, I assert that you have to have more qualities, emotions and skills on the left-hand side of the chart.

Over the course of the next year, the next 365 days, if you would engage with me for just 15 minutes a day in improving your life, in growing and developing, in working on the areas of life that are there to be dealt with, on getting physically healthy, on cleaning out our house or apartment, on doing what there is to do, you will have spent a total of 91 hours moving your life in a positive direction!

That's the equivalent of more than two-40-hour work weeks by just spending 15 minutes a day. Look at the above list of benefits to living life with your whole heart. Does that call to you? Are you ready for a change? It is a total act of courage to take on making changes to your life. It is a heroic act of strength to look at your life and how you have been living it.

**Homework assignment:** Your 1st homework assignment is to start to think about AND write down what makes you happy and what you love. In this assignment you may notice that the first things that come to mind are all the things that make you unhappy or annoyed. That is perfect because it's just as helpful to know what you don't like in the process of creating a vision for your life. Building a life that you LOVE requires that you know and understand what makes you happy and what you love. You will refer to the notes you make on what you love and what makes you happy down the road.

Please post any questions you have for me on this blog because it is absolutely the best way to get a response at this point in time. I personally believe that there is no such thing as a dumb question, so please let me know how I can help you. It is my honor and a privilege to support you on this journey!!

**Level Up Your Happiness**

September 25, 2019

A new survey called "The World Happiness Report", compiled yearly since 2012, indicates that Americans are as unhappy as they have ever been. The United States ranks #19 as the happiest place on earth ranking. This same report states that addictions are causing considerable unhappiness and depression in the U.S. According to the CDC, antidepressant use is up 400% over the last decade. A 2017 U.S. News & World Report Headline reads – "2017 A Record Year of Unhappiness". We live in a world where happiness seems elusive to many. Yet, overall, researchers state that you can control about 40% of your happiness. This post is about you impacting the 40% of controllable factors to boost your happiness.

If you are on this journey of Loving YOUR Life with me then a big part of getting there is growth and development. How intentional are you with respect to how you live your life? In coaching situations when I ask people what makes them happy more often than not there is a silent pause followed by either "that's a good question", or "I don't know", and that is perfectly normal and reasonable. It's just not going to get you a happy life.

Figuring out what makes you happy, and as a subset, what makes you unhappy, is one of the questions on the Road Map to creating a life that you love. Frequently, once someone starts to consider and explore what makes them happy what shows up is all the things that they are unhappy about in their life, or how drained they often feel, or what is annoying. That's normal and actually helpful. Before I get into the specifics of leveling up your happiness I want to mention intentionality.

Abraham Lincoln is quoted as saying, "You can have anything you want, if you want it badly enough." When I say intentional I mean deliberate or on purpose. Because I have a commitment to enjoying my life, I am intentional about how I plan and use my time because having free time allows me *more time to* play and have fun. As you are looking at having a life that you LOVE, intentionality is probably critical. You want to be directing and steering your life not sitting back and letting life happen to you. We could say that the difference is intentionality.

To level up your happiness you have to first know what makes you happy. It might take some soul searching if you are just going through the grind of life. Pause. Think. Consider. You might be in a position where there's not a whole lot of things in your life that make you happy, which would be very sad, but at the same time represent a lot of opportunity. You might have a belief that you are not supposed to be happy. Whatever the case, to level up your happiness you will have to determine what makes you happy and how you can sprinkle your life with the things that make you happy. The things that soothe your soul. The things that make you smile. The things that energize you. What are those things?

The biggest objection or perhaps one of the more common objections I have heard from individuals on this subject is: I don't have the time. Meaning, I don't know what makes me happy and I don't have the time to figure it out. Alrighty then, I can't help you. The balance of this post is for the readers who want to take charge of their lives and have their lives go in a more positive and happy direction.

When people typically begin to explore what makes them happy, sometimes they just don't have a long list of things that make them happy. That is absolutely fine! If you can't think of things that make you happy, then you might consider trying out some new hobbies, joining a volunteer organization that services some community project or area that you support, or at least engage in the exploration of what could make you happy. Maybe you need a new tribe to do social things with. It's hard to say what it will take for you to come up with a list of things that make you happy. All I know is that if you have a commitment you will find a way to get there.

Now, if you have experienced a loss, a trauma, a health problem, or other difficulty, finding happiness might take a lot more effort. Yet I know that it can be done. Let me give you an example. Some. Years ago, when I was really up against it and in a difficult position I recognized that I needed to add more happiness to my life so I made a list of what made me happy. Then I looked at my particular circumstances to see what from my list what was realistic and doable. I ended up combining three things that made me happy – playing with children, doing arts and crafts, and being of service to others – into an offer to a friend that I would babysit her kids for free if I could do arts and crafts with them. It was a beautiful thing all around. We ALL enjoyed it. It made me very happy. There in a very difficult and dark time I found a creative way to be happy. It still makes me happy today remembering those times with someone else's beautiful children on loan to me. There's always a way to infuse your life with happiness.

I am not saying, by the way, that if you have suffered a loss, a trauma, or other problem that you should not be sad. You have to feel your feelings and possibly grieve. And you can feel your feelings or grieve and still have some joy in your life in my humble opinion or in my experience.

If you are new to the concept of doing what you love or having more happiness in your life, I would ever so strongly suggest that you reward yourself for any little activity you do in the process. Rewarding yourself will help you move more quickly to having this as a habit or practice. The more committed you are, the more creative you will become about how to implement this in your everyday living. They say it takes more than 21 days to forge a new habit. If you have not been living your life with intentionality and lots of joy, fun, and love, I would absolutely reward yourself on an on-going basis. Why not? After all, your rewards are supposed to make you happy!

True confessions now…I am such a firm believer in this idea of being happy and having fun that many years ago when I worked in sales for Xerox Corporation and had to make cold calls, I came up with a method for making cold calls fun. I made a little game out of it (with and against myself) to see how many cold calls I could make in a day AND how many people I could make smile in the process. It was actually fun. But it was fun because I made a game out of it. And bonus – it was very effective.

What is it you love? What makes you happy? What soothes your soul? What makes you smile? And then how can you work those things into your life? If you are along for this delicious ride to loving your life, and you get this part done, you will have completed one of the questions on the road map! Woo hoo for you!

Based on a peek at the research on unhappiness there are several areas to move into for the next few blog posts to help you move into a position where you have more happiness in your life. Some of the areas include dealing with health problems since that is a major source of unhappiness in the U.S., training your brain, neuroplasticity of the brain, and managing your thoughts, as well as dealing with depression, numbing yourself to pain, and moving to a higher emotional quotient (or higher emotional intelligence). I have no illusions that life is easy. I know how painful and difficult life can be. I just also happen to know that you can have happiness, joy, and love in those most challenging times. Stay with me on the ride to loving your life.

**Love & Miracles – How to Get More Love & Miracles in Your Life**

January 8, 2020

Love and Miracles. Two of the greatest subjects on earth and two of my favorite things. People who know me well know that I am a big fan of doing all things in love and that I have received many miracles in my life. Do an internet search on the word "love" and you will get over 17 Billion hits. Seventeen Billion. The word "miracles" on the other hand would only get you roughly 106 million hits. Most people want love in their lives yet don't recognize the very things they are doing to repel love. Miracles on the other hand are a concept that are simply too far-fetched for some people to believe in. This post is about how to get more love and miracles in your life.

Let's start with LOVE. The definitions of love include – strong affection for another rising out of kinship or personal ties; maternal love for a child; attraction based on sexual desire; affection based on admiration, benevolence, or common interests; a warm attachment, enthusiasm, or devotion; the object of attachment; a beloved person; unselfish loyal and benevolent concern for the good of another; a score of zero in tennis; and so on. Going back to Sophocles, an ancient Greek tragedy play writer (Born c.496 BCE-died 406), whose quote *"One word frees us of all the weight and pain of life: That word is love."* has been passed on for thousands of years to the present day. Artist Vincent van Gogh is quoted as saying *"The more I think it over, the more I feel that there is nothing more truly artistic than to love people."*

No discussion about Love would be complete without mentioning the relationship between Love and God. It is said that God is Love. Besides the word Love being mentioned in the Bible 310 times, Love is the basis for the Catholic Religion, as well as several other religions although I can only definitively mention the Catholic religion because I am not schooled in the other faiths. You are commanded to Love your neighbor as yourself, and forgive someone seventy times seven times (or about 490 times). Recognizing that God loves us enough to give up His only begotten Son for the salvation of our souls and to save us from sin could be a healing property for someone who believed that. Belief that we can be forgiven by Jesus Christ and God for our sins is another avenue of self-acceptance and healing that religion offers. The context that the Catholic religion offers for suffering can be empowering in difficult times as well. In fact, having religious beliefs and practices can function as a coping mechanism in life – and that's very powerful. The Bible quotes on love are so common that you can find them on coffee mugs, wall art, t-shirts, and tote bags among other things. A few popular Bible quotes on Love include:

*"My command is this: Love each other as I have loved you."* John 15:12
*"And now these three remains: faith, hope and love. But the greatest of these is love."* 1Corinthians 13:13
*"Do everything in love."* 1 Corinthians 16:14

Love songs are very popular just as break-up songs, those songs about the ending of love, are. There endless movies about love. There are both books and novels about love. We even have stamps that bear the word "LOVE" on them. Love is ubiquitous.

Love means being able to say these three things: I am sorry; I made a mistake; and I was wrong. Love means being vulnerable, open, courageous, and willing to be rejected. It means being authentic. It means being compassionate and empathetic with yourself and others. Love means having your heart open to receive love and it means loving yourself. Love means wanting the best for the other person, respecting them and appreciating them as they are. Love is all things good and it requires vulnerability, which is well summarized in this famous C.S. Lewis (1898-1963) quote:

"To love at all is to be vulnerable. Love anything and your heart will be wrung and possibly broken. If you want to make sure of keeping it intact you must give it to no one not even an animal. Wrap it carefully round with hobbies and little luxuries; avoid all entanglements. Lock it up safe in the casket or coffin of your selfishness. But in that casket, safe, dark, motionless, airless, it will change. It will not be broken; it will become unbreakable, impenetrable, irredeemable. To love is to be vulnerable." C.S. Lewis from The Four Loves

Metal Sign made by Nick Spicer of Scrapped, Julian, PA (814)470-2489

Since *Love* is an all-pervasive concept in our world and has been since the early days of man, then why is love so elusive for some people? There are many reasons why LOVE is difficult for some people. Sometimes one bad break-up is enough for a person to withdraw from love. Sometimes it is the culmination of a series of events that have people armor up and close themselves off from love. There is a variety of reasons and circumstances why some find love elusive.

**Obstacles to Having Love:**

This is my list of some of the obstacles for having love in your life. Remembering that I am not a therapist in any way, it's just my observations and beliefs about why it is so difficult for some people to have and keep love in their lives. Anything from this list would be the basis for growth and development. If there is something holding you back from having love present in your life – get to work.

1. Low self-esteem
2. Brittleness
3. Righteousness

4. Being Judgmental
5. Being closed
6. Unwilling to be vulnerable
7. Fear of rejection or hurt
8. Negative attitude
9. Thinking you are better than everyone else
10. Too rigid in your thinking
11. Unwilling to accept other peoples' imperfections
12. Expecting/demanding too much
13. Poor communication skills
14. Low emotional quotient
15. Lack of integrity
16. Addictions
17. Not loving yourself
18. Blaming others
19. Shaming others
20. Lack of boundaries
21. Unable to receive love (damaged from the past)
22. Other psychopathology/neurosis/narcissism/psychopaths/sociopaths
23. Exploiting/Using others
24. Being the victim
25. Believing that you do not deserve love (not good enough or other similar belief pattern)

Some people have been so hurt or damaged by their past either in childhood or adulthood that they simply can't take the risk of being hurt again. While that is understandable, given what we know about the neuroplasticity and neurogenesis of the brain, the hurts and wounds from the past can be healed. It's called doing the work. If you want more love in your life then doing the work of personal growth and development will help you get there. Since the entire point of my blog is to help you LOVE your LIFE, you will find many other tools to help you get love into your life in my past blog posts. To have LOVE in your LIFE- you have to live life – play full out, start making friends, get out there and do things.

## Miracles

The connection between Love and Miracles, in my humble opinion of course, is that I believe you must have Love to have Miracles. Just my opinion, which I am owning. As the recipient of many miracles over my lifetime, Miracles are another favorite topic of mine. Let's start by getting on the same page about what a miracle is and then I'll give you some examples before the process to get miracles to show up in your life. Miracles are defined as: an extraordinary event manifesting divine intervention in human affairs; an extremely outstanding or unusual event, thing, or accomplishment; and a divinely natural phenomenon experienced humanly as the fulfillment of spiritual law.

I have been blessed by so many miracles, some of which would not be appropriate to write about given the involvement with other people. The most well-known miracle of my life started when I asked my Mom to give me a sister, this after she was probably only a few weeks post-partem, which is never a good idea. My mother said that I would never be getting a sister, so my 5-year old retort to that was to put my hand on my hip and toss my head while saying, "Well, then I'll just pray to God." Upon her approval that it was okay to pray to God for a sister, I did that for seven consecutive years. Night after night. Year after year. With such conviction that God would never let me down. I was relentless.

Kind classmates and relatives tried to soften the blow that I would never get a sister with various statements, but I persisted. Just before I turned 13 years old, after 7 solid years of prayer, I received my sister! That's roughly 2,555 days of prayer just in case you were wondering. Have all my prayers been answered affirmatively? Clearly if I am 58 years old and starting over with pretty much nothing, no they have not. Yet, am I totally amazed at my life and the miracles that I have received over the years? Absolutely. I am one very, very lucky woman.

I was told that I would have a hysterectomy and thus never be able to have children due to a 19-centimeter fibroid tumor in my uterus.

Due to the fibroid tumor being 8 times larger than my uterus itself the surgeon felt that a hysterectomy would be the only way to get all of the tumor out. The short version is that the lining of the uterus and a paper-thin layer of tissue was preserved during the surgery, which was the first miracle in this situation. The second miracle of this circumstance is that my uterine tissue grew back to be normal in thickness and health, which is significant because uterine tissue is NOT regenerative. So, I was able to have children against all odds because of these two combined miracles. Due to the extensive scar tissue it did mean that my children were born early and by C-Section to avoid labor complications.

I consider it a miracle that I landed on 3rd Floor Hoyt Hall as a freshman at Penn State University where I had the best Resident Assistant (R.A.) ever and made the most loving, supportive, and all-around amazing friends, 6 or more of whom I am still friends with today. How does that happen? People have been telling me over the past year plus that it is a miracle that I have come out of dealing with 3 concurrent traumas over the past 20 years as a very happy and healthy person. I don't know if that is a miracle or not, but people seem to be pretty certain that it is.

One miracle I experienced had nothing to do with me or my family or actually anyone that I personally knew. I was at an event where I heard some people I knew talking about a very sick man in the hospital and how the next morning they were going to remove his ventilator and that he would simply pass away. I don't know why, but I intervened in the conversation and said that I believed that the man could wake up, sit up in bed and start talking when the ventilator and life support was removed. Oh, the looks that I got in that moment. They said, you don't understand. You have not seen him. He's never going to make it and that is never going to happen.

So, the way it went was that one of the women pointed at me and said, well, if that happens Lisa, I will call you right away. I prayed for this man I didn't know that evening and the next morning I got the call that he woke up, he sat up and talked once the life support equipment was removed. I call this "Holding the Space" for miracles. As I dig into the steps to bring miracles into your life, part of it is your belief that a miracle could happen or holding the space for it to occur.

**How to Have More Miracles in Your Life:**

1. **Unwavering Faith – the size of a mustard seed**-As the Bible says if you have faith the size of a mustard seed (1-2 millimeters in size, much smaller than a pea), then you can move a mountain. Matthew 17:20: "I tell you the truth, if you had faith even as small as a mustard see, you could say to this mountain, 'Move from here to there,' and it would move. Nothing would be impossible." Faith is complete trust or confidence in something or someone.
2. **Resolute Belief/Holding the space**-It could be said that this is just another way of saying faith because the definition of belief includes the word faith. In this instance I use resolute belief and holding the space as you can see the miracle coming to you. You can feel the miracle in your heart. You are holding the space for the miracle to occur if that makes any sense to you. And it is fine if it does not.
3. **Prayer -Continuous/On-going**-As God is Our Father in Heaven, HE hears all of our prayers and petitions. That does not mean that he answers all of them or gives us what we want. For miracles to occur, it is best to engage in continuous prayer. If you get bored with the prayers that you know, then you can always take on, as I did some years ago with my children, the task of learning new prayers. There are many rich prayers worth committing to heart. My most recent one is the "Mary, Undoer of Knots" prayer.
4. **Fasting – Can boost your prayer results**-Fasting is said to be a way to boost your prayer results and as such is included here. What fasting looks like is limiting the hours in any given day where you will eat food, say between 10 AM and 6 PM (an 8-hour window) eating one regular sized meal with two smaller meals, no snacks. Best done with no

sugar or sweets. Obviously done with prayer. I would suggest a Novena, which is a 9-day prayer.
5. **Look for Miracles**-Miracles are not always the thing that slap you in the face. Sometimes you have to sit back, ponder your life and actually look with introspection at what has happened to see the miracles that you have been given. At least that is how it seems to me. Sometimes the totality of the miracle is not evident until you really look at your life. If you are not looking for miracles then for sure you will never see one.

**Concluding Thoughts:**

I am thankful now, looking back over my life, that God said NO to some of my prayers and petitions without getting into detail. Life is so much richer with LOVE. Life is so much better with LOVE. Yes, love of any kind means risk and the potential for getting hurt. The more you work on yourself the more resilient you will become and you will come to understand that if God is in your life in a meaningful way, that things have a way of working out. Have faith. Pray. Do the things that heal your heart. Believe that you are deserving of God's love and thus HIS miracles of love.

I want to leave you with a quote from *"The Velveteen Rabbit"*, first published in 1922 on becoming real:

---

*"You become. It takes a long time. That's why it doesn't happen often to people who break easily, or have sharp edges, or who have to be carefully kept. Generally, by the time you are Real, most of your hair has been loved off, and your eyes drop out and you get loose in your joints and very shabby. But these things don't matter at all, because once you are Real you can't be ugly, except to people who don't understand."*

— MARGERY WILLIAMS BIANCO, THE VELVETEEN RABBIT

---

My wish for you is that you are real and well loved. My wish for you is a happy life filled with people who love you and whom you love. My wish for you is that you can grow and develop in such a way that you know how to live an empowered life even in hard times. How can I help you on your journey?

## How to Generate Your Own Happiness & Why It's THE Skill to Learn this Year

February 13, 2020

Being able to generate your own happiness at any moment is a skill that you can learn, practice and ultimately master over time. Since the point of my blog is to help you LOVE your LIFE, being able to generate your own happiness is right up there at the top of the list for skills and abilities to have. Yet, most people don't have that ability. Instead, many people function where they hold it that they will be happy when…something happens. In statement form it looks like this:

"I will be happy when I am in a relationship."
"I will be happy when I have X amount of money in the bank."
"I will be happy when I have attained X, Y, or Z position in life."
"I will be happy when people like me."
"I will be happy when I get married."
"I will be happy when I feel better or am healthy."
"I will be happy when……."

In other words, many people have their level of happiness linked to or dependent upon something else or someone else. What I am suggesting is that you disconnect your happiness or your ability to be happy to your – financial state, your circumstances, your "state" in life, other people, being in a relationship, or anything for that matter. I am here to state for the record that you can disconnect having your happiness be contingent on some other thing. You can do that. It's entirely possible, and I strongly recommend it. Why?

Because otherwise your happiness is always contingent on someone or something else. Don't give away your power like that. Please.

In one of my early blog posts titled Road Map for Creating a Life that YOU LOVE, September 2019, I listed the question "What makes you happy?" in the diagram for that post coupled with "What makes you unhappy?" Uncoupling your ability to be happy with people and circumstances will increase your ability to be happy in any given moment. You might not know what makes you happy. That's okay. There's no time like the present to figure that out. Start a list. If you don't know what makes you happy, then it's time to engage in the process of self-discovery. How are you ever going to be happy if you don't know what it is that makes you happy? I have no idea. I think it would be a real challenge.

What would it take for you to be happy? What work do you have to do? What is stopping you from being happy? Do you even want to be happy? While that might seem harsh or even idiotic, there are a few people I have known over the years that quite frankly don't want to be happy. You might label it the victim complex or the martyr complex or something else. Yet, there are people who will not allow themselves to be happy. They do exist. Trust me. I hope you are not one of them. And just to be clear, when I ask what makes you happy, I am hoping to God that you are healthy enough that the things that make you happy do not include revenge, harming others, wishing ill on others, or other such horrible things because if that is the case then you are not healthy in my opinion. That is the antithesis of wellness in my view.

Since it is my assertion that generating your own happiness is a skill, I am going to lay out what I believe are the most important components to acquiring that skill. This is not the end-all, be-all list, but a starting place for growing this skill. As with learning any new skill or practice, you start where you are and learn as you go. You practice. You fail. You try again. You keep trying until you arrive at the place where you know that you have mastered it.

**Components to Generating Happiness:**

1. **Self-acceptance, self-love: Love who you are right now**. I don't mean in a narcissistic, self-righteous kind of way. Love yourself and your imperfections. We are all works in progress. Have compassion for wherever you are in your journey right now. Believe that everything is happening for your good.
2. **Be grateful.** If you can't muster feelings of gratitude I don't know how you will ever be happy. There is so much to be grateful for in life no matter how bad things are. I say that from my heart starting over at age 58 with pretty much nothing and a few other hardships that I could never write about. Yet, life is so beautiful if you can open your eyes. Even in very difficult times you can find love, peace, beauty, friendship, laughter, and so much more. Be grateful.
3. **Have a PLAN.** You are either driving your ship, someone else is driving your ship, or you are moored to a dock that you don't like to use an analogy. Create a plan for your life so that YOU are driving your ship! When you have a plan, and your actions are in alignment with your plan – you will have an amazing sense of satisfaction because you know where you are headed. You know what you are up to. You know what you are creating. You KNOW! When you have a plan, you are not floating around aimlessly at sea – you are moving full steam ahead. It's all hands-on deck when you have a plan that you are executing. If you don't have a plan now, that is fine. You can start to create one. Go back to the beginning of my blog posts and start reading from there. I take you through the steps or at least enough to get you started.
4. **Know what makes you happy!** What lights you up? What inspires you? The things that make you happy, light you up and inspire you are the very things that you want to incorporate into your life in one way or another.
5. **Understand that you can be suffering greatly due**

*Love.Life.*

**to circumstances and still be happy.** If you disconnect the dependence of your happiness to people and circumstances, then you most certainly can be happy when times are tough or when you are suffering. Obviously, it's always easier to be happy when times are easy or good. Nobody needs to generate happiness when life is great. That comes with the territory. It's when things are tough that generating your own happiness is the priceless skill worth having and using.

6. **Work on yourself: growth and development.** What are the practices and habits that will help you grow the skill of generating your own happiness? I have written all about them in many of my blog posts. There's quite a few. The more you work on yourself the more freedom and power you will have in life. This is the subject of a blog post titled Top 45 Ways that Personal Growth & Development Will Help You Have a Life You Love, November 29, 2019, just in case you want to get the full flavor of the power of doing the work.
7. **Deal with your issues.** FOR EXAMPLE: Trust issues. Letting go issues. Having to please everyone else. I don't know what life would be like if I had trust issues. Quite frankly, I can't image it. Yet, it's extremely common or so it seems. Whatever your issues are – just deal with them. Like Nike says, just do it.
8. **Find your purpose or mission – and get on it**. It's fine if you don't know what your purpose or mission is at this point. You can either make it up for the time being or you could, just for now, have your purpose to be feeling happy. I am a big fan of having a sense of purpose or a mission. I believe that it's both powerful and helpful to human beings.
9. **LIVE in the NOW**. You are alive right now. In this moment. Be here. Be present. Be in the moment. Right now. The past is over and done. The future is yet to come. If you are working with a plan, then you know what future

is coming because you are actively engaged in creating and causing it.

10. **Identify any negative roadblocks to happiness**. While you might not be able to change some negative things, people or circumstances in your life right now, identifying the negative things, people and circumstances can be very helpful because then you can work to what I call "counter-balance" the negativity. There have been several significant negative things, people, and circumstances in my life over the past 25 years and I was able to counter-balance the negative things that I could not change with positive activities, people, and things. Figure out what it will take to off-set negativity and then put those self-affirming, positive, life-giving things into your life.

**Concluding Thoughts:**

Life can be very difficult. We all know that. Being able to generate your own happiness is a powerful, life-giving skill that anyone can learn, grow and master over time. It will take something to acquire that skill. Anything in life that is worthwhile often involves some effort. It feels good to be happy. To be able to be happy when life is challenging is deeply satisfying and rewarding and possible for anyone willing to do the work to get there. Life is a journey. Can you enjoy the ride? Are you willing to do what it takes to have a LIFE that you LOVE? What can I do to empower and support you in your life? I wish you all good things. I wish you love and peace.

**LOVE Involves Trust: Why It's Time to Deal with Your Trust Issues**

February 27, 2020

You want to LOVE your Life – the entire point of my blog. Hopefully you want to have lots of LOVE in your life. You want all the LOVE you can have! Love involves trust so let's jump right into this worthwhile and significant topic! I will first say that I know more than enough people with trust issues. It seems extremely common if not pervasive in our society. Trust is important not just in your personal relationships but also in business. Plenty of businesses have recognized the almighty importance of being trustworthy to their current and potential customers by making mistakes that cost them financially. What consumers willingly choose businesses that are not trustworthy and reliable? Not too many. There are plenty of books and scholarly articles for business leaders on how to be trustworthy and how to have their business entities be viewed as trustworthy to customers. Trust is the foundation for love and relationships of all kinds.

Trust is defined generally as a firm belief in the reliability, truth, ability or strength of something (synonyms: confidence, belief, faith). In this post I will cover the benefits to being able to trust others as well as the possible negative impact to trusting, the general components of trust, signs that you have trust issues and ways to build your trust muscles. For me, the biggest benefit to being able and willing to trust other people is the gift of LOVE. I LOVE the people in my life. I actually LOVE my life even though some other people are horrified at what I have been through. All that matters is that I LOVE it. There is nothing better than LOVE. Feeling loved and appreciated and showing others that you love and appreciate them. Loving your life! Being trusting, open and vulnerable allows to connect with people on a deep level, which is something that I appreciate because it makes life so much richer for me.

I am, however, guilty of being too trusting. It is my Achilles heel. It is also a choice I have made deliberately after weathering what could only be called an extraordinary betrayal and exploitation. I powerfully decided that I was still going to be trusting. After all, my ability to be trusting was one of the things that I loved about myself prior to the betrayal and exploitation. Why would I give that up because of one bad person or one bad experience? Yes, I will be a lot more judicious about who I trust and to what level, which goes without saying. And yes, I have learned about narcissists, psychopaths, and con artists, which is all very helpful in avoiding people who are not trustworthy. My choice to continue to be trusting is actually therapist approved so woo hoo for me! You don't have to let one or more betrayals completely ruin your ability to be trusting.

Let's say that you already know that you have trust issues. It is okay to have trust issues. You are okay just the way that you are right now and the ways that you are not. You want to have full compassion for how you are organized and how you are not organized. You want to love yourself including your imperfections, your issues and your problems. Okay, maybe not love your problems but at least deal with them. The power for you is in understanding that you have trust issues because then you can use that to set up your life to support you instead of triggering your trust issues. If you are not sure if you have trust issues then you can take a look at the list below of signs that you might have trust issues. You could have one or more of the signs and that is only an indicator that you might have trust issues not necessarily that you do.

You can easily live the rest of your life with your trust issues although you might want to be aware that trust issues are reasonably high on the list of reasons why intimate relationships don't work out. Plenty of people function quite well in life and in relationships with trust issues so it's not a deal breaker. If you are planning on holding onto your trust issues, which I totally understand and validate by the way, you might want to have some frank conversations with your significant other as to how the two of you can work around and support you with your trust issues. That can absolutely be done, but it would take a partner with empathy and the willingness to do what is necessary assuming it is within reason. Who in life has not either been betrayed, cheated on, lied to or otherwise exploited?

It often happens in childhood within the family of origin, or in early intimate relationships or sometimes much later in life. Most people have felt the sting of betrayal, which can even happen in non-sexual friendships. It's what we do with the feelings of betrayal that matters. These events do not have to leave you scarred for life although that happens often enough. You do not have to be defined by any betrayals or exploitations in life. Your understanding of how you are organized or wired as a person can give you power.

Being the proponent of growth and development that I am, of course my thrown way of dealing with life is "Oh, there's an issue – YAY – it's simply an opportunity for growth and development." That's just my approach to life, which I am well aware is not the norm. Regardless of whether or not you ever decide to "do the work" on your trust issues, simply understanding that you have them is very powerful. I also happen to believe that once you can own your trust issues and share them with the appropriate friends, family or partners that you can gain even more freedom and power over that issue. I'm not saying that it will change the issue, but you taking ownership of your trust issues will free you up and help those who love you support you in a loving and compassionate way.

**Benefits of Being Able to Trust People:**

1. Allows you to be in relationships with people – easier, faster, better.
2. You get more love because you are open to it.
3. It's much easier to make friends.
4. It's much easier to be in life – freedom from worry and the side effects of not being able to trust others.
5. Allows you to connect deeply with others.
6. It opens doors – in my opinion.
7. It's got to be way easier than not trusting.
8. Provides for less anxiety in life.
9. Definitely better for your health.

**Risks/Negative Side to Being Trusting:**

1. You might get hurt.
2. You might get betrayed or exploited or used.
3. You might suffer a financial loss – large or small.

I assert that yes, being trusting has risks. There is no doubt about it. Yet, in my opinion, the risk of possible pain or possible betrayal is worth it because when you win you can get deep love, meaningful friendships, and the joy and happiness that comes from love in any form. The components of what goes into trust are not readily agreed upon at this time. The top contenders include reliability or dependability, integrity, good judgement, sincerity, empathy, and good character. Other components to trust, which are not necessarily less important include communication, benevolence, openness, vulnerability, past and present behaviors, the ability to trust, accountability, and transparency.

As I discussed in my past post about integrity (The Sheer Joy and Magic of Integrity, October 9, 2019), people simply are not going to trust you if you don't keep your word. Integrity and keeping your promises have a side benefit of being seen as trustworthy, dependable, and reliable. So, if you want to be trusting I assert that integrity is front and center. There are a lot of variables.

**Signs You Have Trust Issues:**

1. You are viewed as self-righteous, impossible to please or unforgiving.
2. You have difficulty making a commitment.
3. You view simple human error as a breach of trust. Innocent happenings are given a negative slant.
4. Your relationships tend to lack depth (superficial).
5. You expect people to let you down.
6. You feel lonely, isolated or depressed.
7. You are overly cautious or protective.
8. You spy or snoop on people.
9. You sabotage situations or relationships because of your belief that they will let you down.
10. You don't believe that you deserve happiness.
11. You are emotionally closed off or _not vulnerable_.
12. You are overly sensitive or defensive.

13. You cheat.
14. You have feelings of confusion.
15. You constantly test your partner.
16. You don't communicate or shut down.
17. You get triggered and you don't know why.
18. You push away the people who love you or care about you.
19. You feel out of control.
20. You run away from relationships or have short term relationships.
21. You won't let new people into your life.
22. You can't be present or live in the moment.
23. You have to be in control.
24. You are suspicious or paranoid about being talked about by others, lied to or somehow deceived.

**Building the Muscle of Being Able to TRUST:**

1. **Love yourself.** Self-acceptance and self-love, distinct from the narcissistic kind of self-love will help you build the muscle of being trusting.
2. **Personal Growth-** Of course this is on the list! It's on every list! No, it's not on every list just almost every list. Knowing yourself and what makes you tick is incredibly powerful if you want to have a happy life. Almost all of my blog posts are about growth and development on some level so there is a lot of material in this blog to help you.
3. **Be METICULOUS about your integrity.** Take keeping your promises seriously. Ask people to help you if needed. Take your integrity to heart. Where is your integrity missing? Do you keep every promise you make or clean it up if you can't keep your promise? Be intentional with what you say and do.
4. **Have a plan for your life.** Having a plan for your life will help you in many, many ways. Why would you want to

live life without a plan? I know that plenty of people do that but I don't get it. What do you want to have in your life? What would make you happy? Focus on moving your life forward and that will help you build lots of muscles not just the trust muscle.

5. **Manage yourself and your life.** If your life is a mess then get busy. Start making a list and then work off of the list. If you can't manage yourself or your life it should be no surprise that you have trust issues. You can't even trust yourself. You can do this. I know that you can. Start at the beginning of my blog and read the posts. Do the work. One day at a time.

6. **Deal with your problems.** There is no time like the present to deal with your problems. Own up to them. There's no shame in having issues or problems. We all have them. It is just that some people feel like they have to be perfect or have the perfect life. No, you don't need to have the perfect life. Love the life that you have right now – as it is- and work towards whatever would make you happy. Owning your problems is very powerful. Own them and then get to work on them.

7. **Lighten up! Life's too short.** The more you can laugh and play the happier you will be. Life is way too hard to be so serious. Lighten up and have fun whenever and wherever you can!

8. **Deal with your past traumas that are at the core of your trust issues.** It is very likely that past traumas or betrayals are at the core of your trust issues. Deal with them. You can definitely heal from past betrayals and traumas so what are you waiting for?

9. **Open up to friends or family – people who you know love you.** Share with friends or family that you are finally owning the fact that you have trust issues – and they will probably laugh! Or hopefully if they are good friends or good family members. Ask them to support you in building your trust muscles. They are probably already very

aware that you have trust issues. They may have the same issue.

10. **Consider the benefits for trusting others.** I listed some of the benefits of trusting others above. Are any of those benefits of interest to you? I think it's a ton of benefits. Rich and rewarding benefits. Consider what your life would look like if you did not have to worry about people being out to get you, betray you or hurt you. It's both freedom and power.
11. **Get into therapy if needed.** If you can't build the trust muscle on your own then consider a short course of therapy to get some coaching in this area.
12. **Take on learning the habits and practices that will give you a happy life.** If you simply took on the daily, weekly and monthly practices that I list in this blog, you would eventually start loving yourself more and your life more too. The more you can love yourself and your life the easier it will be to build the muscles of trusting others because you will trust yourself more.
13. **Live in the NOW with an eye to what you are creating.** If you are being present, in the moment, right now, you are not worrying about the past or anything but BEING in the PRESENT moment. The more you can practice being PRESENT, the less you will worry about life. Of course, this is best done when you have a plan for your life and you know what you are creating.
14. **Practice.** Life offers plenty of opportunity for trust. Practice. Try it. Fail. Try it again. Don't give up. You will get there if you persist.
15. **Choose to be trusting.** What if trust was a choice? What if you could simply choose to be trusting? At least when the opportunity presents itself – choose to be trusting.
16. **Ask people to help you with this.** You probably have lots of people in your life who have trust issues. Ask people to help you. Why not? The worst thing that could happen

is that they could say no. So, what. Who cares. Stop caring so much about what other people think of you and get busy working on yourself and your life.

**Concluding Thoughts:**

I personally can't image dealing with some of the signs that having trust issues includes like being worried that people are out to get me, always waiting for the other shoe to drop, feeling alone or isolated, believing that I don't deserve happiness, feeling hurt by every little thing someone does or says (or doesn't do or say) or constantly getting triggered or defensive. I just cannot imagine living life that way. Many, many people live with those feelings and fears every single day. Life is difficult as we all know. Building your muscles to be able to trust the people in your life will help you get more love and happiness in your life as well as give you more freedom, power and less anxiety.

There is definite power in simply owning that you have trust issues and being able to name that area of your life. You don't have to fix it or change it although you certainly could. If you wanted to you could make a commitment to working on it. You will be able to build muscles to trust others out of your commitment when you back up the commitment with actions that align with the commitment. Regardless, trust is an important component of living life. Anything you can do to build your ability to trust or even to be trustworthy in life will help you in many ways. I am here to help you along the way. Do you have trust issues? What do you have to say about trust issues? How can I support you in having a life filled with more love, happiness and freedom? How can I support your journey in life?

*Love.Life.*

**The Power & Magic of Vulnerability: Top 10 Ways You Can Start Increasing Your Ability to be Vulnerable**

March 10, 2020

Everyone wants to feel loved, connected, happy and alive, which are just a few of the amazing benefits of having the ability to be vulnerable with people. Vulnerability is one of the key components to intimate and deeply loving relationships and friendships. It is at the core of LOVE in my opinion. What it means to be vulnerable in real life is to be able to share your heart openly and freely with people that you know or possibly even strangers. It means being able to connect with people at a very deep level. It gives life meaning that is simply not possible without it. Part of vulnerability is openness and authenticity, which are extremely important facets of life to me and are a natural expression of who I am in the world.

When I say the magic of vulnerability what I mean is to be able to walk around in life being your authentic and true self – you as you really are – relating to others and being with people without particularly caring if they like you or not. It means being alive and free of anxiety and constant worry. It gives you an extraordinary sense of peace, joy and love. It is absolutely magical. It is also extremely powerful. Long before concepts like self-esteem and vulnerability were a "thing" some of us were walking through life being vulnerable as a natural expression of who we are. To be able to simply be who you are is beyond freeing. It allows for a childlike wonder. It is the most awesome thing in the world and so necessary for you to feel love.

Back in late 2018, I was looking for some documents and ran across some pictures from high school and college. My thought at that time was, gee I should post these to my private Facebook page because if anything ever happened to me these pictures would never see the light of day. So, over a month or so I posted a few pictures every day and it was a real hoot! Facebook friends of mine saw pictures of themselves from their youth that they had never seen before. It was fun and a very rich walk down memory lane. What started out as the innocent sharing of pictures so that the people could then download the pictures and have them morphed into me sharing personal information – a.k.a. me being vulnerable about what I was dealing with at the time.

As a result of me sharing myself with no shame and no apologies, after all, I did nothing wrong nor am I at fault for what happened, I got richly related to new people. I received tons of fantastic suggestions and advice. I got reconnected to people I used to know back in the day. I made new friends that I see almost weekly. All this happened because I was vulnerable in sharing my life and some (note NOT all) of my circumstances. It became apparent to my Facebook friends that I don't have this "perfect" life. Haha! It actually became obvious that I have some pretty awful circumstances to deal with on a regular basis. As a result, people started putting themselves on my team – a team that I didn't even ask for with the hashtag #TeamLisa. It was quite moving to be frank.

Were there criticisms? Of course! Were some people rolling their eyes? For sure! Did I care? No. In the sharing of myself and my circumstances, again not nearly all my circumstances, I was being vulnerable. People could relate to what I was going through. People could identify with me even if their situations were very different. It's not about being perfect. It's about being comfortable with who you are and what you are up to. I am completely moved by the prayers and love people have shown me through my private Facebook page. It touches my heart deeply. While most people would never be so vulnerable in a social media format, it has worked for me in so many ways. I would do it all over again.

Prolific writer C.S. Lewis, author of *The Chronicles of Narnia* and *The Lion, The Witch & The Wardrobe* was also known for many of his nonfiction books wrote about vulnerability and love in his *The Four Loves* book (1960). Here is a quote from his book:

*Love.Life.*

---

"To love at all is to be vulnerable. Love anything and your heart will be wrung and possibly broken. If you want to make sure of keeping it intact you must give it to no one, not even an animal. Wrap it carefully round with hobbies and little luxuries; avoid all entanglements. Lock it up safe in the casket or coffin of your selfishness. But in that casket, safe, dark, motionless, airless, it will change. It will not be broken; it will become unbreakable, impenetrable, irredeemable. To love is to be vulnerable."

— C.S. Lewis, The Four Loves (1960)

---

Currently, Brenè Brown, a research professor at the University of Huston where she has spent over two decades studying shame, empathy, vulnerability and courage, is the leading author and speaker on vulnerability having many excellent and bestselling books on the market. Her 2010 TEDx talk on vulnerability is one of the most viewed TED talks with over 40 million views. She is bringing subjects like shame and vulnerability into the public arena. And while she has so many phenomenal quotes on vulnerability, this is the one that speaks the loudest to me:

---

*"Vulnerability is not knowing victory or defeat, it's understanding the necessity of both; it's engaging. It's being all in."*

— Brenè Brown

---

I assert that the traits or characteristics that are necessary for being vulnerable or having vulnerability are some of the same characteristics that are required for having a life that you LOVE. And I am all about having a life that you LOVE. I am enthralled with YOU having a LIFE that YOU LOVE. Oh, gee whiz, I am pretty much just an over-the-top fan of LOVE in any capacity. Love your friends, love your family, love what you do, love your life and everything in it. Or at least as much as you can. You might not be able to remove some people or things in your life, but you can still have a pretty happy and joyous life. Trust me. I know. Vulnerability is critical.

And for the majority of human beings we are simply not wired to be vulnerable. We have had too many hurts, wounds and bad experiences to walk around with our hearts wide open to life. To be vulnerable does mean taking a risk that you will be rejected for who you are. I understand that all too well. I just don't happen to live like that. I am okay with rejection. I want to be around people who love me for who I am – with all of my imperfections, unconventional, and quirky as I am. And I want to know my peeps for who they are. Not what they do. Not what they have. Just who they are as human beings. I am crystal clear about the benefits of being able to be vulnerable with people as well as the risks.

In this post I will share the top reasons why people avoid being vulnerable, the benefits to vulnerability, the main components or traits necessary to be vulnerable, and what you can do to be more vulnerable as well as what I will call a cautionary tale. Let's start on a positive note. This is my list of benefits to vulnerability from my own perspective. It makes life so much richer.

## **Benefits to Vulnerability or Being Vulnerable**

1. It's the one thing that will help you get more LOVE in your life both romantic and platonic.
2. It's easier to make instant connections with people.
3. It's easier to develop deeper and more meaningful relationships because it builds intimacy.
4. Freedom – if you have the ability to be vulnerable then you have the practices, habits and characteristics to be more freed up in life and have LESS anxiety, fear and worry.
5. It's a very powerful way to live life.

6. You will have more friends because of #2 and #3 above.
7. You will have better health because you will have less anxiety, fear and worry.
8. You will have a sense of peace.
9. You will experience less loneliness because of #1, #2, #3, and #6.
10. It can change your life in an extremely positive way.
11. You will feel connected.
12. You will feel deep love and intimacy.
13. You will feel happy and alive.
14. People will be drawn to you for your vulnerability.
15. It's definitely way more fun to be authentic, open and real.

When I looked up the definition for vulnerability and vulnerable – I would run too if I wasn't so clear about the absolutely compelling benefits of vulnerability and the gifts it gives me in my everyday life.

The definition of vulnerable as an adjective is to be susceptible to physical or emotional attack or harm. Is it any wonder that people flee the scene when it comes to being vulnerable? The definition of vulnerability, a noun, is the quality or state of being exposed to the possibility of being attacked or harmed either physically or emotionally. I would add financially, a component that I address in a moment.

**Top Reasons Why We Avoid Being Vulnerable**

1. Fear of getting hurt
2. Fear of being used or exploited
3. Fear of rejection
4. Fear of being judged as less than or inferior
5. Fear of being laughed at or ridiculed
6. Feelings of shame or embarrassment
7. Incomplete with a past experience or event
8. Being stuck
9. Feelings of inadequacy or worthlessness

10. Fear of losing your money or assets * Addressed below*

There is no question if you open your heart that you might get hurt, used or exploited. It's possible you could be rejected, judged, laughed at or ridiculed. Some people are not who they say they are – even if you meet them through someone you know and even sometimes if they are highly recommended by someone you know. Some people just never let you know who they really are, which is one of the risks you take. You have to weigh the benefits of vulnerability with the risks. You have to consider what you want in your life. If you want love and friendships then that involves some risk. You have to consider the benefits of being vulnerable that I listed above.

It's even possible that you could lose your money or assets. However, in this day in age pre-nuptial agreements and other legally binding contracts are the way to prevent you from losing your money and assets. I just happen to be of the opinion that this fear is extremely reasonable and is one that can and should be handled by a pre-nuptial, legally binding agreement. I know that some of you can and will disagree with my stance on this, which is fine. It happens all the time that both men and women lose significant amounts of money and assets due to relationships gone bad and for that reason alone it's reasonable to handle that fear with a legal document. I would have serious questions about anyone unwilling to sign a pre-nuptial or other legally binding document handing the protections of either party's assets. Why would you not want to protect someone else's money or assets? I say that having lost significant money in prior relationships so I might be biased.

**Cautionary Tale**

I can't write about being vulnerable without making some mention of con men and women, predators, narcissists and psychopaths. They exist in decent numbers in our society as in 1 out of 100 people fit the bill for psychopaths with many more being con artists, predators and narcissists. Even when you do your due diligence and meet people through friends or business contacts, you might have the great misfortune of getting involved with a con artist, a predator, a narcissist or God forbid – a full blown psychopath. It happens to people of all professions and walks of life. Full blown psychopaths can be dangerous. And I believe it behooves all of us in the world to have a tad bit more understanding about psychopaths because I believe that education is power.

The premier expert in psychopaths is Dr. Robert Hare, a Canadian psychologist who developed what is called "The Psychopath Checklist" (PCL). The Psychopath Checklist was later refined into the Psychopath Checklist-Revised (PCL-R) and sometime later a screening version was released known as the Psychopath Checklist-Screening Version (PCL-SV). Dr. Hare's PCL-R and PCL-SV are the gold standard as a diagnostic tool for psychopaths according to the research I looked at. I found the PCL-R and PCL-SV online when I was researching psychopaths a few years ago. I found it extremely helpful as a layperson to see a copy of these tools. I used the PCL-SV to score a person I was dealing with. That person got just below a perfect score on the test. Above a certain test score means an increased likelihood of violence.

In fact, I found it so helpful that I will probably drop Dr. Hare a personal note soon letting him know how helpful his tools are to a layperson and asking him to make a PDF available of the tests. If you are dealing with a person who you suspect could be or might be a psychopath, look up the PCL-SV or PCL-R online. Hopefully you can find a printable version of the PCL-SV, which is what I would look for first or the PCL-R. It is a very helpful tool that I believe every domestic violence organization and every law enforcement organization should be trained in, which is not the case presently. I further believe that the contents of the PCL-SV should be fodder for public conversations. We should all understand the criteria of what makes up a psychopath. Just my opinion. Maybe I'll include that in my note to Dr. Hare. Doing your due diligence doesn't mean you won't end up dealing with someone with ill intent so this is my word to the wise.

What is important is that when you do the work on yourself – the growth and development work that I write about – you do not have to end up with your spirit crushed. You do not have to end up balled up in a corner unable to function. Often times men and women who have the unfortunate circumstance to be in a relationship with a con artist, predator, narcissist or psychopath come out of the relationship badly damaged. They have experienced a trauma for which they are not equipped to deal with. I am here to say that you can heal from any trauma or painful experience or event. It takes work. It won't happen overnight. I can say with authority and experience that bad people, events or circumstances don't have to damage you or take away your ability to function or have happiness. While that is more often the case than not – it simply does not have to go that way.

Everything I write about is how to function in life – at a powerful level. When you have the habits, practices, attitudes and beliefs for a powerful life no one can take that away from you. In my mind, my spirit is not crushable because it belongs to God. Completely and fully. People who are in the narcissist or psychopath genre intend to crush the spirit or soul of another by their actions. You don't have to end up in a bad state. Do the work on yourself. Some of the people who are con artists, predators, narcissists or psychopaths are exceptionally good at fooling people. And, if you don't really know about those personality types you could fall prey to their actions. You shouldn't fault yourself if you do. You just pick yourself up, dust yourself off, and move forward powerfully. I recommend laughing as you do that. As in "Haha! You tried to crush my spirit, but I WIN!" At least that has worked for me. I am not kidding about the laughing part.

Even though what I have been through is horrific in every way and was of course extremely painful, I am a better person for what I have been through. I STILL choose to be vulnerable. Why? Because the benefits to feeling love, being able to give and receive love are too extraordinary for me to pass up. I am the embodiment of love. I will never give up LOVE in any form. That's way too valuable to give up. So, work on having a functional life. Work on yourself. You can survive anything with the right coping mechanisms, attitude, work ethic, habits and practices. That is what this blog is about. Having a happy and joyful life even when times are difficult.

**Requirements to be Vulnerable**

This is just my take on what I believe vulnerability requires. I don't know how or if this matches up with what the psychology books say, so do take it with a grain or perhaps a pound of salt.

1. Self-confidence/Self-Esteem: Being clear about who you are in the world without apology.
2. Openness
3. Ability to laugh at yourself
4. No perfection: There's no room for perfectionism if you are living a real and authentic life.
5. Courage & Bravery: It's an act of courage and bravery to be vulnerable UNTIL you grow and develop yourself until it is a natural expression of who you are. Then, it is just what you do and who you are.
6. Not caring too much what others think of you – or the ability to not be worried about being judged.
7. Compassion for yourself and others – a sense of humanity.
8. Empathy for others. Being able to put yourself in someone else's shoes.
9. Authenticity – the ability to be the real you.
10. BE PRESENT.
11. Trust – yourself and others (just have a pre-nuptial or other legal agreement to protect your money and assets, which is often important for young people too).

## What You Can Do to Become More Vulnerable

1. **Practice Self-Love & Self-Acceptance**: Embrace your imperfections.
2. **Growth & Development:** Pretty much everything I blog about is in the growth and development category. The more you work on yourself the easier it will be to allow yourself to be vulnerable.
3. **Practice being vulnerable.** Bit by bit, give yourself opportunities to open up a little and practice being vulnerable with people in your life.
4. **Build Your Self-Esteem.** I just blogged about this in a post titled Is Low Self-Esteem Stealing Love, Joy & Happiness from Your Life? Top 29 Tips for Boosting Self-Esteem Like a Boss on March 6, 2020. Anything you do to increase your self-esteem will go a long way to helping you become more vulnerable.
5. **Do self-care** because you will look and feel better, which is always helpful. I blogged about this in a post titled Self-Mastery, Self-Motivation & Self-Care: The Holy Grail of Happiness & Joy, January 30, 2020.
6. **Be PRESENT!** You can't be authentic and real if you are not present. Being present is an important ability or trait for living an amazing life. Be in the moment. Be here now!
7. **Recognize the commonality of the human condition and humanity**. We all want to be loved and appreciated. We all have hurts, wounds and pain. We are all doing the best that we can. When you come from a place of the human condition, it seems to me that it takes a lot of pressure off of you.
8. **BE FOCUSED on YOUR LIFE - & making it great.** If you spend your time and energy on your life and making it the best life possible you will not care nearly as much about what other people think or say about you. Drive your life fully and completely and a great deal of issues and problems will resolve themselves.

9. **Practice doing new things** because that builds the muscles of courage and overcoming fears.
10. **Take on the practice and habits that give you a life that you** love in time management, planning your life, having fun, making friends and pretty much everything that I blog about.

**Concluding Thoughts**

You want a life filled with love, joy, happiness and freedom. You want to feel alive and connected. You want to have an easier time in life. Vulnerability can help you get there. How guarded or vulnerable are you as you go through life? Are you willing to take a chance in life – take a calculated risk – for all of the benefits that feeling love, having friends or a romantic relationship has to offer you?

I assert that if you did the work to have self-confidence, be open to life, drop the need for perfection, be able to laugh at yourself, be present, and have compassion for yourself and others that you would find being vulnerable not as difficult. If you did the work to have those traits or characteristics, perhaps being vulnerable would come easy. It could become a natural expression of who you are in the world. Where are you with being vulnerable? Can you do it? Are you willing to be vulnerable? What is stopping you? How can I help you? Let me know!

**LOVE in the Midst of Chaos – And, Yes I love you!**

March 31, 2020

The obvious question some of you might have right now is how could I love you if I have not even met you? How could I love you if I don't even know you? The answer to that question lies in my deep-seated sense of humanity. When you get the human condition and have a big sense of humanity then it is easy to LOVE. When you have dealt with your own issues and can accept yourself for who you are it is much easier to LOVE everyone for who they are, which is a separate distinction for loving people for what they do for you, what they have, and so on. Everyone wants to be loved and valued and to be accepted for who they are. I can say that I love you even though I don't know you because I know who I am, I love and accept myself (not in a hubris filled or narcissistic way), and I have compassion for the human condition and life itself. I actually deeply love people and humanity.

Two essential questions have been pondered, researched and written about since the beginning of time from what I can tell. Those two questions are: (1) What is the meaning of life? and (2) What am I here for? Or what is my purpose in life? It seems to me that the greatest thinkers and philosophers of all time have written about that. It appears that every generation throughout time have pondered those two exact questions. I am not a philosopher, in fact I don't even think that I did very well in a college philosophy class, however those two questions have captivated me and held my attention for decades.

From my perspective, the meaning of life is all about LOVE. Giving love. Receiving love. Loving your life, your friends, your family, what you do on a daily basis, your coworkers, your neighbors, your hobbies and organizations. For me, LOVE is at the core of everything that I do – or almost all of it. Love is the most powerful of emotions and causes people to get out of their own way and do extraordinary things – for either the people that they love or for society and humanity. Abraham Lincoln, Martin Luther King, Jr., Mahatma Gandhi, and Mother Teresa are examples of people who have gotten out of their own way and done what was needed for the love of their cause, the love of their people, or the love of the world.

I believe that my purpose in life is to bring LOVE into the lives of the people I come into contact with and to help others LOVE their LIFE. I believe in loving people. I believe that LOVE is very healing, delightful and fun. I also am well aware that love, in the context of either platonic friendships or romantic relationships, involves risk. The risk of rejection. The risk that your offer of friendship will not be returned in kind or returned at all. The risk of loss and of betrayal. Yes, there is no doubt that love in either context involves some risk.

Young children, unless they are abused or grow up in a very toxic and unhealthy living environment where they are not well cared for or where their needs are not met, are usually very loving, care-free, and open. Children walk around curious and filled with wonder about the world - until they have their first experience of shame or some incident where they are left feeling abandoned or not good enough. It happens at various ages for children. Then they become more cautious, guarded, not so open and less willing to take risks. It's just kind of the evolution of human beings. It is both my experience and assertion that you can heal your past hurts, wounds and traumas and become open to love and letting love be the field that you play in.

Of course, I have had many hurts, betrayals of a significant level, and loss over my lifetime. Yes, because you know that if someone is 58 years old and starting over in life with pretty much nothing that something bad happened. That's probably very obvious. I am never going to stop loving people. Loving my life. Sharing love. It's too wonderful to give up. I know some of you gave up on real love a long time ago and for probably very good reason(s). I can totally understand that. You are not wrong for that. I am simply inviting you to a new way of looking at life and love.

In the midst of the chaos that is enveloping the world, there has never been a better time for healing and love in my humble opinion. There are more people suffering in the world right now than just a few months ago. There are more people who need to feel love and be loved right now than in the past. Bringing LOVE to the table in the midst of the chaos is just what is called for – says me. I know. Who do I think I am? Nobody. Just someone who has a lot of experience, both good and bad, with love. And I am still a huge fan of love.

The chaos offers you the opportunity to reconsider where you stand about love. It offers those of you who are not working or even those of you who are still working the gift of time to contemplate love and where love is present in your life or where love is missing. We are all given this one precious life to live however we choose. Some people make bad choices and don't treat others well. Some people get so badly wounded at some point in their lives that they just put up walls and don't let people in. And there is a lot of in between. It's not all or nothing for some people.

What is the meaning of life for you? I am well aware that is not a question that too many people think about. Oh, trust me, I know that. What if you could use this chaos to redesign your life to be more pleasing to you? What if you could have more love in your life – either through friendships or a romantic relationship? What if you could love more parts of your life than you love right now? Given the level of unhappiness, anxiety, depression and other problems that was present in the world before the chaos – I assert that, prior to the chaos, too many people were living their lives in a way that didn't make them happy.

This is the core essence of what I write about – how to design your life in a way that inspires you and makes you happy as well as the habits, practices, skills and attitudes that will leave you functioning well no matter what happens. It boils down to being able to be happy with your life and able to deal with hardship and unexpected turns in life. My last 4 blog posts were specifically designed to help you deal with the pandemic and help give you tools and tips to get through it. There are over 33 blog posts to help you start living a life that you are both happy with and would be proud to have lived.

One of the biggest fears about love is rejection. You want to make new friends but are concerned about being rejected, which is a reasonable fear because that happens from time to time. Or perhaps you want to be in a romantic relationship or just start dating but you are worried about being rejected. Again, a reasonable consideration. But here's the thing about rejection. You don't have to take it personally. Yes, you might be rejected if you try to make a new friend or group of new friends. You might be rejected if you start dating or even if you begin a new relationship. IF you find yourself rejected in either case, what IF you said to yourself, well God has better people HE wants me to meet? Or there is someone better for me to date. What if you stopped taking the rejection like there was something wrong with you?

I am suggesting that you stop taking rejection as if you were not good enough. You ARE good enough. You are already good enough. Maybe you could grow and develop. Maybe you could adopt some new habits and practices to make your life happier. Maybe you could look inward and find happiness within yourself. If you are waiting to be happy until you have a perfect life, or until you have that perfect relationship – good luck with that. I don't support that philosophy although you are clearly welcome to keep that way of thinking.

If you were willing to accept that rejection of any kind DOES NOT mean that you are not good enough, I assert that your whole world would change. I assert, as someone practiced and skilled at being rejected (not kidding), that you would experience a whole new freedom in life. You would be willing to take more risks and I say that you would have more love in your life. To get there might mean doing what I call the work on yourself. It might mean growing and developing. It might mean healing past hurts or wounds. It might mean developing better coping mechanisms for life. It might mean a few different things. Who knows what it would take for you to change your view of rejection? I don't know what it will take for you to do that. I do know that what I write about will help you get there over time.

Loss and betrayal are two other components that prevent people from allowing love into their lives. Yes, having LOVE in your life might mean a potential loss or betrayal. I have written about loss and betrayal in a post titled The Power & Magic of Vulnerability: Top 10 Ways You Can Start Increasing Your Ability to be Vulnerable, March 10, 2020, because to be vulnerable you have to deal with that on some level. Being able to trust is a part of allowing love into your life and you can find out about how to deal with that in my post titled LOVE Involves Trust: Why It's Time to Deal with Your Trust Issues, February 28, 2020. The other post that deals with LOVE that might be helpful to you is titled Living Life with Your Whole Heart September 2019. The post titled Love & Miracles – How to Get More Love & Miracles in Your Life, January 8, 2020 also relates to this topic of LOVE. Can you tell that I LOVE anything to do with LOVE? Chuckling to myself. It's true.

I know exactly who I am. I am comfortable in my own skin. I accept my imperfections and how I am as well as how I am not. I am just me doing life the best that I can. I am crystal clear that some people don't like me. I am too happy, too organized, too loud, too colorful, to this and too that for some people. I mean I am clear that I get on some people's nerves quite easily. I am fine with that. I mean I never intentionally annoy people because that's not my style. I have a tribe of people who accept me for who I am and who love me dearly. I am blessed beyond measure. I treasure life. I treasure people. I treasure humanity and everyone in it. I am passionate about living life to the fullest and being happy!

Where do you stand with LOVE? What is the meaning of life to you? What are you here for or what is your purpose in life? Are you willing to go on a delicious journey to create a life filled with love and happiness? Are you willing to let go of the past? Are you willing to hit the re-set button and start anew? Are you willing to let love in? Are you willing to be happy? Are you open to love?

It's really your choice on how you live your life. I am well aware that there are some people who are so attached to negativity and unhappiness that they just can't let go of that. We probably all know people who fit that description. You did not choose this chaos. You did not choose to have your life upended and the rug to be pulled out from under you. Nobody chose that. You do get to choose how you react to it. You do get to choose how you will move forward. You do get to choose if you are going to make any changes to your life as a result of it. You do get to choose if this chaos will permanently disrupt your life or IF it will be the start of something better.

With the state of things and all of the chaos, we need love now more than ever. We need the healing touch of love. We need the generosity of love. We need the kindness of love. We need the united feeling love can provide. We need people to stretch themselves to be better. We need love in generous amounts spread all around. We need to help people like never before. We need people to love each other and be kind.

I know times are hard. I am an expert in hard times. Trust me. You have no idea. I want you to have a wonderful life. Even though I don't know you, I feel love for you. I am here to help you find your way through the chaos to love. Are you willing to go on the journey? How can I support you? What are you struggling with? What do you need to be successful? What is stopping you? Please let me know!

**The Miracles of Gratitude**

June 30, 2020

Gratitude could change your life for the better and permanently if you understood how powerful it is for human health and wellbeing. Given the level of unhappiness in the world, I believe that it is a safe assessment that some gratitude is missing because one of the benefits of gratitude is happiness. If you want to increase your happiness levels then this is one excellent way to accomplish that. If happiness is what you need you can find more about happiness in a previous post on happiness or you can learn how to generate your own happiness in this post. Gratitude has been written about since the beginning of mankind and is the inspiration or content of songs, books, quotations and much more. Yet, the research in the area of gratitude is fairly young in comparison.

Gratitude is defined as the quality of being thankful; readiness to show appreciation for and to return kindness. The academic definition of gratitude includes a two-step process which includes recognizing you have received a good result or outcome coupled with recognizing that there is an outside or external source for this positive outcome or good result. Two different ways of stating the same thing. We all mostly recognize gratitude when we hear it or see it.

---

*"He is a wise man who does not grieve for the things which he has not, but rejoices for those which he has."*

— EPICTETUS (EPICTETUS WAS A GREEK STOIC PHILOSOPHER BORN A SLAVE IN HIERAPOLIS, PHRYGIA IN 50 AD.)

---

I am a huge fan of gratitude. It is a way of life for me. Because I have lived this way for so long I actually had to do some research on the benefits of gratitude to see what the science shows. It was amazing! This is the compiled list, which only includes the known and agreed upon benefits – not the ones still being researched and proven.

**Staggering Benefits of Gratitude**

1. Increases happiness
2. Reduces pain
3. Releases toxic emotions
4. Improves sleep quality
5. Reduces cardiac diseases
6. Reduces inflammations
7. Reduces neurodegeneration significantly
8. Increases energy
9. Increases vitality
10. Increases enthusiasm
11. Helps in stress regulation
12. Reduces anxiety
13. Reduces depression
14. Helps build emotional resilience

15. Helps you focus on the good things in life
16. Helps you stay in reality, the present, even when things are bad
17. Promotes solution-oriented thinking
18. Improves relationships
19. Provides increased motivation via serotonin, dopamine & oxytocin transmitters that make you feel good
20. Increases self-esteem
21. Helps people meet their basic psychological needs

Let that sink in. Isn't that amazing? Awesome? Simply overwhelming? The science is in and gratitude is miraculous in terms of benefits for human health and wellbeing. What this means is that gratitude is one powerful thing to focus on if you want to be happier and healthier. It means that gratitude is absolutely the muscle to build unless you just want to whine and complain about your life. Unless you just want to be the victim to your circumstances, your life, your past or whatever. You get to choose.

Then why are we not more grateful? Here's a first pass at some of the reasons why we struggle at being grateful.

## Reasons Why People Struggle with Being Grateful

1. They are having serious issues and are in pain and suffering.
2. They are spoiled or have an entitlement mentality.
3. They have unrealistic expectations.
4. They have low self-esteem.
5. They are prone to negative thinking or are a pessimist.
6. They feel sorry for themselves or have the victim mentality.
7. They have addictions like drugs or alcohol that are problematic.
8. They are narcissists or have some other psychopathology.
9. They are bitter or envious of others.
10. They are simply self-centered.

11. They have the temperament that they are never satisfied.
12. They might have boundary issues.
13. They simply don't know enough about poverty and other serious issues facing people in the world.
14. They don't know people who are worse off than they are.

---

"Gratitude is not only the greatest of virtues, but the parent of all others."

— CICERO (CICERO WAS A ROMAN STATESMAN, LAWYER AND ACADEMIC SKEPTIC PHILOSOPHER FROM ITALY BORN IN 106 BC.)

---

I understand all too well that some of you have great difficulty with being grateful or having gratitude in your life. To help you with that I am going to give you a helpful hot list of things that most of you can be grateful for in your life. Notice that I said that most of you can be grateful for...

**Things You Could be Grateful for (as they apply):**

1. Having sufficient food
2. Having clean water
3. Have safe shelter or a place to live
4. Family/spouse/relationships
5. Friends (Read this if you need to make new friends or more friends)
6. Neighbors
7. Employment or income
8. Nature
9. Good weather

10. Pets
11. Children/Nieces or Nephews
12. Beauty…in art, people, nature and so many things
13. That you are alive today
14. For your health
15. For financial security
16. For your hobbies (read this if you need to hobby up)
17. That your mind/brain is working
18. That you can read this
19. That you can create your life as you want it to be (read this for how to start that)
20. That you are not in jail
21. For laughter
22. That you can change
23. That you are a good person (read this if you have doubts about that)
24. That you have time (read this for ideas on time management)
25. For your skills and abilities
26. For God and your faith
27. That you have the gift of speech, vision or hearing

As someone who is more often than not in a state of gratitude, I express my appreciation for people in my life on a daily basis. I say thank you everywhere I can to everyone I can. I write handwritten thank you notes as often as needed. You would be surprised the impact that a handwritten thank you note has on the receiver. One time I was in line at the car dealership and a man said hello to me as if he knew me. Shortly thereafter when he realized that I didn't recognize him, he explained who he was and that he had my written thank you note taped to his locker. That thank you note had been written a few years before our chance encounter. What I learned then was that it can be deeply meaningful for a person in a paid position to receive a thank you note for simply doing their job.

I not only write thank you notes, I take little treats to people who matter to me and help me along the way. For me gratitude is a natural expression of loving my life and the people in it. There are so many things we can each be grateful for. Practice that muscle and it will grow and grow until it is the most natural expression of you and your love of the little things in life.

**How to Increase Your Gratitude Muscle:**

1. Keep a gratitude journal or list. Do that until the practice of gratitude is so natural that you don't have to think about it – it just comes automatically.
2. Personal growth and development. Do the work. See this post on the benefits of personal growth and development or this post on emotional intelligence.
3. Stop the negative thinking and pessimism.
4. Have a road map for your life or a plan or vision and execute your plan!
5. Find those less fortunate and help them! Volunteer and get involved in your community. There are lots of people who could use your help!
6. Be present. Be here now. Live in the moment.
7. Write thank you notes to people who you are grateful to and snail mail your note! Do this as often as you can!

---

"Gratitude is the sign of noble souls."

— Aesop

---

**Call to Action:**

Being grateful is free because it is a state of mind hopefully coupled with words expressed to another person. Are you willing to allow yourself to have the miracles of gratitude in your life with all of the benefits of health and wellness? How can I help you grow your gratitude muscles? Who do you know who could benefit from reading this post? Please leave me a comment if you have a question that I can help you with. Please share this post with your friends or family or on social media. I am here to lovingly support you in your journey through life. How can I help you?

**The Road to Happiness Starts Here**

August 20, 2020

While life is hard, even extremely hard at times especially during a pandemic, that doesn't mean that you can't find happiness and be happy. This is month two in the Year of Freedom – freedom from depression, anxiety, overwhelm, feeling stuck, worry, anger, resentment, suffering, negativity and your past – stepping into love, happiness, peace, contentment, increased self-esteem, personal satisfaction, control over your life and your destiny. All of that is possible with new skills, habits, practices, attitudes and beliefs. And for the next year you can win prizes in the Year of Freedom Giveaway, so please enter to win.

The theme for August theme was being AWAKE and AWARE. Are you awake and aware to how you live your life? Are awake and aware to how you are feeling moment to moment? Are you aware of how you spend your time? In the Awake & Aware month of August, I covered the absolute critical nature of self-care and dug deeper into self-care with a post on Pandemic Sleeping Tips since so many more people are having trouble sleeping, which is extremely important to happiness if you look at the research.

Happiness doesn't have to be an elusive, someday-maybe you will be happy. You can learn what it takes to be happy. It's not just one thing that usually makes people happy. Overall happiness is a function of several things, which I am covering today. There are things you can do – actions you can take every day to be happy just like there are actions you can take to stave off depression, deal with low self-esteem, or deal with feelings of overwhelm.

## Benefits to Happiness

1. Happiness feels great
2. Happiness is good for your heart (protects your heart).
3. Happiness helps build your immune system.
4. Happiness helps you combat stress more effectively.
5. Happy people have less aches and pains.
6. Happiness helps combat disease and disability.
7. Happiness can lengthen your life span by up to 10 years.
8. Happy people are less likely to get sick.
9. Happy people have more friends.
10. Happy people are more successful.
11. Being happy makes life easier.
12. Happy people have more rich and meaningful conversations.
13. Happy people smile more, which makes them perceived as more generous, trustworthy and extroverted.
14. Happy people exercise more and eat better.
15. Happy people are more productive.
16. Happy people are more creative.
17. Happy people earn more.
18. Happy people are more satisfied with their jobs.
19. Happy people are kinder.
20. Happy people are more loved.
21. Happy people are viewed as better, well-regarded leaders.
22. Happy people are happy with themselves and what they have in life.
23. Happier parents engage in more positive parental behaviors and also influences positive outcomes in their children (child's motivation, achievement and peer relationships).
24. Happiness is sexy and an attractive quality.

*Love.Life.*

**Reasons Why People Are Unhappy**

There are many, many reasons why people are unhappy in life. These are just a few of the more common reasons.

1. Lack of purpose or meaning in life
2. Comparing yourself or your life to that of others
3. Boredom
4. Lack of social connections or friends
5. Lack of self-care
6. Lack of sleep (in particular even though sleep falls under self-care)
7. Low self-esteem
8. Feelings of remorse, shame, guild, anger, resentment
9. Negative thinking or being a pessimist
10. Being unhealthy either physically or mentally or both
11. Blaming others for your state in life or problems
12. Not setting attainable goals
13. Not being present (living in the past)
14. Unresolved (current or past) trauma
15. Difficult life circumstances (financial, relationship, job, caregiver, etc.)
16. Lack of assertiveness (you get exploited, used, etc.)
17. Lack of gratitude
18. Poor time management
19. You don't know how to manage, process and deal with your emotions effectively
20. Being overly self-critical
21. Self-sabotage or addictions
22. Being a people pleaser at your own expense
23. Feeling stuck
24. Having disempowering beliefs, attitudes or thinking
25. Engaging in catastrophizing or over-thinking
26. Feeling alone in life
27. Living in fear of rejection, failure
28. Being a perfectionist
29. Having a victim mentality

30. Living in resignation

While most everyone says that they want to be happy, in my experience not everyone is willing to take the appropriate actions necessary to bring happiness into their lives. I believe that happiness is both a choice and a function of how you live your life. I am also sure that you can learn to generate your own happiness separate and distinct from your circumstances, which you can hear about in this video. I know that you can eventually be happy if you are willing to take the actions and build the habits and practices that help you be happy.

**September Theme: Building a Base for Happiness**

I selected building a base for happiness for the September Year of Freedom theme because constructing your life is much like building a home – you get to pick and choose how you are organized, what you do with your time, how you view life, who you spend your time with, what goals you set and so much more. Thanks to the science field of neuroplasticity, we know that you are not stuck in life being the way you are now. You can teach an old dog new tricks (video). The science on neuroplasticity is so exciting. You can change. Your brain can develop new pathways leading you to a whole new life. You can be happy. You can be freed up from old hurts and wounds. This month I want you will dig in and start to build a base in the most critical areas of having a functional and happy life.

This month I am asking you to begin building your base for happiness in these key areas:

1. **Building a base routine of self-care**: Everything you need to know about self-care is covered in this post on self-care including why people don't do it, and why it is important as well as what it is. Personally, I just don't see how you can be happy if you are not taking care of yourself. In my post on Pandemic Sleeping Tips I shared that the research shows that people are more emotionally

and socially sensitive when they don't get the proper sleep. Yet the negative consequences for insufficient sleep are way more serious than just being "touchy" or sensitive. This month go to work on establishing a routine of self-care that helps you be energized, rested and recharged. A solid self-care routine will go a long way to happiness and having more energy.

2. **Building a base of social connections and friends**: The research is very compelling that dealing with feelings of loneliness and isolation are more positive for human health than dealing with obesity and other health issues. If you are one of those people who possibly needs to make more friends you can find out more here or watch this video on making friends. Even with the constraints of the pandemic there are ways to be connected to your friends or family by phone, by video calls or with social distancing. The important aspect of this is that you establish a foundation or a base of social connections because that will help you in the area of happiness and good health.

3. **Building a base of emotional vocabulary**: While you are building a base for happiness I highly recommend that you print out an emotional vocabulary sheet and begin increasing your emotional vocabulary because that will help you increase your emotional intelligence, which is extremely valuable in the area of happiness. I explain the emotional vocabulary sheet this in a video here. You can find an emotional vocabulary word sheet here. Really, this is so important. Do it!

4. **Building a base of hobbies or enjoyable activities**: On the road to happiness it is very helpful if you have hobbies or activities that you enjoy and that make you happy! If you don't have an array of hobbies at this time, I have a post about getting a hobby because they really can help you love your life as I discuss in this video. If you don't have the time to start a hobby right now you could at least begin to explore what hobby you would begin when the

time is right. Beyond hobbies you can find enjoyable activities that you appreciate and make you happy. Walking is one of my activities that I just love. Find activities that light you up even if it is volunteering, doing charity work, or helping those in need – all really great activities that can boost your sense of wellbeing.

5. **Building a base of integrity:** We live in a world where integrity is sadly often lacking. I am a huge fan of integrity because I believe that living your life with integrity gives you huge emotional and psychological benefits. I have written about integrity including 10 benefits of a life of integrity. One benefit not listed in that post was you will probably sleep better and that is just an opinion not a fact. Look at yourself and how you live your life. Do you keep your promises? Do you do what you say you will? Where can you add integrity into your life? This month start to boost your integrity and do what you say you will do.

6. **Building a base for a reward system:** When you are working on establishing new habits or behaviors it is extremely helpful to have a personal reward system or watch my video here. Last month I recommended to people to have a buddy to make the most of the Year of Freedom and changing their life because it's helpful to have a person who is committed to changing their life as well. I really, really hope that you will implement a reward system because I have confidence that a well put together reward system will help you stay motivated as you start to build the base for happiness with your new habits and practices.

**Some of the Reasons Why I am Happy**

1. My belief and faith in God
2. Reasonably strong in self-care
3. Having an attitude of gratitude

4. Being present or living in the NOW
5. Able to deal with, manage and process my emotions (emotional intelligence)
6. Healed from the past by doing my own personal growth and development
7. I purposefully do things that make me happy (intentionally)
8. I have a vision and life plan for my life that makes me excited and happy
9. I am working on my life plan on a regular basis
10. I rarely do things that make me unhappy OR I find a way to be happy doing something that I don't particularly like (like ironing for example)
11. I don't watch the news
12. I have a child-like sense of wonder about life and the world
13. I have strong time management skills
14. I have a solid prayer life
15. I have amazing friends and family
16. I avoid negative people and situations whenever I can
17. My heart is filled with love for people and humanity as well as the human condition
18. I don't compare myself to others
19. I am not materialistic
20. I appreciate life and just being alive
21. I have empowering beliefs and attitudes (like good things happen to me)
22. I appreciate my imperfections
23. I have firm boundaries
24. I am assertive (distinct from being passive, aggressive, or passive-aggressive)
25. I deal with problems directly and head on
26. I appreciate and value all of the difficulties and traumas I have had in my life and how I have grown from them
27. I choose happiness and love

**Call to Action:**

What are you willing to do to increase your own happiness? What support do you need to make the changes in your life that will lead you to being happy? Who can you get to be your buddy in changing your life? Who do you know that needs to read this blog post? How can I support you in building your base of happiness? Will you share this article on your social media so that you can help someone who needs to see this? Please let me know how I can help you with your journey because that would make me happy!

October Theme: Healing Your Heart

October 1, 2020

**Heart Break & Wounds to Your Heart**

I am a fan of healing broken hearts and living life with your whole heart as opposed to half-hearted living or being one of the walking wounded. You are in excellent company if you have suffered a broken heart and have not yet healed from it. Really, really good company if that makes you feel any better. There are too many people who become jaded, wounded, or otherwise broken after experiencing heart break. Many of those people will tell you directly that they are just jaded. While that is fine and that is one way to live, I am a fan of love and healing your heart, which can be done.

I recently blogged about dealing with emotional pain and how to use it to your advantage. Heart break is a special form of emotional pain, which in and of itself can be a big source of loneliness and isolation. When I speak about heart break I am specifically addressing the heart break caused from an intimate, significant relationship that ends due to either death or a break up although there are other things that can cause heart break, which I addressed in the post about emotional pain.

Twenty-eight sources or causes of emotional pain are included in that emotional pain post. All of life involves some form of emotional pain now or then because it is just a part of life unpleasant as it may be. Unless you close yourself off to people, happiness, love, joy and being connected to people - emotional pain and heart break is unavoidable. What is helpful is to learn the skills, habits, practices, attitudes and beliefs that will enable you to live a happy and powerful life regardless of what is going on in your life especially when times are tough. Dealing with heart break often causes people to develop trust issues. You want to be able to heal your heart so that you can be vulnerable with people because that is a critical part of close relationships.

Here's where I make a shameless plug for you to enter to win free stuff! Yes, you read that correctly! I am giving away cool stuff every single month until July 2021 in my Year of Freedom Giveaway. Why? Because if you took on your own growth and development you could have a completely different life. You can read more about the Year of Freedom here.

Hopefully you want to have a happy and healthy life. I want you to have a happy and healthy life. Even if your life up until this very moment has been filled with stress, strife, negative events and people – you can change that. You are not stuck with a future that is filled with negativity or unhappiness. We know that the brain can be rewired thanks to a concept called neuroplasticity of the brain, which means that you literally can teach an old dog new tricks (video). You can change your life regardless of what your past includes. It takes motivation, the willingness and openness to want something better for yourself, and support. Even if you are in a situation that you cannot change because of the circumstances – you can go to work on yourself (growth and development) and feel better. You can also create a vision for your life or a life plan and start working on that.

If you think that this is simply impossible for you, then I would strongly suggest that you get familiar with the concept of the self-fulling prophecy and what that means in life, which I happen to have a short video on. Life is hard. There's no doubt about it. That's why you need to have every tool and technique to make it easier. Harness the self-fulling prophecy to your advantage because otherwise you are making use of the self-defeating prophecy, and just like the name implies – that's a negative thing.

**Physical Manifestations of Heart Break**

My recent post on emotional pain includes a section on how emotional pain can manifest in physical pain in the body, which I am not going to repeat here. I will however add some new information on the subject. If you have never heard of emotional pain causing physical pain in the body that falls under the mind-body connection and is worth learning about since there is plenty of evidence to support that. Consider that over 2,000 years ago, Hippocrates – a Greek physician who is considered to be the father of medicine, wrote that all forms of illness had a natural cause when at that time (460 B.C. to 375 B.C.) people believed that sickness was caused either by the wrath of God or some superstitious beliefs. All that means that the mind-body connection has thousands of years of history and practical use.

According to the American Heart Association, physical manifestations of heart break can include a condition called Broken Heart Syndrome, which can include chest pains (angina), shortness of breath, irregular heartbeats (arrhythmias) and cardiogenic shock (a suddenly weakened heart can't pump enough blood to meet the body's needs) – a condition that can be fatal if not treated immediately.

The bottom line is that emotional pain of any kind can cause physical pain in the body or heart issues in the case of a broken heart. This should provide some motivation to deal with and process your emotions and do the work to heal your emotional pain, which can be done if you put in the effort and keep at it.

## Benefits to Healing Your Heart

There are significant benefits to doing the work to heal your heart regardless of the source of heart break. This list is only a partial list of the top benefits.

1. It gives you access to love.
2. It helps you form healthy relationships.
3. It helps you feel connected to people.
4. It will increase your happiness.
5. It will give you freedom from emotional pain.
6. It will increase your vitality.
7. It feels better.
8. It will increase your self-esteem.
9. It provides significant health benefits.
10. It will help you feel back in control of your life.
11. It will give you a sense of real freedom from the past.
12. It will increase the joy you experience in life.

## 20 Steps to Healing Your Heart

Healing your heart will not happen overnight. It typically takes time and actions on your part. This is both an outline of the process and the steps.

1. **Own that your heart if broken.** Put into words how you are feeling.
2. **Be committed to your own healing and wholeness.** Everything in life that matters starts with a commitment. To really heal, you need to commit yourself to healing. Make a decision that you will do whatever it takes to heal your heart and mean it.
3. **Accept that it's okay to feel this way**. Being in denial is not going to help you heal one iota.
4. **Go through the grieving process step-by-step**. Feel your feelings. Don't make yourself feel guilting for being human.

5. **Increase your self-care right away.** When you are reeling from a broken heart it is absolutely imperative that you bump up your self-care and make sure that you are getting plenty of sleep because it will help you feel better and heal. Do not skip this step! This is the step that will accelerate your healing and help you function in life. This is a foundation for living a happy and powerful life. It's really not optional if you want a great life.
6. **Forgiveness is powerful.** Sometimes heart break includes anger whether it be anger over a break up or anger that someone died "leaving" you alone. It can include resentment and other feelings that call for forgiveness. You want to take a look at what you are dealing with and determine if you need to forgive yourself for anything or perhaps forgive the other person(s). Anger and resentment zap you of energy and vitality. It takes so much more energy to remain angry or resentful than it does to forgive. Forgiveness is for you not the other person. I highly recommend forgiveness over anger and resentment for health, happiness and vitality – it is a path to healing.
7. **Practice gratitude as a tool for healing.** Gratitude is one of the big sleepers in having a powerful life from my view. It doesn't cost anything. Anyone can practice the skill of being grateful and it is easy to do. The benefits of gratitude are extraordinary. It might not make sense to ask that you start practicing gratitude when you are suffering from a broken heart, which I can understand. That doesn't change the benefits or the fact that getting into the operating practice of being grateful will change your life for the better. Feeling grateful every day will help accelerate healing your heart break.
8. **Limit pity parties to a reasonable time period.** If you are prone to excessive self-pitying, self-loathing, catastrophizing, negative thinking, low self-esteem, anxiety or depression, you might tend to overdo the pity parties. If you are in doubt about whether your pity parties are

reasonable or beyond reasonable start talking to the people who care about you and want to see you feel better. Do a survey. Ask several people and get a consensus and then take the appropriate actions. Just be mindful that excessive pity parties are not going to help you move on and will prolong your pain inhibiting healing in the process.

9. **Implement healthy distractions.** While you are processing your emotions and allowing some time for actual healing to take place, set up some healthy distractions for yourself. Examples include: setting an attainable goal that will make you happy and going to work on that goal; cleaning and/or organizing anything or doing yardwork; volunteering at a local charity or service organization. These are examples of healthy distractions that will help you fill up your schedule and take your mind off of your heart break.

10. **What can you learn from this?** Ask yourself what you can learn from your heart break. While not every situation has some value, I do find that I can learn and grow from almost everything in life, which means that I am a huge fan of asking this question and being open to using heart break to my advantage.

11. **How can you use this to become a better person OR help make the world a better place?** In my very early 20's when I experienced the death of a friend, I used the heart break of it to make sure that I made every moment in life count in part to honor my young friend who didn't get that chance. How could you use your personal heart break to be a better person? How could it be used to make the world a better place. This falls under using emotional pain to your advantage.

12. **Create a life plan or vision that excites or inspires you.** Everyone needs to have a purpose or feel needed or useful. It is part of being human. Yet all too often people float through life just letting life "happen to them" without intentionality. I am a big fan of having a plan or vision for

your life because when heart break hits it is extremely powerful to have one in place because it is a powerful tool to pull you forward when you are feeling down. The bonus is that it is never too late to make one.

13. **Get out there and socialize even with the current limitations.** What we know about loneliness and social isolation is that it is extremely bad for your health as you can read about here. You are much more likely to be feeling lonely or isolated when you are dealing with a broken heart. It just goes with the territory. Even though you might not feel like it, get out there and socialize. If you don't have enough friends, which is an extremely common problem in our society and the world, then put that on your life plan or vision or set a goal to make more good friends. Having good friends and/or a good family can go a long way to help you heal from heart break. The problem is that too, too many people don't have good friends or a good family (tips if you have a bad family or parents video).

14. **Ask for help.** If you are going through heart break it's okay to ask for help. You can call friends or family and say I need a pick me up or let's meet for coffee. No one is going to think less of you for asking for help because you are human. Human beings need each other for health and wellness. Go to therapy if you need that. Get the help that you need.

15. **Be watchful of the decisions you make as a result of heart break.** It is particularly important if you are healing from heart break to pay attention and be awake and aware of what you are thinking, feeling and deciding as a result of a broken heart. If you are not awake and aware, then you could subconsciously make a decision that you are simply not aware of, which could negatively impact your life and your future. For example, after some people experience a broken heart they unconsciously or subconsciously decide that they are never going to let someone get that close to them again. That type of

unconscious/subconscious decision cuts you off from love, relationships, happiness and all the good stuff. It happens all the time that people make decisions after heart break that they are not awake and aware of so please pay attention.

16. **The self-fulfilling prophecy is key to a better future and healing.** What you believe matters moving forward as you heal. You can create your future and take advantage of the self-fulfilling prophecy (video) by consciously deciding what your future will hold. What that would look like after a broken heart might be along the lines of – God has a better man (or woman) in mind for me. Or it could take the form of -I have learned and grown and I will have love in my future. It could take many different forms. The important point is that you author and create how it will go. I decided after a huge betrayal and heart break that I was still going to trust people. It was a conscious decision on my part and I am happy with it because being able to trust is important if you want to connect with people in intimate relationships.

17. **Use tools that are appropriate to heal.** There are plenty of tools available to help you heal. Use whichever of them resonates with you. Some examples include: affirmations, cognitive behavioral therapy, psychotherapy, praying, meditation, tapping (emotional freedom technique).

18. **Engage in hobbies or activities you find enjoyable (healthy ones).** Hobbies are one of my favorite things and they can provide a pleasant distraction while you are healing. If you don't currently have any hobbies that you enjoy now is the perfect time to go hobby shopping and find one that you love. Ask people about their hobbies. Have fun with this. Make a list of activities, healthy ones please, and start doing those.

19. **Get complete with what happened.** Whether it is heart break caused by the death of a person or a

relationship that ended, heart break can leave people incomplete with things that were not said or otherwise unfinished business. That includes the things that you wish you had said or done and that sort of thing. I suggest that you write a letter to the person in question – *without sending it* – and say what there is to say. Obviously if the person is deceased you would not be able to send it. Notice that I am NOT recommending that you send these letters to a living person. You are doing this as an exercise to get complete. In an ideal world, you would get complete with an individual face to face, yet that is not always possible or appropriate in break some or all ups. Do this over and over until there is nothing left to say.

20. **Avoid Rebound relationships.** Whether your heart break is because of the death of a beloved spouse or partner or the ending of an intimate relationship it is best to work on healing your heart and avoid getting into a rebound relationship out of fairness to both parties involved, to avoid regrets, and to avert other problems that can result.

**Call to Action:**

There is no question dealing with a broken heart is painful, hard and not what you want to go through. At the same time would you rather cut yourself off from love, joy, happiness, feeling connected and related to people? I hope not! Learning how to heal your heart is a valuable skill that will help you in life. Are you dealing with a broken heart? Are you taking prudent and appropriate steps to go through the healing process? What do you need to help you through the process? Do you know someone who is going through this? Will you share this on social media to help other people? Will you let me know how I can help you? I want you to have a happy and healthy life.

# PERSONAL GROWTH & DEVELOPMENT

### Road Map for Creating a Life that YOU LOVE

September 9, 2019

Very few people would get in a car and start driving to a new destination without first putting the address in their phone, their GPS or doing a MapQuest or something. Yet we are kind of thrown into life without a road map to having a life that we love. There are absolute practices, habits or routines that those of us who are blessed enough to have a life that we love engage in -on a regular basis. While I love to laugh, play, and have fun – I take my happiness and my life seriously. If I want to have as much fun and play as much as I can (and YES, I DO), then I can't allow people to waste my time or energy or waste *my own time* doing things that don't serve my greater purpose.

Many people complain that they don't have time to do the things that they love, and at the same time they are not engaging in the practices and habits that will free them up to do whatever it is they want to be doing. Many of the practices that people tease me about are the very things that a person must do to have lots of energy, focus, and have a fun life that is full of love and happiness. Before we look at a simplistic visual for some of the elements to creating a road map for a life that you love, I want to cover some aspects that will help build a strong foundation for the journey.

**Love Your Imperfections**

What is going to be exceptionally helpful on this journey to a life that you love is to be able to LOVE your Imperfections, to love who you are right now, to be able to LOVE YOURSELF. If you have really low self-esteem that is likely going to be a significant challenge. You could "fake it till you make it" or use affirmations in the interim until you grow enough in your personal growth and development journey that you can say in earnest that you really love yourself. There is incredible power and freedom in being able to own up to your imperfections or even *others perceived view of your imperfections.*

To put this into context for you, some years ago I was told that I was "loud and colorful", which wasn't exactly the view that I held of myself at the time (subject for an entire future blog post). As I pondered that assessment, eventually I had to admit that I am loud and colorful and accept that as who I am. To some people this is a flaw or an imperfection of mine. And yet, that is not how I view it at all. I am also very happy and get excited over little sometimes mundane things, which some people find really annoying. And I am happy with myself even when people tell me to "calm down" or "take a chill pill" when I am happily excited about something. It just doesn't faze me. I just go on being happily excited.

I am not the same person that I was years ago although I apparently have many of the same personality characteristics that I am "known for". What has changed over the years is my ability to fully love myself and embrace who I am. It's the ultimate freedom and I suggest that you open your heart to yourself. You are enough. You are ALREADY enough. We are talking about practices that will

*Love.Life.*

allow you to love life and let's start with the premise that you are good enough, loveable, and perfect the way that you are.

## Mastery

As you take on creating a life that you really LOVE, I want to pause and have a brief conversation on the topic of mastery. Mastery is defined as comprehensive knowledge or skill in a subject or accomplishment OR control or superiority over something. Research shows that the number of hours it takes to become masterful or have mastery in a given subject or field is 10,000 hours. Malcolm Gladwell talks about this in his book *"Outliers – The Story of Success"*. A different author, Cal Newport states in his book *"So Good They Can't Ignore You"* that ridiculously successful people are that way because they practice. While there has been some controversy or disagreement on Malcolm Gladwell's 10,000 hours concept, the point I am making is that you get good at something most often by doing it over and over and over. By practicing. By being willing to do whatever it is – even if you are bad at it – until you get good at it.

Having a life that you LOVE is most likely going to involve you taking on some new practices – things that you are not used to doing. If you have the proper expectations going into this journey, it's going to produce a much better result. And I am all about results. If you have not spent the last decade or more making lists, setting goals, thinking about what makes you happy, doing what makes you happy, creating a vision for your life – then ALL of this is going to feel foreign and uncomfortable to you. And that is good. And at the same time, you want to expect that there is going to be a transition period until you have practiced so much that you are masterful – regardless of the hours it takes for you to get there.

## Thinking Big

As you contemplate the life that you want to create, I highly recommend that you think big! Thinking big is not a common phenomenon in our culture. We tend to think that you have to start at the bottom and work your way to the top. We tend to think that you can't double your income or triple your income in a year. We tend to put limits on what we can achieve. An excellent classic book on this subject is *"Think and Grow Rich"* written by Napoleon Hill back in 1937. It's a great read.

Another way to consider this topic is to start to look at what miracles you would like to have in your life. What things, unexpected as they may be, would you love to have happen? What would you be doing if you could do anything? What would your life look like if you had a magic wand or if you were granted 3 wishes by a genie? What are your dreams? What are your hopes? What is it that you want that you might not even be able to tell yourself or your friends? If you can answer these questions that will put you on the path to thinking big.

## Simplified Road Map to a Life You LOVE

To create a road map for a life that YOU LOVE, there are many aspects that you will have to consider and flush out over time. To help you get started on this exciting journey, I have sketched out a diagram of things to contemplate or ponder. It's an incomplete sketch because I have not included formulating an action plan and other necessary steps and practices. Creating a life that you love doesn't happen overnight. It takes thought, consideration, planning, action, growth and development, and more.

You might be surprised to learn that only about 3% of Americans write their goals down on paper according to the research, and less than 1% review and rewrite their goals on a daily basis. And I can just hear some of you moaning and groaning right now at the thought of writing down goals or making lists. Yes, you will have to make notes, eventually write up goals, and yes, review them on a regular basis. I will be covering time management, one of my passions – seriously I LOVE time management, in a future post. People with goals that they have written down are 50% more likely

*Love.Life.*

to achieve their goals. And YES, I have been doing these things for pretty much my entire life. And YES, this is just a practice to embrace!

Here is a visual of a very simplified starting point to creating a road map for your Life:

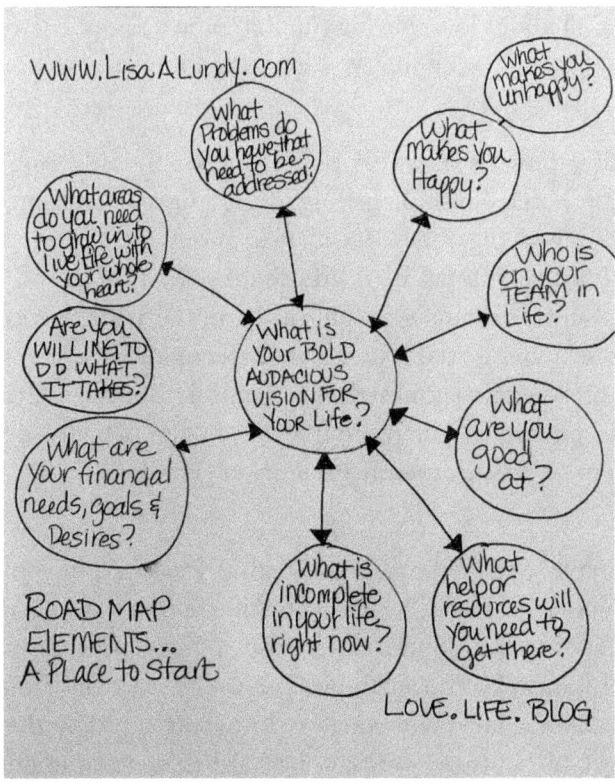

However, you do this or whatever form it takes, these are the questions that you are going to have to answer to start creating a life that you love! If you are in a dark place or as I call it "up against it", it could be overwhelming to embark on answering these questions. Do it anyway. Your life is never going to change if you don't start doing something different. In my Living Life with Your Whole Heart post I mentioned that if you devoted 15 minutes a day for a year to improving your life that would equal over two 40-hour work weeks. So, what are all the things that you can accomplish in 15 minutes?

You could start answering the questions on the road map sketch. And clearly write the answers down! Will you use a notebook? Scrap paper? Get a fancy blank journal? Well, I would recommend that you do it in a way that brings a smile to your face. Remember this journey is all about love, having fun, happiness and the good stuff. If you look at having a life that you love as a chore…it's kind of counterproductive.

Completing things is very, very powerful. Whether it's a job, a task, a project, or a relationship, getting things finished, cleaned up, or done is a life-giving force. I will talk about that in a future post because I am such a fan of it and the results it produces. The best advice on answering the questions listed in the visual is to be honest with yourself. No denial. No inflated exaggerations. Just the hard, cold truth. And sometimes that is painful. But so is living a life without love and joy. The more honest you can be with yourself, the more likely you are to attain the goal of you living a life that you love.

I am extremely excited to be supporting you on your journey to a life that you love! Please let me know if you have any questions by posting them in the comments section. I hope you are excited for yourself because I am over the moon excited for you! Count me in as one of your fans, someone to love you through the process, encourage you, nurture you, say the hard things you might need to hear, and just cheer you on!

**What Tripping Over the Truth Looks Like in Real Life- Ker splat**

October 8, 2019

If you are on this journey with me moving towards Loving Your LIFE – as in really being in LOVE with your life – then you understand that part of getting there is personal growth and development, a subject that I LOVE! I want to give you a glimpse of what that personal growth and development looks like in real life with an example of how last week I "Tripped Over the Truth" and what that means. I will start with the phrase 'tripping over the truth'.

## Tripping Over the Truth

I first heard of the phrase 'tripping over the truth' from a book titled "The Power of Moments" by New York Times Best-selling authors Chip Heath and Dan Heath, also the authors of "Switch" and "Made to Stick". Tripping over the truth has 3 components to it: (1) it is a clear insight, (2) that is compressed in time, and (3) the insight is discovered by the audience themselves. It is something that you didn't see coming, yet at the same time you know is viscerally correct. Another word for tripping over the truth is epiphany, although personally I feel that there is some distinction between the two concepts. There's a great YouTube video of Dan Heath explaining this concept: https://www.youtube.com/watch?v=KZ_N77OquQA

Sidebar – I have to mention that I LOVE the book "The Power of Moments" for so many reasons. It is about celebrating milestones and making magic moments and so much more. It is about how to cause them and really make a difference based on solid research. Since I love celebrating people, connecting with people, and having delicious moments with people, of course I would LOVE this book. Great audio book for driving in my opinion. If you want to be the cause for more joy in your life AND your work, also a great book. That is also where I became familiar with the phrase "level up". It's my kind of book.

## Tripping Over the Truth – In real life: Ker splat

I woke up crying in my tripping over the truth moment completely stunned because this truth was the _very_ thing that people had been trying to get me to see about myself for my entire life. Flashes of conversations with people spanning decades were right there in that exact moment. Shock and awe does not cover it. How could I have missed the very point that people, as in lots of people, had been trying to get me to see? As I popped out of bed still crying to get ready for my day since I still had work to do I began to process my emotions something that thankfully I have a good amount of practice with. I was a raw bundle of emotions sadness, shock, a touch of oh no, maybe a little anger, and a ton of gratitude and love – all swirling around in the same mass of tears. And throughout the day as I kept to my schedule the tears came and went and I got more grounded in the fact that this was the undisputable truth. Part of the shock was in the fact that this truth had been spoken to me by countless people over the years. How could I have not seen it especially in light of all of the work I had done on myself?

What was my moment of truth? What did I finally see for myself? I am reluctant to say, and I will be brave and do it anyway. What I saw for myself was my level of innocence, naivete, and goodness in a way that shook me to my core. Why? What's so bad about that? Well, tripping over this truth leads me to understand my point of vulnerability – my Achilles' heel so to speak. And while I tend to be more vulnerable in life than many, even I don't love being vulnerable.

Let me tell you as a fiercely independent woman, actually getting my point of vulnerability made me really unhappy. And as someone who has spent decades purposefully working on my own personal growth and development, I also knew in that moment that this was a very good thing. True power comes in knowing and understanding yourself. Yet, seeing my own level of goodness, innocence and naivete as those close to me had been trying to get me to see meant that on some level I would need some level of protection. That meant that my tough girl, "I can do it on my own" story was just all baloney. So, I cried periodically throughout the day as I let it all sink in noting how many people had actually said that directly to me over the years.

Yes, when we actually trip over the truth about ourselves, even when we know conclusively that it is a good thing and FOR our benefit, there could be a few tears at least for someone like me. Part of the tears were quite simply gratitude because I could see in my tripping over the truth moment how God had protected me from so many bad things in the people that HE sent into my life. I mean I cannot tell you the gratitude I feel even now writing this. God has provided me with so many Angels on Earth as I like to call them to help protect me. With all of the really, really BAD things that have come my way, I remain unjaded, with a heart that is not hardened, with LOVE for people and humanity. That in and of itself is pretty miraculous and would not have happened without the LOVE of some very special people.

It's actually a little funny, I'm out in the world pretending to be a tough girl, when everyone who knows me can see my heart (gee, since I wear it on my sleeve, it's pretty easy to see) and I'm the only one who can't see my blind spot. Okay, maybe you don't see any humor in that, but I do! All of this leads into the topic of self-awareness.

**Your Self-Awareness**

The Greek phrase for self-awareness is "know thyself", and this concept has been studied by philosophers dating back to Socrates (469-399 B.C.). The psychologist and author, Daniel Goleman, who wrote "Emotional Intelligence" defines self-awareness as "knowing one's internal states, preference, resources and intuitions." Please note that self-awareness is distinct and different from self-focused attention or just thinking about ourselves.

Self-awareness is the cornerstone to emotional intelligence and one of the most fundamental issues in psychology. Self-awareness runs contrary to the culture we live in. According to psychologists Matthew Killingsworth and Daniel T. Gilbert, we run on automatic pilot about 50% of the time meaning we are unconscious of what we are doing or how we feel. To live a life that you truly LOVE as I stated in a previous post, you have to bring some intentionality to your life. You have to become conscious of what you LOVE for example, conscious about what you don't like, conscious about where you want to be in a year or two or five, conscious about how you feel, awake to life. To have a life that you LOVE, it will take many things and self-awareness is one of them. Tripping over the truth may come in very handy along the journey.

And in all my years of doing the personal growth and development work as I have, I have never found anyone person who did "the work" so to speak that found out something really horrible about themselves. Doing work on yourself in my opinion will result in a happier, more peaceful and more joyous life. Almost a week after I tripped over the truth and I am more content and still chuckling about it. And fully empowered by what I now see and know about myself. It's all good. Where are you in your self-awareness? We will get further into emotional intelligence (a.k.a. emotional quotient) in a future post. Wherever you are is perfect. Just come along for the ride!

## Top 45 Ways that Personal Growth & Development Will Help You Have a Life You Love

November 29, 2019

Personal growth and development is another topic that I LOVE. As in LOVE! I completely LOVE this subject! I was fortunate to have my first real introduction to growth and development in the early 1980's when I was in a Counselor Education course to become a Resident Assistant (R.A.) at Penn State. In the course you had to listen to two positive and two negative or constructive pieces of feedback from each person in the class. When I heard one young man say, "You were the first person that I met in this course, and you welcomed me into the classroom with a huge, warm, inviting smile" – I thought to myself oh, this is his positive feedback, until he continued with, "And I felt so intimidated by you." Oh NO! I will never forget the dichotomy of my warm inviting smile and actions leaving someone feeling intimidated. It was a powerful lesson that impacted me, in a positive way, from that day forward. I could intimidate someone with my smile and warmth. That has been hugely helpful to this day.

So, what is growth and development? I will boil it down to working on yourself or self-improvement. My philosophy is that we either grow and develop through a crisis - think death, divorce or other trauma or we can intentionally take on our own growth and development. There are plenty of people who are simply unwilling to grow and develop. They remain stagnant throughout their lives, and that's okay. It's my opinion that growth and development offers significant benefits – the topic for this post. Before I give you the list of benefits let me set the stage for personal growth and development and some ideas of tools that can help you in this area.

Personal growth and development requires that you be open for starters. You have to be open to consider looking at yourself, your life views, your habits and ways of doing life. You have to be willing to consider other thoughts and views. I am not talking about giving up your values or those things that are core to who you are. I am talking about getting a real-world assessment of yourself, how you occur in life, and what would be helpful to you in having a more powerful life. Growth and development can happen through a conversation with a friend or co-worker when you have a eureka moment realizing something newly for yourself. It can happen through a variety of tools that are in your everyday life. Or it can happen with a commitment and a serious focus. Regardless of how it happens, this is powerful stuff.

Pretty much what I write about is personal growth and development and what it takes to have a life that you love. In my post titled "What Tripping Over the Truth Looks Like in Real Life – Ker splat", I wrote about a distinction of growth and development that has been labeled "tripping over the truth" – which is worth a read. Regardless of how you get there or what vehicle you use – it's my opinion that any time or investment in your own personal growth and development has a very high yield. We can all agree that life is difficult and at times can be extremely harsh and hard. The skills and abilities that you pick up on the path of growth and development while they won't prevent bad things from happening in your life, they most certainly will make dealing with the tough stuff easier or perhaps less difficult.

**Examples of Personal Growth and Development Tools:**

1. Reading THIS Blog and doing the work
2. Courses, programs, seminars, training, podcasts, etc.
3. Books
4. Programs like Toastmasters International*(see mention below)
5. Movies or DVD's
6. Conversations with people
7. The Bible and religious programs
8. Setting stretch goals and attaining them
9. Going to college or a university for a degree program
10. Getting a coach
11. Doing therapy
12. Doing things outside of your comfort zone
13. Implementing new habits that improve your life
14. Journaling for insight and understanding

**Buyer Beware**

Without naming any names of businesses or programs, I have to say as strongly as I can that you must be cautious and beware about some personal growth and development programs, courses, companies and even coaches. There are some organizations and/or individuals that have a history of exploiting people and are even abusive. There are some cults and cult-like organizations. Since 2003, I have participated in Toastmasters International, an organization that helps individuals become better public speakers and leaders. Toastmasters International has been around since 1924 and offers a low-cost and proven program for personal growth and development in a safe environment. It is one organization that I feel comfortable in recommending as one vehicle for personal growth and development. Just understand that it is a buyer beware arena in my opinion. I would say more however that would not be prudent.

**Top 45 Reasons Why Growth & Development Will Help You Have a Life You Love**

1. **You will deal with your problems head on.** The first area of growth and development is dealing with reality and not a fantasy life. Once you start to acknowledge your life is your life – you will begin to deal with your problems head on. There will be no denial about what your life is and what your life is not.
2. **You will avoid future potentially bigger problems and could save a lot of money in the process.** As you become situated in reality and begin dealing with your problems head on, you will gain the benefit of avoiding potentially bigger problems in the future, which could save you a lot of money in the long run. That is one of the huge benefits of living in the real world is that you can anticipate and plan and AVOID problems but not if you are in denial or minimizing the current status of your life.
3. **It will help you take control of your life. You – in the driver's seat.** How often do you hear people say that they can't do this or they can't do that because of X, Y, or Z? When you take on your growth and development, and you begin to act on the things that make you happy and begin making choices about what you want your life to look like – you will get back in the driver's seat and take control of your life.
4. **You will be happier.** The whole point of growth and development, in my opinion, is about getting happy.
5. **You will get freed up.** The more you deal with your problems head on, the more you take control of your life,

and the more you understand the potential problems you could avoid, you will feel freed up. Or at least freer than you were before you started.

6. **You will feel more peaceful and contented.** While I am committed to happiness, some people would be satisfied simply to feel contented and peaceful. Feeling contented and peaceful is a byproduct of growth and development.
7. **You will have less anxiety.** The more habits and practices you put in place to manage and direct your own life – to your own design I might add – the less anxiety you will have. The more you work on yourself the less you will be concerned about what other people think of you – one of the big sources of anxiety for many people. There are many reasons why you will have less anxiety by doing the work – keep reading.
8. **It builds self-esteem.** When people are directing their own lives and creating their life to go a certain way – that builds long-lasting self-esteem.
9. **It will help you or should help you in every area of your life.** The more you take control of your life and the more you work on yourself, the less you will tolerate a dysfunctional mess in your life. Growth and development will permeate every area of your life and therefore you should reap benefits in all areas of your life.
10. **It will help you be more authentic and real.** To be able to be authentic and real with other people is so freeing. The more growth and development work you do will allow you to drop the facade of being perfect, having it all together, of having a problem-free or perfect life. You will be able to be with people with all of your imperfections and all of their imperfections – and enjoy people in a whole new way.
11. **You will be able to deal with your past and make peace with it.** While not everyone deals with their past in doing growth and development, it is often the case that the past comes up and is dealt with in some form or another. It

*Love.Life.*

is never as bad as people think it will be and it is exceptionally powerful to make peace with your past.

12. **It will give you tools to help when life is hard.** One of the most powerful benefits of doing the growth and development work is that it will give you amazing tools for when life is hard. You grow and develop and, in the process, you learn new things, gain new tools, adopt new attitudes all of which can be extremely beneficial when things get tough.

13. **It can be very fun.** Knowing me as I do, I have to say this – if it's not fun then I am probably not doing it. Having spent more than a few decades doing growth and development, I can say with all sincerity that it is fun or I would have stopped a long time ago.

14. **The people who engage in growth & development are pretty cool – get into that tribe.** The people who you will meet if you jump into growth and development are some of the best people that you would ever want to meet! Without question, these are the people who you want to have in your tribe (with only a few rare exceptions).

15. **There's really no reason not to.** What would be the reason not to get into growth and development? You are a multimillionaire with a perfect life? Yeah, that would be a reason. For the majority of Americans, that is just not the case. There is really no good reason not to get into growth and development.

16. **It makes you more likeable and relatable.** The more you can be authentic and real, the more likeable and relatable you are. It's just easier to be around people who tell it like it is, aren't trying to impress anyone, and have some emotional quotient as well as compassion for their fellow men.

17. **You will be less annoyed by other people.** The more growth and development work you do on yourself, the less annoying other people will be in my opinion because you

will understand that they are doing the best that they can and you will have compassion for how they behave.

18. **It's an act of self-love.** In my most humble and earnest opinion, doing the work of growth and development is a gift that you give to yourself. While everyone else who knows you may benefit greatly from the work that you do, you are and always will be the number one recipient of the benefits. It is a gift you give to yourself.
19. **It helps you be more compassionate and empathetic.** As you see yourself as a human being with areas to work on and grow, you will begin to see other people in the same light, which usually leaves you with compassion and empathy for others.
20. **It will help you increase your emotional intelligence or quotient, which usually translates to higher pay.** You will absolutely increase your emotional intelligence or emotional quotient, which translates to higher pay typically. See the post I wrote titled "Top 17 Benefits to High Emotional Intelligence and Why It's Important" for the lowdown on this benefit.
21. **You are never going to find out that you are a worthless scumbag (or it's very unlikely unless you are really evil).** Save for the really evil people in this world, you are never going to find out that you are a worthless scumbag. And quite frankly those people who are really evil are most likely suffering from some deep psychopathology as to not even recognize that they are evil and a scumbag. So, not to worry on finding out something really awful or terrible about yourself.
22. **It can help you restore and clean up relationships.** As you take on your life and begin dealing with your problems head on, cleaning up and restoring relationships will likely surface. The skills you gain in growth and development will help you restore and clean up relationships.
23. **It is wonderful happy hour conversation starters.**

Growth and development can be a fascinating happy hour conversation starter. From my experience, the people who have never done growth and development work are often kind of curious – the kind of curiosity like I'd like to do bull riding, but I think I will just watch – and as such they often want to hear what YOU have learned and how YOU have benefitted from the work. Those people who have done growth and development work will, of course, love to exchange stories with you and you will have a delightful conversation about how you have grown.

24. **It makes life less painful.** There is no doubt that life is painful at times. Having tools, skills, and practices, etc. available through growth and development simply makes life less painful.
25. **It's why we are here in life.** From the beginning of time the great thinkers and philosophers have written about growth and development. It's embedded in the two historic questions that have been written about since the earliest days: (1) what is the meaning of life? and (2) why am I here?
26. **You are either growing and expanding or shrinking and contracting.** Growth and development offers you the ability to expand yourself and your thinking, which is better for you than shrinking, contracting or being stuck.
27. **It will help you appreciate yourself and others.** As you do the work, you will begin to appreciate yourself in a whole new way and in the process, you will be able to appreciate others as well.
28. **It will inspire you.** It's my opinion that growth and development work is inspiring. To see people grow and change – is cause for celebration! I frequently celebrate my own growth and development! Why not?
29. **It's very good for your brain – doing actual thinking.** As I have written before, much of what we do in life is repetitive, which conserves energy for the brain.

Doing actual thinking as required in growth and development – while it uses more energy – it is very good for your brain.

30. **You will be able to empower others by your own empowerment.** The more skills you pick up along the way, the more you can share those skills and empower others.
31. **It can help you deal with traumas.** The work you do on yourself can help you deal with either past or current traumas and that is a very good thing.
32. **It's not as scary as you think.** It is really not scary to do growth and development because you are not going to find out you are some horrible person. You will find compassion for yourself and others.
33. **It will help you not take things so personally.** When you do the work, you will not take things so personally because you simply don't have to. And, if I may be so bold – you don't even have to take things personally that ARE personal! How's that for amazing! To not take things personally that actually were personal? That is power my friends. Absolute and real power!
34. **It will make you a better leader or manager.** The research on emotional intelligence or emotional quotient makes it pretty clear that individuals with higher emotional intelligence or emotional quotient are better leaders and managers and usually make more money.
35. **It's very fascinating.** The whole arena of growth and development is very fascinating to me. I am not the only one given the plethora of books, courses, training programs and life coaches available at this moment in time. It's been the subject of books and writings since the earliest of days including the Bible.
36. **You will be less concerned about what other people think of you.** As you grow and develop and gain more confidence and self-esteem and become clear in what

you are up to in life, the opinions that others hold about you will have less weight. That's both powerful and freeing.

37. **It can be more effective and cheaper than therapy (operative words can be).** I am of the opinion that doing the work of personal growth and development can be more effective and cheaper than therapy. The operative words are can be. It really depends on your commitment and actions.

38. **It can help you deal with and/or reduce your addictions.** As I have said repeatedly, I am not a therapist or licensed medical professional in any capacity, that being said, it is my thought that people use addictions to avoid feeling pain or dealing with their lives. Assuming I am correct, it stands to reason that doing the work of growth and development would lessen the need to numb yourself to life and would thereby reduce addictions.

39. **It can help you connect with your purpose and passions in life.** Often when people do the work, they open themselves up to connecting to their purpose and passions in life. I have asked my beloved readers over and over to identify what makes you happy and then to sprinkle your life with what makes you happy. Doing the work allows you to take the time to begin to identify and/or create the things that will bring you happiness.

40. **It can help you identify and break dysfunctional family patterns.** Doing the growth and development work can definitely help you identify and break dysfunctional family patterns. Frequently, we are unaware of the dysfunction or level of dysfunction in our families until we do the work. It's very powerful to be able to identify and break family patterns that do not empower you.

41. **It is a high return use of your time and energy.** In my humble opinion, there are very few things that you can do that will result in such a high return for your time,

energy, and sometimes money. Looking at this list of benefits – this is a lot of goodies for your investment.

42. **It will boost your self-confidence.** The more you know yourself, the higher your self-confidence will be. I am not talking about an arrogant kind of self-confidence. I am talking about a sense of humility about humanity and life that is at the core of this kind of self-confidence.
43. **It builds character.** There is no question that doing the work of personal growth and development is an act of courage and bravery – even though it is not difficult. These are the things that build character over time.
44. **You help make the world a better place every time you grow and develop.** I assert that when you grow and develop and in essence become a better version of you – you help make the world a better place. You are more compassionate, empathetic and kind. All of the benefits offered by growth and development help make the world a better place with you in it.
45. **Blatant judgements and criticisms from others will not impact you so deeply or at all.** You will always be judged and criticized in life. It's just part of life. When you do the work, I assert that the judgements and criticisms from others will not impact you so deeply or possibly at all.

**Concluding Thoughts**

As someone who has actively participated in the actions necessary to produce personal growth and development for over 35 years, I believe without question that this is critical and necessary to having a life that you LOVE! It doesn't have to be hard. It can be fun and quite engaging. In fact, if it's not fun and engaging, try another approach. There are numerous ways to find a path to growth and development. There really are so many ways to get there. What matters is that you make a commitment, first off, to having a life that you LOVE. Then get busy to do what it takes to get there.

Wouldn't it be nice to be happily engaged in moving your life forward? Wouldn't it be lovely to have the tools in your toolshed to deal with the tough times life can bring you? Wouldn't it be wonderful to have less stress, less anxiety and more fun? Looking at the benefits I have listed above, aren't those benefits something you would enjoy and make your life easier? I would venture a guess that they are benefits that would give you a better quality of life. I am committed to you having a life that you LOVE- one that you design and create for yourself. How can I support you in your journey? Do let me know!

## Self-Mastery, Self-Motivation, & Self-Care: The Holy Grail of Happiness & Joy

January 30, 2020

On the road to having a LIFE that you LOVE, your ability to manage yourself, motivate yourself and take care of yourself (self-care) are the holy grail of happiness and joy in my view. There is an intricate relationship between these three areas as I will cover. Before I dive in, I am asking you to read this particular post with LOVE of yourself in mind. I am asking that you do not read this post and say to yourself, "Oh, great – something else I am not doing, or not good at, or…" or some other negative, self-defeating thought. I invite you to read this post with the curiosity and wonder of a child saying to yourself instead, "Oh, let's explore what new things there are for me to consider on my journey to a happy life." Use the content of this post to say to yourself – how can I start making my life better? What is one thing I can start doing now? Use this as an opportunity for self-assessment and growth – not to beat yourself up for what you are not doing.

The concept of self-mastery, which is defined as self-control, self-discipline, or the ability to control one's own desires or impulses, has been written about since man's earliest days. Epictetus (Greek Stoic philosopher born 50 AD – died 135 AD) is credited with saying: "No person is free who is not master of himself". The Greek philosopher Aristotle (384 BC – 322 BC) is quoted as stating: "The hardest victory is the victory over self." Author Napoleon Hill wrote about it in his 1937 book *Think and Grow Rich* -a book I highly recommend. It's still being written about as I write this.

Self-mastery is important if you want to have a happy life. From my perspective, self-mastery has at least 4 components. I don't know what anyone else has to say about it, but this is what makes sense to me as I deconstruct something that I have been good at for a long time. I have written a great deal about the individual items listed in this post so I won't repeat myself with explanations. I sincerely doubt that anyone who doesn't take care of themselves can attain self-mastery because they are woven together in my view. The same goes for coping strategies or mechanisms. You could attain some level self-mastery, again in my opinion, without necessarily understanding what stops you but it seems unlikely to me that you could really have self-mastery without understanding yourself to the level of knowing what stops you. But then, what do I know? What I know is the more LOVE you put into your LIFE in any capacity, any form, any amount – the better your life will feel.

## Self-Mastery Components:

1. Self-motivation
2. Self-Care
3. Coping Mechanisms or Strategies
4. Understanding what stops you

## Understanding What Stops You

I'm starting with this first because I think it is a helpful place to start. Many people have never thought about what stops them in life. I find it a powerful place to look every now and again. This is not a comprehensive list, but a good general list.

1. Fear- of failure, of success, of…you name it.
2. Something new or something that you lack the experience or skills for
3. Something that you don't want to do
4. Something that you are resentful about
5. Something that is painful
6. You lack time or other resources

## Coping Skills, Mechanisms or Strategies

We all understand that I am not a therapist, so here's my take on coping skills or mechanisms based on experience. How you cope with life is very important, yet it is not a topic that we typically talk about unless you are in therapy or a group therapy session. We see the by-product of a lack of coping skills or mechanisms in our societal problems today. We have the escalating rate suicide of our youth, obesity across all ages including very young children, drug and alcohol addictions as well as other problematic behaviors. It seems pretty clear to me that, as a whole, we are not too good at coping skills. Life is hard. We know that. Bad stuff happens. Coping skills can make the tough times more manageable. Frankly, really rock-solid coping skills can see you through trauma or even multiple concurrent traumas. I only learned about coping skills or mechanisms in late 2018 when I was told that I didn't need therapy because there was nothing wrong with me because while I have endured a long-standing trauma, I have amazing and very strong coping skills or mechanisms.

1. Religion
2. Positive Outlook or Attitude
3. Time Management/Organization Skills
4. Exercise

5. Socializing
6. Hobbies
7. Self-Care-recognizing that you are emotionally drained, stressed out, anxious or physically tired and then immediately engaging in the self-care activities to soothe yourself and recharge your mind, body and emotions.
8. Quality Sleep
9. Problem-Solving Abilities (& Resourcefulness)
10. Health
11. Personal Growth & Development
12. Forgiveness & Letting Go

**Self-Care**

This is a critical aspect of self-mastery in my opinion because taking care of yourself is extremely important if you want to be happy and healthy and have a LIFE that you LOVE. I have witnessed people work themselves almost to death, saying that they can't take time for themselves because they have too much to do, and they are lifeless. They are unhappy. They have lives with no joy. And they did it to themselves although they can't see that. Some people take better care of their cars than they do of their bodies and minds. It's a combination of taking care of your physical body, your emotions and your mental state – those three aspects need to be cared for. We don't drive our cars for 24 hours a day and expect them to keep working. Our vehicles get to sit in the garage overnight or at least for X number of hours. Yet, we charge at life, eating junk food, drinking soda, not getting enough sleep, working without playing and we wonder why we are not happy. It's no wonder so many people are unhappy. I am not saying, by the way, that you can't eat junk food. Everything in moderation. You just should eat enough healthy foods to allow for the periodic less than healthy foods and beverages.

*Love.Life.*

You can work self-care into your daily routine. At least that's how I do it. I know that I function much better when I have stayed true to the things that work for me. There are other things that qualify as self-care, but I think that this list is enough to get you started.

1. Sleep-good quality and sufficient amount
2. Diet-rich in nutrition (or take supplements to hedge your bets)
3. Exercise – walking counts
4. Meaningful relationships, friendships, family – social connectedness and outings or visits
5. Things that make you happy- intentionally put into your days
6. Hobbies
7. Rewards
8. Living space that makes you feel good
9. Ways to recharge, rewind, recover – whatever they might be so long as they are not self-sabotaging, addictions, or other behaviors that are negative or harmful.
10. Something to look forward to-make it up if you have to

**Self-Motivation**

1. Have a vision for your life – one that excites you, one that energizes you and touches your heart.
2. Create a reward system (or Level UP) that is both meaningful and financially responsible for where you are in life and where you want to be. This should be FUN! You get to decide what the rewards will be for the various milestones or projects or tasks that you complete. A reward system that YOU design should provide ample motivation. If it does not, then simply go back to the drawing board and consider what is missing or change the rewards. Change something if it is not motivating you.

3. Have goals for your life – hopefully ones that come from the vision you have for your life.
4. Lists-Lists can provide motivation if you are driving your life forward. Even on a very bad day, having a list can help you turn things around IF you are driving your life forward towards a vision you love.
5. Time management practices or habits -using your time effectively gives you more time to do what you love.
6. Social Engagement/Outlets – connect with people.
7. Create a TEAM or partnership to propel yourself and others forward.
8. Growth & Development -will help you get to the life you LOVE, help you stay motivated, reduce obstacles, and help you solve problems. The better you know yourself the better you will be at self-motivation.
9. Visual Signs to encourage yourself onward. This may sound hokey, but it really does work and can be fun and funny!
10. Celebrate milestones, accomplishments and progress – on top of any rewards that you have received along the way! I mean really celebrate all that you can in your journey in life. Why the heck not?

**Putting It All Together**

If I put this into an "If/Then/Else Do" loop, it might look like this… (Haha on me that I am even attempting such a thing). At least I am chuckling.

- IF you are overwhelmed by this post and have nonetheless kept reading to this point THEN -pat yourself on the back! That's power and courage in one action. THEN you will also want to read my blog post titled *Dealing with Overwhelm: How to Put an End to Feeling Overwhelmed with Life Once and For All Plus 29 Tips to help you in the Meantime*, November 6, 2019.

Some people have an on-going and never-ending struggle with overwhelm. Deal with that once and for all. That is possible.
- IF you are <u>not coping well with life</u> THEN- consider making a list of all the people, organizations, and groups who could help you. Ask for help. Then look at the coping skills and decide which ones will benefit you the most and start doing it. Look at the list of self-care and implement what you can from that. Seek mental health counseling or call the national suicide hotline if you are having thoughts of death or suicide.
- IF you <u>DO NOT Have a powerful vision for your life THEN</u> follow these instructions – First, don't panic. Breathe. If you don't have a vision for your life you can either put that on your list to think about and create, or you can start working on one or more areas of your life knowing that it will come to you eventually. Your vision for your life could be as simple as making a difference in the world by volunteering. Those of us who volunteer regularly know that the world needs volunteers – and many more than we have now. You could alternatively make up a vision for your life and change it later. Whatever you do, don't worry about this. Look at how you can improve your life starting right now and get to work on that. A happy life is waiting for you. A happy life is calling your name. And it takes you and your actions to make it happen.
- IF you <u>DO have a powerful vision for your life</u> THEN- simply assess what you could do to improve your coping skills, self-motivation, or self-care strategies. Pick one or two things that you could add or change in your life and start doing them.
- IF you have <u>poor coping skills and lack motivation</u> THEN - focus your efforts on self-care because that will help you feel better, in theory, sooner rather than later. Secondarily, I would suggest that you take on learning or working on your

coping skills. Improvements in self-care and coping skills will help you start to get motivated.

**Closing Thoughts**

One of my all-time favorite sayings is "Carpe diem", which translates roughly to seize the day. Given that, I must include an ancient quotation from Horace, one of the leading Latin lyric poets and satirists under emperor Augustus (Born December 65 BC – Died November 8 BC):

> *"Carpe diem! Rejoice while you are alive; enjoy the day; live life to the fullest; make the most of what you have. It is later than you think."*
>
> — HORACE

That pretty much sums up my life philosophy or part of it anyway. There is no time like the present. Live life with no regrets. Do what you can to help your fellow man – any time you can, any place you can, in any way you can. Be clear on what you want out of life. Take actions commensurate with your goals and desires. Be unstoppable. But above all – get to know yourself because that is where the real power in life is. Understand what makes you tick. The better you get to know yourself and how you operate, the more control and power you will have over your own life. The less people can push your buttons. The less anxiety and stress you have.

One day at a time – do what you can. I am here to love you through this process. And, trust me it is a process. It won't happen overnight. It won't happen in a week or two. But bit-by-bit, if you do the work you will reap the benefits. Please let me know how I can support you with your self-mastery, self-motivation, self-care, and life in general!

**August Theme: Awake & Aware**

It's the first month of the Year of Freedom & Giveaway Program and I couldn't be more excited for you!! If you are new to my blog you might not realize how intimately I understand dealing with hardship, depression, anxiety and all that I write about. I started my life over last year at age 58 with basically nothing. So, I know all too well how extremely difficult life can be. At the same time, I know the specific actions to take to overcome life's trying time. It's time for you to step away from depression, anxiety, worry, fear, anger and resentment and into the emotions of love, joy, happiness, peace and contentment. I have written about dealing with depression, dealing with overwhelm, how to be happy when you are suffering, how low self-esteem can steal your love and happiness and I know what the research states about the specific actions that can be taken to alleviate such negative feelings. You will come to know that I love research. It's just one of my things.

You have this amazing chance to change your life for the better (and win some cool stuff)! The theme for August is Awake and Aware. If you are super charged up about changing your life for the better and actually feeling better right now, there are 40 previous blog posts that will help you so you don't have to wait. You could start reading them right now. Each month will start with a theme, some small assignments and new content. Content that will expand and supplement what I have already written. I am not a fan of recycling content.

I can't tell you how it touches my heart to see someone improve their life. It's incredibly moving. It's the stuff that magical moments are made of. It is one of those things that inspires me to no end. To be a part of that is an honor and a privilege beyond compare. If you are willing to do the work, I promise you that you can and will have a different life in a year! Note that my promise is conditional that you do the work. At the end of this post I have the promises of the Year of Freedom as well as my requests of you. Now, let's dive in.

. . .

### Why is the theme Awake & Aware?

I have thoughtfully selected the theme of Awake & Aware for the first month of the Year of Freedom for a few reasons. Often times in life people get in a rut or go through the motions of getting through the day without stopping to think about why or what they are doing. That's normal, reasonable and fine. It's just not helpful to creating a life that you love and one where you are in control, happy and empowered. To start our journey together the most powerful place to start is to start observing yourself in life and just notice, hopefully with a childlike wonder, what you do, how you feel and so many more things.

If you want to go on a road trip typically you pick out your destination and then plan the trip. Likewise, if you want to have a life filled with lots of happiness, joy, peace, contentment, and lots of positive things it's helpful to know where you are starting from as well as where you are going to. A peek at the topics that we will be getting into in the Year of Freedom is covered here.

### Buddy UP

Life is more fun when you have someone to pal around with, someone to hang out with and someone who supports what you are up to. That's just a fact assuming we are talking about someone who is actually nice to you and wants the best for you. I request that you find someone to buddy up with for the coming year! Why? Because you have a better chance of being successful based on the research regardless of what you are trying to accomplish. I am suggesting it because I believe having a buddy who is also committed to improving his/her life will make this journey more FUN. I am a huge fan of fun!

If you are in the position where you feel that you don't have someone to buddy up then it's probably a sign that you need to make new friends, which is fine. This gives you the perfect excuse to make a new friend. Can you say this: "Hey, I'm doing a self-improvement program to give me a better life, would you be interested in being my buddy? It's a free and fun program?" Of course, you could say that. Would you? I don't know. Why not? What do you have to lose? Nothing. You have nothing to lose. Regardless of how you do it, I highly recommend that you get a buddy and that you and your buddy support each other for the coming year. Make this journey FUN.

## Self-Care: A Golden Gateway to a Happy Life

Self-care is critical to health and well-being. While I superficially mentioned in in a prior post, the topic of self-care is entirely deserving of what I call a dedicated post, which is coming soon. In the meantime, I am asking that you do all that you can to take care of yourself meaning get enough sleep, try to eat healthy foods, work on managing those things that make you feel good and so on because it is extremely important. And you can look forward to a full-on dedicated post on self-care soon.

## Being Confronted – What That Looks Like

I ask that you pay attention to what happens in your mind and body as well as within your circle of people when you take on changing your life for the better. First of all, you might get symptoms of being "confronted" in your physical body or mind. For me, what that looks like is sometimes I get an overwhelming sense of being tired like I need a long nap. Sometimes my skin will break out in little cuts on my hands, like paper cuts that miraculously heal up within hours once I get the thing that I am being confronted by. Once in a blue moon I will get a stuffy head that seems to go on for a day or two when I am literally not sick at all. Mental confrontation can show up physically in the body is what I am telling you.

Next, there are the people in your life that might not want you to change your life for whatever reason(s). They might really take issue with you starting to feel happy and be in charge and in control of your life. It would be good to pay attention to what the people in your life are saying and doing as you begin to move into a happier time in your life. Just watch and listen and be awake and aware.

What I want you to do for this month, assignments are included at the end of this post, is to be awake and aware to how you do life. To help you with this I am including a list of things that you could pay attention to, if you wanted to. This is just a start. These ARE NOT questions that you need to answer. These are just to get you thinking. This IS NOT an assignment but rather things that you could start to observe in your life.

**Be Awake & Aware of Points to Ponder:**

1. What you are thinking?
2. How you are feeling?
3. What do you desire in life?
4. What do you want in life?
5. What are your dreams?
6. How are your relationships with family?
7. How are your relationships with friends? Neighbors? Co-workers?
8. What are you surrounded by in life?
9. How do you take care of yourself (or don't take care of yourself)?
10. How do you treat others?
11. How do others treat you?
12. How do you use your time?
13. Do you have enough time?
14. What makes you smile?
15. What makes you happy?
16. What makes you angry or annoyed?
17. What you think of yourself?
18. What upsets you?
19. How often are you upset in any given day?
20. How often are you happy in any given day?

*Love.Life.*

21. What makes you sad?
22. Do you compare yourself to others or your life to others' lives?
23. What have you always wished for or wanted for either yourself or someone else?
24. How do you feel about your life?
25. How your living space is organized and how does it feel?
26. What are the areas of your life that are working well?
27. What are the areas of your life that need a boost or major overhaul?
28. What problems do you have that you need to deal with?
29. How is your diet (the foods you eat daily)?
30. Is your diet filled with nutrition or junk food?
31. How much sleep do you get each night?
32. Are you getting enough sleep?
33. Do you wake up well rested or tired?
34. How much of your time do you spend laughing?
35. What is missing from your life?
36. What inspires you?
37. What excites you?
38. When are you the happiest?
39. Who are the people in your life who drain you of energy or that you avoid?
40. What needs to be cleaned up in your life?
41. What are your core values?
42. How often do you keep your promises to other people?
43. Will you allow yourself to be happy?
44. Will you allow yourself to have a great life?
45. Do you have people in your life to support you?
46. Are you committed to having a wonderful life?
47. What will get in the way of you having a wonderful life?
48. Can you be gentle and compassionate with yourself?
49. Can you let go of trying to be perfect?
50. Can you promise to enjoy the journey and have fun?

## August Assignments: Awake & Aware

1. **Keep a journal, notebook or notes** on what you are waking up to, what you are noticing for the first time, what you are seeing for yourself, how you are feeling. Try not to judge what you are making notes on – just jot down what you are becoming awake and aware of. Go easy on yourself.
2. **Self-Care Daily:** Take care of yourself. Each day engage in practices that nurture and care for your body, mind, emotions and spirit. A full dedicated post on this coming very soon.
3. **Try to Play and Laugh as much as you can!**
4. **Notice how you feel** moment to moment. How much of your day are you feeling happy and good? How much of your day are you in a negative state?

## Promises of the Year of Freedom

If you read the blog posts with an open heart and mind…
If you do the assignments with intentionality…
If you are willing to have a different life…

Then I promise you the following:

## Promises of the Year of Freedom (12 months): Assuming you do the work…

1. You will be awake and aware like never before in life.
2. You will learn new things.
3. You will hopefully look at life a little differently.
4. You will be happier.
5. You will take on new habits, practices, attitudes and beliefs

that put you in control of your own life regardless of your circumstances.
6. You will be living a life of your own design and feel empowered.

## Request of the Year of Freedom (12 months):

1. Be open. Open minded. Curious. Bring childlike wonder to your life.
2. Laugh and play. As much as you can.
3. Go easy on yourself.
4. Make self-care a big priority. Every day. You matter.

## Call to Action:

It's time for you to have a wonderful and happy life. It's just time. You don't have to wait for the pandemic to be over to start. You don't have to wait for a job. You don't have to wait one more day. Today is the perfect day to begin. Grab a friend or make a new friend just for this express purpose. Who do you know who could use some joy, happiness, and freedom from fear, anxiety and depression? Share this post with them right now and on social media. It's time. Please leave your specific questions below and dive into being awake and aware! I am so excited for you!!!

# EMPOWERING PRACTICES, SKILLS, HABITS, ATTITUDES & BELIEFS

**LOVE the TIME of YOUR Life**

September 12, 2019

Time, time management and all things related to TIME is one of my many great LOVES!! I am wildly passionate about all of the components of time because the benefits of being good at time management are gigantic. And I have been around long enough to know that this is a subject that drives some people crazy. They hate time management, making lists, or anything involved in time management. As someone who has coached individuals and given seminars and workshops on this subject I am extremely aware that this is a negative topic for some of you. With the focus of my blog being LOVE LIFE and specifically you loving your life, I have to say that the more you can master your relationship to and with time, the more in control and positive you will feel, which moves you in the right direction to loving your life.

There is already plenty of research available on how much time people and CEO's, in particular, waste. Wasting time is defined as spending time doing something that is either unnecessary or does not produce any benefit or in a way that is LESS beneficial than it could have been spent. One research study stated that the average American spends 2.5 days each year looking for lost items. Humm. What would you do with 2-1/2 days of free time? I am pretty confident that if you looked at the research on how much time is wasted by various individuals doing different activities that you would not be left feeling empowered. My point is that to have a life you love, time is where the rubber meets the road. We each only have 24 hours in a day. It's just that some people are more effective and efficient with their time leaving them more play time, more happy time, more time to do what you love!

So, let me share with you what I believe are the key benefits to getting better at time management:

1. You will have **more time** to do what you want.
2. You will have **more energy**.
3. You will have **more freedom** in your life.
4. You will have **more control** over your life.
5. You will be **making better choices** in life.
6. You will *feel more confident and powerful.*
7. You will *feel happy*.
8. You will **have a sense of accomplishment**.
9. More often than not, people **begin to act on and execute life goals and plans**.
10. Usually people **expand themselves and take on new challenges**.

This is just my view of it having spent decades practicing my skills and habits until I had a high level of mastery. This topic will have to be dealt with over multiple blog posts simply because there is so much juicy good stuff to share. Today I will deal with the high points including some pointers to get you started, which might be insufficient for you readers with a moderate to high skill set. I will start with asking you to examine and think about how you feel and what you think about time management, making lists, or anything having to do with this topic. And I will start by dealing with those people who are at the lower or lowest end of the scale.

Here's a sampling of what people often say to me when this subject comes up:

*I don't have enough time to consider time management.

*I'm not good with time.

*I'm too busy.

*I have too much to do.

*I'm overwhelmed with all I have to do now.

*I hate time. I wish it were yesterday.

*I'm not that organized – it takes too much time.

*I tried that but it didn't work.

*Are you kidding me, I don't have time to make a list!

Let's start with your own mental consciousness. To help you explore where you stand with how conscious or unconscious you are with respect to time, I am providing my own continuum. Yes, I made this up (laughing to myself now). I don't know if it will be helpful or make sense to you, but it obviously makes sense to me. I assert that to have a life that you LOVE, you will want to start becoming very acutely aware of your time, how your time is used and how your time could be used. I say this with no faintness of heart. I am shall we say very rigorous about my time because the better I use my time translates into more free time for me. I'm not too obnoxious about it, I hope. People that I meet with for business or personal meetings seem to appreciate that my awareness of time helps them stay on track and demonstrates that I care and respect their time as well.

I am a firm believer that once you gain mastery or some level of mastery in time and time management and you can see and feel the benefits, you will start making better and/or different decisions about how you use your time. The more aware you become and the more practice you have with practices and habits in time management, you will begin, sometimes, to question whether or not someone, something, some organization, or some event is worth your time, which is a good thing. It means that you are now much more conscious about your life.

How conscious or unconscious are you with respect to time? If you want to get the joys of love and loving your life I assert that it's going to be so, so much easier if you are present and conscious to how you use your time and what is worth your time, and how your time could be used if it wasn't being eaten up by certain tasks and activities. I fully understand that there are some things in your life that you are unable to change, and yet I have found that when individuals become conscious about where their time is being used they most frequently begin to make better choices with their time. That simply can't happen if you are asleep at the wheel.

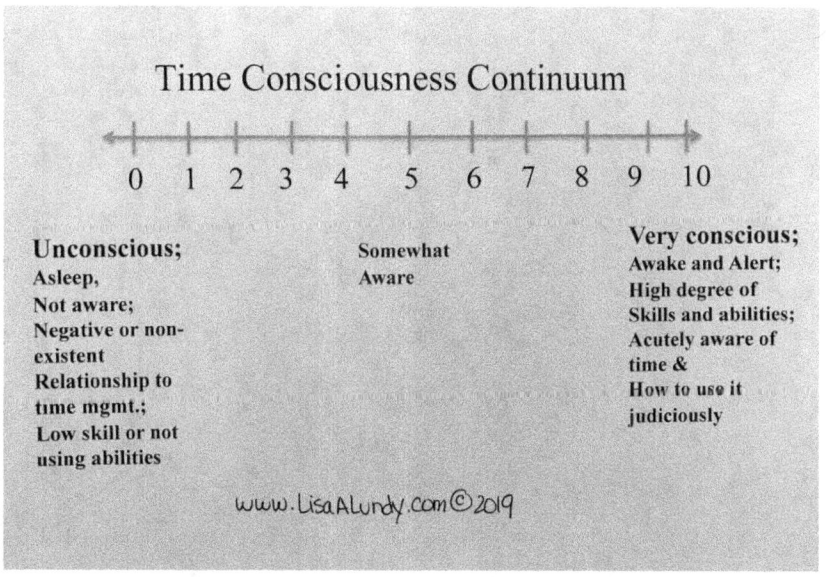

Next, I would like you to consider how you feel about time and time management and all things related. And, yes! I have a continuum for that as well! These were from one of my time management workshops, so I didn't have to create them for the blog. And I think visuals can be very powerful. Do you complain that you never have enough time? Do you feel that people waste your time? Are you often feeling overwhelmed? Are you neutral? For you to have an effective relationship to time and begin to take on the practices and habits to move your life in a more positive direction, you are first going to have to make up your mind that you are going to enjoy time! Change your attitude and the world changes. It can actually be as simple as changing your mind.

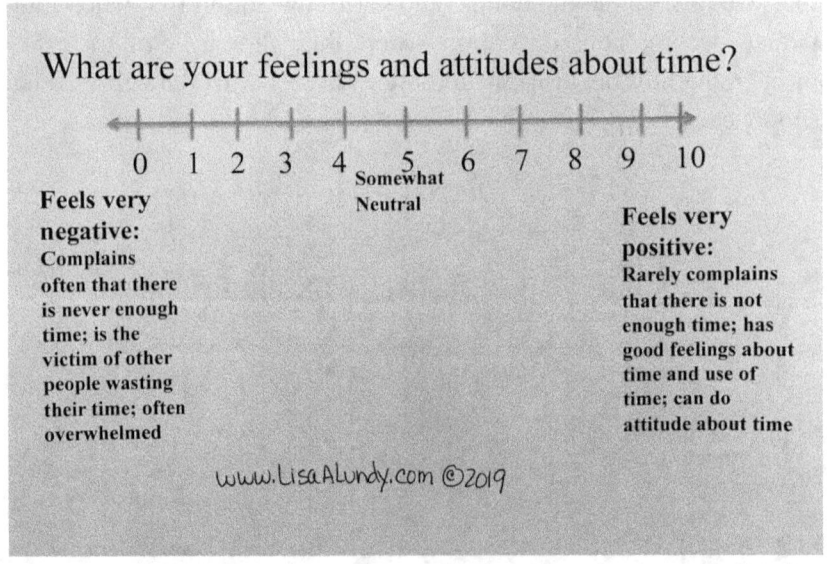

## Level Up

Level up is apparently the new lingo for reward yourself or so I understand. The terminology "level up" coming from gaming where you work towards the next level in a computer game. I am introducing you to the concept of rewarding yourself for embarking on the journey to being so in love with your life that you just are elated. I know, sadly, some of you can't image a life where you feel so much love and joy. While that breaks my heart, I believe that anything is possible. What I have found to be extremely powerful is having a self-designed reward system to motivate and inspire me to get things done. When I say "level up" I am saying "reward yourself" so we are all on the same page.

I suggest that you begin to flush out rewards for yourself. Only you can say for yourself what a good or great reward would be. If you are on a tight budget then you will want to be creative and come up with things that are either free, or cost little money. Some of the things that I have used in the past to Level Up include: taking road trips, having a meal with a friend, making matching dresses and skirts for my daughter and I, giving myself time to engage in a favorite hobby, doing something that I wouldn't normally do or buying myself something that feels like a reward. This is individual and you will figure out what works for you. My point is that I suggest that you include leveling up along the way and not just rewarding yourself for crossing the finish line. Do this on an ongoing basis.

## The Practices or Habits of Time

In my last blog post, titled Road Map to Creating a Life You Love, I had a visual of elements for making a life that you love. These are basically questions that you have to answer to create a bold and audacious life – the life you love! While you may not be in a position where you have answered the questions listed on the Road Map diagram (sketch actually), the bottom line is that you will be driving your life with goals, a vision or your commitments. If you have no vision, no goals and no commitment, then what is driving your life? Someone else's requests, demands, vision for your life? I don't know. But in the absence of goals, a vision, and commitments, something else is driving your life.

## Making Lists is a Core Practice of Loving Your Life – Or Until You Get There

It doesn't matter how you make your lists, when you are on the road to loving your life, I assert that making lists is going to be part of the process. Once you arrive at the point where you are in love with your life – you can ditch the list making if it makes you happy. I am only speaking about this as a tool to help you get there. Once you arrive – woo hoo it matters not what you do! I have a "Master List" of projects, goals, and things to do based on the vision I have for my life. This "Master List" then serves to drive my weekly and daily lists. Yes, I do weekly and daily lists. I do this because I am so crystal clear about the benefits – see the above-mentioned list. I do this because I am up to something in the world and it serves me.

My "Master List" holds all of my projects, tasks, meetings, events, and other things that I either have to, need to, or want to be doing. And it contains my level up rewards. When I make up a list for the week, I am looking at my Master List and triaging what is most important from that Master List that I can fit into the week. My daily list is driven by my list for the week that I have carefully crafted from the Master List. Done in this way, making lists serves to be a PAUSE in your life where you can reassess, re-evaluate, and prioritize or triage all that has to be done. There is no right or wrong way to make lists. One practice that I love once I have made a new Master List is to "Cherry Pick" as many of the items that can be done quickly ~ as in an hour or less because then I get the satisfaction of getting items completed and crossed off early on. Trust me, while this might not seem like much fun, you can even have fun with making lists. Really! You can!

What matters is that you are actively engaged in being the driving force in how you want your life to go and that you are taking actions that forwards you having a life that you LOVE. Clearly there is much more to say in the subject of time management and how to be more efficient and effective with the time that you have. That will come in a future post. For now, the take away is for you to make the decision to do whatever it takes to become better at using your time starting with raising your consciousness about it and moving to a position where you can feel positively about making lists. For some of you just doing that will be a major milestone and accomplishment. Let me know what questions you have by posting them in the comment section! Thank you for visiting my blog and I hope you are on the road to loving your life!

## The LOVE and POWER of Completion

September 16, 2019

Completion is one of my LOVES! I assert that getting complete provides a very real source of power and boost of energy. To have a life that you LOVE it's wildly helpful to have energy and power. It can also provide the opportunity for something new to be created. While sometimes getting complete can be sad or mean the ending of something, there is still power available in completing – a project, a task, an event, a relationship, or an unfilled dream or promise. Complete, as a verb, is defined by the dictionary as to finish making or doing, or to make (something) whole or perfect. As such then, completion is simply the act of finishing something. This blog post is about three topics: getting complete, completion lists, and Master Lists, which are all things that I have been teased about since my college days. Unfazed about all the kidding and ribbing, and there has been a whole lot of that, I do the things that give me a life that I love.

It seems to me that we have some level of cultural agreement that it is acceptable to leave things unfinished, incomplete, or undone. And there's some psychology to why people start things and don't finish them. While I'm a fan of emotional quotient or emotional intelligence and psychology in general, this post is not on the psychology of getting complete – it's about the power, results, and actions to move yourself with intention to finishing more things or relationships. For now, just trust me that overall, or in general, finishing what you start will give you power, freedom, a sense of accomplishment, and possibly happiness and excitement depending on what you are finishing.

Before I get into completion lists, I will briefly mention completion as it relates to relationships even though this is a topic for a future blog post, it is significant enough to merit a paragraph.

Being complete in a relationship, to me, is when you have said what you have to say and nothing is left unsaid. In some cases, getting complete in a relationship means the ending of the relationship. It's been my experience when I get complete in a relationship and it's clear that the relationship is not going to continue, I have a profound sense of peace. Often times relationships can be tricky, problematic, or troublesome, and we just don't have the skills to clear the air, to say what needs to be said, or otherwise clean it up. I assert that walking around with relationships that are incomplete is not a powerful place to be. I believe in saying what needs to be said at the risk of losing a friendship, or having people not like me. I already know that plenty of people don't like me. I'm not in life to win a popularity contest. I'm in my life to have the most fulfilling and joyous life that I can. I'm in my life to contribute to others – to help make the world a better place, to make a difference. Caring what people think of me doesn't serve me or my purpose in life. So, you might have to brush up on some interpersonal skills to start completing relationships in your life – subject for a future post – but I would highly recommend that you at least start thinking about the status of your relationships as we will get to the power of cleaning up relationships soon enough. Just not in this post.

## Completion List

For me, a completion list is a catch-all for anything and everything that is incomplete, unfinished, needs work, or is an intention that has never been executed. We all have those "good intentions" that we never seem to get around to. In 1998, after a move to Buffalo, New York, my completion list had something like 57 or 58 tasks, projects, and things to finish many of them related to the move, unpacking, getting organized, or home improvement projects. I use my completion list as a place holder for anything that calls to me to be done. It matters not how many items you have on your list; what matters is that you make a list and then eventually review your list. Here is an example from my life of how having this practice or habit changed my life in an unexpected way.

In January 2009, when I wrote up (typed up actually) my completion list for the year, I had 26 items listed. Number one on the list was to have Diane Gregor over for coffee. Diane and I had gotten to know each other from working to bring Landmark Education classes to the Buffalo area. We worked well together however we just didn't know each other well. We were teammates working on a group project who liked each other well enough. When I called her up to say that she had made my completion list, she just laughed and asked what that meant. I explained to her my completion list process and system, and that she was on my list to have her over for coffee. With three little children, it was easier for me to have her over than get out to meet her. She happily agreed and we scheduled her to come over. Over the ensuing months, we became good friends. When Diane later became sick, I was honored to be in her inner circle of friends to come to her house to help out until she passed away. For me, caring for someone who is ill, or otherwise struggling is of the highest of honors and a real privilege. It's one of the 7 Corporal Works of Mercy in the Catholic faith – to visit the sick. Had I not been an avid list maker, a person clear about what I am up to, a person who infuses my life with fun and joy, a person who acts upon good intentions, I would have missed out on getting to know a beautiful soul and having Diane as a good friend. Someone who I still miss and cry about on occasion – like in thinking about her for this post.

Just making a completion list, which I typically do in either very late December or early January serves as a PAUSE. In fact, making any list acts as a PAUSE button for life. It's a chance to contemplate how your life is going. It's the moment to assess, evaluate, prioritize, reflect on how you want your life to go, what you want to accomplish, who you want to be with, and all kinds of things. List making is extremely powerful if you want to be in control of how your life goes and having more LOVE – in my opinion. You are welcome to have a dissenting or different opinion. For myself, I have proven over and over through the years that having and making lists is a practice or habit that helps me have more fun, accomplish more in less time, and have my life moving in the direction I SAY it should be going in as opposed to drifting aimlessly along or letting life happen to me.

The other thing that making lists does is that it provides a visual representation of the marking of time, and of accomplishments. It's not about how many items you put on your completion list. It's about you stopping and pausing to consider what is unfinished, what either needs to be or has to be done. It's about taking control of your future and your time. While I almost always type up my completion list – it's really irrelevant how your completion list is done. It just matters that you have a place to catch not only the things that have to get done, but also your dreams and wishes. Clearly, I didn't have to put Diane Gregor on my completion list, yet I wanted to get to know her better. I didn't want another year to pass by where we would each say to each other, we should get together sometime.

This is the first year in forever that I did not make a completion list! The reason that I did not do one this year was because I was actively engaged in a major downsizing move and I was pretty much getting rid of most of my belongings keeping very little. My only priorities were getting rid of things and stuff, finding a new place to live, and moving. In preparing for this post, I began to think about what would go on my completion list for the balance of the year IF I were to write one up. Pretty much nothing. The two things that are incomplete is organizing my pictures and dealing with old papers, which I did start earlier this year and stopped when I decided that it was not a priority. It was simply not important enough for me to complete – at least not this year.

After my April move, I coined the phrase "Summer of Fun" to commemorate having fun after a grueling few months. As the summer wore on, I changed the slogan from "Summer of Fun" to "Summer of Love", which ultimately changed to "Year of Love" because I simply was not going to get to do everything I wanted before the summer ended. So, after a very stressful period in life, it is frequently appropriate to take a moment, or the rest of the year in my case, to do what Stephen Covey called "sharpening the saw" in his *The 7 Habits of Highly Effective People* book. As I mentioned in a previous post, the newer lingo for this is "Level Up", which means reward yourself in whatever form that takes.

While I don't have a completion list for the year, I am actively using the "Master List" and I will move onto that even if the distinction between the two is not clear to you at this point.

## Master List

When I go to re-write my Master List I have feelings of excitement, happiness, anticipation, and introspection. I love the opportunity to reassess, re-evaluate, prioritize and triage the things that I have to, want to, or need to get done. When I have a completion list for the year, I will select the most important items to go onto my Master List. The process is fairly simple. I first draft on scrap paper the things that I think merit my time. Then I will sleep on it and often think about it for a few days. After all, this list is what will be driving my weekly lists for the coming weeks or month. Once I have thought about the draft of my Master List, I will write up the actual or real Master List. I do this on oversize paper because it works for me. It doesn't matter what form you use to create a Master List as long as you have one – if you are going to ramp up your game and take this on as a practice or habit.

In the past I have written up my Master Lists with a more chronological approach to when things needed to be completed. I try to put the most important items in the first few numbered items. Since I do my Master List on oversized paper, when new tasks pop up, I will write them in the margins – adding them to the list in a very informal and messy kind of way. I do a new Master List when the mood strikes. Sometimes I will have accomplished 25% or upwards of 65% before I make a new list. It sometimes depends on how messy the list gets. There is no right or wrong way to do this. You will figure it out as you go.

I am a huge believer in a reward system to bring levity and joy to this process or habit. I level up my Master List by including small or not so small rewards, which I write into my Master List. For example, I love water color painting so this is a great reward or level up for me. I include some time for painting as well as special road trips, or other things that are rewarding to me. I am of the opinion that for beginners this is an absolute must. One year my reward for doing a ton of projects was to make matching dresses for my daughter and I. It was a great level up for the self-discipline of completing many projects and tasks.

If you have read this far, you might be thinking that I am out of my mind. You might be thinking does she really do this? Yes, I have friends from college who can attest that I have been roasted in college for doing exactly this. Like Nike says – Just Do It! My promise to you is that if you take on this practice or habit, you will, over the course of time, become clearer about what is important to you, how you are spending your time, gain skills in prioritizing what has to get done, and gain greater control and power over your life. All of that should help you move towards doing what you love and having a life that you love. Let me know if you have any questions or what your comments are! Love you!

## The Sheer Joy and Magic of Integrity

October 9, 2019

For me, there is sheer JOY and Magic in integrity. If you want a magical life then one area to look at, consider, assess and work on is integrity. From my point of view, operating with high integrity is a requirement to having a life that you LOVE. That is not a fact – just my opinion although given the plethora of books and research on integrity I would say there's some backing to my stance. Integrity is defined as (1) the quality of being honest and having strong moral principles; (2) the state of being whole and undivided. Integrity is often thought of as honesty, truthfulness, authenticity, reliably the same regardless of the circumstances (or usually), trustworthy, consistent or consistency of actions, and moral courage. It takes something to operate with high integrity and I assert that the benefits are well worth the effort.

If you are on the journey with me to having a LIFE that you LOVE then you recognize that personal growth and development are key components to arriving there. How accurately can you assess yourself on this subject? How accurately can you assess yourself in general? We rarely see ourselves as others see us, which means that you could get considerable value by enlisting the help of trusted friends or confidants to help in your assessment. Engage in a conversation for your own benefit – am I reliable? Am I trustworthy? Do I do what I say I will do? You could actually have some fun with this – and I recommend that you do have fun with this. Why not? What is the worst thing that you could learn? That you have little or no integrity and people don't trust you? Or you could find out the little thing that you do, and perhaps were not aware of, that would make all the difference in the world.

What operating with high integrity looks like in real life is keeping your promises, doing what you said you would do, telling the truth, not gossiping, knowing and believing that what you say and do matters, treating others the way that you would like to be treated, having compassion for yourself and others, and reliably being the same person with everyone in your life. It takes courage. It takes being brave, feeling uncomfortable, embarrassed, vulnerable, disappointing people and being judged. And maybe every once in a while, making an ass out of yourself. For certain, it takes being honest with yourself, which can be really hard sometimes. Tall order? Maybe. Or maybe it could be the most freeing, peaceful and powerful way to operate your life.

At the risk of being vulnerable and of giving you the opportunity for a good laugh at my expense – I will share an example of integrity from my life. A high school yearbook co-editor and I used to go to my house after school to work on our yearbook pages because it was convenient and probably because my Mom fed us dinner and snacks. In the process of doing the yearbook pages at my house, several supplies were stored at my house. A stapler belonging to the high school ended up in my dorm room at college, which bothered me, yet I kept forgetting to pack it up and take it home to return it to the high school. For more than 35 years that stapler moved everywhere I moved and I thought about returning the stapler too many times to count. When I moved back to my home town and unpacked the stapler yet again I knew that it was time to reclaim my integrity and I seized the opportunity to return the stapler even though I was incredibly embarrassed about the fact that so much time had elapsed. I knew that the high school probably would not care yet it was important to me as a matter of my own integrity.

At that time one of my kids was doing yearbook at my old high school, so I gave the stapler with a little card attached explaining the journey that the stapler had taken to my child so it could be returned "home". I felt quite relieved and incredibly embarrassed about the lapsed time. The two journalism advisors got quite a kick out of the returned stapler and the journey it had taken. I heard a rumor that the stapler and card was given a special place in the new journalism room when the new school building opened. I don't know if that is true or not. Although this story could be fact checked. Ha-ha. Not kidding though.

*Love.Life.*

Here is my own personal view of the benefits of operating with high integrity. My list might not match up with other lists or what the authors of books state or even therapists say, but this is what I believe are the top 10 benefits for having high integrity.

**10 Benefits of High Integrity**

1. Trustworthy – If you want to win friends and influence people then being viewed as trustworthy is critical. No one wants to be friends or even work with people that they can't or don't trust. Trust is crucial to healthy relationships. When you keep your promises and do what you say you will do that helps build trust.
2. Reliability – Operating with high integrity helps you be viewed as a reliable person after all you can be counted on to do what you say you will do, show up when you have promised to show up (or communicate that you can't keep your promise). We all want to have reliable people in our lives so this is a good thing.
3. Build Connections – In a world where loneliness and social isolation continues to grow, operating with high integrity helps you build connections – social connections – because people gravitate to people that are trustworthy and reliable. Loneliness and social isolation increase premature death by up to 50% making it a bigger threat than obesity according to two meta-analyses from Brigham Young University (see my post titled 8 Ways to Improve Your Health & Look Younger for more details on this), so building connections helps you be healthier than not having connections.
4. Builds Relatedness   Once you have a connection with a person, having and operating with high integrity helps to build the feeling of relatedness, which is a critical stage prior to a relationship forming.
5. Builds Relationships – Having high integrity contributes in

a very positive and healthy way to any relationships you have or will have in the future.
6. Builds Courage – Sometimes operating with high integrity takes courage and being vulnerable so over time the continued practice of saying and doing the hard things will build courage.
7. Builds Self-Esteem – When you practice doing what you said you would do, telling the truth, being authentic, not gossiping, and the other components of operating with high integrity you will naturally feel better about yourself.
8. Builds Character – Every time you do the right thing, even when no one is watching or will know, it builds character. Operating with high integrity helps you build character day after day.
9. Brings Inner Peace – When you operate with high integrity you will not feel conflicted, you will not feel bad, you will have the inner peace of knowing that you did the right thing, you are trustworthy and reliable.
10. Adds LOVE – I assert that the higher your integrity the more LOVE you will have in your life. Trust is the foundation of healthy relationships and you simply can't have trust if you operate outside the bounds of integrity.

I say that operating with high integrity gives my life joy and magic. It gives me connectedness, relatedness, and rich relationships. Since I am constantly striving to make sure that I get into Heaven someday (not anytime soon though), it aligns perfectly with my religious values and beliefs. Now, who is up for a little integrity experiment? When you notice that you are out of integrity in some area of your life or with someone – get into action to reclaim your integrity – make that call, apologize for X, Y, or Z, do that thing that you said you would do OR come clean about the fact that you are never going to do that thing. Do whatever it takes to put your integrity back in place. Then, observe how you feel and what happens! And, please let me know! It's joy and magic that you don't want to miss.

## 10 Ways to Get Yourself Motivated for a Happier Life

October 15, 2019

Motivation we will define as the general desire or willingness of someone to do something or the reason or reasons one has for acting or behaving in a particular way. Procrastination, which is kind of the opposite of being motivated, is classified as a form of self-sabotage in psychology. As human beings we tend to push away uncomfortable situations, or we procrastinate because of the fear of doing something new or the fear of failing. Harvard University Psychology Professor Ron Siegel suggests that bringing optimism and fun back into the picture can help with motivation.

According to the research, motivation leads to happiness in life and understanding and developing your own motivation skill set can help you take control of many other aspects of your life. The benefits of being self-motivated include (summary list from multiple sources): higher self-esteem, higher confidence, more trust, strength for challenges, helps you overcome indecisiveness, helps you be more open and positive, helps you be more organized, helps promote good time management skills, and can help you get faster promotions at work. That all sounds good on paper.

If you have been following my blog then you realize that my intention is to help you get to a point where you LOVE YOUR LIFE. Most people are just not wildly in LOVE with LIFE. If you want to be self-motivated then you will have to be intentional about your life, your time, and what actions you are taking. Of course, you would not be motivated if you feel like you are on a treadmill or just meandering through life. Of course, you would not be motivated if you are feeling like you have no control over your life. Of course, you would not be motivated if you feel depressed or overwhelmed. (Sidebar: If you are experiencing depression, please see a licensed psychotherapist for help. Depression can be very serious.)

Just like taking a trip, you have to know where you are going. You have to know what your goal or goals are. As I discussed in the

Creating a Road Map to a Life You Love post, you are going to have to do some work to get there. A Life that YOU LOVE is simply not going to magically appear one day. We call that magical thinking, and I don't recommend it. Ever. Motivation is one of the cornerstones to success according to the research. But how do you get motivated? Well, it starts by getting clear on what you are out to accomplish. What lights you up? What is fun? What do you love. Once you have laid out a path, it's much easier to muster up the motivation. Motivation, and especially the self-motivation aspect, is a skill or muscle like so many other attributes and skills that can be honed and practiced over time.

While I happen to be fairly strong in this area, this past weekend I bumped up against a lack of motivation, which is very unusual for me. As a result, I began considering and looking at why was I not doing what I had planned? What was holding me back? I had set up a reward for completing the project, yet even that was not providing the motivation called for.

As the all too familiar story goes, I had set aside or planned for X numbers of hours over a weekend to make a dent in a complex and large paper filing project. And the weekend flew by, as weekends often do, without one piece of paper being filed! It was really rather shocking for me. That's not how things go for me once I set a goal. So, I thoughtfully considered the situation to determine why I was not being my word and getting the papers dealt with. Once I had done that there were a few significant reasons that were stopping me, and some changes would have to be made. This is the power of personal growth and development – to be able to distinguish or ascertain in any given moment what is going on internally and then make changes to keep moving forward. It's extremely powerful to be able to engage in that kind of process for any area of your life.

While I have not included having a positive attitude in my list of 10 ways to get yourself motivated, that kind of goes without saying. The negative vs. positive attitude is the subject for an entirely separate post. Suffice to say for now, most things go better with a positive attitude. Nor have I included playing music that you love, or several other things in this list. This is just my own view of the top things that I have found increase self-motivation from my own life and from coaching individuals over the years.

## 10 Ways to Get Yourself Motivated to a Happier Life:

1. **Emotions** – Your emotions are exceptionally powerful and if you want to be motivated then harnessing your emotions is by far one of the best tools that exists. To make use of your emotions in a positive way, I suggest that you distinguish for yourself the emotions you will feel when you accomplish the task at hand – regardless of what you are doing. In the paper filing conundrum example from the weekend, once I looked at the emotions I would FEEL once I was finished – relieved, excited, happy, proud, accomplished, satisfied, organized, complete, energized – well that was a big part of what I needed. Yet, there was more. Part of what was stopping me was that so many decisions would have to be made about (a) whether or not to keep certain papers, (b) the filing of the papers would inevitably lead to some new projects, (c) given the complexity of some of the documents it was overwhelming about how to file and store some of the papers. So, as I contemplated why I was not doing the paper filing, it also became clear that I needed focused time – not time in between my social outings as I had originally set up. The papers carried with them some importance and keeping them or not keeping them was no small matter. This type of job requires brain power and focus, and the recognition of that meant scheduling a focused time for the job. That was both freeing and motivating. Using your emotions to bring motivation to the table is extremely powerful and effective, and I would suggest starting with this if you are looking for a boost in motivation even if it means dealing with a fear of some sort.

2. **Clarity of Vision or Purpose** – Sometimes getting clear on your vision or purpose can provide motivation. Why are you doing this or that? What purpose does it serve? Does doing this thing support your goals in life? Is it critical? Will the end result make you happy? Is it on your "Master List" or weekly or another list?
3. **List the Benefits** – In some instances when you are really resisting doing this thing or that thing, it can be powerful to list the benefits for doing X, Y, or Z. In my paper filing conundrum, I also listed the benefits to getting it complete, which was helpful and powerful in getting me back on track.
4. **Rewards or Level Up** – By now you all know that I love rewards or leveling up and I use this technique all the time! The trick with using a reward system is getting the right reward that will actually motivate you. Continuing with my paper filing conundrum, I had established a reward but it was insufficient for the daunting task of handing so much paper. I was not in the right frame of mind, and as such my reward did not provide the motivation called for with this project. If you have never used rewards in life, then you will likely have to do a little tinkering until you have a system that works for you.
5. **Transform or Reframe your thoughts** – To transform is to make a thorough or dramatic change in form, appearance, or character. To reframe is to express words, a concept or plan differently. When you transform or reframe how you think (and feel – don't forget #1 above), things should immediately shift. You might need to get some support, coaching, or advice on this especially if you are stuck.
6. **Use a Timer** – Sometimes just getting started is half the battle. I often use a timer and frequently find that once I am started on a project or task that I have been avoiding, things really get going. When that is not the case, I still use a timer to keep my commitment to whatever I have agreed

to (note: agreed to with myself). In an earlier blog post I suggested that if you just worked on improving your life, making your life happier for 15 minutes a day that would equate to just over 2 40-hour work weeks over the course of 1 year. I actually use a timer a lot for many things because it works for me.

7. **Break it down into manageable parts** – Often when you are faced with a big task or job it's overwhelming. Break down the task or job into manageable parts. While in the end it is the same amount of work – it will be perceived as more doable. If you can't figure out how to break it down into more manageable parts, then ask someone to help you do that. This can really be a helpful way to get motivated.

8. **Get a Partner or Accountability Coach** – While we are not in life alone, many of us, myself included, do life like we are on our own. Getting a partner for a project or task can help you get motivated. Who likes (or loves) to do the task at hand? Can you barter or trade? People would probably be glad to help you if you let them know that you could use a hand! I know! One of the perpetual criticisms I have faced over the years is that I am not the easiest person to contribute to! Yes. Guilty. And I know how much I love to help other people, so consider getting a partner. An accountability coach is someone who will hold your feet to the fire.

9. **Visual Aids or Signs** – This is a favorite of mine because it works for me. Truthfully, before I have company coming over, I have been known to take down some of my signs, reminders or other visual aids that support what I am up to in life! I know. You have to be in my inner, inner circle to see that stuff! In the past I even did laminated signs that were designed to empower and motivate me (no lamination now because it's so bad for the environment). Signs or visual aids can be exceptionally powerful to remind you what you are up to, what needs to get done, etc. Whether

you make them or buy them, signs or visual aids can be a powerful reminder of what you are committed to, what you are up to, what matters as you move to a life that you LOVE.

10. **Make a Game Out of It** – This is one of the techniques that I really enjoy and have been doing since my cold calling days of Xerox back in the day as I discussed in a prior blog post! If there's a will then there's a way. If you wanted to make a fun game out of a task or job, you can figure it out. You could make a game out of losing weight, getting organized or…filing papers! The more fun and play that you can bring to anything in life, the better it is to me.

You absolutely can have a life that you LOVE. And to get there you will need self-motivation, to be intentional, to figure out what it is that you want. You can have lots of joy and happiness if you are willing to do the work to get there. For those of you who are new to this kind of purposeful, intentional, goal-oriented life, this might seem a bit over-the-top. It would probably feel extremely weird if you began implementing such new behaviors. Do it anyway! The likelihood that you are just going to "fall into" a life that you LOVE is so miniscule that it's just not likely. So why not figure out what you want and go for it! I am here to love you through the process.

## Top 35 Ways that Making a List Will Help You Have a Life You LOVE

November 18, 2019

When life is hard, overwhelming or depressing making a list can be extremely helpful. I know. If you missed the comments I made in my last post I will repeat it for emphasis - I am 58 years old and my retirement money has been taken as well as most of my assets. I am starting over with pretty much nothing. Yep. I know about how hard life can be. I also happen to know that there are certain practices or habits that can pull you forward when the going gets tough. Having been a list maker since before college, I am extremely practiced in making lists and more importantly the topic at hand today, which is the ways that making lists can help you get through difficult times or simply create the LIFE that you LOVE.

If you are not a list maker by habit, then embarking on a new practice of making a list will not feel natural. I am hoping that you will place some level of trust in me that if you persist in making a list that you will ultimately see and feel the benefits I am laying out in this post. Making a list is part of having a clear vision for your life, which is something that many people simply do not have. It's part of being intentional. If you want to have a life that you LOVE, then you have to be the director of your life. You have to live intentionally into the future that you are creating. While it is a lot more involved than that as you can read about in prior blog posts, one foundation to having your life go the way that you say it will go starts with making lists.

Specifically, you will want to look at the blog post titled "LOVE the TIME of YOUR LIFE" for a look at the topic of managing your time, how to use rewards as an incentive to build the habits (called level up), and a brief overview of Master Lists. We all have only 24 hours in a day. It's just a fact of life. Assuming you work 8 to 10 hours a day, 5 days a week, that means that you have at least 118 hours a week (that is predicated that you work 50 hours a week) to use as you see fit. Hopefully you are sleeping 7-8 hours a night, which subtracting that from your 118 hours leftover after work time is deducted would leave you with 62 hours a week (assuming you sleep 8 hours per night). How are you using your 62 hours per week? I understand that some of you are working more than 50 hours a week, but a lot of you are not.

What ARE YOU DOING with your 62 hours per week, which assumes you are working 50 hours a week and sleeping 8 hours a night? I mean what are you really doing with your time?

I understand that you have shopping, cooking, cleaning, household chores, and so much more. But the bottom line is that most people have chunks of time that are wasted. More people than not do not use a list to manage their life. If you had a vision of your life that you were excited about – a vision for your future that you really wanted – trust me you would not want to waste a minute messing around with unimportant stuff. You would be motivated and on fire to get that future for yourself. There's no way around making lists if you want to have a happy and powerful life filled with joy and the things that you love.

While there's plenty more to say about the process of making lists, one of the most powerful ways to make sure that making lists becomes a habit and a routine that you will not let go of is to use a reward system for yourself while you are making your lists and building the muscle of making lists as a tool to get you your delicious life – the life that you actually deserve. I can't say enough about using rewards to motivate and inspire yourself. I mention it in the "LOVE the TIME of YOUR LIFE" blog post, but it has to be mentioned here again. I am a staunch believer that a reward system, also called LEVEL UP, is critical while you are establishing new habits.

Only you can determine what is a good or great reward for yourself. Only you can determine what is appropriate, financially responsible, and a good fit for yourself. Rewards or leveling up can be anything that you determine would be motivating and rewarding. If you have not been a list maker in the past, or perhaps not a reliable list maker, then please implement a reward system for yourself. It could be allowing yourself the time to work on a hobby that you normally don't allow yourself the luxury to do. It could be meeting a friend, neighbor, or family member for coffee or a meal. It could be planning a trip or other event. I have used all of those as rewards in the past. And even though I am as committed to making lists as anyone ever could be, I still use a reward system for myself. Why? Because I love rewards. I am worth it. And quite frankly, rewards are fun!

The bottom line is that after coaching individuals for more than a decade, I know that rewards have worked for everyone that I have worked with in the past. The key element is selecting rewards that work for you. That's not something that I can help you with other than to give you ideas on rewards. If you can just trust me and come up with some rewards that you would be motivated to receive and use the rewards as an incentive, that would be the best thing you could do.

Having a reward system does not, by the way, guarantee your success. There are other factors involved, which is the subject for another day. Rewards or leveling up, however, are one of the best tools that I know of to increase the likelihood of your success. Another part of it is your attitude. Yet another part is how badly do you want more love and happiness in your life. There are many components that will affect how things go for you. A reward system will be helpful.

**WORD OF CAUTION:** I ask that you be mindful in your early days of gaining skills in making lists. It will be easy for some of you to mentally beat yourself up for not doing everything on your list, or not doing enough on your list, or not making the right list, or not thinking of something that could or should have gone on your list. THAT is NOT going to be helpful. What I want you to be doing in the early days until you are very practiced in making and using lists is to celebrate that you are embarking on a new habit or practice. Please don't judge yourself for not doing enough or all of your list or anything like that. Instead, celebrate and acknowledge yourself for taking on your life. Pat yourself on the back for doing what few people will ever do. Love yourself for making the effort. Love yourself for trying. Love yourself for working towards the life that you love. You have probably been way too hard on yourself for too many years. Cut that stuff out.

As a lay person, I can say these are my thoughts about the benefit and value of making lists, which I am not representing is what other people say are the benefits of list making. I have no idea what other individuals say are the benefits. This is my list and what I say are the benefits.

## Top 35 Ways Making A List Will Benefit You

1. **You will get more done**: Here I am talking about an increase in productivity. There is no question that having a list helps people be more productive.
2. **You will save time**: Having a list helps you be more efficient, which frees up time. Think about the time you waste because you are not clear in your thinking. You make an extra trip to the store because you forgot something primarily because you didn't have a list or you didn't look at your list. That happens to everyone – some people more than others. There is no doubt that you will free up time to do things that you love if you engage in making lists.
3. **You will be more focused**: Making a list requires that you do actual thinking, which means that you are focused. Hopefully you are driven and focused on doing the activities that will move you closer and closer to a life that you LOVE. After all, that is the intention.
4. **It will be harder to distract you**: When you are practiced at making lists and hopefully reaping the rewards you have set up for yourself, it will become harder and harder for you to be distracted from your goal and purpose.
5. **You will feel good – eventually if you stick with it**: While making lists might feel awkward, uncomfortable, and weird in the beginning, if you stick with it you will feel good because you will notice the changes and see how you are more efficient and productive, which means that you will ultimately realize that you have more free time to do what you want.
6. **You will have a visual to see your accomplishments:** Many times, we get to the end of the day and wonder what did we do all day. Having a list gives you a very definitive and visual representation of what you accomplished for the day. It can be a powerful tool for feeling good even on bad days.

7. **It can provide a structure for difficult times to pull you forward**: When life is very painful or difficult or you are suffering, having a list – once it is a firm habit – can pull you powerfully towards the future you are creating. It is an exceptionally amazing tool for dealing with tough times. Trust me, I know all about this.
8. **It will help lower anxiety**: Most of us have some level of anxiety now and then – some more than others. Having a list can help you lower your anxiety because it is a visual sign that you are moving forward with your life. If you are using lists to move you to a life that you love, then the lists that you make should be comforting and help you reduce your anxiety. There are other reasons that are mentioned below which are additional points why list making should help you if you have anxiety.
9. **It will help you create a life that you love**: There is no question that making lists will help you create a life that you love because you are the one making the list and you are determining what goes on your lists with the exception for the constraints that happen if you have other people in your life – primarily if you are a care-giver, a parent, have a spouse or significant other, etc. While having those responsibilities involving other people will impact your list, you are still the driver and the bottom line for having a life that you love and lists will help you get there.
10. **It will force you to prioritize what matters the most**: Making lists forces you to decide day to day and week to week what will go on your list. Simply put, making a list helps you triage and sort out the most important tasks and activities that either have to be done or that you want to do.
11. **It will reduce your stress levels**: Making a list helps reduce your stress levels in a couple of ways. One, you are being more productive and efficient- two factors that right away should help you bring down your stress level. Additionally, you are forced to prioritize what has to

happen versus what could happen, which should help you feel more in control of your life, which in theory should make you feel better. Having a list will also help you not forget things that could be costly and help you avoid negative consequences for not doing things that have a bad impact (like paying bills, filing taxes, being where you are supposed to be, keeping agreements, and so much more). I assert that the more lists you make and the more habitual you are in making lists (and actually working on getting stuff done), the less stressed you will feel.

12. **It will save you money**: Making lists absolutely will save you money. You don't make a second or third trip to the store. Ca-Ching. You don't pay a late fee on paying a bill because you paid it on time. You don't have to pay a higher shipping costs because you are ordering something late like a gift or something. There are a multitude of ways that making lists can save you money.

13. **It will motivate you (or it should or can)**: Making lists can clearly motivate you if you are working towards a life that you love. Even if you are simply in a depressed or overwhelmed state, making a list can motivate you. You want a better life for yourself, I hope that is the case if you are reading my blog posts, and making lists will help you get there eventually. Stick with the program.

14. **It will help you feel more confident**: While it is just my opinion based on years of experience in my own life and with coaching others, I stand by the fact that when people take on the practice of making lists they feel more confident. They are choosing what to do with their time. They are selecting what is important. And they are taking charge of their destiny. That is the formula for confidence.

15. **It can be a handy reference for what is going on**: Making lists is a very handy reference for what is going on AND what you WANT to be going on. When you have had a long day, or perhaps a hard day, it's easy to forget what matters because you are just exhausted and worn out.

*Love.Life.*

Having lists helps you remember what is going on. It's also very helpful to keep you on track for not missing deadlines, and what not.

16. **It can help you clear your mind:** Personally, I know that making lists can help you clear your mind. It's one of the reasons that I often recommend to the people I coach to make their list for the next day before they go to bed at night. Making a list definitely helps you clear your mind because what is in your mind should go on the list – or if not the list then a "catch-all" list for things that need to be done later.

17. **It can definitely help you sleep better**: When you have less anxiety, less stress, when you feel more confident, and are more productive and efficient – is there any doubt that you would sleep better? I hope not. People who seriously engage in making lists that is the people I have coached over the years have reported that they sleep much better than prior to starting the list making. There is solid reason that would be the case. It's also the reason that I recommend making your list before you go to bed at night so your mind is clear.

18. **It will help you avoid problems**: Making a list can help you avoid both big and small problems. If you are managing your life using lists, then you will avoid late payments, missed deadlines and other things that can be quite problematic or even expensive.

19. **It's a tool that can help you corral other areas of life and deal with them**: Once you get into making lists, you will use your lists to get other areas of life in order and deal with them once and for all – if you are like most people. As you become more productive and efficient and have more free time, you will begin to take on other areas of life that you may have been avoiding or that you simply didn't have time to deal with.

20. **It can serve as a reminder of what you are up to**: Life is hard. Having a list can serve on your worst or most

trying days as a reminder of what you are up to in life and that can be extremely powerful and helpful. When times are tough, it's easy to feel sorry for yourself and like you can't win. A list will remind you that you are up to having a life that you love, which is always helpful.

21. **It's free**: One helpful benefit to list making is that there are no costs involved. It's free. You can use recycled scrap paper for making your lists. It doesn't have to be fancy.
22. **It's easy**: In the scheme of life, making lists is just not that hard. It takes you doing some thinking and some way to record your list. Pencil or pen and paper. Computer and printer. It's not rocket science. Anyone can do it.
23. **It can help you say NO and mean it**: What I know about using lists and training people in list making and time management is that once people get clear about the life that they want, the life that they COULD have, it becomes infinitely easier to say NO to things that don't support your future and mean it. When you have clarity about your life and future, you simply don't want to do what isn't necessary. And most of us do things that are not necessary and don't serve our greater vision.
24. **It is good for your brain – doing actual thinking**: We do things repetitiously because it conserves energy for our brain. Doing actual thinking requires brain power, which is very good for our brains. You have to think about what you want your life to look like. You have to think about what you want in life. You have to make decisions about what actions match up with the vision you have for your life. That is actual thinking. It's good for you.
25. **It can help you of you are dealing with depression or overwhelm**: Life is very difficult if you are depressed or dealing with overwhelm as my previous blog post on overwhelm should make clear. Having a list can be very helpful, comforting and pull you forward if you are depressed or dealing with overwhelm. I should know. Haha. But not kidding at all.

26. **It will help you build the muscle of integrity**: Making lists helps you increase your integrity muscle. The more lists you make ongoingly, the more you will keep your promises and do what you said you would do because you will become clearer and clearer on what you are doing and what you said you would do.
27. **You will be more trustworthy**: Nothing breeds trust more than doing what you said you would do when you said you would do it. Making lists will help you do exactly that. People generally LOVE trustworthy people. We want to be around people we trust and run from people who are unreliable or not trustworthy. It's a really great benefit to making lists.
28. **It forces you to pause**: This is one thing that I LOVE about making lists. It forces me to pause. I pause when I make my Master List, my weekly list and my daily list as I contemplate what actions serve me the most. What are the most beneficial things that I could be doing with my time? It is a good thing if you are committed to having a life that you love!
29. **It can help build your self-esteem**: Given all of the benefits that I have already covered in this list, is it any wonder that it would help build self-esteem? Hopefully you can see that as a given.
30. **It will help you control your own life**: The practice of making lists is absolutely the way to help you get control of your own life. I understand that many of you have circumstances that are beyond your control. Even with that, making lists will help you get control of the part of your life that is in your hands and likely take back more control in other areas of your life.
31. **It is a grounding activity that grounds you in reality**: It's always helpful to be grounded in reality as opposed to wishful thinking or denial. Making lists helps to get you out of denial and into reality. It's a grounding activity that helps propel your life forward.

32. **It will help you become more self-disciplined**: The habit of making lists on a daily basis can absolutely help you become more self-disciplined and that is always powerful and helpful if you are up to creating a life that you LOVE.
33. **It improves your reliability factor**: When you implement the regular habit of making lists and increase the number of times that you do what you said you would do and keep your promises then people will begin to view you as someone who is reliable. You will be viewed as someone people can count on, which is distinctly different than trustworthy in my opinion.
34. **It will help you reach your goals**: While I have listed this as #34, this is the number one reason to make lists. It will, in fact, help you reach your goals. That is the reason for making lists – to have the life that you LOVE. To reach your goals. To have something other than the life that you have been having.
35. **You get rewards**: If you are taking my advice, then you are absolutely going to get rewards by making your lists. While I can't force you to come up with a reward system and give yourself rewards or level up, why would you skip over that? That's fun! You want to make every area of your life as much fun as you can – or at least that is my operating philosophy. Create fun rewards for the practice of making lists – and take the rewards! And enjoy the process.

**Concluding Thoughts:**

I absolutely LOVE making my lists. I look forward to checking things off my list and to making new lists. I was roasted in college for having "lists of my lists", which was pretty funny and at the same time very accurate. The reason that I LOVE making lists is because I am clear as a bell about the benefits I have listed in this post. You might not be looking forward to making lists. That's okay. Do it anyway. Create some rewards that you WILL look forward to. Have some fun with this. Even though I am masterful in time management and list making, I still use a reward system for myself because it really works and it's fun!!

My purpose in blogging is to help you gain the tools, perspective, habits and practices that allow you to move to a LIFE that YOU LOVE. Making lists is a part of living intentionally and getting the life that you deserve. How can I support you in this practice? What did I miss? What questions do you have? I want you to have a life that you LOVE. Now, go make a list!

## 21 Reasons Why Making Friends Will Help You LOVE Your Life & 17 Ways to Make New Friends

December 3, 2019

Making friends is hard. We all inherently know that but yet it's not something that we talk about. Making good friends is, in my opinion, a life skill that we should be teaching young people. This is a topic that, of course, I LOVE, and one that I have something to say a few things about. I am deeply Blessed by God that I have many good friends – people that I can count on. People who have my back. People who have my best interests at heart – and who know that I am likewise there for them. Today I will give you the 21 reasons why making friends will help you LOVE your Life, 17 ways to make new friends, the obstacles to making friends, and who knows what else!

Making and keeping friends and spending time with friends is by far one of the best investments you can make to improve your health. As I wrote in a previous blog post titled 8 Ways to Improve Your Health and Look Younger: "Loneliness and social isolation increase premature death by up to 50% making it a bigger threat than obesity according to two meta-analyses from Brigham Young University." The bottom line is this – you can do many things to improve your health, but making friends and spending time with friends is one of the best things that you can do that is proven (assuming you have good friends) to make a difference in your longevity and health.

I want to start with defining friends. There are rock-solid good friends, acquaintance friends, Facebook friends, BFF's, Besties, work friends, neighbor friends, church friends, and so on. What really makes a good friend? Someone where there is reciprocal caring. Someone who is as good to you as you are to them. It is NOT the person who rejoices in your hardship. It is not someone who puts you down. It is someone who lifts you up, hopefully makes you laugh – and you them, and someone who makes you feel loved and supported. Anything else is not a friend. And you might have friends in your life currently that are not so great to you. That would be helpful and powerful to recognize. You deserve to have friends. You deserve to have good friends who appreciate and support you – and you them.

Life presents many circumstances where you have to make new friends. You go off to college, get a new job, move to a new city or town, get married or divorced, or become a widow or widower. Life offers many situations where making new friends is simply what there is to do. If you are open and willing to take risks, you can make friends in the most unlikely places or with the most seemingly unlikely people. I met Susan over 26 years ago. She and I were both having work done on our cars at the Good Year store in Whitehall, PA. We were both single and close in age. So, I approached her about if she would ever want to go out and have a drink sometime. I was relatively new to the area and had broken up with the boyfriend who was the reason for my move. I gave her my card. I think she was laughing and thinking – who is this crazy woman. We eventually did meet up for drinks and laughed ourselves silly. Together we eventually built a posse stitching together strangers we met along the way and had many fun times. We are still friends and still make each other laugh!

Helen was my neighbor before I built my house. She seemed very nice although she was about 48 years older than I was. Who could have predicted that she and I would become friends? Well, we did become friends and kept in touch even after I built my house. I was there for her first ever surprise party for when she turned 80! She said often to me that everyone should have friends that are significantly younger because once you get to be her age all your friends pass away. When I ultimately moved out of state, we kept in touch by phone calls and letters. She was a sweetheart and we would laugh together like crazy. She passed away at age 101 with us having been friends for 23 lovely years. You never know who you COULD become friends with if you are not open to it.

Why is it so hard to make friends? What's really the obstacle in making new friends? My assessment and opinion is that what holds us back from making new friends is the fear of judgement, fear of being assessed as not good enough, and other anxieties that stem from fear of rejection. Yes, some people will reject you. So what? I have mentioned in prior blog posts that we need to love our imperfections. We need to LOVE ourselves. If you are comfortable in your own skin and with yourself – making friends becomes a whole lot easier. Until you get to the point where you can authentically love yourself and love your imperfections, making friends is a pure act of courage and bravery. It takes being authentic. It takes being willing to put yourself out there. It takes being willing to fail or be rejected.

Most people I know could use a few more good friends. Maybe that's not you, but I know that most people could. The worst thing that could happen by taking an action or several actions to make new friends is that people might think you are weird or strange. Who cares? You want to have a rich and powerful life. You want to have a life that YOU LOVE. You want to have a life that inspires you! You have to stop caring at some point about what other people think about you. You have to get to the point where you are clear about what your intentions are and you are acting upon those intentions. It is living life intentionally. Maybe making more friends could be one of your goals or intentions for the coming year.

Maybe you not giving a flying hill of beans about what other people think of you would be a breakthrough of gigantic proportions. I just don't know. I know that making friends is powerful and not that hard if you are willing to give up your fears of being judged and assessed. And the benefits are clearly worth it.

## 21 Benefits to Having Good Friends

1. It's one of absolute best things you can do to improve your health.
2. Friends love you (receive love and give love).
3. Friends validate you (give and get validation).
4. Friends support you and vice versa.
5. Friends make you laugh and smile (or so that's how it goes in my world).
6. It's FUN!!
7. It takes a bite out of loneliness.
8. You have people to do things with.
9. Friends call you on your s**t (or should).
10. It's great for your emotional health and wellbeing.
11. It is how human beings are meant to be – in tribes.
12. It builds self-esteem.
13. It makes life so much more interesting.
14. You will learn new things (unless you are friends with clones of yourself).
15. It helps mitigate or stave off depression (or it can).
16. It's great to have a fan club to cheer you on in life.
17. Friends can help you survive dark times.
18. Friends can remind you of who you are and what you are capable of -for those times when you might need reminding.
19. Friends make life easier.
20. Friends can help you with your growth and development.
21. Friends can help you celebrate the good times in life.

Before I get into the ways to make new friends I should probably be a little forthcoming. According to the Malcolm Gladwell book "The Tipping Point", I am probably the kind of person that he calls a "connector". I connect with people, often at a very deep and personal level. Beyond that, I have been since the 7th or 8th grade the kind of person who doesn't give a bleep about what people think of me. You would understand that fully if you knew that in the 7th or 8th grade I wore my headgear to junior high school – the kind that goes over the back of your head and around the sides of your face – to school. During the day! Yes, I knew that the other kids might make fun of me – and I didn't care. Good for me.

That's not most people. What it might take you to make new friends assuming you are even committed to that is starting to care about your life and your happiness MORE than you care about what other people think of you. People have made fun of me for most of my life for different things. And I simply don't care. I know what it takes to have a wonderful life even in very dark times and that it what matters. Be brave. Be courageous. Do whatever it takes to put yourself out there and make new friends. I promise you that it will be worth it. Yes, you might get rejected. And you can deal with that.

The following list is a compilation of the various ways that I have made friends over the years. They work. They are not an overnight fix. This is not something that will happen just because you go to an event, volunteer, or take one specific action. It takes intention. And for the record, I did not help to start a chapter of Alpha Omicron Pi Sorority in order to make friends although that was a byproduct of helping to charter the chapter. I did, however, start two different Toastmasters International Gavel Clubs in two different states to help my children make friends. Just do something with intentionality.

**17 Ways to Make New Friends:**

1. Get out there in life – get out of your head, get out of where you live – get out there in life!
2. Join a club or organization. Joining an existing club or organization is a great way to meet people and to make friends.
3. Volunteer some place – anyplace that appeals to you. Volunteering is another way to increase the number of people you meet and help you find friends.
4. Talk to strangers – all the time. Of course, I am a fan of talking to strangers. It is fun or it can be fun. Let's face it, some people are just not so fun. But I find more people are fun than are not. Start talking!
5. Reconnect with old classmates. Reconnecting with old classmates or childhood friends represents another opportunity to make meaningful friendships.
6. Organize a reunion, charity event or something. Yes, I have done this in the past and it was delightful on every front. While this takes some time and energy, if you are putting together a new tribe, this is one way to do it.
7. Take classes that interest you. This is another way to meet people with shared interests, which is always a plus when you are looking to make friends.
8. Share yourself authentically with people you meet. Being vulnerable and sharing yourself authentically (okay, not over sharing) will go a long way to drawing people into you and making them think that you might be someone that they want to connect with.
9. Get your local restaurants to start "communal tables". While "communal tables" are not so common, this is a fantastic way to meet people. Restaurants that do this set aside a table where customers who are dining alone, can meet other people who are also dining alone. I think it's the best idea since sliced bread.
10. Invite other people to do things with you. You might be

*Love.Life.*

surprised how many people are sitting at home wishing they had people to do things with. Get out there and invite people to go places or do things with you. What do you have to lose?

11. Start a new hobby and connect with people who do that hobby. I am a super fan of hobbies, which I will be writing in a future post. I believe it is really good for people to have hobbies. If you don't have one – go start one. If you already have hobbies – connect with people who have that shared hobby.
12. Meet and organize your neighbors. Yes, yes, yes to this. I did this in Pennsylvania and New York. I am a fan of this. It just takes one person to host a coffee, or initiate a cookout, or suggest that the neighbors come together in some way. It just takes one person. Be that person.
13. Read the paper or local on-line calendar for events that interest you and then go to some!
14. Start a local club in your area. I started two Toastmasters International Gavel Clubs so that my children, who were being home schooled at the time, could meet other kids and make friends because I believe making friends is extremely important. If you can't find a club that interests you – start your own.
15. Ask people to introduce you to other people. It's not unreasonable to ask the people you do know to introduce you to other people. Nothing ventured nothing gained in my book.
16. Meet up with co-workers, if appropriate. While it is not always appropriate to socialize with co-workers, often times it is okay.
17. Use social media to help you. I have made some of the most wonderful friends through social media. I mean lovely, lovely, precious friends. I have used social media to reconnect with childhood friends. Social media can be a tool to help you connect with people and make friends.

**Concluding Thoughts:**

This is a very important topic and I hope that what I have written has given you pause to think about the friends you have in your life and hopefully the inspiration to go out and make more friends as needed. The more work you do on yourself, growth and development as I call it, the easier it will become to make new friends. The more work you do on yourself, the less you will care what other people think about you and quite frankly what other people say about you. You will be clear about what you are committed to in life and how your life is going to go.

I want you to have an amazing and spectacular LIFE that YOU LOVE. Having friends is part of that in my opinion. I just can't image a life without people to share it with. The love. The laughter. The good times. The bad times. Life is meant for sharing and friends are part of that. Now, what is holding you back from making more friends? How can I support you in making new friends? Please let me know!

**Here's How to Have the Best New Year of Your Life**

December 5, 2019

New Year's has been celebrated around the World for thousands of years – approximately 4,000 years from about 2,000 B.C. to the present time. I absolutely LOVE this time of year because it is a time to pause and reflect, a time to plan and set goals, and a time to create the LIFE you LOVE. If you have had a bad year, then all the more reason to close the chapter on the current year and start fresh. With the New Year approaching I am laying out the process to use the milestone of New Year's to create an amazing New Year for yourself. According to the research, about 88% of people who set New Year's resolutions fail! Why is that? What does it take to be in the 12% of people who are successful with respect to New Year's resolutions?

I assert that the 88% of people who fail with their resolutions fail because they do not have the habits, practices and support that is required to succeed. Intentions alone are nothing but good thoughts or ideas. Intentions have to be executed into action to be anything more than a thought. Resolutions are just thoughts or ideas. It takes action to translate the thought into something real.

If you want to be in the 12% of people who reach their goals and succeed in attaining resolutions, there is a process to put into place.

Before I layout the process, I want to go back to the theme and intention of my blog – to help you have a LIFE that you LOVE. That takes you getting clear, eventually, about what you want your life to look like. How do you want your life to go? What do you want in your life? What makes you happy? As I have said before, if you want a happy life you definitely need to know what it is that makes you happy. Unfortunately, a lot of people just simply don't know what makes them happy. That is – I think – our societal norm. It might take exploring. It will definitely take actual thinking. Your New Year's resolutions will hopefully spring from what you want your life to look like. What else would you base them on?

If you are coming off of a bad year, which happens to a good number of people through no fault of their own, I want you to be compassionate with yourself. I want you to make peace with whatever happened and be able to create a fresh start. That might be easier said than done depending on what happened this past year. Regardless of what has gone down, it's important that you make peace with it to be able to create a better future for yourself. If you are coming off of a fantastic year – that's awesome – celebrate like crazy! Regardless of what kind of a year you have had – it's good to keep steering your life in the direction that you want it to go in.

Yes, I do this process. Every. Single. Year. I love this process. For many years, I even made my kids come up with a list of goals for themselves. It's a great practice for any age. It is the process that sets the tone for the year. It is the process that supports me in having a life that I love. Yes, I have had plenty of bad things happen in my life, but when I look back over my life it's not the bad things that I recall or remember. I remember all the really great stuff.

Having a life that you love takes intentionality. You have to be really intentional. Otherwise you get sucked into the drift we call life. Life just happens. Maybe that works for you. I am asserting to really be wildly passionate about your life you have to be in the driver's seat and take control. Don't just let life happen to you. I invite you to enjoy this process. The reason that I love this process is because I know that it works. It really works. If you have never done this before then it will feel unusual or unnatural or perhaps weird. Just do it.

## Process to Be Successful with Your New Year's Resolutions:

1. **Pause** – Start with a pause to think. You simply have to stop doing life and pause.
2. **Reflect** – Reflect on how your life has gone so far up to this point in time. What works about your life? What doesn't work about your life? What would you LOVE to have in your life that is not present currently? What inspires you? What is missing? What do you want more of in the coming year?
3. **Close the Book If You Have Had a Bad Year** – Some years are better than others. If you have had the proverbial "bad" year, then close the book on that. Get complete. Do whatever it takes to put the past year to bed. Don't start the new year by dragging the past into your fresh start. Maybe you have had a series of bad years. Get complete on that. Maybe you need to journal about that. Maybe you need to talk to a friend. Or talk to a coach. Do whatever it takes so that you are complete and ready for a fresh start.
4. **Vision for Your Future** – As you reflect on your life up to this point, you want to create a vision for your future.

*Love.Life.*

You want to be clear about what it is that you want in your life and possibly what you want less of in your life.

5. **Think Big** – While you are creating a vision for your future I invite you to think big. I request that you think big. If you have never read the book "Think and Grow Rich" by Napoleon Hill, written in 1937 and still sold today, I would highly recommend it. There's really no harm in it unless you are going to beat yourself up for not making the 'thinking big' kind of goals.

6. **Plan of Action & Goals** – As you create a vision for your future, you want to take the vision and use the vision to create a plan of action and some specific goals. Perhaps you want to make more money, while that's great – what is even better is to list out X dollars more money. Or maybe you want to make more friends. That's a fantastic goal and it will likely take some actions to attain that goal. Goals are specific with a measurable result and a deadline. Without the specific result and deadline, it's just a dream. Possibly a pipe dream. You should write down your plan and goals on paper or type them up on your computer. Regardless of how you do it, you want to end up with a hard copy of your plan of action and goals.

7. **Specific Actions Required** – From your overall plan of action and goals you will then drill down to list very specific actions to take to attain your goal. Your specific actions can then go on your Master List of Tasks to do. I have written a bit about making lists and Master Lists in past blog posts most notably the blog titled "Love the TIME of your Life". Write down all of the actions that you will need to take to be successful. Write them down. Not kidding.

8. **Reward System** – If you have been reading my blog since the beginning then you know that I am a huge fan of rewards or leveling up! I mean I am a super HUGE fan of rewards or leveling up. I have a great amount of self-discipline, and I still use a reward system. It's fun. It provides motivation. It can be super cool. You get to say

what a reward is for yourself. No one else can dictate or tell you what a good reward for you is. I hope you will simply trust me on this one. If you want to significantly improve your chances of attaining the life that you love, a reward system will absolutely help you get there.

9. **Commitment** – It takes commitment to loving your life to have a life that you love. Review the vision you have created for your life as well as your plan of action and goals. Are these the things that you are excited about? Does your vision inspire you? You have to have commitment, so if you are not excited and inspired about your future I would suggest that you either go back to the drawing board and revisit your vision and action plan OR find a way to get excited about what you are creating. Either approach can work. If you look at what you have laid out and are not inspired and excited, something has to change because you are unlikely to be able to maintain your commitment to that vision and plan. And, why would you do that anyway? Because you think you should?

10. **Inspiration/Motivation** – Being inspired and motivated will go a very long way to helping you attain the vision you have created for your future. Carefully crafting a reward system that you love will help you maintain motivation over the long haul – or it should if properly done. Sometimes even with a reward system you might find yourself not taking the actions that you should. In those instances, you will want to get some coaching, talk to a friend, or find some way to distinguish what is stopping you. I know from experience that even with a reward system, there are times when you will get stopped. You have to be willing to recognize that you are stopped and then take an action to get moving in the right direction.

11. **Support** – Frequently people fail in goals or with their vision because they do not have support. It is important, in my opinion, to have support for creating a life that you love. This blog is support. You can post questions to get

supported. You probably, and hopefully have people who love you who would support you in what you are doing if you let them in on what you are committed to. Making lists and following good list management practices will absolutely support you as will a good reward system. Read my past blog posts to determine what habits or practices you might need to consider that will support you in being successful.

12. **Create a TEAM** – I absolutely love working in teams because I just happen to believe life is better in a group than alone. Join forces with someone or multiple people who are committed to having a life that they love. Name your team – the dynamic duo, the terrific trio, the four musketeers. Have fun with this. If you don't have enough people like that in your life then it's time to add more people to your tribe. I just blogged about making new friends so that will help you if you want to do that.

13. **What could stop you** – There are lots of things that happen in life that could stop you in making progress or thwart your intentions. Lots of things. Right out of the gates, I believe that it is powerful to recognize what are the kinds of things that could stop you. You might get depressed or feel overwhelmed. An unanticipated event might happen. The more you get to know yourself and what makes you tick, the better you will be able to recognize and distinguish what are the things that could stop you. And regardless of what happens, you can still make progress towards your goals and vision. Trust me. You can.

14. **Monitoring Progress** – If you are committed to having a life that you love, you will want to monitor your progress. That is a given. One of the best ways to monitor your progress is through the list management practices that I have written about in previous blog posts. Each time you make a new Master List, for example, you will have a visual representation of the progress that you have made. Each

time you make a new Master List you will be taking a pause and reflecting on what are the most important tasks that should go on your new Master List. As I have said before, I don't see how you can have a life that you love without some level of list making in it. I just don't believe that the human brain, with some rare exceptions, is wired for that. Regardless of how you do it, you are going to want to periodically check in and see that you are moving forward and making progress on your goals and vision. Otherwise, why bother?

15. **Celebrate Every Step Forward** – Life is hard. We all know that. Why not celebrate every step forward? I believe wholeheartedly in celebrating everything possible. As you make progress, assuming you have established a reward system, you will be rewarding yourself or leveling up. And there are other milestones or accomplishments along the way that are probably worthy of celebration. Celebrate all that you can. Why the heck not?

**Concluding Thoughts:**

I know that life is hard. Trust me I know. Yet, I also know that even in the darkest of times you can have happy moments and good times – great times even. There has never been a better time to take charge of your life and start having it go the way that you would like it to go. And that probably means doing things – habits and practices – that you are not used to doing. Hang in there. The more you do a new habit – the more comfortable it becomes – until eventually it just feels right to do that habit.

With a new year approaching I am hoping that you will get excited about your life and your future! I hope you will get excited about celebrating yourself and your life. Why not? What else are you going to be doing? I hope you will try on this process. I mean I really WANT you to try on this process because I know that it works. How can I help you? How can I support you? Post a question on this blog and I will do my best to support you!

Love.Life. That is what it is all about.

## How Hobbies Can Help You Love Your Life and the Top 23 Reasons You Should Hobby Up Now

December 11, 2019

Hobbies are one of my favorite subjects not just because I LOVE my hobbies or because I have so many of them. They are one of my favorite subjects because hobbies are so GOOD for people! Hobbies are great for people of all ages. Hobbies are generally described as those things you do in your leisure time for pleasure or amusement. Hobbies can include collecting items, doing creative or artistic endeavors, playing sports or engaging in other activities that provide enjoyment like watching sports.

Before I get into the glorious benefits and joys of hobbies, I am going to digress and address the number one objection I have heard over the last few decades from people about WHY they don't have any hobbies: they don't have the time. While I am not a fan of repeating myself, this bears repeating (from my Blog post titled "Top 35 Ways that Making a List Will Help You Have a Life You LOVE). We all have only 24 hours in a day. It's just a fact of life. Assuming you work 8 to 10 hours a day, 5 days a week, that means that you have at least 118 hours a week (that is predicated that you work 50 hours a week) to use as you see fit. Hopefully you are sleeping 7-8 hours a night, which subtracting that from your 118 hours leftover after work time is deducted would leave you with 62 hours a week (assuming you sleep 8 hours per night). How are you using your 62 hours per week? I understand that some of you are working more than 50 hours a week, but a lot of you are not.

What ARE YOU DOING with your 62 hours per week? I mean what are you really doing with your time? I understand that you have shopping, cooking, cleaning, household chores, and so much more. But the bottom line is that most people have chunks of time that are wasted. You are clearly not spending all 62 or more hours per week doing chores, shopping and cleaning. My point is that you have more time than you realize – and time enough for a hobby or two if it was a priority.

The second objection I have heard over the years from people who don't have hobbies is that they don't have the budget for hobbies, so let's deal with that pronto. Contrary to popular belief, hobbies do not have to be expensive. Many, if not most hobby supplies can be picked up at yard sales and flea markets. If you are not a fan of garage sales then you might not realize the things that you can pick up on for next to nothing. Plus, if you receive gifts for your birthday or Christmas – you can ask for supplies, tools, or things that would support your hobby. Don't let a limited budget stop you from getting a hobby that you LOVE.

The point of my blog is helping you have a LIFE that you LOVE. Hobbies are a great way to get there. They are not something that you should wait until you retire to find. They are treasures that can nurture your well-being NOW. They are things that can ramp up your happiness and level of satisfaction in life. Why would you wait for that? Why would you avoid doing something that brings happiness to your life?

I have had hobbies since my early teen years starting with collecting small tea cups, collaging with words cut out of magazines, cooking, reading, embroidery and sewing, and refinishing furniture. After college I expanded my hobbies to include biking, quilting, counted cross stitch, candle making, soap making, scrapbooking, paper crafting and collecting antique children's furniture. As a mother, I required each of my children to find hobbies that they enjoyed, which was an interesting experience since I have two sons. My daughter was on easy street when it came to hobbies.

To help my sons find more masculine hobbies, I visited YouTube.com and found a wealth of hobbies for teenage boys. One of the hobbies was metal casting, and Noah took that on and has made several items from aluminum cans like hooks to hang things from and a phone stand. He then went onto watch videos on how to make knives and has made several knives from scratch. He found videos on what is called plastic smithing, which is fascinating. As the name implies, it is making objects out of melted plastic. For plastic smithing, you melt plastic grocery store bags in a toaster oven (OUTSIDE or in a garage with the doors open) to reduce the plastic to a hard block of plastic, which will be extremely hard. Then objects can be filed or cut out of the hard-plastic block.

I personally believe that EVERY SINGLE PERSON should have at least one hobby that they can do and enjoy. The benefits, in my humble opinion, are over-the-top amazing! While I am not sure that everyone will agree with my take on the benefits of having hobbies, it is nonetheless my view on the benefits of hobbies. As the purpose of my blog is to help you LOVE your LIFE, having one or more hobbies will help you accomplish that goal.

**Top 23 Benefits to Hobbies**

1. Hobbies are FUN!
2. Hobbies are relaxing.
3. Hobbies make you happy (if it doesn't make you happy, then it's not a hobby and stop doing it.)
4. Hobbies can reduce stress and anxiety.
5. Hobbies can help you with social connections or at least many hobbies have that potential.
6. Hobbies help build self-esteem.
7. Hobbies make you more interesting. In some cases, much more interesting.
8. Hobbies can soothe your soul.
9. Hobbies are a great way to kill time and are much better than doing nothing.
10. Hobbies provide fantastic cocktail or happy hour conversation pieces.
11. Hobbies give you something to look forward to.

12. Hobbies can be used as part of your reward system.
13. Often hobbies give you an end product that provides additional enjoyment. Food from cooking, artwork from painting, and so on.
14. Hobbies can help you stay out of trouble.
15. Hobbies are good for your brain.
16. Having hobbies will leave you much better prepared for retirement.
17. Hobbies can help you stay young.
18. Hobbies can sharpen the saw – recharge and rejuvenate you.
19. Hobbies can help you with depression by giving you something to look forward to and something that makes you happy.
20. Hobbies are great coping mechanisms for life – especially when times are tough.
21. Hobbies can be exciting and inspiring.
22. You can make money from some hobbies.
23. There is absolutely no reason not to have hobbies.

If you don't have a hobby that makes you happy then maybe I would suggest that you consider finding some new hobbies. Back when I only had two children, I decided that I would learn 3 new hobbies a year. I started by taking the Wilton Cake Decorating class taught at a local craft store. That was very fun and allowed me to develop a very handy skill. While cake decorating is not something that I do on a regular basis any more, it is something that I can still do when needed. I took a stamping class at a local rubber stamp store, which led me into paper crafting as a hobby – a hobby that I still do now and then. Eventually I realized that I was pretty good on the hobby side of life and I ended my practice of trying three new hobbies a year.

Then came my Mom encouraging me to draw with my children and start water color painting. That I finally said yes to my Mom on drawing and water color painting is and will always be one of the best decisions of my life (even though I had plenty of hobbies at the

*Love.Life.*

time) because I love it more than I can say. Some hobbies I have retired from. While I still have my collection of antique children's furniture and small tea cups I am no longer collecting them, yet they still provide me with happiness and joy.

The most important thing is to find one or more hobbies that you enjoy. If you are on the low end of hobbies or are looking for some hobby inspiration, I put together this list of hobby ideas.

**Hobby Ideas**

| | | |
|---|---|---|
| Hunting | Metal Casting | Knife Making |
| Fishing | Plastic Smithing | Interior Decorating |
| Biking | Woodworking | Repurposing Objects |
| Running/Racing | Making Stained Glass | Ceramic Painting |
| Reading | Music (making or playing) | Wood Painting |
| Cooking | Traveling | Button Collecting |
| Sewing | Crafting | Model Trains |
| Quilting | Jewelry Making | Model Airplanes |
| Knitting | Beading | Kite Making/Building |
| Crocheting | Antique Cars | Wood Turning |
| Painting | Souped-Up Cars | Glass Collecting |
| Throwing Pottery | Showing Cars | Showing Dogs |
| Candle Making | Antique Collecting | Scuba Diving |
| Making Soap | Stamp Collecting | Watching Sports |
| Refinishing Furniture | Coin Collecting | Playing Sports |
| Scrapbooking | Paper Crafting | Collaging |
| Photography | Braided Rug Making | Batiking |
| Figurine Collecting | Milk Bottle Collecting | Calligraphy |
| Gardening | Cultivating Plants | Drawing |
| Making Doll Houses | Writing Poetry | Writing Novels |
| Playing Cards | Playing Poker | Volunteering |

## Concluding Thoughts

Assuming that you agree with the math used in this post for your free time, what are you doing with your 62 hours a week? If you don't have any meaningful hobbies that you love and look forward to doing then I would suggest that you put that on your list of personal goals. You could make it a fun project to just simply explore what hobbies you might really love. Some hobbies you won't know until you do them. I have tried knitting and crocheting more than once and they are just not my thing. Lots of people love knitting and crocheting, but it's just not for me. Find what works for you.

To have a powerful life and one that you LOVE, you simply have to fill it up with the things and people you love. Hobbies are a great way to put some fun and joy into your life. How can I support you in the area of hobbies? Do you have hobbies that you LOVE? What are your thoughts about hobbies? Let me know.

**Self-Motivation: The Nuts & Bolts of Leveling Up with a Reward System**

February 18, 2020

One of the best ways I know to keep yourself motivated is with a reward system, which is also know these days as 'leveling up' – that phrase coming from computer gaming where you work to get from one level to the next level. I am a huge fan of a reward system because I know that it can work exceptionally well based on decades of experience. It not only works, but it is also fun! If you have the perfect life and life is easy then you don't need one, but you could still definitely get benefits from having one. The key benefit to a reward system is that it will help you maintain your motivation and get things done. Hopefully you are on this journey to having a LIFE that you LOVE, and as such you have things that you want to accomplish to help you get there. A well thought out reward system will help you get there without a doubt and I sincerely hope that you are going to use FUN rewards that YOU WANT! Otherwise, what are you doing?

Over the years as I have coached individuals I have heard a few key objections about why some people say they can't do a reward system so let me first address that. The 3 primary objections to a reward system are: (1) someone has little or no self-discipline and would take the rewards without doing the work; (2) they can't figure out what rewards to use; and (3) they don't have the time. If you lack self-discipline, that is a muscle that you can build over time and I highly recommend it for a variety of reasons. In the meantime, you can ask a friend, relative or someone to be your accountability coach to hold your feet to the fire and help you maintain your integrity. Self-discipline is a function of keeping your word to yourself. You can get outside help with that while you get to work on building the muscle of self-discipline.

Figuring out what rewards will motivate you is a bit of an art. Some people have a much easier time in figuring out what will inspire and motivate them in the rewards category while others have to do a little more work to figure it out. Like anything else in life, if you want something bad enough you will figure out what it takes to get it. I will be saying more about figuring out your rewards in a bit. The objection about not having the time to implement a reward system is often a cover for something else in my opinion. It's almost like saying yes, I would like to be more motivated, but I don't want to invest the time to create the very thing that I want – more motivation. It takes a little time, but let's face it this is not rocket science. It's just not that hard.

## Creating Your Reward System

1. Know yourself. The better you know yourself, the easier it will be to include rewards that inspire you, motivate you and spur you on to get your stuff done.
2. Experiment/Play. If you have never had a self-designed motivational reward system then I highly recommend that you experiment and play with it. Try different rewards. Brainstorm for ideas on what you might really enjoy but didn't initially think of when you started. Ask people for ideas.
3. Self-Discipline. If you are not highly self-disciplined, then there's no better time like the present to get to work on that. It's very helpful to be self-disciplined. In the meantime, get a friend or two or someone who can help you keep your promises while you do the work to build the muscle of self-discipline.
4. Create a list of possible rewards. Be creative. Be financially responsible. Have fun with this. Think outside

of the box. I will add more thoughts on the rewards below.
5. If the system you design is not producing the results, then stop and figure out what is missing. Is the reward not big enough? Are your tasks too large and perhaps might be better broken down into more manageable parts? Get into a conversation about what is stopping you? Get into a conversation about how you have your reward system set up and what you might tweak.

**Picking Your Rewards**

In a self-designed and self-determined reward system, you and you alone pick the rewards although you can certainly get ideas from other people. The question is what would be a good reward for you? I highly recommend that you make sure your reward system is in alignment with your finances. This is extremely personal. What is a reward for you might occur to someone else as a chore or work. You get to decide what would make you happy and be a good reward. There is no right or wrong way to do this excepting perhaps spending money on a reward that you don't have. Here are some examples of the categories that rewards can fall into – not an exhaustive list, but enough to give you the idea of it.

1. Small purchases of something you want/need/desire.
2. Hobby time.
3. Social outings – meeting for coffee, lunch, dinner or something.
4. Road trips.
5. Massages/nails/spa time.
6. Projects that you "don't allow for" – this means allowing yourself time to do something that you normally "don't allow yourself to do", which could mean anything from sorting old pictures, to tackling a nagging issue, or whatever.

7. Doing things that make you happy. Hopefully if you have been reading my blog for a while you have a handy dandy list of the things that you like or LOVE that make you happy! That is a great place to look when picking your rewards.
8. Concerts, movies, or other events.
9. Volunteering or doing something that you would enjoy but would otherwise feel guilty about doing. There could be a broad range of activities or things that could fall into this category. What would you like to do but might be prone to feeling guilty if you did it?
10. The activities that re-charge your heart and soul. I am always about the heart and soul and as you get to know yourself better, hopefully you will get to know what activities re-charge your heart and soul. What lights you up? What touches your heart? Anything in this category is a good option for a reward.

**A Few of My Most Memorable Rewards**

One of my early rewards back some 30 plus years ago was to take a group of charms that I had from my childhood and get them placed on a bracelet. It was not terribly expensive, and I don't remember what the project was, but I still have the bracelet - a cherished treasure – and it was a wonderful reward. About a decade ago, one of my memorable rewards was to make matching dresses for my daughter and I. I got the fabric and patterns and then made the dresses – about a year later! I was so on fire with getting my stuff done that I just didn't take the rewards I had "earned". However, having a young child waiting in anticipation for the matching dresses I eventually had to be my word and make them. It was a huge success and that launched the rewards of matching skirts over the years for a total of three matching skirts I believe.

Now, I am well aware that the thought of making matching dresses or skirts would absolutely not seem like a reward to some or many of you, but for me it was a fantastic reward, which is why rewards are personal. Another memorable reward was a road trip I took with one of my kids last summer. We visited old friends and neighbors, listened to music and had a wonderful time. That was an excellent reward. I am a big fan of hobbies and I often use hobby time as a reward. Make your rewards fun! Make them things that you want!!

## The Physical Structure of Your Reward System

While you can have the physical structure of your reward system done in any way that pleases you, I strongly suggest that it is in writing! I am an advocate of what I call a "Master List" of tasks, jobs, projects, etc. that move you forward in the life you are creating. I have a small section at the bottom of my Master List that is labeled "rewards", and that is where I list my tentative rewards. As I have written about my Master List previously in my post titled LOVE the TIME of YOUR LIFE – September 12, 2019, a few points bear repeating. I suggest that you have your Master List written out and displayed in a location where you will see it every day. This is your guide for getting to where you want to be in life. You want to be reminded about what you are up to. I happen to do mine on oversized paper. It doesn't matter what size or kind of paper you use. Just get it in writing and put it up where you can see it! And I would definitely list your rewards even if you just have a list of rewards to pick from without a concrete commitment to which rewards you will use.

## The Reward to Work Done Ratio

This is the question people ask when I am coaching them in setting up their reward system. The answer is you take rewards as often as you need to in the beginning. I mean as often as you need to because once you get your life cooking and you are "on fire" you won't need the rewards. When you are "on fire" you can still take the rewards, but you might find yourself skipping the rewards altogether. I always put a list of rewards on my master list of tasks, but I don't always take them. Sometimes I take no rewards for months. It's all dependent on how I feel. There's no concrete ratio for how much work you have to do in order to earn a reward. In the beginning, however, it seems to help people to take more rewards more often.

## When Your System is Not Working

Every now and then I will notice that my reward system is not working. To be factual, it's not the reward system that typically is not working – it usually has to do with a project or task that I am avoiding. A few months ago, this happened with a massive paper filing project that I actually needed to do. By doing the mental work to figure out what was stopping me, I realized that I was trying to do the paper filing at night when I was tired. The nature of the paper filing I had to do required a lot of mental decision making – to keep or discard important documents – and it simply was not something I could do at the end of a long day. Once I realized that I needed a fresh mind for the task at hand, I changed the project to be done at the start of a day. When your motivation system is not working it is either that your rewards are not inspiring you or they don't have enough draw on your heart OR the project you have to do might need to be broken down into smaller parts or changed in some way. So, if you set up a reward system and you find that it's not working, then do the work to figure out what needs to be changed, tweaked, or revised.

## Concluding Thoughts

Of course, you want to have a LIFE that you LOVE. Of course, you want to be the captain of your own ship and steer it in the direction that you want to go. So, what is stopping you? Life stops us. Most of us at some point or another. Life is hard. Life is infinitely easier when you are in charge of it. Life is always better when you are moving in a direction of your choosing. Having a reward system to level up can help you keep on track for a LIFE that you LOVE. Have you ever used a reward system in your personal life?

I am so excited for you! I hope that you will consider setting up a reward system for your life! Why the heck not? I mean really? Why not? Let me know how I can help you LOVE your LIFE. Let me know if you have any questions about a reward system.

**Do You Have these 8 Things That Will Help You Flourish in Life Regardless of What Happens? Hint: It's not too late to get them!**

April 28, 2020

The world and the largest percentage of the population is suffering in enormous and excruciating ways with the current pandemic. The level of uncertainty that exists has not been known to the majority of us living today. The negative emotions of fear, panic, anxiety, depression, anger, resentment, upset and so on seem to rule the day as does boredom for many. While the full emotional toll this has taken remains to be seen, the predictable outcome is extremely bad. This is a trauma for many and as such there are expected impacts as a result. The economic toll is unfathomable. It is a disaster that is catastrophic for too many people on a variety of levels. The present circumstances of the pandemic are impacting people differently. Some individuals are being much harder hit than others. Why is that? What does it take to flourish in life regardless of what is going on? What are the things that will help you function really well despite trauma or hardship?

As someone who has flourished in the face of trauma over and over again, I have some thoughts about the habits, practices, attitudes and so on that contribute to making people functional. If the concept of being functional is new to you then you can check out this post, which will help bring you up to speed https://lisaalundy.

*Love.Life.*

com/empowerment/the-one-coronavirus-article-that-could-change-your-life-for-the-better-forever/.

Can you image feeling peaceful in times of great difficulty? Can you imagine being able to cause moments of happiness and joy in dark times? It is possible to be happy separate from your circumstances. It is a skill set that anyone can develop, which you can read about in my post on generating your own happiness https://lisaalundy.com/empowerment/how-to-generate-your-own-happiness-why-its-the-skill-to-learn-this-year/.

Today I am distinguishing the top 8 things that – in my humble opinion – will help you flourish in life no matter what is going on. That does not mean, however that you will not have to grieve a loss, process sadness, or deal with your emotions. I am not saying that you will never be sad, unhappy or grieving a loss. What I am saying is that you can get to a certain level of skills, abilities, attitudes, practices and habits that will allow you to flourish even when you have suffered a huge loss. The fantastic and great news is that all of the things I am listing can be developed over time so there's no reason to be blue if you are missing several or many of the items. In other words, it's never too late to learn and grow. This is what I blog about and my passion – helping people be empowered and happy and love their life even when it's hard.

**1. LOVE**- Love almost always makes my lists because I believe in love. I believe that LOVE is the most powerful emotion on the planet and is extremely healing. I believe that love can heal so many hurts and wounds from your past. I also believe in loving life and the things and people in your life. I am a fan of LOVE and I believe that most people could benefit from putting more love in their life. Here's the thing about LOVE though – you have to be able to open your heart to let love in. You could be extremely well loved, but if you can't open your heart to let love in – you won't feel it. You will feel alone and lonely and quite frankly your life will be much harder than it has to be.

Love involves or centers around gratitude, generosity, compassion. The world clearly could use more gratitude, generosity and compassion. Love your friends. Love your family. Love your neighbors. Love your hobbies. There's so much to love in life. Open your heart and let love in. GIVE LOVE. Give of yourself generously. It's so amazing and beautiful. And yes, there's some risk to it. You can read more about LOVE and getting LOVE in your life in this post, which includes some of the risks to love and opening your heart https://lisaalundy.com/empowerment/love-in-the-midst-of-chaos-and-yes-i-love-you/ and a separate post devoted to dealing with your trust issues because it's hard to let love in if you can't trust other people https://lisaalundy.com/empowerment/love-involves-trust-why-its-time-to-deal-with-your-trust-issues/.

**2. Attitudes/Beliefs/Values (Including Character)**-I have lumped these together for the sake of brevity and because it can be difficult to distinguish between an attitude, belief and quite frankly sometimes a value and while this item is worthy of a standalone post today it gets a mere mention. Beliefs are assumptions and/or convictions we hold to be true based on past experiences. Attitudes come from core values and beliefs that we hold. Our core values include what is important or critical to you based on religion, concepts, people, things and ideas. Our behaviors are the expression (or mismatch) of the core values, beliefs, and attitudes that we hold.

There are empowering attitudes and beliefs and there are disempowering attitudes and beliefs. To flourish in life, I believe that it's very helpful to sort out any disempowering beliefs and attitudes you have and swap them for empowering beliefs and attitudes. Here are some examples of disempowering or negative beliefs or attitudes:

- I'm not good enough.
- I can't win.
- People always leave me.
- People always betray me.
- No one will ever love me.
- I don't matter to anyone.

- Nobody loves me.
- It doesn't matter what I do, my life never works out.
- Everyone else is better than me.
- No one cares what happens to me.
- People don't like me.

These beliefs or attitudes will never allow you to have a life that you love. They are not only negative, but they provide the basis for the self-fulfilling prophecy, which means whatever you believe will come true does in fact come true. In other words, it is exactly like the athletic coaches tell their players – if you think you can – you can. If you think you can't then you can't. If you have negative or disempowering beliefs and attitudes then you want to replace them with empowering ones. Over time you can convert your thinking. Over time. Not overnight. Here are some examples of empowering or positive beliefs or attitudes:

- I am good enough.
- I am enough.
- People love me.
- I make a difference in the world.
- My life has a way of always working out.
- I am blessed beyond all measure.
- I am lucky.
- People really care about me.
- I have so much to be grateful for.
- Things happen for a reason.
- I am responsible for my own happiness.
- I get to choose how I respond to life.

One way to change your thinking from disempowering beliefs or attitudes to empowering beliefs and attitudes is through the use of affirmations. I have a post that will give you some insight and more information on how your beliefs and attitudes can impact your health and on affirmations, which you can find here https://

lisaalundy.com/empowerment/stress-kills-your-brain-cells-heres-19-strategies-to-prevent-that-and-help-you-to-be-happy-healthy/

While I am not going to get into the aspects of character and what defines someone of good character, I am going to mention that I personally belief that integrity is at the core of having a life that works. I believe that integrity is a must. If you want to know more about how integrity can impact your life and help you have a life that leaves you feeling good, you can read my post on the magic of integrity https://lisaalundy.com/empowerment/the-sheer-joy-and-magic-of-integrity/. I am an absolute integrity freak. It is extremely important to me personally.

**3. Resilience**- Psychological resilience is the ability to mentally or emotionally cope with a crisis or to return to pre-crisis status quickly. The condition of resilience happens or exists when a person uses mental processes and behaviors in taking care of oneself and protecting oneself from the possible negative impact or effects of the crisis or stressors. This is the raw essence of my blog posts and intention – to have you have a life that you love where you are resilient and can get through whatever happens. I very recently blogged about this aspect of life, which you can read here https://lisaalundy.com/empowerment/the-coronavirus-tipping-point-which-way-will-you-tip/

**4. Making a Plan**-I am an absolute fan of having a plan, setting and attaining goals and being the captain of your life. You steering your life in the direction that you want it to go in as opposed to being adrift at sea. Life happens. Have a plan. When you have a plan for your life as in one that you have created and one that you LOVE, you will automatically have a different feeling about life. You should be happier. You should be excited. If not, scrap that plan and make a new one that makes you happy and excited.

If I can be candid, most people don't have a plan for their life. Most people don't set goals on a regular basis. So, while it might not seem "normal" it is the path to having control over your life and having life go the way you want it to go – or at least more so than not.

There are several aspects you have to consider in putting together a plan. You can find out more about the elements to think about in this post: https://lisaalundy.com/empowerment/road-map-for-creating-a-life-that-you-love/

**5. Executing Your Plan & Staying Motivated**-Once you have a plan, and by golly, it better be one that lights you up and inspires you or what are you doing -the next critical points are executing your plan and staying motivated while you execute your plan. There are tricks and techniques that I have used for decades to keep myself on track and my actions in alignment with my plan. It takes self-discipline to execute your plan, which is a habit or skill that you can practice and build on over time.

I definitely recommend a personalized reward system, which you can read about here https://lisaalundy.com/empowerment/self-motivation-the-nuts-bolts-of-leveling-up-with-a-reward-system/. Self-motivation is a subject that I covered in this post https://lisaalundy.com/empowerment/self-mastery-self-motivation-self-care-the-holy-grail-of-happiness-joy/

**6. Self-Esteem & Self-Care**-Self-esteem is how you feel about your self-worth or how much you value yourself. Self-esteem can be measured on a continuum from low self-esteem to high self-esteem. While psychologist William James first introduced his theory on self-esteem in 1890, the self-esteem movement didn't really take off until the 1960's. The difference between someone with low self-esteem and high self-esteem can be quite remarkable. Whereas a person with high self-esteem is focused on growth and development, a person with low self-esteem is focused on not making a mistake.

While children typically have high self-esteem that often declines through adolescence and teen years, there are things that can cause self-esteem to plummet at any age including: unsupportive parents or caregivers, friends who are bad influences, stressful life events like divorce, moving, trauma or abuse, and mood disorders like depression or anxiety. The higher you can get your self-esteem the easier your life will be. And there are things you can do to improve your self-esteem.

I wrote about low self-esteem here including ways to boost your self-esteem https://lisaalundy.com/empowerment/is-low-self-esteem-stealing-love-joy-happiness-from-your-life-top-29-tips-for-boosting-self-esteem-like-a-boss/.

Self-care is very important and, in my opinion, relates to self-esteem. Some people with low self-esteem can't generate the interest or don't have the ability to care for themselves, which makes sense to me based on what I know. Self-care is extremely important if you want to have a great life. You can find more ideas on self-care in this post: https://lisaalundy.com/empowerment/self-mastery-self-motivation-self-care-the-holy-grail-of-happiness-joy/. Whatever you can do to increase your self-esteem and engage in self-care will be extremely helpful.

**7. Social Connections & Friends**-Most people are shocked to learn how important social connections and friends are to health and wellbeing. I am going to repeat what I wrote in an October 2019 post because it is significant:

*Loneliness and social isolation increase premature death by up to 50% making it a bigger threat than obesity according to two meta-analyses from Brigham Young University. Social isolation is defined as a lack of contact with other individuals. Loneliness is described as a feeling that one is emotionally disconnected from others, so you can feel lonely even if you are in a group of people. Compelling research by J. Tanskanen and T. Anttila (Am J Public Health 2016 November; 106(11): 2042-2048. NCBI.NIM.NIH.GOV) indicates that a lack of social connections is as influential a mortality risk as traditional health-related indicators such as alcohol, smoking or obesity.*

What this means is that having friends, family, neighbors to connect with, even if it is by telephone or a remote connection, is extremely important if you want to be healthy. It means that we should all make connecting with other human beings a priority. Let me put it another way, if you want to be healthy then you need to be connecting with people. I know that can be difficult for some people.

I understand that. So get paired up with a friend or family member who will drag you out to things because some people just need a nudge.

For some of you that might mean that you need to make new friends. I have always been a big fan of having good friends. Making friends is difficult for many people so you can read 17 ways to make new friends in this post https://lisaalundy.com/empowerment/21-reasons-why-making-friends-will-help-you-love-your-life-17-ways-to-make-new-friends/. Now that applies more than ever before.

**8. Emotional Intelligence/Emotional Quotient**-This is the ability to identify, manage and process your emotions as well as have empathy and recognize the emotions that other individuals are likely to be feeling. I simply can't emphasize enough how important this is to having a life that you love. We are not born into this world and given lessons on how to identify, process and manage our emotions. If we all knew how to do that there would be a lot less depression, anxiety, suicide, and mental health issues in the world. Yet, these are skills that you can learn over time. This particular item, in my opinion of course, is an extremely rich area. When you can control your emotions and identify how others might be feeling in a given situation it is both rewarding and powerful.

I summarized the top 17 benefits to having high emotional intelligence and traits of people who do have it in this post: https://lisaalundy.com/empowerment/top-17-benefits-to-high-emotional-intelligence-and-the-29-traits-of-people-who-have-it/. It is really amazing stuff.

While you are working on growing your emotional intelligence or quotient, there are things you can do that will help you. One of those things is to learn how to change your emotional state by "Flipping the Switch", which I have a blog post devoted to because it is a game changer. That will help you right now. Here is that post: https://lisaalundy.com/empowerment/disaster-relief-how-to-flip-the-switch-on-your-emotions-and-feel-better-now/

. . .

**Call to Action:**

What can you do today that will make your life better or help you feel better? Are you willing to do that? Was this article helpful to you in some way? If so, please share it on social media! If not, what is missing or how can I be helpful to you? My mission is to help people live lives that they LOVE. Are there any areas that you are struggling with? Let me know in the comment section – as in here is what I would love to read about in your next blog post (or whatever you have to say).

I am here to love you along the way. I know that life is hard. Trust me – I know. Yet I also know that life can be delicious and joyful more often than not. Sending you love and good energy!

**Feel Better Now with Self-Care**

August 4, 2020

**What Is Self-Care?**

If you want to feel better now self-care is one of the best ways to accomplish that. Self-care is finally getting the attention it deserves with more research being devoted to this worthy subject because the benefits are extraordinary. I am a huge fan of self-care and engage in self-care actions myself on a daily basis, which might be one reason that people often think that I am years younger than I actually am. As we continue the August Year of Freedom theme of being Awake & Aware (don't forget to enter the Giveaway to win free stuff), I hope you will read this with an open mind and consider the information I am providing because this is extremely important.

Self-care as a noun is defined as: (1) the practice of taking action to preserve or improve one's own health; and (2) the practice of taking an active role in protecting one's own well-being and happiness, in particular during periods of stress. What self-care looks like in actuality is different from person to person yet there are some research-based actions that are a solid foundation for taking care of yourself. I will start by giving you some of the major benefits of self-care in the hopes that this will get your engines running and give you some motivation to get started in self-care.

**Benefits of Self-Care**

1. You will feel better.
2. It helps keep you healthy.
3. It increases your psychological well-being (your mental health).
4. It increases your motivation.
5. It makes it easier to deal with stressful situations.
6. It helps you be more productive.
7. It boosts your immune system by activating your parasympathetic nervous system giving you resistance to disease.
8. It increases your self-esteem.
9. It increases your self-awareness.
10. It increases your energy.
11. It can reduce psychological symptoms (depression, anxiety, worry, etc.).
12. It can lower your healthcare costs.
13. It helps promote a healthy relationship with yourself (self-love, self-compassion, self-kindness).
14. Other people benefit when you feel good about yourself and are taking care of yourself.
15. It helps increase your resilience.
16. It might help you look younger.

Now, let that list sink in deep. Pause. Would you like to feel better? Would you like to have an easier time when stressful things happen? Would you like to be more productive and have more energy? Would you like to have more resistance to disease? Do you want to be healthy? It's a robust list of benefits. So why wouldn't you just do everything you could to take self-care actions?

. . .

**Obstacles to Self-Care:**

1. They don't have time.
2. Their comfort zone does not include self-care.
3. They lack motivation.
4. They are attached to unhealthy behaviors.
5. They don't feel that they are "worth it" on some level.
6. They have never seen self-care role modeled so they are simply unaware of it.
7. They have difficulty maintaining healthy behaviors overtime.
8. They prioritize other people over themselves.
9. They are engaging in a form of self-sabotage by not caring for themselves.
10. They lack some form of support or encouragement to change.


**Physical Self-care**

1. **Sleep:** One easy way to increase your self-care is to get more sleep. The research is conclusive that making sure that you get both enough sleep (quantity of sleep) and good sound sleep (quality of sleep) is by far one of the key ways to improve your health and vitality because the only time your body can repair itself is when you are sleeping. If you are too busy to get more sleep then I would urge you to work on your time management skills because increasing your time management abilities will free up some time, which you can then use for sleeping! You will never regret making this a priority.
2. **Diet & Nutrition:** You eat and drink food every day. That's just a fact of life. Your body depends on nutrition from your food to stay healthy. Any little changes you make to improve your diet and provide better nutrition for your

body will yield big results. If you became awake and aware to what you are eating and make some substitutions throughout the day, it would add up. If you want to avoid cancer and other very significant health problems focusing on your nutrition is a proven way to do that because there is a direct relationship between cancer and nutrition in the cancer research that I have amassed over the last 16 years. I eat reasonably well and I also take supplements based on what I have learned over the last few decades.

3. **Move Your Body:** Moving your body creates a chain reaction of positive benefits in your body. Walking is one amazing way to move your body and get the benefits of exercise without stressing the body. I have a personal goal of walking 12,000 steps a day, which is 6 miles. I don't accomplish that every single day, but I get there more often than not. Make it a goal to walk more or find some form of exercise that you enjoy and then do it as much as you can. Make it fun because you are more likely to do it if you can work fun into it.

4. **Grooming:** Taking a hot shower or bath, doing your personal grooming, putting on a nice outfit will actually make you feel better. I am a huge fan of doing personal grooming on a daily basis because it simply feels better. Look your best and you will feel better.

5. **Environment:** Take a look at your surroundings – where you live, your car or vehicle, all the places that you spend time in. Are they comforting? Visually appealing? Clean and organized? It is well established that people feel better when their environment is clean, organized and appealing. Over time you can get to work on cleaning and organizing your space.

## Emotional Self-care

1. **Increase your emotional vocabulary:** Print out an emotional vocabulary sheet from the internet and start increasing your ability to pinpoint not only the emotions that you are feeling but the intensity as well. I have a YouTube video on this to help you. We live in a world of language and the more you can identify your emotions the better you will be at dealing with them.
2. **Learn how to process and manage your emotions:** You don't have to be held hostage to your emotions. You can actually learn to process and manage then in such a way that you are not victim to your feelings. This is a skill set that anyone can learn. In the meantime, while you are growing and developing new skills, learning how to flip the switch on your emotions can be very helpful.
3. **Use Affirmations to rewire your brain:** You can use affirmations to rewire your brain without having to unpack your pain, traumas, betrayals or other negative things. An affirmation is a short sentence or phrase that helps to build your self-esteem and help you feel better, which you can watch in this video.
4. **Ditch the negative thinking, catastrophizing, or disempowering beliefs:** You won't feel good if negative thoughts are ruminating around in your head, if you are catastrophizing, or if you engage in disempowering thoughts or beliefs. That's just not helpful. You can turn that around. I would suggest doing affirmations multiple times a day until you have turned the corner.

## Establish Boundaries

Boundaries are critical to self-care because they establish guidelines and practices that lead to good mental health and well-being. Poor boundaries can lead to resentment, anger, burnout and other negative consequences. If you are unfamiliar with the term boundaries – well you are in good company. It's not something that we talk about too often in society, but we definitely should. Boundaries help set limits for what you will and won't do, what you will or won't tolerate, who is responsible for what, and so much more. Boundaries are personal and vary. What is important is that you have them in some form.

## Learn to Become Assertive

Assertiveness goes a long way to help you implement and maintain boundaries. The healthiest position in life is to be assertive as opposed to passive or aggressive. There are excellent books available on the difference between being passive, assertive, or aggressive. There is actually a huge difference. Many interpersonal relationship problems could be resolved through assertiveness and boundaries. If you are not in a position to be assertive in. your life right now, perhaps you could take it on in this Year of Freedom because I promise you that you being able to be assertive in your life will give you a lot of freedom.

## Spiritual Self-care

This is your sacred space. For some of you it is your relationship with God. For some of you, I don't know what it is. For me it is my relationship with God and Jesus Christ and it is my relationship with following my heart. My religious beliefs provide the guidelines for my behaviors, which makes life so much easier if I can be frank. Having solid religious beliefs eliminates confusion and provides clear and compelling rules for living. It's really very helpful. Plus, when you believe in God, then "With God, ALL things are possible", which is like have a super power! It's totally cool.

### Life Plan/Vision/Road Map

A life plan, vision or road map will provide three key things that are extremely helpful to self-care and feeling happy: it provides motivation; it provides a source of happiness; and it provides clarity. You can also see my video on this topic. This should be something that lights you up, makes you happy, inspires you. I love this subject if you can't tell!

### Doing What Makes You Happy

When I say, do what makes you happy, I don't mean at the expense of other people although if you have toxic people in your life they might be unhappy with you taking control of your life and starting to be empowered. I have written about the skill of being able to generate your own happiness, how to be happy when you are suffering, and how to level up your happiness. I trade in happiness. It's one of my things. I want it to be one of your things. Sprinkle your day, week, and life with the things that make you happy.

### Time Management

Time management gives you the time for self-care. Time management gives you time to execute your life plan, vision or road map for your life. Time management also gives you time for playing, hobbies, socializing – all the good stuff. You want to have a positive relationship to time and time management, to making lists, and begin to learn the techniques that will give you more free time because that will support you in every area of your life.

### Get a Reward System

If you are looking to change your behavior it can be extremely helpful to have a personal reward system in place to provide inspiration and motivation. I have personally used a reward system for decades because I know that it works if you have the right rewards. I strongly urge you to have a reward system as you work towards having a life filled with self-care, things that make you happy and are fully empowered to deal with whatever life brings you. Yes, do it!

## Other Examples of Self-Care from My Own Life

I do a lot to take care of myself because after all, if I don't take care of myself who is going to? No one. These are examples of things that I do to take care of myself, which you are free to judge in any capacity. I'm not saying that you should do these things. I'm just sharing some of the practices that I have adopted for my well-being, which work for me or I wouldn't do them.

1. Not allowing someone to exploit my generous nature, which could come in the form of saying no to a request that feels exploitive.
2. Distancing myself from negative people or people who lack integrity or character because that's just a no-go for me.
3. Staying clear of people who lack boundaries, who are mean to others or who look down upon other people because that just doesn't work for me personally.
4. Being extra compassionate with myself if I have had some added stress or an emotional thing to deal with, which could come in the form of taking a nap, going to bed earlier than normal, or easing up on my schedule.
5. Being assertive and speaking my truths, which could also come in the form of standing up for myself and not tolerating abusive behaviors from anyone in my life regardless of the relationship.
6. Terminating "discussions" or "quasi-conversations" where someone is projecting, gaslighting, monsterizing, being irrational or manipulative, which can be done in a very polite but firm way.
7. Refusing to accept other peoples' monkeys (not my circus, not my monkeys).

8. Taking myself out of any situation or setting that feels or appears to be either toxic or somehow unhealthy.
9. Not holding grudges, which comes in the form of forgiveness and letting things go – a healthy practice that is good for me.
10. Not taking things personally even IF they were personal.
11. I don't put myself in situations that I am clear I won't enjoy, will be unnecessarily painful, will be disrespected or treated badly unless it can't be helped, which is highly irregular and extremely infrequent.
12. Not allowing people to waste my time.

**Call to Action:**

Yes, I do the self-care actions I have just written about. What can you start doing in the area of self-care? Who can you get to be your buddy? I wrote about buddying up in the last blog post for the Year of Freedom. I was totally serious. Did you get a buddy yet? Right now would be the perfect time to get someone to share your amazing ride to your new life. How can I help you? Who do you know that needs a little nudge in the area of self-care? Share this with your people who need a boost. What are you waiting for? Your life is ready for you to step into with love, happiness and joy.

**Pandemic Sleeping Tips**

August 14, 2020

Having trouble sleeping? You are in very good company if that makes you feel any better. I think most people would be surprised to learn that sleep-deprived people have a tendency to overreact to situations in comparison to people who were not sleep-deprived according to the research. "In other words, we tend to become much more sensitive emotionally and socially when we are sleep-deprived. That is what I like to call the 'who was at my desk or who touched my coffee cup?' phenomenon," says Dr. David F. Dinges, Ph.D. in the journal article *The Extraordinary Importance of Sleep*. So, some of those "touchy" people who fly off the handle on a regular basis may actually be very nice people who are just sleep-deprived.

Approximately 50 to 70 million people in the U.S. had at least one sleep disorder prior to the pandemic according to the research. With the pandemic it is predictable that more people than ever are having trouble sleeping, which is completely understandable and reasonable. At the same time, there are steps you can take to sleep better. If you were not a good sleeper prior to the pandemic, then it is very likely that any sleeping problems have been exacerbated. I am a very sound sleeper and I make sure that I get plenty of sleep. This is a topic that I love because it is so rewarding to help someone who has sleep issues get it turned around. It's really remarkable and life-changing.

Few people look at their sleep time as sacred. More people look at their sleeping time as a time slot that they can take time from if they get too busy. If you find yourself doing that – skimping on sleep because you are too busy, then I would suggest that you consider how you might use your time better with this post on time management, or how making a list will help you love your life. If you short change yourself on sleep because you are too overwhelmed with life then I would ask you to consider dealing with overwhelm once and for all. If depression or anxiety are preventing you from sleeping that is worth getting a jump start on as well.

## Reasons Why People Have Trouble Sleeping

1. Stress & Emotional Concerns – including depression, anxiety, worry, anger, resentment, grief.
2. Mental health disorders
3. Trauma
4. Sleep apnea
5. Diet

6. Lack of exercise (yes, exercise can help you sleep better if you don't do it too late)
7. Pain
8. Medical causes including side effects of medications, neurological causes, hormone changes, restless leg syndrome and more
9. Poor sleep habits
10. Improper sleeping temperature (too hot or too cold)
11. Alcohol
12. Caffeine (too late in the day)
13. Eating too late at night
14. Going to bed too hungry
15. TV/Phone/Electronics
16. Inconsistent sleeping patterns or schedule
17. Age (Teens and older people fall into this situation more often than other ages)
18. Your environment is not conducive to sleep
19. Dust mites (allergy related)

We all inherently know that getting enough sleep and good quality sleep is good for us, yet I don't believe that most people understand the significant benefits of good sleep or on the flip side the extremely negative health consequences of a lack of sleep so I am providing those for your review, which I have summarized from multiple sources.

**Benefits of Sufficient Sleep**

1. Improved mental performance (cognitive)
2. Improved behavioral performance
3. Improved mood (emotional regulation)
4. Improved memory consolidation
5. Improved immune system functioning
6. Decreases mood disorders
7. Decreases feelings of loneliness

8. Preventative measure against dementia
9. Decreases risk for obesity
10. Decreases risk for heart disease
11. Decreases risk for diabetes
12. Decreases risk of early death
13. Less emotionally sensitive
14. Less socially sensitive
15. Decreases stress (perception)
16. Helps insight formation

## Negative Impact of Insufficient Sleep

1. Impacts judgment
2. Negatively impacts mood (emotional regulation)
3. Negatively impacts your ability to learn & retain information
4. Can cause an increase in the risk of serious accidents
5. Causes profound impairments in cognitive performance
6. Causes profound impairments in behavioral performance
7. Contributes to obesity
8. Contributes to diabetes
9. Contributes to heart disease
10. Contributes to an early death
11. Impaired immune system functioning
12. Increases mood disorders
13. Contributes to dementia
14. Contributes to loneliness
15. Makes you more emotionally sensitive
16. Makes you more socially sensitive
17. Ramps up stress levels (perception of stress)

## How Much Sleep Should I Get

According to Dr. Dinges, Ph.D., Professor and Chief of the Division of Sleep and Chronobiology in the Department of Psychiatry at the University of Pennsylvania Perelman School of Medicine, the consensus of evaluations conducted by the American Academy of Sleep Medicine and Sleep Research Society jointly concludes that between 7 and 7 and a half hours is what people should be aiming for. It is important to know that when you are experiencing high amounts of stress, a trauma, or other unusual circumstances that you might need more sleep. Sleep is the only time that the body has a chance to repair itself so increased stress might mean bumping up your sleep to help offset the stress.

## Steps for Better Sleep

**1. Mindset**-What is your mindset about sleep? Specifically, what are your attitudes, beliefs and expectations regarding sleep? What do you say about sleep? This is the foundation for good sleeping because if you expect that you won't sleep well or that you usually don't sleep well, then my guess is that you absolutely won't sleep well. Not surprisingly all of the people who I have coached on improving their sleep stated at the outset that they were very poor sleepers. That is not an accident. There are three key foundations for becoming a good sleeper:

- You EXPECT to sleep well.
- You RESPECT that you will function better with the proper amount of sleep.
- You BELIEVE that you can learn to sleep soundly.
- You TREAT SLEEPING like it is sacred, extremely important and you just don't let life get in the way of your sleeping.

If you are not going to have the proper attitude about sleeping can you really expect to become a great sleeper? No. You won't become

*Love.Life.*

a great sleeper if you have the wrong attitude, beliefs and expectations.

**2. Commitment**-Are you committed to doing what it takes to become a great sleeper? Are you willing to make the changes necessary to become a great sleeper? Are you willing to become awake and aware to the obstacles that might be preventing you from getting good sleep? It doesn't matter what I say from here on out, if you are not committed to becoming a good sleeper – nothing matters. Everything starts with a commitment. Make a firm commitment or resolution that you are going to do whatever it takes to start sleeping very well and soundly. That in and of itself will make a difference.

**3. Rule out underlying medical issues**-There are many underlying medical issues that can cause sleep problems or sleep disorders including undiagnosed Celiac disease, gluten intolerance, nutritional deficiencies and hormone imbalances to name a few. Certain prescription medications can also cause sleep to be disrupted so you might need to speak to your doctor about your medications.

**4. Set the stage for great sleep – Your Environment**-Some people discount the impact that your physical environment can have on sleep saying that your environment is just not that important. Research shows that too much light, or a messy room, or things like dust mites can disrupt sleep. If your room is messy clean it up. Put clean sheets on your bed. Look around to see how you could make your bedroom more inviting for sleep. Make the changes to your bedroom, as needed, to set the stage for blissful slumber. It's an investment that will provide high returns.

**5. Clearing Your Mind**-It is critical that you clear your mind before going to bed if you want to get really solid and restful sleep because when your mind is clear you will not be fussing, stressing and worrying. To clear your mind, I suggest that you go through these steps. Of course, it's really helpful if you have a life plan or purpose and you are working having your dream life. But even if you are not, this usually works – in combination with the steps listed above and below. Clearing your mind is a skill set that takes time to develop. Hang in there. Keep at it until you are good at it. I know you can do this!

- Make a list before you go to bed of what needs to be accomplished the next day or in the coming days or anything that needs to be recorded on paper.
- Deal with your emotions so that you are not tossing and turning trying to sort yourself out in bed. For some of you that might mean learning how to flip the switch on your emotions, or it might mean that you start dealing with your low self-esteem issues, or start growing your emotional intelligence. I have written extensively about how to have a powerful life and be free from stress and anxiety. This is one area that can easily prevent you from getting good sleep. It is well worth the investment of your time to learn how to manage, deal with and process your emotions. Trust me. It's well worth it.
- Once you get in bed if you have any thoughts like – "Oh, I hope I don't forget to do X, Y or Z tomorrow" or "I should try to remember bla, bla, bla…" GET OUT OF BED immediately and write it down on your list - the list that you made before you got in bed. I am not kidding about this.

**6. Create Your Fantasy Dream**-Once you are in bed, hopefully in your bedroom that is an environment that is conducive to sleeping and you have cleared your mind using the above steps, then close your eyes and create your fantasy dream. Of course, in the beginning you will actually be awake, but as you keep going on in your fantasy dream you will fall asleep. Make this fun. Make this amazing. Why not? You have nothing to lose by going to bed and starting your sleep with a fantasy dream of your own making.

**Call to Action**

What is preventing you from sleeping well? Are you committed to improving your sleep? Are you willing to do whatever it takes? Hint – you might need to re-read either the benefits of good sleep or the negative impacts of insufficient sleep to get some motivation. I think there's plenty of juicy benefits that should give you the incentive to make the changes you need to. How can I help you? We have more people than ever struggling in life right now. Help them by sharing valuable information. Please leave me a comment on how I can help you!

## The Healing Nature of Self-Compassion

October 15, 2020

**What is Self-Compassion**

Self-compassion is not something that we talk about every day or even often as a matter of fact and it is something that we need to bring front and center because of the extreme value it brings to not only ourselves as individuals but also to the people we love. While I have written about dealing with low self-esteem, depression, overwhelm, trust issues, worry and fear, and how to be happy or generate your own happiness – self-compassion is a new topic that deserves your full attention if you want to be happy and contented in life.

Self-compassion is treating yourself like you would a good friend and understanding that we don't have to be perfect in life. Compassion is defined as the ability to show love, empathy and concern for people who are having problems or experiencing a hardship in life or the desire to help someone who is suffering in life. According to Paul Gilbert, Founder of the Compassionate Mind Foundation, the foundation of self-compassion is rooted in courage. Gilbert believes that self-compassion is one of the most important declarations of strength and courage in humanity.

The opposite of self-compassion is self-criticism or having a self-defeating tendency. When we say the phrase "inner-critic" we are referring to those negative thoughts that you have about yourself and the negative things that you say about yourself that are condemning in nature, which often times people are not awake and aware of. Being highly critical of yourself however does not mean you are a perfectionist although it can be an aspect of perfectionism. Having a strong inner critic can lead to very serious problems including a host of serious mental health problems so it is a destructive behavior that would be healthy to interrupt. If you want to learn more about the psychological impact of a strong inner-critic and the psychiatric disorders that come in to play, you can find a good at www.Self-Compassion.org (Self-Criticism.pdf).

Self-compassion involves understanding that failure is a part of life and treating yourself with empathy when it comes to personal failures, shortcomings or painful situations in life. Understanding that failure is part of the human experience and gives rise to a greater appreciation for humanity and the human condition. Building the skills for self-compassion will give you greater resilience in life and promote psychological wellbeing plus it will feel better to you once you get on the path of self-compassion.

You want to free yourself up from worry, fear, anxiety, depression and all of the negative emotions so I hope you will join me for a Year of Freedom stepping into love, peace, happiness, and all of the good stuff life has to offer and while you are doing so you can enter to win free prizes until July 2021. I want you to have a happy life filled with love, joy, happiness, freedom and that is possible for you with growth and development. Why not?

## 15 Years in: My Journey into Self-Compassion

My journey into self-awareness started when my Mom gave me a book on assertiveness when I was in high school, which was amazing and changed my life for the better. Thus, I began my interest and love for personal growth and development, which continued in college with the counselor education course required to be a resident assistant (R.A.) and has never stopped. The issue of a lack of self-compassion was only raised about 15 years ago and it was a shock. I had never thought about the fact that I was hard on myself – an extremely common phenomena I hate to say.

Once I became awake and aware to the fact that this was an area I needed to grow and develop I started by asking my three young children to help me notice when I said or did things that might show that I was not being kind to myself. I think we were in the car when I asked for their help on this at the tender ages of 8, 6 and 4 years. Well, we had not gotten far in our car ride before one of the kids quipped up – Oh, I think that you are being hard on yourself! Oh my. Some moments in life are just memorable. Over time, my children were very helpful in pointing out when I was being hard on myself.

Of course, I also talked to my adult friends about this as well and at least one or two of them took on looking at this area for themselves. While I can't remember every single detail of the process of building self-compassion, I can tell you that for me it was a gradual process starting with me waking up to the fact that I lacked self-compassion and followed by my commitment to be kinder to myself.

After all, I was very compassionate with other people. Why not be compassionate with myself? Having mastered and built the skills in the area of self-compassion, I can easily say that this is extremely freeing, valuable in untold ways for physical and mental health, and something that I recommend strongly. Put this on your list of things to grow and develop because you will never regret learning self-compassion.

With self-compassion under my belt or in my proverbial toolbox it is easier to recognize when people I know are being hard on themselves. It provides for a good conversation with most people. Yes, if you can be compassionate with other people, why not be compassionate with yourself? There is no good reason not to build the skills of self-compassion and there are too many reasons why skipping over this skill set will be extremely bad for your mental health.

**Obstacles to Self-Compassion**

1. Feeling unworthy
2. Controlled by negative emotions like shame, sadness, etc.
3. Feeling like you are not good enough
4. Feeling too overwhelmed with life
5. No experience or role model of self-compassion
6. Low emotional skills or abilities
7. Trauma – past or current
8. Viewing it as a selfish idea or concept
9. Childhood maltreatment or abuse
10. PTSD
11. Mental health issues like psychopathy, antisocial personality disorders, borderline personality disorders, narcissistic personality disorders, and more
12. Fears
13. Viewing it as weakness
14. Having trust issues
15. Negative thinking or pessimism
16. Very strong inner critic
17. Burnout
18. Viewing it as some kind of failure
19. Perfectionism

**Benefits of Self-Compassion**

1. Happiness
2. Optimism
3. Wisdom
4. Increased personal initiative

5. Increased curiosity and exploration
6. Agreeableness
7. Conscientiousness
8. Extroversion
9. Builds resilience
10. Builds personal strength
11. Decreases stress
12. Increases productivity
13. Provides peace of mind
14. Lower levels of anxiety and depression
15. Improves body image
16. Provides greater life satisfaction
17. Strengthens mental health
18. Increases motivation to improve oneself
19. Better able to face life
20. Activates oxytocin – the love hormone making you feel safer and secure
21. Greater sense of humanity

**Negative Effects of Self-Criticism**

1. Can lead to psychopathy
2. Personal maladjustment
3. Social maladjustment
4. More interpersonal problems
5. Associated with loneliness
6. Associated with depression
7. Associated with a lack of intimacy
8. Associated with increased likelihood of rejection
9. Associated with marital dissatisfaction
10. Associated with eating disorders
11. Predictive of anxiety disorders and phobias
12. Associated with PTSD
13. Increased unhappiness

14. Increased stress
15. Decreased motivation

## Steps to Developing Self-Compassion

1. **Claim that you are hard on yourself.** Just own it. Claim it. Owning it gives you power over your inner-critic. Claiming it provides the steppingstone for change. And this is something to change as soon as you can.
2. **Ditch any shame or embarrassment about it.** When we live in a world where most people lack self-compassion there is no reason to be ashamed or embarrassed about it. It is how people are raised – to be hard on themselves.
3. **Acknowledge this is an area to change.** With an understanding that developing self-compassion is extremely important for your mental health as well as resilience, happiness, and other health benefits that should nudge you into the space of recognizing that this needs to change.
4. **Tell people you are working on this area of your life.** Yes, you can tell people that you are working on growing your self-compassion. Why not? When I am working on growing new skills in an area of life, I have found it to be immensely helpful to let my friends know what I am working on because they will support me.
5. **Create a TEAM of friends to work on this with you.** You could create a team, which I highly recommend, and make a fun journey out of this process. I mean you could do that. Operative word here is could. I am a fan of teams and working in groups for so many reasons.
6. **Become awake and aware to your verbal statements and internal thoughts.** Until you are awake and aware of how much time your inner critic spends condemning you, shaming you, or making you feel

*Love.Life.*

bad – you won't have the opportunity to really make a difference with self-compassion. You really have to pay attention to what you say out loud and what you are thinking. We live in a world where too many people are not self-aware and lack emotional intelligence to understand what is happening with their own emotions.

7. **Make a list of your strengths or good qualities.** I am not kidding. Write down your strengths and good qualities as a human being. Look at it. Let it sink in.
8. **Begin the practice of appreciating your goodness as a person and your strengths.** You want to begin to practice the skill or habit of appreciating your goodness and good traits or strengths. This will go a long way to help reduce the air-time that your inner critic gets.
9. **Use affirmations or visual signs to help rewire your brain.** Affirmations can help rewire your brain using the scientific principle of neuroplasticity of the brain. Use affirmations and visual signs to help create new pathways in your unconscious and subconscious mind, which overtime will help.
10. **Use psychotherapy or cognitive behavioral therapy if needed.** There should be no shame or embarrassment to use psychotherapy or cognitive behavioral therapy to help you develop self-compassion or deal with your issues for that matter.
11. **Reward yourself for small victories.** I am a huge fan of using a personal reward system because change can be hard. Rewards can help you stay motivated while you are working on establishing new habits and skills.
12. **Get to work on growing yourself in other areas.** Personal growth and development is the road to access a happier, healthier and more satisfying life. Why not? What else are you going to do with your time? Watch TV? Sure. You can do that. You could also spend a little time having fun improving your life.
13. **Boost your self-care right away.** I am a huge fan of

self-care and this is a foundational skill set to living a happy and healthy life. There is no time like the present to implement self-care practices, which are guaranteed to improve your health and help you feel better.

14. **Practice or grow your assertiveness skills.** Having assertiveness skills will help you in every area of your life including feeling better about yourself. It can also help you have a better outcome for any difficult conversations you have to have in life.
15. **Catch yourself not being kind to yourself and get back in the game.** When you are learning new habits, practices and skills you will catch yourself here or there back in old habits. Once you catch your inner critic talking – get right back on track to practicing self-appreciation and self-compassion.
16. **Notice how it feels to be kind to yourself – really notice.** It really feels wonderful to be kind to yourself. As you begin to take on the practice of self-compassion, notice how it feels. I mean really notice. That will be helpful to keep you on the journey to building skills and habits in this area.
17. **Prayer or meditation can be helpful.** When you are working on developing new attitudes, beliefs, skills, habits or practices – prayer or meditation can be helpful in calming your mind and helping you focus or get grounded.
18. **Being present – right here, right now – can be very helpful.** This is extremely valuable for many reasons. Being present has so many benefits. It will definitely help you get away from the past and hopefully your inner critic.
19. **Be patient.** Developing self-compassion is a process that takes time. It is a journey that typically does not happen quickly. Have patience and keep at it. This is too good and too juicy to skip over.

## Call to Action

How compassionate are you with yourself? Are you kind and gentle or loving with yourself? Are you ready to take on growing and developing self-compassion? What do you need to be supported in this process? How can I help you get there? Who do you know that could use a dose of self-compassion? Are you willing to share this post with them to help them? Please let me know how I can help you be more self-compassionate in the comment section. I want you to have an amazing life. Let me help you!

## The Healing Nature of Assertiveness

November 9, 2020

## What is Assertiveness

Assertiveness is a core social skill that can help relieve feelings of depression, anxiety, low self-esteem, overwhelm and improve relationships, improve mental and physical health and help you be happier. The reason why assertiveness is healing is because it can help you grow your emotional intelligence, help you be more authentic and vulnerable, and help build healthy friendships and relationships – all of which are extremely valuable to your health and happiness. We know that social isolation and loneliness are very bad for your health. Assertiveness skills have a lot to offer in helping you build the social connections and relationships that will help you be well loved and happy, which is the point of my blog and YouTube videos.

So exactly what is assertiveness? We can't base our definition of assertiveness on some dictionary definitions because some of them clearly get it wrong. Assertiveness is NOT being confidently aggressive or aggressive or forceful. That is not what assertiveness means in any way. Let's look at the components of assertiveness as a way to define it:

1. Communication between people where you are expressing

your wants, needs, feelings or thoughts while being respectful of the rights of others.
2. Respect for others- this is an integral ingredient of assertiveness.
3. Sets boundaries
4. It is not passive nor is it aggressive

Both passive behaviors and passive-aggressive behaviors are at opposite ends of an assertiveness continuum. Passive behaviors would include being emotionally dishonest, being indirect, denying your own needs, and self-inhibited. This is not healthy behavior. Passive-aggressive behavior is not healthy either and because it is so common, I have included in this post behaviors that often indicate someone is being passive-aggressive as well as the negative impacts passive-aggressive behavior can have on your life and wellbeing.

This is a skill set that we are not usually born with. Depending on the level of dysfunction in your family growing up, you may have more or less trouble learning to be assertive. The research indicates that between 70-96% of Americans have grown up or are growing up in dysfunctional families, which often leaves people feeling wounded and unhappy. And all of which means that it is time for healing and self-compassion. And while you are on this journey to healing and having a happy life, I hope you will enter my giveaway for free prizes going on until July 2021.

**My Personal Journey into Assertiveness**

My Mom gave me the *"Your Perfect Right"* assertiveness book by Robert Alberti and Michael Emmons when I was in high school! What a blessing that was. I mean I can't even put into words how that changed my life – how I looked at life, how I felt about myself, and how it changed the way I looked at life. It was a pure gift. It was a defining moment in my life and at such a young age. It was helpful with my friends, some teachers, my clubs and activities and at work – all as a high school student. While I can't go back and say how my life would have gone without this skill, yet it is clear to me how I grew because of it. It changed some of the decisions I made before graduation because I knew that I had value and worth and my feelings mattered. Thank you, Mom!

Assertiveness is a skill set that anyone can learn, practice and grow over time. To make the most out of assertiveness skills it really is extremely helpful to understand some basic psychology concepts like projecting, gaslighting, denial, passive-aggressive behaviors and cognitive dissonance because that will help you better make sense of life and what is happening when your assertiveness skills don't seem to be enough, which is why I recommend that in the steps to becoming assertive section.

There are so many actions that you can take, which will help you become more assertive. For me, I found becoming assertive to be very freeing. I am such a fan that I believe that this should be required in grade school because we have too many adults who can't be assertive.

**One Assertiveness Technique**

While there are several different assertiveness techniques, for the sake of simplicity I will share one that I find easy and direct: "I – Statements". With "I – Statements" you are stating your own thoughts, feelings, needs, wants and desires in first person. By owning your thoughts, feelings, needs and wants you remove the blaming others and take responsibility for yourself.

Examples:

- "I understand that you have several critical jobs to do and you are very busy, however I need your help with this particular project. When can you meet with me?"
- "When you don't invite me to lunch with the guys, I feel excluded and unimportant."
- "I know you are busy with life, and I want you to know that

I understand that. I would like you to try to keep to the schedule we established or give me more notice if you have to break your commitment."
- "When you do X or say Y at our office meetings, I feel that my contributions to the team are less important than other team members. When is a good time for us to sit down and talk about this?"
- "When I have to keep asking you to do the same thing repeatedly, it makes me feel that you don't respect me or value our relationship."
- "I feel dismissed and demeaned when you do X, Y or Z, and that doesn't feel good. Let's talk about what is going on that you are doing that."
- "I love it when the girls all get together. Could you please include me the next time you are going out because I have been feeling a little left out?"

**Roadblocks to Being Assertive**

1. Low self-esteem
2. Lack of knowledge or skills
3. Not believing that you matter
4. Fears: ridicule, rejections, failure, retaliation, etc.
5. Looking for or wanting love and acceptance
6. Uncertainty-you are unclear about what you want
7. High stress
8. Personal insecurities
9. People pleaser: overly sensitive or considerate of the needs of others
10. Lack of emotional skills
11. Lack of communication skills
12. Not wanting to be viewed as selfish
13. Worried about hurting the feelings of another person
14. Misguided beliefs about assertiveness

15. Bad past experiences with being assertive
16. Abuse or maltreatment in childhood
17. Passive personality: let other people decide for you
18. Lack of clarity of purpose, desires or boundaries

**Benefits to Being Assertive**

1. Raises self-esteem
2. Increases self-confidence
3. Helps facilitate better communication
4. Improves your relationships
5. Better for your mental health
6. Better for your physical health
7. Provides for an authentic life
8. Helps grow your emotional intelligence and abilities
9. Improves outcomes of different situations
10. It feels better
11. Helps reduce depression and anxiety

**Negative Impacts of Passive-Aggressive Behavior**

1. Divorce, friendships ending family estrangements
2. Increased stress in relationships and social connections
3. Poor credibility at work
4. Increased frustration
5. Communication issues
6. Poor personal or professional reputation or both
7. Lack of connectedness to people
8. Physical health problems
9. Emotional problems
10. Feelings of isolation
11. Higher stress levels in general

12. More unhappiness
13. Anxiety disorders
14. Depression
15. Addictions

**Possible Signs of Passive-Aggressive Behavior**

These are possible or likely signs that passive-aggressive anger could be in play.

1. Negative gossip
2. Hostile joking
3. Repetitive teasing
4. Negative criticism
5. Sullen behaviors
6. The silent treatment
7. Social exclusion
8. Backstabbing
9. Two-faced behaviors
10. Intentional button pushing
11. Overspending
12. Neglect
13. Procrastination
14. Stonewalling
15. Withholding
16. Blaming
17. Breaking agreements
18. Forgetting
19. Deliberate failure
20. Victimhood
21. Dependency
22. Addiction
23. Self-harm
24. Resistance
25. Rigidity
26. Negative orientation

**Steps to Becoming Assertive**

1. **Growth and Development:** Becoming awake and aware of what you are thinking, how you feel, how you are perceived by others and understanding how other people feel is extremely valuable. Everything under the broad umbrella of growth and development will help you have a rich and happy life.
2. **Read up or watch YouTube videos**: The book titled *"Your Perfect Right"* by Robert Alberti and Michael Emmons, first published in 1970, is a classic resource on this subject. There is plenty of free material online to help you grow your assertiveness skills.
3. **Take on Self-Care like it matters:** Self-care is one of the foundations for a happy and healthy life and it is going to help you feel better in life. The better you feel about yourself the easier it will be to be assertive since low self-esteem is one reason why some people find it challenging to express themselves. While self-care includes several components, getting enough quality sleep is one significant part of it. It is critical and you can find ways to make it both fun and enjoyable. I highly recommend making your life fun and enjoyable as much as you can!
4. **Growing your self-compassion:** Taming your inner critic will go a long way to helping you to appreciate yourself and your good qualities, which is very helpful in becoming assertive particularly in people who are hard on themselves – a very pervasive condition in society.
5. **Be Well Loved:** Feeling well loved is not only amazing, but it will also help you feel good enough about yourself to understand that your opinions, feelings, thoughts and desires matter, which is one of the things often missing when people don't feel like they can be assertive. You want to have being well loved on your list of life goals.

6. **Have really great friends:** Having great friends who love and support you will go a long way to not only help you feel like you matter but also to helping learn assertiveness skills. Friends are really important to human health because they can help reduce feelings of loneliness and isolation and really bring joy to your life. Most people I talk to will admit that they don't have enough good friends and making friends is hard. Making friends is actually a life skill worth learning, so I have several YouTube videos on making friends (a whole playlist). Everyone needs friends – and no bad people, shady people, backstabbers, or the like. You want people who have character and integrity.
7. **Practice difficult conversations:** Being able to be assertive is a skill set. Being able to have difficult conversations and have them go well is also a set of skills. I strongly suggest that you practice any conversations that might be difficult because that will increase the likelihood that the outcome will be positive or at the very least better than if you didn't practice at all.
8. **Ask for help:** There is no reason to be ashamed or embarrassed if you need help in life. We are meant to help our fellow human beings. If you are feeling ashamed or embarrassed that you need help, then it is definitely time for growth and development for you (see #1 above). You are not expected to be perfect. Everyone needs help now and then. Just ask for the help that you need!
9. **Don't let fear stop you:** Fear is one of those emotions that stops people in life. It grips people and they don't know what to do. This is a powerful emotion to master and it can be mastered as a skill set – dealing with fear.
10. **Grow your emotional abilities:** Growing your emotional abilities will help you in every single area of your life. It will help you feel better, do better professionally, make more money, and provide life satisfaction. It will definitely help you become assertive. One particular emotion that would be helpful to grow and develop is your

anger skills. We are not very good as a culture or society with anger, yet anger can be healing in nature.
11. **Learn a few basic psychology concepts:** Understanding a few basic psychology concepts, especially the self-fulfilling prophecy and passive-aggressive anger will help you in every area of life and will be extremely helpful when you are learning to become assertive.
12. **Don't give up:** You might get discouraged if things don't go as well as you expected when you try being assertive. Don't give up! This is an extremely valuable skill that you want to have in your life. You want to have this skill in your life. It will help you in every single area of your life. If your first few attempts at being assertive don't go your way, keep trying. Practice. Just don't quit!

**Call to Action**

How assertive are you in your life? Is this an area that you can see would be helpful? I sure hope so! Being assertive has so many benefits! You want to be able to share your feelings, your thoughts, your desires, wants and needs in a positive, respective manner that doesn't diminish or demean other people. This will help you in so many ways! What are you willing to commit to today to get going on the road to assertiveness? What help do you need? How can I help you? Please leave me a comment with what you need! And, don't forget to share this with the people you know who could benefit from this content!

# NUTRITION, HEALTH & GENERAL WELLNESS

### 8 Ways to Improve Your Health & Look Younger

October 2, 2019

The current statistics indicate that nearly 45% of Americans have a chronic illness defined as an ongoing, generally incurable illness or condition such as heart disease, asthma, cancer or diabetes, and that this number has increased dramatically over the last 30 years with predictions that it will continue to rise. According to the Mayo Clinic almost 70% of Americans are on at least one prescription medication with more than half of the population taking two prescriptions. The last two decades have provided me with an intense opportunity to learn about health, medicine, the different kinds of medicine, and what it takes for your body to be healthy and well. Disclosure: I am not in the medical field and nothing in this blog post can be construed as medical advice. You should get medical advice from a licensed medical practitioner. What I am sharing today is my personal opinion, based on what I have learned and implemented in my own life. I am not on any prescription medications although some people think I should be medicated – Haha. Joking. Not joking. I have the energy I had when I was in college and only a few gray hairs – as in very, very few. And I work at being healthy.

It's very hard to LOVE LIFE if you don't feel well. In fact, it would be exceedingly difficult to be happy if you are in pain, don't feel well, or have other challenges caused by a health problem. If you are with me on the Journey to Loving Your Life, then taking your health seriously – as if it really mattered – would be a crucial step. And, yes, I do the things I am recommending with rigor because I know that they make a difference for me. Each one of these 8 items merit an individual blog post devoted entirely to that item. Today you get the highlight of why. I will eventually drill down on each one separately in the future.

**1. SLEEP**

According to the CDC (Centers for Disease Control & Prevention), 1 in 3 Americans don't get enough sleep. Sleep is the ONLY TIME that your body has a chance to go to work on repairing itself. The Division of Sleep Medicine at Harvard Medical School states that insufficient sleep is linked to weight gain, diabetes, cardiovascular disease and stroke, mood disorders, depression anxiety, mental distress, and a lower life expectancy. They also state that insufficient sleep takes a toll on perception and judgement – mental performance. There is the amount of sleep that you get each night and then there is the quality of sleep that you get. For your body to function well, it's a fact that you need to get the right amount of sleep and good quality sleep. Most recommendations for how much sleep you need is between 7 to 9 hours per night.

**2. Connectedness & Relatedness**

You may be shocked that I have listed this as number 2, but wait until you hear why. Loneliness and social isolation increase premature death by up to 50% making it a bigger threat than obesity according to two meta-analyses from Brigham Young University. Social isolation is defined as a lack of contact with other individuals. Loneliness is described as a feeling that one is emotionally disconnected from others, so you can feel lonely even if you are in a group of people. Compelling research by J. Tanskanen and T. Anttila (Am J Public Health 2016 November; 106(11): 2042-2048. NCBI.NIM.NIH.GOV) indicates that a lack of social connections is as influential a mortality risk as traditional health-related indicators such as alcohol, smoking or obesity.

All this means that getting connected to and related to people will greatly enhance your health! That might be easier for some of you than others, but regardless of the level of difficulty, if you want improved health and the potential to live longer, it is important to develop relationships and put yourself in situations where you can connect with people. How to do that is a lengthy enough topic for a future blog post. Bottom line – dealing with any feelings of loneliness and social isolation will boost your health and surely make you feel better.

### 3. Walking or Exercising

While many Americans despise the thought of exercise, walking is a doable option for most – not all – but most people. Walking or some form of exercise has the benefit of being preventative for: stroke, metabolic syndrome, high blood pressure, Type 2 diabetes, depression, anxiety, some specific cancers notably colon and breast, arthritis, and falls. Additionally, walking or some form of exercise has been proven to improve mood and cognitive function, boost energy, help you sleep better and it's good for your sex life. Walking is my preferred method of exercise because it is easy on the body, can be done almost anywhere (even while you are waiting for your turn at the phone store), and it is relatively low cost – the cost of a good pair of walking sneakers.

If you have an ongoing health issue you should consult with your physician before embarking on any exercise program. Period. I use an old-fashioned pedometer to track my daily steps and record them in my planner. Regardless of what exercise you do – walking or other – any exercise carries significant health benefits. Like Nike says – Just Do It.

## 4. Improving Your Diet

Even people who do not own an automobile understand full well that a motor vehicle will not go if the gas tank is empty. We inherently understand that cars require not only gasoline (or diesel fuel), but also transmission fluid, brake fluid, antifreeze, and so on. Your body operates in much the same way. Your body is fueled by what you eat and drink. Therefore, any small changes you make to improve your diet will go a long way to help you be healthier and feel better and potentially look younger. The more I have learned about nutrition, the more respect and value I place on nutrition. This doesn't mean that you have to give up red meat, French fries, or deep-fried chicken. It simply means that any changes that you are willing to make to improve your diet will help you improve your health.

As the author of an Allergy & Celiac Cookbook, which contains a whole chapter on nutrition and special diets, this subject is worthy of multiple blog posts. Suffice to say for this post, consider substituting a beverage loaded with nutrition like a fruit or green smoothie for one of your less nutritious drinks (soda, coffee, tea, etc.). Consider adding one more green vegetable per day. Substitute a healthier entrée for a less healthy entrée. Start thinking about what you eat and drink and the nutritional density of those foods and beverages. And if you are unwilling to improve your diet, see item #8 in this post, which is all I can offer you.

## 5. Attitude & Gratitude

According to Psychology Today (2015), there are 7 scientifically proven benefits to having an attitude of gratitude including: gratitude opens the door to more relationships; improves physical health; improves psychological health; enhances empathy and reduces aggression; provides better sleep; improves self-esteem, and increases mental strength. Researcher Dr. Barbara Fredrickson, one of many researchers in the area of positivity, indicates that a positive attitude yields a faster recovery from cardiovascular stress, better sleep, fewer colds, and a greater sense of overall happiness. There now exists a sufficient body of evidence to state that you will benefit from a positive attitude and being grateful. That might be a tall order if you are pessimist (or a realist…) -and I am not even going there folks.

The bottom line is that whatever you can to do be more positive and grateful will benefit your health. If you need help moving to this as a practice, then one of the old standby recommendations is to keep a gratitude journal and write down on a daily basis what you are grateful for. Certainly, getting to know others who have much bigger problems than you have should be helpful in moving you to a perpetual state of gratitude.

## 6. Managing & Reducing Stress

Chronic stress can actually decrease your lifespan by shortening our telomeres, the "end caps" of our DNA strands, which cause us to age more quickly. I understand how difficult it is and can be to manage or reduce stress. I totally get it. Yet, sometimes there are choices that we could make that would reduce or stress that we don't recognize or see. For example, years ago I thoughtfully decided not to work with a person on a project because it would have increased my stress levels too much. As much as my decision shocked some people, I knew that I was going to be so much happier not working with said person. Once I declined the celebrated invitation to be on a special select team at work because the meetings were going to be in New York City and I was just unwilling to have that stress. In that instance, the company moved the meetings to a location that was agreeable so I would join the team.

What are the things that cause you stress? What can you do to manage or reduce it? Sometimes the choices you make to manage or reduce your stress will cause other people to be unhappy. Deal with it. Or let them deal with it. Any work you can do in this area will definitely yield health benefits. You can also see my past blog posts on Leveling up your Happiness for suggestions.

## 7. Reducing Exposure to Chemicals or Toxins

If you have never seen the video called "Ten Americans" by Ken Cook, one of the founders of the Environmental Working Group (EWG), then you are probably wondering what I am talking about. In research done by the EWG, they obtained 10 umbilical cord blood samples from newborn babies and did chemical testing on the blood. Here is a statement from Mr. Cook's Testimony before the U.S. Senate Committee on Environment & Public Works:

*"EWG tested these 10 Americans in 2004 and found more than 200 synthetic industrial chemicals in their blood, including dioxins and furans, flame retardants, and active ingredients in stain removers and carpet protectors. We also found lead, polychlorinated biphenyls (PCBs), and pesticides that the federal government banned more than 30 years ago."*

We are birthing babies that have high levels of toxic chemicals in their blood. You are unwittingly exposed to carcinogenic chemicals in many personal care products like perfume, cologne, personal care products that list "fragrance" as an ingredient, as well as cleaning products, and many more indoor chemicals and toxins that can be mitigated. Choose natural products for your personal care and cleaning. Open your windows for fresh air to improve your indoor air quality. I have so much more to say about this subject having tested one of my kids for toxic chemicals in their blood and what it took to address that, which will be covered in a future post.

## 8. Offset Your Not So Hot Diet with Supplements

According to the CDC and U.S. Department of Agriculture (USDA), 50% of Americans are deficient in Vitamin A, Vitamin C, and magnesium; greater than 50% of the general population is Vitamin D deficient; 9 out of 10 Americans are deficient in potassium; 7 out of 10 Americans are deficient in Calcium; and the statistics just go on and on. While many U.S. physicians' rail against Americans taking supplements, the statistics simply do not support that advice.

If money were no object I would suggest that you get nutritional testing, which would give you concrete medical data about where your body stands with respect to nutrition. However, even if you are diagnosed with malnutrition, most insurance companies will still not pay for nutritional testing. What to take and how much to take in the way of supplements is not something that I can answer for you because that would be irresponsible. I take a good number of supplements because I have experience in this area. I only take high quality products that are recommended by the kinds of physicians I tend to prefer.

**Happy & Healthy**

Can you truly be happy if you are unhealthy? Probably. And clearly it would take a lot more effort if you are in pain, having a health problem or challenge to be happy in life. To be healthy in our current society and culture takes some effort, a willingness to make changes that are either needed or called for, awareness, and some commitment. For me these above things that I do on an ongoing basis provide me with huge rewards or I would not do them. They are habits or practices that are ingrained in how I live life. They can become habits or practices for you. My wish for you is fantastic and glowing health where you feel well and have plenty of energy to do what you LOVE. Let me know if you have any questions.

**The Ultimate Consumer Guide to Nutrition, Why It Matters & How It Could Save or Change your Life**

October 29, 2019

I used the right kind of physicians and nutrition to save the life of someone I love preventing a cancer diagnosis in the process as well as other rather horrific diagnoses that were predicted. Imagine my shock in about 2010 when I attended the American Dietetic Association (now called the Academy of Nutrition and Dietetics) and the Registered Dietitians who came to my booth there could not believe

*Love.Life.*

that my child was not on a feeding tube. I am not sure who was more shocked, me that having a feeding tube for a failure to thrive diagnosis with other complications was the norm, or the Registered Dietitians that I had managed to avoid both a feeding tube and an NG tube. One of the reasons for this post is that this subject comes up a lot when I talk about how to be healthy. Having this post allows me to refer consumers here for both information and downloadable images. Here's what I am going to be covering for consumers relative to nutrition:

1. The Significance of Nutrition to Health, Wellness and Disease Prevention
2. The Lack of training of American Physicians in Nutrition
3. Malnutrition – What It Looks Like (Hint: It's not what you are thinking)
4. Advanced Nutritional Testing -Why, What, Where and How
5. Correcting Nutritional Deficiencies – What you must know (or your Doctor must know)
6. Malabsorption – Yes – You could even have this without knowing it
7. Supplements – The Pros and Cons and Some Thoughts

Medical disclaimer: I am not a licensed medical practitioner of any kind. You should get your medical advice from a licensed medical provider. What I am sharing with you does not constitute medical advice of any kind. I am merely providing my experience and research in this area, which is not medical advice. If you have a health problem, you should seek help from a licensed medical doctor or other licensed healthcare provider.

Personally, I have 14 years of experience with malnutrition, advanced nutritional testing, correcting malnutrition, malabsorption and the diagnosis of malabsorption, and IV nutrition therapy. In 2004, over a period of 5 months, once a month for 5 months one person per month who was in the medical field instructed me to research cancer even though I had a two-year old with food allergies. After the 5th person in 5 months told me to research cancer I began researching cancer even though I was pretty angry about it. Two years later, in 2006, that research paid off as I was able to recognize through my research that without some immediate and significant change in this 4-year old's nutritional status that a cancer diagnosis was on the horizon. The specialist at the time confirmed my research as a matter of fact. The next medical challenge for my little one without an immediate turnaround in nutrition was either cancer, leukemia, or a heart attack.

At that time, I was not schooled in the relationship between nutrition and cardiovascular disease or much else. I was in the infancy of my nutritional education. With a diagnosis of malabsorption, which came a year after intense supplementation to correct nutritional deficiencies that were demonstrated through advanced nutritional testing, I requested IV nutritional therapy because based on my research at that point, the only way to bypass malabsorption was either IV therapy or by injection. IV nutrition therapy made the most sense to me as an educated medical researcher – layperson that I am was then and still am. Repeat advanced nutritional testing was used at yearly intervals to determine the success and then alter the IV nutrition therapy based on the current results. It's not easy getting a young child to sit still for a 2-hour IV. This proved to be one of several critical and pivotal turning points in getting my child on the road to wellness. So, I am a huge fan of advanced nutritional testing and correcting nutritional deficiencies. Fast forward 14 years and I know more about nutrition and the impact that a lack of nutrition has on the body.

## 1. The Significance of Nutrition to Health, Wellness and Disease Prevention

Even people who don't own a car understand that for a car to run it requires certain things like gasoline, as well as transmission fluid, antifreeze, brake fluid, and so much more including tires. Likewise, the human body runs on a complex makeup of nutritional components. Without the correct nutrition, it is impossible to be healthy in the long run with emphasis on the phrase long run. The relationship between nutrition and good health is well established although not well practiced in American medicine with traditional physicians. Good nutrition is essential to disease prevention. Why this matters is because according to the research Americans are not meeting the Federal Dietary Recommendations for nutrition (The Journal of Nutrition: J Nutr. 2010 Oct; 140(10): 1832-1838. Susan M. Krebs-Smith, et al).

The likelihood that anyone of us is meeting the nutritional standards or recommendations set forth in the Federal guidelines is slim to none. According to the American Society for Nutrition, which was established in 1928, millions of cardiovascular deaths (worldwide) are attributed to not eating enough fruits and vegetables (Baltimore, MD, June 8, 2019 ASN Staff). The National Cancer Institute, the U.S. government's principal agency for cancer research and training, studies have reported malnutrition in 30% to 85% of patients with cancer.[1,2] Let that sink in for a moment if you want to grasp the significance in preventing cancer. Our principal cancer agency states on their website 30% to 85% of the patients with cancer have some reported malnutrition (National Cancer Institute: Nutrition in Cancer Care (PDQ)-Health Professional Version). It should alarm you and wake you up IF you care about being healthy and well and avoiding cancer, heart attacks, strokes, and other chronic diseases.

To quote myself from my blog post on 8 Ways to be Healthy and Look Younger: According to the CDC and U.S. Department of Agriculture (USDA), 50% of Americans are deficient in Vitamin A, Vitamin C, and magnesium; greater than 50% of the general population is Vitamin D deficient; 9 out of 10 Americans are deficient in potassium; 7 out of 10 Americans are deficient in Calcium; and the statistics just go on and on. What we know is that the majority of Americans are deficient in one or more nutrients. And we also know that nutrition is a recognized determinant in 3 of the 4 top leading causes of death in the U.S. (The American Journal of Clinical

Nutrition: Am J Clin Nutr. 2014 May: 99(5): 1153S-1166S. Penny M. Kris-Etherton, et al.)

You simply cannot be healthy over the long haul if you lack nutrition in your body. Period. End of story. This is part of the reason for this post. If you are not healthy, then get advanced nutritional testing done. When you take your car into the shop for service, they hook it up to sensors to do the diagnostic work. If the mechanic said, our sensor is broken, but I can tell by looking at your car or listening to it what is wrong – you would say no thanks. You want your car to be hooked up to the electronic sensors because you know that is reliable. Likewise, you want laboratory tests to tell what your nutrition is inside your body if you want to avoid cancer or other diseases and conditions.

## 2. The Lack of Training of American Physicians in Nutrition

To quote a recent research article: "The importance of including nutrition in the training of health care professionals, as well as in the continuing education of practicing clinicians, remains a low priority. The absence of required medical nutrition education within medical and other health care curricula, and the lack of curricular coordination between health professions, bears witness to this problem." – The American Journal of Clinical Nutrition (The American Journal of Clinical Nutrition: Am J Clin Nutr. 2014 May: 99(5): 1153S-1166S. Penny M. Kris-Etherton, et al.)

So even though we know that nutrition can prevent diseases, and by the way saves money not to mention lives – we still have no focus on training physicians and health care professionals in the area of nutrition. So, what that means to you, my beloved consumers, is that you have to know where to go to get the right kind of nutritional testing and you have to find the right kind of physician who can order the proper tests, interpret the results and then correct any deficiencies. It has been my personal experience that the physicians (M.D., D.O., and N.P.) who have taken the time and energy to get trained in nutrition and how the body works are *integrative physicians*.

Let's define an integrative physician: an integrative physician is a licensed medical doctor who goes to get specialized medical training outside of his or her original medical training. All physicians who are licensed in the U.S. receive their medical training, for the most part, from mainstream medical schools. Thus, a physician who becomes an integrative physician was at one time a mainstream medical doctor before he or she went for specialized medical training. If you are looking for an integrative physician, I would consider looking up the following organizations: American Academy of Environmental Medicine (AAEM), American College for the Advancement in Medicine (ACAM), International College for Integrative Medicine (ICIM). It is extremely critical that you have a highly trained integrative physician before you start correcting nutritional deficiencies. Continue reading for why.

### 3. Malnutrition – What It Looks Like (Hint: It's not what you are thinking.)

Malnutrition, according to the World Health Organization (WHO), refers to deficiencies, excesses or imbalances in a person's intake of energy and/or nutrients and covers 2 broad groups of conditions. When we "consumers" think of malnutrition, we think of emaciated children in third world countries. We do not think that someone who is 20, 30, or 50 pounds overweight could be malnourished. You simply cannot tell by looking at a person if they are malnourished UNLESS they are emaciated, then yes, it's clear that they are malnourished. But by the medical definition, it is blood work that would indicated if a person has malnutrition.

In other words, anyone could have an instance of malnutrition and based on the previously mentioned National Cancer Institute research that studies have reported malnutrition in 30% to 85% of patients with cancer – it should be pretty clear that malnutrition is more abundant than you might think in a country where obesity is a national problem. Malnutrition should be determined by advanced nutritional testing – the next item up for discussion.

## 4. Advanced Nutritional Testing – Why, What, Where and How

Advanced nutritional testing is testing for nutrition in the human body done by specialty laboratories usually not covered by insurance although that is just too upsetting to discuss. This type of testing is typically only ordered by integrative physicians who have the training in knowing when this is appropriate, how to read the results and then in what order to correct any deficiencies. If you have had cancer, a stroke, a heart attack, or have a chronic disease or illness, then in my most humble of opinions, this is the absolute thing - advanced nutritional testing – that you must have. Because this has been confusing in the past when I have discussed this with consumers, I am including a sample of one type (brand) of nutritional test.

In my humble opinion the individuals who should have this kind of testing are those who have had cancer, a heart attack, a stroke, or who have a chronic health condition or who are interested in preventing these health conditions (and you have the money to pay for it). We know that chemotherapy kills about 40% of your healthy cells, and that requires your body to do more work. It seems to me that this type of testing would be extremely valuable to anyone who has had chemotherapy (and possibly radiation). Due to the preventative nature of this testing, individuals who have a family history of cancer or other genetic diseases can use this testing to prevent an array of diseases by getting their nutrition in order.

There are many pictures of the different pages of the tests. This is so that you can print these out and use them as a reference when you are speaking to your physician. Let me be honest, a mainstream physician is not going to be able to understand or comprehend these test documents. I know this because I have shown them to enough mainstream physicians to have a pulse on this. These are to help guide you through the process of what things you should be tested for.

These images are from actual lab results and are not presented as an endorsement of the particular laboratory nor are they presented in any special order.

## 5. Correcting Nutritional Deficiencies – What you must know (or your Doctor must know)

Assuming you get some advanced nutritional testing done, and you are deficient in one or more nutritional elements, then the thing that you MUST know is that you can't go off willy-nilly and correct the nutritional deficiencies all together. The correction of nutritional deficiencies must be done in a special sequence fixing one before another. This takes specialized knowledge and expertise, which is why you must see a physician who has the training and expertise to not only order and interpret that testing, but then have the skill to know what to correct first, second and so on. This is critical! A lack of knowledge in this area could make things worse for your health.

## 6. Malabsorption – Yes – You could even have this without knowing it

This is my layperson's version of explaining malabsorption. To get a diagnosis of malabsorption, you must first get nutritional testing that shows a deficiency. Once a deficiency is determined, you begin oral supplementation designed to correct the deficiency. After a prescribed period of time, typically 6 months to a year depending on the deficiency, if the deficiency is not sufficiently improved or not improved at all, then you would be able to qualify for a diagnosis of malabsorption. On a non-clinical level, if someone has a very high dietary intake of calcium for example, but has a deficiency of calcium in their blood work, then it would be suspect that there is an absorption or malabsorption because of the lack of correlation between the dietary intake and the blood levels.

And yes, even YOU could have malabsorption. And you would have to have the medical testing to know for sure.

## 7. Supplements – The Pros and Cons as Well As Some Thoughts

If you believe the American governments numbers on the numbers of citizens who are deficient in the various nutrients stated previously in this post, and if you believe the previously stated research that Americans are not eating properly to meet the Federal dietary guidelines, then you might consider supplements. In a perfect world, the advanced nutritional testing would be a routine part of well visits because it would save billions of dollars in health care costs. That day is decades away or never unfortunately.

If you have a health condition, then you must absolutely discuss taking any supplements with a licensed healthcare provider. Based on the nutritional research available today, it seems to me that taking a high-quality supplement would be advantageous in preventing health problems. I take supplements although not every day. By high quality I mean not sold at my local pharmacy or grocery store. I mean the brands that integrative physicians would recommend. Some of those brands include, but are not limited in any way to: Thorne, Cardiovascular Research Ltd.,

Klaire Labs, Pure Encapsulations, Douglas Laboratories, Life Extension, Jarrow Formulas, and Kirkman Laboratories to name a few. I am not endorsing these manufacturers. Nor have I been paid to list them here. They are simply some of the ones that we have used over the years.

**Concluding Comments**

For 14 years I have been talking to consumers about nutrition and health and wellness. For the same period, I have been researching cancer and other health conditions. The book *"Dr. Folkman's War:*

*Angiogenesis and the Struggle to Defeat Cancer"* by Robert Cooke is a medical history book on cancer and well worth the read if you can manage it. If you have any interest in cancer then this is the book I recommend – it's a stunning inspirational story about Dr. Folkman and his amazing efforts to prove the concept of angiogenesis, which by the way is now a medically recognized thing. If you have a health condition that is not being resolved to your satisfaction, or if you are not healthy, then it makes sense to me to consider advanced nutritional testing. The same thing goes if you are simply interested in preventing a future health condition.

Unfortunately, advanced nutritional testing is often not covered by health insurance which is an indictment of our health care system in my humble opinion. There are some health care practitioners that are using kinesiology of sorts to determine nutritional status, but I am not informed or educated about that so I will leave that alone. Those practitioners are welcome to leave comments on this post.

Whatever you can do to bump up your nutrition will go a long way to helping you be healthy. Ideas for what you can do to increase your nutritional status is a weighty enough subject to merit a separate blog post in the future. For now, let me know if you have any questions. Hopefully this gives you enough to speak to your health care provider about with respect to nutrition and quite possibly gets you thinking about your own nutrition and what you are eating.

## Stress Kills Your Brain Cells – Here's 19 Strategies to Prevent that and help you To Be Happy & Healthy

January 2, 2020

The research tells us that chronic stress, fear and anxiety can damage the brain and increase the risk of major psychiatric disorders, which is not good news for the largest segment of the population. The good news is that due to the neuroplasticity of the brain, the ability of the brain to form new connections and pathways and change how circuits are wired, and neurogenesis, the ability of the brain to grow new neurons, there is a lot you can do to combat stress and keep your brain and body in good health. If this idea that stress can kill your brain cells is too far-fetched for you to believe, consider that back in 1996 Stanford biological sciences Professor Robert Sapolsky published a review article in the August 9, 1996 edition of the journal *Science*, showing links between long-term stressful life experiences, long-term exposure to hormones produced during stress, and shrinking of the part of the brain involved in some types of memory and learning.

Sapolsky, an expert on stress and the brain, is the author of the book *Why Zebras Don't Get Ulcers*, and complied the research using magnetic resonance imaging (MRI) scans. A more recent study published in 2014 titled *Neuropathology of Stress* by Paul J. Lucassen, et al (Acta Neuropathol. 2014: 127(1): 109-135) discusses the science about how *"Exposure to chronic or severe stress has profound effects on the structural and functional integrity of the limbic brain areas that not only coordinate the stress response, but are also exposed to the altered expression levels of different hormones, neurotransmitters and trophic factors."* The *Neuropathology of Stress* article has 247 cited references in the paper.

**Start with Your Thoughts, Beliefs and Attitudes**

If you are new to growth and development then you might not be too hip to what thoughts you have rolling around in your head let alone be paying attention to some of the words that come out of your mouth. If you want to get ahead of the impact of stress, fear and anxiety then it will be beneficial for you to wake-up and really start paying attention to what thoughts pop into your head during the day, as well was some of the sentences that you speak. Doing this will be the gateway for you into where you need to grow and develop. Many people have very self-defeating or negative thoughts. We think that we are not good enough. We are not this or not that. We think that we don't deserve all the good stuff life has to offer. So, in paying attention to what you think and what you say, you will uncover some of your underlying beliefs and attitudes about life that will be critical to moving you into a more positive and happy position.

For example, once you start paying attention to what you are thinking and saying, you might uncover that you have a belief that "You can't Win", which would be exceptionally powerful if that is the case because there is a long-held concept in psychology called "the self-fulling prophecy" that hold what you believe basically is what will happen. There's an alternate corollary to that called the "self-defeating prophecy" that hold the same thing but with a negative slant. Understanding your beliefs about life is very powerful if you want to manage stress, fear and anxiety as much of where stress and anxiety as well as fears comes from is our own thoughts.

In the book, *The Hidden Messages in Water*, author Masaru Emoto shows photographs of water crystals before and after they have been exposed to various stimuli like soothing music or heavy metal music and while it is a very small and short book – it is nonetheless a compelling visual on the impact of our environment on something so simple as water. I highly recommend a peek at the book or at least some of the videos on that book. You are exposed to your thoughts on a never-ending basis. What are you feeding your soul and mind with? That is the question. While you might not have an answer to that in this moment, it is worth looking at and discovering.

Let's say for the sake of example that you are or become aware that you have a never-ending supply of negative thoughts. While that would not be good or helpful, the cause for celebration is the recognition that you have a steady stream of negative thoughts entering your mind because that is something that you can change. I would understand if you are skeptical or doubtful, but I ask you to trust me on this. This is not a post about how to convert from a true pessimist to an optimist, that is entirely another subject. I am assuming that if you are reading this you have some motivation to want a better life for yourself and that you are willing to do whatever it takes to get there. If that's not you, you need not read any further because nothing I say will make a difference for you. It just won't. If you are that attached to having a negative and unhappy life – and there ARE people like that – then nothing will change that for you. And you are welcome to keep your attitudes and beliefs – even if they are not serving you. Life is about choice.

**Ways to Preserve Your Brain Cells & Be Happy**

There are a multitude of ways to combat stress and be happy, which is the goal if you want to preserve your brain cells. I am providing my own list with some minor explanations. Basically, if you do the work to create a life that YOU LOVE and sprinkle your days and weeks with doing things that make you happy, you are on the path to counter-balancing the negative impact of stress on your life. This is the core point to my blog – that you set up your life to be what you want it to be - a life that brings you happiness. How happiness affects your body is the subject for an entirely separate post. For now, here are some of the options to help you stave off damage caused by stress, fear and anxiety.

1. **Being Present**- Being present means having your full attention to the task at hand or what is going on in the moment. If you are having a conversation with another person it means that your full attention is devoted to the conversation and you are not obsessing with your own thoughts or doing something else. You are "in the moment" with that person. The reason that I have listed being present as one way to interrupt stress, fear and anxiety is that you can't be present in the moment if you are obsessing about other things because that is the opposite of being present.
2. **Exercise** – If you detest exercise then consider walking, which has health benefits much like that of any other form of exercise. Exercise is good for your physical body and has been shown to reduce stress and the effects of stress. If you have a medical condition, check with your physician first before embarking on an exercise program. Except for those

individuals with mobility problems, walking is an easy, cheap and available form of stress reduction. Shoot for getting more steps each week until you can get to 10,000 steps a day. Old-fashioned pedometers, which is what I use, function well to help you monitor your progress. Regardless of what form of exercise you opt for, exercise will help you avoid some of the impacts of aging – and that alone is worth your consideration.

3. **Affirmations**-While you are on the road to creating a life that you LOVE, which I hope is the road you are on – doing affirmations can help you curb some of your negative thoughts. Affirmations if you have never done them are simple statements that you repeat to yourself throughout your day. Affirmations are deeply personal and can be highly effective if you actually do them. Examples of simple affirmations include statements like: I am enough; Happiness is a choice and I choose to be happy; God provides for all my wants and needs; or I love myself. Some might consider this in the vein of "faking it until you make it" and that's fine. I know that affirmations can be very powerful and can help you while you are on your journey of personal growth and development.

4. **Prayer**-If you are not religious or have not been exposed to prayer, it can be a powerful tool in reducing stress, anxiety and fear. According to a National Review.com article by Clay Routledge (April 9, 2018), prayer is positively associated with welling-being and health, can contribute to perceptions of meaning in life, which promotes psychological well-being, and religious faith increases self-control and reduces (or can) unhealthy behavior. I find prayer to be refreshing, calming and reassuring.

5. **Meditation**-Meditation has plenty of benefits for health and in particular in reducing stress and anxiety and improving brain function. While I personally have only tried meditation a few times, probably because prayer

works for me, there's plenty of support in the internet about ways to go about it.

6. **Cognitive Behavioral Therapy (CBT)**- Cognitive Behavioral Therapy is a particular type of short-term psychotherapy that has the goal of changing patterns of thinking or behavior that are behind people's difficulties and thus change the way that they feel. Cognitive Behavioral Therapy works by changing attitudes and behavior by focusing on the thoughts, images, beliefs and attitudes that a person holds (their cognitive processes). One DVD series that I believe falls under the cognitive behavioral therapy category is the Dynamic Neural Retraining System by Annie Hopper, which I happened to view with someone who could benefit from the DVD series. I found it quite riveting. This DVD series, I believe, is intended for individuals with chronic illnesses like chronic fatigue syndrome, fibromyalgia, multiple chemical sensitivity, and electric hypersensitivity syndrome. However, it seems to me that it might have broader applications, but then what do I know? It is at least a resource that I am comfortable putting out there. The brain science that was included was compelling. I enjoyed watching it and I think that the exercises she includes to retrain the brain are reasonable.

7. **Tapping or Emotional Freedom Technique (EFT)**- Founded by psychologist Dr. Roger Callahan in 1979, whose student, Gary Craig, later organized the sequence of the tapping method developed by Dr. Callahan and renamed it the Emotional Freedom Technique. According to a recent research article, the Emotional Freedom Technique is an evidence-based, self-help therapeutic method and over 100 studies demonstrate its efficacy (Bach D, Groesbeck G, Stapleton P, Sims R, Blickheuser K, Church D. Clinical EFT (Emotional Freedom Techniques) Improves Multiple Physiological Markers of Health. *J Evid*

*Based Integr Med.* 2019;24:2515690X18823691. doi:10.1177/2515690X18823691.

8. **Personal Growth & Development Work**-It is my personal opinion that any work you do to improve yourself a.k.a. personal growth and development will go a very long way to help you permanently enhance your tool shed in dealing with stress, fear and anxiety. As I mentioned in a past blog post there are many avenues for obtaining growth and development including but not limited to: reading this blog, courses, program, seminars, trainings, podcasts, books, programs like Toastmasters International, movies or DVD's, conversations with people, The Bible and religious programs, setting stretch goals and attaining them, going to college or a university for a degree program, getting a coach, and so on. Personally, I have a great affinity for growth and development, so I highly recommend it. See my November 29, 2019 post titled *"Top 45 Ways that Personal Growth & Development Will Help You Have a Life You Love"* for my take on this.

9. **Neuro-Linguistic Programming (NLP)**-Developed in the 1970's in California by John Grinder, a linguist, and Richard Bandler, an information scientist and mathematician, Neuro-Linguistic Programming (NLP) is a psychological approach that involves analyzing strategies used by successful individuals and applying them to reach a personal goal. It relates to thoughts, language, and patterns of behavior. The research on NLP, despite being in existence for 40 plus years, does not confirm the validity of the theories behind NLP nor the effectiveness of the approach. Literature reports that it remains popular, however it lacks the scientific support of things like Cognitive Behavioral Therapy or Tapping (Emotional Freedom Technique) for what it is worth.

10. **Journaling**-Journaling has been around since the beginning of time and is easy, inexpensive and effective in

helping people deal with stress, anxiety, fear and their thoughts.

11. **Practicing Gratitude as a way of life**-It's really hard to feel stressed out, fearful or full of anxiety if you are practicing gratitude. While I am not saying that you can't feel stressed, fearful or anxious at the same time you are feeling grateful, being filled with gratitude has the benefit of reducing those negative feelings. Gratitude does not come naturally for some people. You might have to work at it. You might have to consciously look for things to be grateful for and write them down.

12. **Positive Attitudes/Self-Fulfilling Prophecy/Beliefs**-A thorough examination of your attitudes, beliefs, and your outlook on life can help you reduce stress, fear and anxiety if you uncover limiting beliefs, attitudes or outlooks. As I previously mentioned the self-fulfilling prophecy, this is only one aspect that can help you or hurt you when it comes to dealing with stress and anxiety. If you believe that your life will never get better than it's completely likely that it will never get better. The sports world and famous coaches have lots of quotes about what it takes to win like the Vince Lombardi quote: "Winners never quit and quitters never win." What is it that you believe? What are your core beliefs about life?

13. **Get out and socialize**-The medical research on this is so compelling that it bears repeating and I quote myself from my October 7, 2019 post titled *"8 Ways to Improve Your Health & Look Younger"*: Loneliness and social isolation increases premature death by up to 50% making it a bigger threat than obesity according to two meta-analyses from Brigham Young University. Compelling research by J. Tanskanen and T. Anttila (Am J Public Health 2016 November; 1106(11): 2042-2048.NCBI.NIM.NIH.GOV) indicates that a lack of social connections is as influential a mortality risk as traditional health-related indicators such as alcohol, smoking or obesity. (end quote of myself) Yes, you would do

well to get out there and socialize. You can also refer to my post about how to make new friends. This will help you with stress, fear and anxiety – both getting out there and socializing and making new friends.

14. **Create a Life You LOVE-** In my humble opinion one of the best and most powerful ways to vanquish stress, fear and anxiety is to create a life that you love! Create a life that you have designed with all of the things that you love in it. That takes intentionality and time. This is what I write about, what I am passionate about and what I believe is the most important thing you could do with your time – create a life that YOU LOVE! That IS what this blog is about!

15. **Volunteer for organizations that inspire you** – Yet another way to help reduce stress, anxiety and fear is to spend your free time volunteering for organizations that inspire you. It will give you a good feeling. While you won't get the same payoffs as you might by doing some of the other options I have listed above, it is one activity that will help you.

16. **Start helping people who are worse off than you are** – If you want to be jolted into a new reality quickly start helping people who have a more difficult life than you do. These people are not hard to find if you are looking. There's nothing like a dose of the harsh reality that as hard as your life is – and I am not saying that it is easy – is seeing how utterly impossible some people's lives are compared to yours. That is not to minimize your problems or compare your problems to others, but it can really help add some perspective that is often helpful. In this day in age when the Autism numbers are skyrocketing, there is an endless supply of parents who have no choice but to care for their child with Autism without respite or help of any kind. Then there's people caring for an aging parent with little resources. In our great nation, there are plenty of people in need of help and who are likely much worse than you are.

17. **Hobbies, Hobbies, Hobbies-**Hobbies are a wonderful

way to offset stress, fear and anxiety and this is a subject of a blog post titled *"How Hobbies Can Help You Love Your Life and the Top 23 Reasons Why You Should Hobby Up"* from December 11, 2019. I am a FAN of hobbies because they are so good for us!

18. **Implement Time Management Practices** – Another way to reduce your stress, fear and anxiety is to improve your time management practices – yes, I am talking about making a list. I have blogged about time management in previous posts because it is the way to free up time, be more efficient and garner other amazing benefits. See my post titled *"LOVE the TIME of YOUR LIFE"* from September 12, 2019, and *"Top 35 Ways that Making a List Will Help You Have a Life You LOVE"*, from November 18, 2019.

19. **Draw a Line in the Sand/Defining Moment** – Sometimes the way to alter your future is by taking a stand and drawing a line in the sand or creating what you might call a defining moment. You could take the stance that you are simply going to have your life go a certain or particular way. You could be so firm and resolute about it that not one person would doubt you. You could do that. We mostly don't do that. I highly recommend it. It's invigorating. It's freeing, and it's your right to do so. Why not??

**Concluding Thoughts:**

The research is in – stress, anxiety and fear are really bad for our brains, longevity, health and mental abilities. The good news is that you can take definite and definitive actions to counter-balance, reduce or eliminate stress in your life. You can do that. Most people don't do what it takes to remove, eliminate or counter-balance stress, anxiety and fear. They just live with it. That's not the powerful life for you my beloved reader. The powerful life for you is embracing the habits and practices that make you happy.

If you focus on being happy, you will automatically or over time eliminate those things that make you unhappy, which would be negative things that stress you or cause you anxiety. I want you to have a happy and healthy life that you LOVE. What support do you need? What questions do you have? How can I empower you to do what you need to do? Let me know!

# DEALING WITH EMOTIONS & PROBLEMS

**Top 17 Benefits to High Emotional Intelligence and the 29 Traits of People Who Have It**

October 25, 2019

I have been in LOVE with the concept of Emotional Intelligence (EI), which is also referred to as Emotional Quotient since I became aware of it as a "thing" back in 2005 or so. I remember being so taken with the idea of it that I spent much too much time taking an on-line test to measure my emotional intelligence or emotional quotient! I have dug into this topic to bring you the most relevant summary of information on this topic because if you are on the journey with me to moving from wherever you are in life to having a life that you LOVE, then this is a subject that simply has to be dealt with. It's part of your growth and development process, which is part of what it takes to have a Life that you LOVE.

We all know what I.Q. is – a measure of your mental intelligence (Intelligence Quotient) or how "book smart" you are. The idea of emotional intelligence (EI) or emotional quotient (EQ) was popularized by author Daniel Goleman in his 1995 book "Emotional Intelligence: Why It Can Matter More Than IQ", who as a science reporter for *The New York Times* read an article in an academic journal by psychologists John Mayer (University of New Hampshire) and Peter Salovey (currently the President of Yale University) who offered the first formulation of the concept they called "emotional intelligence." But even before psychologists Mayer and Salovey offered this concept, history shows a variety of individuals who wrote, both directly and indirectly, the significance of being able to have abilities with emotions going back to at least 1920.

In the 24 years since Goleman's "Emotional Intelligence" book hit the market, the concept of emotional intelligence or emotional quotient has taken hold in business, educational markets, corporations and with the general public because it offers a wide range of benefits for any individual or entity. Let's define emotional intelligence or emotional quotient before we get into the benefits. Emotional Intelligence or emotional quotient is generally defined as: the ability, capacity, skill or self-perceived ability to identify, assess, and manage the emotions of one's self, of others, and of groups. This definition taken from "Understanding and Developing Emotional Intelligence" by Olivier Serrat, Asian Development Bank, June 2009, courtesy of Cornell University ILR School (http://digitalcommons.ilr.cornell.edu/intl).

According to the research, emotional intelligence or emotional quotient has 5 distinct components: self-awareness, self-regulation, self-motivation, social awareness, and social skills. Each of those 5 areas is further broken down into the attributes inherent in each component. For your convenience and hopefully your curiosity, that list would be as follows:

1. Self-Awareness: emotional awareness; accurate self-assessment; self-confidence.
2. Self-Regulation: self-control; trustworthiness; conscientiousness; adaptability; innovativeness.

3. Self-Motivation: achievement drive; commitment; initiative; optimism.
4. Social Awareness: empathy; service orientation; developing others; leveraging diversity; political awareness (not related to governmental politics).
5. Social Skills: Influence; communication; leadership; change catalyst; conflict management; building bonds; collaboration and cooperation; team capabilities.

The literature outlines the attributes for each competence listed above, which is more depth than this post calls for or most of you would be interested in at this time. According to Goleman's website, *The Harvard Business Review* has hailed emotional intelligence as "a ground-breaking, paradigm-shattering idea," one of the most influential business ideas of the decade. And part of that might be due to the fact that emotional intelligence in the educational environment or "social and emotional learning" (SEL) as it is called involves the neuroplasticity of the brain, the shaping of the brain through repeated experience. So, whether you **LOVE** it or hate it, emotional intelligence or emotional quotient is here to stay. It's a thing. And I believe it is a **BIG** thing!

As I combed through the internet researching what is being said about emotional intelligence and emotional quotient with respect to the benefits from having high emotional intelligence, I was struck by the variety or lack of consistency of the listed benefits for high emotional intelligence. I have compiled a comprehensive list of what has been stated as the benefits for having high emotional intelligence or EQ and the subsequent list of the 29 traits of people who have high EI/EQ by merging and sorting lists from the following on-line articles on emotional intelligence: John Rampton (Inc.com), Rhett Power (Success.com), Justin Bariso (Author of "EQ Applied: The Real World Guide to Emotional Intelligence" from his post on ThriveGlobal.com), Kimberly Zhang (Editor in Chief of Under-30CEO.com), Marcel Schwantes (Inc.com), the Daniel Goleman website, as well as the Olivier Serrat article listed previously in this post.

## 17 Benefits to Having High Emotional Intelligence:

1. Helpful for depressing situations in that it provides a broader perspective for handling challenges and problems
2. Helps facilitate better and more rewarding relationships with people
3. Helps you deal with stress more efficiently
4. Helps reduce anxiety
5. Helps diffuse conflict
6. Allows you to empathize with others
7. Provides calmness and clarity of the mind
8. Helps build resilience
9. Allows for better communication
10. Builds integrity
11. Helps you manage change better
12. Increases confidence
13. Increases creativity
14. Helps increase performance and productivity
15. Highly correlated to top work performance, promotions and higher pay
16. Makes for more effective leaders and managers
17. Links strongly to concepts of love and spirituality

These are significant benefits that carry a lot of weight. Who wouldn't want to have reduced anxiety or deal with stress more efficiently? Or have more rewarding relationships with people? It is more evidence as to why this concept is here to stay. After looking at the benefits for having high emotional intelligence or emotional quotient, I wondered what are the traits of people who have high emotional intelligence or quotient.

## 29 Traits of People with High Emotional Intelligence:

1. They are change agents. (think growth and development)
2. They are aware of their strengths and weaknesses. (self-aware)
3. They are empathetic.
4. They are not perfectionists.
5. They are balanced and healthy. (sleep and outside, non-work interests)
6. They are curious. (an inborn sense of wonder and curiosity)
7. They are gracious and thankful.
8. They are focused. (not easily distracted)
9. They are self-motivated.
10. They do not dwell on the past.
11. They focus on the positive.
12. They set boundaries.
13. They are great at managing their own emotions.
14. They are creative and deep thinkers. (**NOT** over-thinkers)
15. They are hard to offend.
16. They know when to say no.
17. They can distinguish between wants and needs.
18. They can determine the moods and energy of a group.
19. They think about feelings both their own and others.
20. They ask others for their perspective.
21. They pause or know when to pause.
22. They ask why.
23. They are open to criticism.
24. They apologize.
25. They forgive.
26. They have an expansive emotional vocabulary.
27. They respond rather than react.
28. They show up as their authentic selves.
29. They handle difficulties better.

## Growing Your Emotional Intelligence

Do the 29 above listed traits embody characteristics that you would like to have in yourself? Do the benefits of having high emotional intelligence appeal to you? I would certainly hope so. How do you grow your own emotional intelligence? Perfect question, and I will give you my thoughts on how to dip your toe in that water starting with how I worked to help my own three children grow their emotional intelligence more than a decade ago.

With my children I printed out a what I will call a "feeling words chart", which was basically a 2-page chart with one page dedicated to pleasant feelings and one page dedicated to difficult/unpleasant feelings. Each general category, say for example ANGER, had a subset of feeling words. ANGER listed feeling words like irritated, enraged, hostile, upset, resentful, worked up, boiling, fuming, infuriated, insulting, annoyed, offensive, and so on. The HAPPY category listed feeling words like great, joyous, thankful, elated, lucky, fortunate, ecstatic, delighted, glad, satisfied, and so on. The GOOD category, just to drill down and make sure you get the nuances and flavor for this included calm, peaceful, comfortable, pleased, relaxed, blessed, reassured, at ease and so on. To me, this is not an exact science because it seems to me that there is some cross-over with words under say, GOOD or HAPPY, that could be swapped. My point being that this is not precise. The feeling words chart was a tool.

With the feeling charts in the background, when a situation arose I would ask my children to give me 3 feeling words to pinpoint how they were feeling. In the beginning, my children would just give me a general word like anger, happy, or good. So, at every opportunity that I could or that I thought of, I would ask my children to give me 3 feeling words for any situation. As you can imagine, they got better at coming up with more than one word in a feeling category. And as you can also probably imagine there came the day when one of the kids asked me – why 3 feeling words? Is that arbitrary or is there something magic about the number 3. No, it was rather arbitrary because I am not some clinical researcher who knows exactly how to increase emotional intelligence, but it made sense to me at the time (meaning it was logical), and it seemed to be effective.

So, in looking at my kids old feeling word charts, it seemed to me that for a beginner, it might be helpful to simplify the feelings into broader categories. Plus, as adults you are much more aware of feelings and the words that can describe how you are feeling. To that end, I have made this diagram of over-simplified emotions. I have reduced the total number of categories by half to make this first pass less complicated and hopefully less overwhelming to those of you who are looking to increase your emotional quotient.

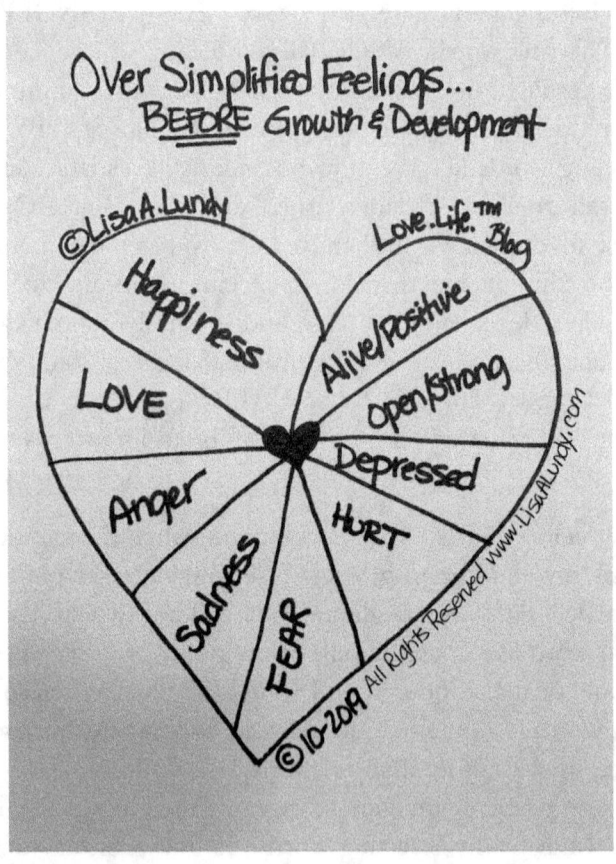

Love.Life.

Now, it is my opinion, my assertion, and my belief (note that I am not presenting this as a fact borne out by research, which it may or may not be), that once you really go to work on yourself, once you work on growing and developing yourself, your emotions will shift. You will become less annoyed with people. Less in life will bother you. You will become freed up in countless ways. There will be less anger, less resentment, less upset. There will be more love, more joy, more happiness, more peace. So, I have made a visual for this. Here you will see that I am representing that the positive emotions of love, joy, happiness, gratitude, peace, contentment, etc. occupy much more space than the negative emotions.

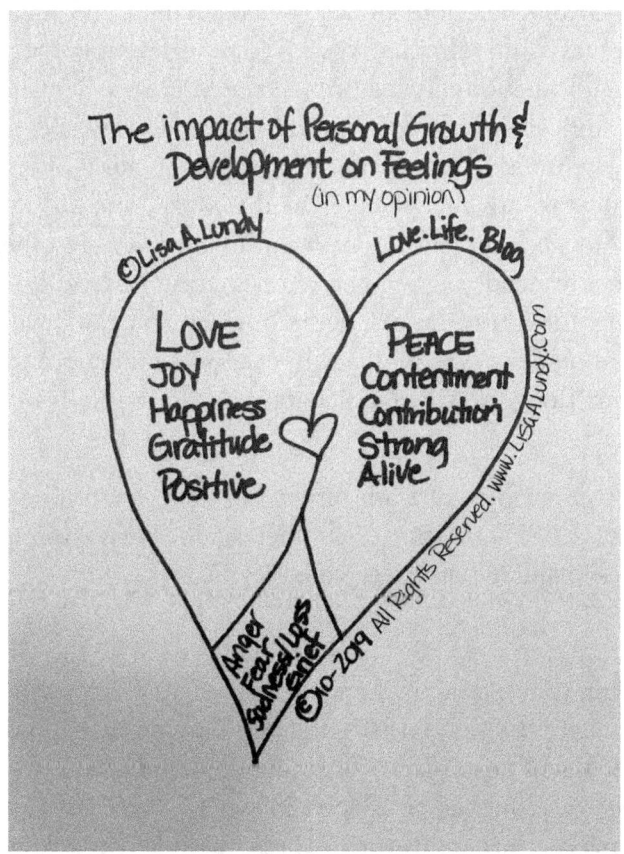

Since we are talking about increasing your emotional intelligence or quotient, I am going to introduce you to what I am calling (because I don't know if there is even a term for this, probably there is), advanced emotional intelligence! How's that for a bad name?

## Advanced Emotional Intelligence

I sincerely apologize if there is an actual name for what I am about to describe. If there is, please post it in the comment section and we can all have a great laugh on me! To have advanced emotional intelligence you will first have to have some ability to identifying your emotions in any given situation and that requires self-awareness and familiarity with the wide range of emotion flavors or distinctions if you will. Once you have some ability in naming and claiming your emotions, and I would definitely suggest you use at least 3 feeling words per situation, then you can move onto this advanced stage. In this stage you will distinguish opposing feelings present in one event or situation. In other words, the more advanced you become in distinguishing how or what you are feeling, the more you can figure out that you can have opposite feelings about one situation. You can be both happy and mad about something. You can feel happy and sad about an event or situation.

To help you grasp what I am presenting here, I will give you three examples. Oh! There's that 3 number again. Very arbitrary. These are made-up and hypothetical examples.

1. Seeing your old family home = 80% excited, happy, nostalgic; 10% angry; 10% sad. You are mostly happy, excited and nostalgic about seeing the home where you grew up. However, on a closer internal inspection of your feelings or perhaps as you get better at identifying your feelings, you realize that you are angry about some of the things that happened in the family home even if you found

out about them much later in life. And you are a little sad about some of the memories.
2. Discovery of a betrayal =75% angry, furious, hurt; 25% relieved, validated. Discovering a betrayal would make most people angry, furious, and hurt to name the top emotions that come to mind. However, a person might feel relieved and or validated if there was some suspicion about the betrayal before it was confirmed. Or put another way, it is freeing for most people to know the actual truth even when the truth is painful.
3. Starting a new job = 85% happy, excited, curious; 15% nervous, apprehensive. Most people starting a new job are happy and excited and maybe curious. Yet we can probably agree that starting a new job often brings with it some anxiety, apprehensions, and other feelings.

## Special Note about Anger, Grief, Loss and Betrayal

I would say with a certain level of clarity that we in our society are not so great in dealing with the negative emotions in particular anger, grief, loss, and betrayal. It is extremely important, in my most humble opinion, that you begin to grow your skills in dealing with the negative emotions. Why? Why would you ever want to do that? For starters, there is research to suggest that we hold emotions in our bodies, especially the negative ones. To be really healthy, it is just prudent to deal with your emotions. This, by the way, is worthy of an entire blog post. So, bear with me for I am just skimming the surface of this topic. The inability to deal with anger, grief, loss and betrayal can negatively impact your relationships, your job, your friendships, and more. And we are just not great at these unpleasant or negative emotions unfortunately.

If you don't have anger skills then it is either likely or somewhat likely that you will behave in a passive-aggressive way, which is really not cool. Or you might gravitate towards acting out, which is not good either. If you suppress or repress your anger, that's not going to get you where you want to go in life. And people on the receiving end of misplaced anger are not going to be happy with you. There is tremendous freedom in being able to accurately recognize you are angry (hurt often being the underpinning of anger), to name your feelings and then as appropriate express them or not depending on the situation.

Our society is also not so great in the areas of loss and grief. We simply have never been trained in how to grieve or handle some losses. The more you can manage and handle your feelings in the area of loss and grief, the better you will be able to hold and support someone else who is feeling a loss or grieving. In addition, there is an extreme amount of power and freedom to be able to grieve a loss. I say this having some practice in loss and grieving. We are no better, again, in my opinion, in dealing with betrayal. Ultimately betrayals often or most often involve anger and loss and grief. The more willing you are to dip your toe in the water of feelings and the more you practice feeling your feelings, identifying your feelings, and talking about them, the more you will be increasing your emotional intelligence – so I say.

## Closing Comments on Emotional Intelligence and Emotional Quotient

I have covered 17 benefits to having high emotional intelligence and 29 traits of people who have it. Do the 17 benefits appeal to you? Would you like to be the kind of person represented in the list of 29 traits of people who have high emotional intelligence? I sure hope so. If you want to have a life that you LOVE then being able to identify, manage and process your emotions, as well as recognize the emotions of others will give you power and freedom. Like any new habit or practice that you embrace or take on, it might feel awkward or weird at first. The more you do it, the more comfortable it will feel. I am not saying, by the way, that you can't be successful in life with low emotional intelligence. I am not stating that at all.

What I am saying is that if you develop skills and abilities in the area of identifying, managing and processing your emotions and the emotions of others you will have a richer and more powerful life. Why? Because not dealing with painful situations or events that upset you or make you angry don't make the situation or event go away. When you can feel anger, pain, betrayal, loss, grief, you (in my opinion) will be able to feel MORE happiness, more joy, more LOVE, and more peace. Do you have to do this – work on your emotional intelligence? Of course NOT! You should never do anything that you really don't want to do if you can help it. I promise you that any work you do in this area will ultimately be well worth it.

How can I support you in this area? My commitment to you is to help you move towards having a life that you LOVE. And in my most humble opinion, having a life that you LOVE means being able to deal with ALL the aspects that life encompasses – not just the good stuff. We are pretty good already at the happy emotions. This is just more growth and development on the way to a life that you LOVE. What questions do you have? Does this make sense to you? What is your assessment of this subject? I can't wait to hear what you have to say about this!!

## Dealing with Overwhelm: How to Put an End to Feeling Overwhelmed with Life Once and For All Plus 29 Tips to Help You in the Meantime

November 6, 2019

Overwhelm. Everyone has felt it at some point in their lifetime. Some people live it every single day. It's the opposite of feeling powerful. It's unpleasant. It's hard. It's the thing that nearly pushes some people over the edge. There are some people who absolutely should be feeling overwhelmed by their circumstances because they have situations that are extremely hard and more than any one person can actually manage. If you struggle with overwhelm either periodically or on a regular basis the first thing you should know and understand deep in your bones is that it is not your fault. The second thing you should know and understand is that you, as a human being, are enough. You are good enough. You are perfect just the way you are and just the way that you are not. LOVE. You have to LOVE your imperfections.

This is not about something being wrong with you. This is about how you do life. It's about living an intentional and happy life. We are simply not taught some of the things that I discuss in my blog posts. IF overwhelm is one of your "things", then I would suggest that you get really excited. It's time to celebrate the impending growth and development that is on the horizon as you take on the challenge of overwhelm. It's an act of LOVE, self-love, to grow and develop. It's just time to deal with any overwhelm you have in your life and get freed up to be happy and love life.

Let's start with getting on the same page about what I mean when I say overwhelm. Overwhelm is defined as a verb in the following ways according to the dictionary: bury or drown beneath a huge mass; defeat completely; to give too much of a thing (to someone); inundate. The synonyms for overwhelm include: swamp, submerge, engulf, bury, deluge, flood, overload, and overburden.

If you have been following my blog then you know my purpose in blogging is to help you have a life that you LOVE. Part of that process means dealing with issues and problems – the things that are hindering you or hampering you from loving your life. Dealing with overwhelm is one of those things and it will require, most likely, some growth and development on your part. I am presenting my take on overwhelm and what it requires to put an end to it or have it be a fleeting, passing feeling instead of a lingering, hanging on feeling. I am not asserting that this is the only way to deal with overwhelm. It's a compilation of years of growth and development and experience. We all know that I am not a therapist, a medical professional, or anyone licensed to give out mental or physical health advice. What follows is my attitudes and beliefs about the sources of overwhelm, how to fix that at the source level and tips for coping while you do the work required to deal with overwhelm.

I am going to start with a breakdown of the mind in a completely simplistic fashion. The human mind is broken down into three distinct parts: the conscious mind, the unconscious mind and the subconscious mind. Due to the nature of what we are dealing with in the subject of overwhelm, it is going to be powerful for you to understand that there are these separate areas of the mind and that we begin to have the conversation about how these areas impact your thinking. If you have never heard of this concept before then for certain this is going to sound foreign to you and it might be something that makes you go – what is she talking about? Stick with me. This is very important. I'm going to show you how powerful it can be to access what is going on in your subconscious or unconscious mind a bit later in this post.

**Conscious Mind**: This is the part of your mind that you are conscious of. You are aware of what you are thinking. You are or may be aware of what you are feeling. You are aware of what is going on around you. The conscious mind has been represented as being about 10% of your mind – give or take.

**Subconscious Mind & Unconscious Mind:** I am lumping these two categories together for the sake of simplicity even though they are separate and have distinguishing features. The makeup and operation of the mind as well as how to train your brain or mind is the subject for a future post. For the purposes of dealing with overwhelm, it is helpful to understand that the largest percentage of your mind is not something that you typically have access to that being the subconscious (or preconscious) mind and unconscious mind. Yes, there are steps you can take to access what is lurking in your subconscious and unconscious mind, but that's not the subject at hand. If you understand that the largest part of your mind is not something that you currently have control over or access to – it can be helpful in cutting yourself some slack. And sometimes that in and of itself can be extremely powerful. It has been written that these two parts of the mind represent about 90% of the mind, give or take, which makes them powerful and will be discussed in a future post on neuroplasticity of the brain, training your brain, etc.

**Sources of Overwhelm:**

I am owning this list as my own. This is my assessment of the general things that are the cause of overwhelm for people. I provide it here because to fix the issue of overwhelm you need to get to the source of the problem.

1. **Mental** -I am defining this as negative thinking, pessimism, and the lack of mental habits or practices that support inner mental peace. This includes negative self-talk, low self-esteem, the inability to effectively manage anxiety, fears or other emotional states, abuse from other individuals, and a host of other situations that are not conducive to happiness and love.
2. **Physical**-This category includes both environmental sources of overwhelm like a living place that is too messy, dirty, unorganized, possibly hoarding, and anything that does not provide you with a positive and peaceful way of living and it includes your physical body and health since being unhealthy can provide a constant source of overwhelm.
3. **Situational or "Too Much on your plate"**-There is a vast array of things that can leave you either permanently or temporarily with too much on your plate. This is a very common source of overwhelm for people. The kinds of things that can cause situational overwhelm include being a care giver of any kind, having a special needs child or special needs adult child, having a sick family member or friend, working multiple jobs, being the executor of an estate, going through a divorce, the end of a relationship, the loss of a job, and the list goes on. These are situational sources for overwhelm and

sometimes or more often than not you have no control over these events except to put in place a strategy for dealing with the overwhelm it causes and the event or situation itself.
4. **Emotional**-I am listing emotional overwhelm as the state where you are not or have not processed feelings that need to be dealt with typically in the areas of grief, loss, sadness, anger, resentment, betrayal. The emotional overwhelm may be caused by a situational factor or event listed previously that throws you into emotional overwhelm. This may or may not involve a trauma or PTSD. This could be from the death of someone, a significant loss of any kind like the loss of a job, a relationship, a home, a marriage, a financial loss, or any of the situations listed above. Feelings need to be dealt with and processed if you want to have freedom, power, and happiness. The power begins with you recognizing your feelings and then processing them appropriately.
5. **Structural**-Separate from the physical category listed above, I am including in this item the organization and time management practices and habits that give you a life that you love, or in the absence of the organization and time management practices leave you feeling overwhelmed as often as you are. Also included in this category is over-scheduling that process by which you schedule more than you can or should handle. In over-scheduling you are either making commitments that are too much for you given your life or are possibly just not appropriate given where you are in life.

## Dealing with Overwhelm – LONG TERM FIX

Here are the steps that I assert you will have to go through if you want to put an end to overwhelm in your life for good. Yes, it will take some time. And yes, yes, yes it will be well worth it in the end. Image your life and you are happy! Imagine your life and you are functioning well and feel peaceful. Imagine your life and things are working. It takes some effort to have that. It takes intentionality to have that. It just doesn't happen overnight.

1. Get an accurate (outside) assessment: Would most or some people be overwhelmed in the same circumstances? I say get an outside assessment for a few reasons one of which is that sometimes you can't see the forest for the trees and someone who cares about you and has been good to you should be able to give you an honest assessment.
2. Determine the sources(s) of your overwhelm: See previously listed sources above.
3. What are the habits and practices that will help you cope with life and then eventually flourish? Hint: You can read my previous blog posts for several ideas.
4. What things could a TEAM, if you had one, do to reduce the load you are carrying?
5. Who could be on your team? I have more to say about this, so keep reading.
6. Make a plan on what needs to be done based on your accurate assessment and the sources of your overwhelm.
7. Get supported and validated.
8. Engage in self-care and start executing your plan with your TEAM (see below).

## My Unconscious or Subconscious Mental & Emotional Process of Overwhelm:

I have done a good deal of work, that means growth and development, to access my subconscious and unconscious mind. One of the areas that I worked on many years ago was the area of overwhelm. The following diagram is one rendering of what would happen both in my mind and with my emotions when I fell into a state or moment of overwhelm. For me at the time, I was dealing with 3 concurrent traumas and while I was functioning pretty well, there would be some incident or something would happen that would

*Love.Life.*

temporarily throw me into a state of overwhelm. By doing the "work" on myself, I was able to piece together the process for myself. Your overwhelm is likely to be completely different than mine.

I have represented my personal overwhelm in a circle because this makes sense to me. Once I got that this IS my mental and emotional processing for overwhelm, my conscious brain took over and would tick through the process in a matter of seconds. It's the most amazing thing ever! Back before I had this clear understanding of the overwhelm process for myself, being in a state of overwhelm could last for a few hours or if it was bad more than a day or two. Once my brain got this cycle, overwhelm was something that my brain could recognize as a temporary state that would pass almost instantly. It's incredible. On the outside of the circle I have listed the thoughts that would run through my mind. On the inside of the circle I have listed some of the feelings that I was feeling when I was in overwhelm.

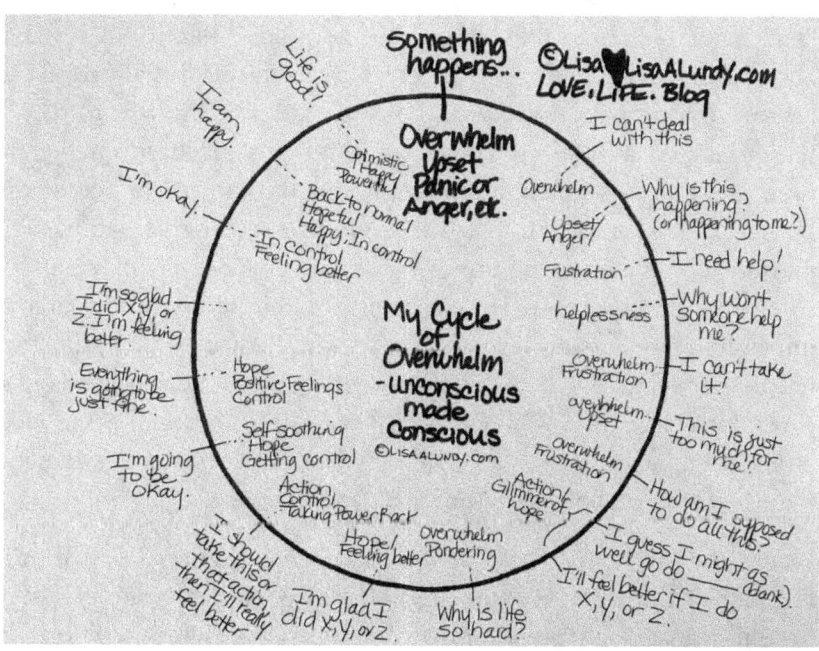

Accessing your subconscious or unconscious mind will have to be covered in a separate post. You might be able to use my process to start to understand your own mental and emotional processing. This is very powerful stuff.

**Creating a TEAM**

This subject is worthy of a separate blog post and eventually I will do that. For dealing with overwhelm, however, it needs a little mention and some ideas. There are those of you who have overwhelming circumstances and you actually need help because you have more on your plate than any human could handle. It's just a fact. You will have to deal with your feelings and emotions if you are going to allow and create a team for support. Let me share two examples from my own life. First of all, I'm not the easiest person to contribute to. I know this about myself and while I'm not proud of that, it's not the worst thing in the world. Given that, it takes a lot for me to admit that I could use a hand.

Back in the day when I was dealing with 3 concurrent traumas (can't say more about that or trust me, I would), I had to ask for and accept help. I needed to go to the University of Buffalo Medical Library to do medical research, but I couldn't see my way to spend the money for a baby sitter that was required with three small children. So, friends and neighbors helped me out for free so I could go do my medical research. This was a God send!! Then I had friends and neighbors who came to my house for my kids' birthday parties when the immunocompromised health of one of the kids made it impossible to have kids around. These adult ladies would come and be the party guests when the kids were little and made birthdays a cause for celebration. Of course, it wasn't the same as having kids attend the parties, but it was the best I could do given the danger that the common cold represented at that time.

Here's the kicker for those of you who have circumstances where help is called for – those who are helping you will get more joy and benefit from helping you than you could imagine. Let that sink in. If you can find your way to allowing others to help you, they will get equal or greater benefit. It's what we call a win-win-win. They win. You win. And your life wins. Ask family, friends, neighbors, co-workers, people at your place of worship, local community organizations or even your Facebook or social media peeps for the help that you need.

**Short Term Tips for Dealing with Overwhelm**

These are my tips for getting through overwhelm until you actually deal with the source of your overwhelm and execute a plan that fixes the problem at the source. These tips are not the long-term solution. You can also read my past blog posts which have content to help you move forward powerfully for practices on how to live an intentional life that you love.

1. Live MOMENT to MOMENT-If you have a great deal of overwhelming circumstances then I suggest that instead of living day to day as is often recommended – you live moment to moment. One problem at a time. One moment at a time.
2. Attitude Adjustment-Pay attention to what you are thinking. I mean really pay attention to the thoughts that pop into your mind. If you are having negative and disempowering thoughts then it's time for an attitude adjustment because negative self-talk is not helpful when you are in overwhelm.
3. Triage what has to be done-Create a list and triage the most critical and essential things that have to get done. Use this to ground yourself in the urgent matters that have to be completed.
4. Ask for help-While asking for help is not easy, there are huge benefits for the people who are willing to help you not to mention the benefits you will receive.
5. Beef up on your sleep and/or naps-While sleep is essential for all human health, being under high stress adds volumes to the significance of sleep. Do what you can to increase your sleep or grab a cat nap when you can.

6. Take vitamins-Being under stress is hard on the body so I believe it can't hurt you to take some extra vitamins if you are dealing with overwhelm. Of course, you should always check with your licensed medical provider before taking vitamins.
7. Do things that make you happy-Figure out what makes you happy and add that into your life wherever you can. I understand that might not be an easy or simple suggestion depending on your circumstances, but I know that it can be done if you make up your mind to do it.
8. Find a way to laugh-The more you can laugh the better. Whether it is a comedy show on TV, a Netflix special, reading something funny or laughing with friends or family – laughter is good for the soul and body.
9. Socialize with friends or family-Compelling research speaks volumes to the negative impact of loneliness and social isolation, a problem often that comes with situations that cause overwhelm, so anything you can do to socialize is a plus. Ask friends and family to come over and help you and you can socialize while they are helping you.
10. Pray or meditate-I find prayer very soothing and calming. If you don't believe in prayer then you can meditate. Taking any action to calm your mind and soul is going to be helpful in times of overwhelm.
11. Go for a walk-If your health allows for this, then try to walk for 15 minutes a day. Even if it just means parking further away from a store. The research is significant for the positive health benefits for just walking for 15 minutes a day. If you can do more walking than that by all means do it!
12. Fill your mind and space with positive things-I highly recommend that you turn off the news and anything that is negative or upsetting. You are better off filling your mind and your space with positive and uplifting things.
13. Go easy on yourself-Having some compassion for yourself will also be helpful. We may be wired to be hard on

*Love.Life.*

ourselves, or most of us anyway, but it is really not helpful when you are dealing with overwhelm.

14. Dress up-Take a shower, put on nice clothing and do your hair and makeup (or other grooming). You will look better and feel better and that is always helpful.
15. Have faith-In difficult situations it can be challenging to have faith, yet having hope, which is what faith brings with it, is essential. Believe that things will get better and they usually do or eventually do. Believe that things will get worse, and guess what – they usually do. Have faith that things will turn out and in the interim, do the work.
16. Journal-Taking a few minutes every now and then to journal can be very therapeutic and can also help you access your subconscious or unconscious mind.
17. Read an empowering or inspiring book-Fill yourself with things that lift you up and there are plenty of books that could fill this bill.
18. Do something to "sharpen the saw"-Refuel and re-energize yourself. What does that mean? What do you do that fills your heart and soul? If you don't know, then that is a good place to start.
19. Look at what needs to change and make a commitment-Making a commitment to change your life for the better is empowering and inspiring to most people. Look at what you can change and get to work on that.
20. Make signs to inspire yourself-I know it sounds hokey, but in my experience, signs can be very helpful! Have fun with this!
21. Keep it in perspective-Perspective can go a long way to changing our attitudes and feelings. Everyone should know someone who has it harder in life than you do. It is jolting especially when you think that life is hard. If you don't know anyone who has it harder than you, then you can certainly find people using the internet who have dire situations.
22. Do little things to help others (or allow contribution)-

Helping others gives you a good feeling. If you can't find a way to help others, then consider allowing contribution to your life.
23. Plan something to look forward to-Everyone loves having something to look forward to. If you don't have something to look forward to, then make it up. I organized two reunions in the past so that I would have something to look forward to.
24. Make up your mind how your life is going to go-It's exceptionally powerful to make up your mind, in a decisive way, about how your life is going to go – and then live from that place.
25. Fill your heart with gratitude-It's hard to be unhappy if you are feeling grateful. And while gratitude might not come easy to you, it's a practice that you can learn to become good at. Start by making a daily list of what you have to be grateful for.
26. Smile-There are benefits to smiling and the more you smile, the better you will feel. You might have to work at it, but smiling more will help you.
27. Don't take things personally-easier said than done. If you believe that the things in life that have happened or that are happening now are happening for your benefit, then life will instantly look different. It's much more empowering to believe that what is happening is happening for your growth and development, or for your good.
28. Listen to music that soothes your soul or lights you up-music can be very good for you if it is the right kind of music *for you*.
29. Start a new hobby or continue with a previous hobby-I am a HUGE fan of hobbies! They are good for people of ALL ages for so many reasons. If you don't have any hobbies then consider exploring what you might really enjoy. Hobbies can bring you joy, happiness, peace and satisfaction.

## Concluding Thoughts

We live in a world of unhappiness and overwhelm. Sometimes we have no control over situations or events that happen to us, which rightfully leave us feeling overwhelmed and in many cases with more to do than anyone could handle. It does not have to be that way. The more you take control of your life and live intentionally, the more happiness you will have in your life and the less overwhelm you will have in your life. These are new practices and habits, new ways of thinking and doing life. If you have not lived with intentionality in the past then this is going to feel different. It might possibly feel very weird. You might be thinking that this is ridiculous and no one really does this stuff. Yes, I do this stuff. Yes, it works. Regardless of how it feels or what you think of the actions it requires to deal with overwhelm, it takes something to have a life that you love. I know that you can absolutely have love, joy and happiness even in times of great difficulty and suffering (more about that coming in a future post).

We live life on a treadmill going through the motions. We live life in the grind of day to day operations. We want a different life but the question is what are we willing to do to have that wonderful happy life? I know how to be happy even when life slaps me down. I don't have a perfect life, but I have a happy one. And I know how to be happy even in the face of dark times and periods of great suffering (coming post on that). I am here to support you along the way. What is causing your overwhelm? What are you doing to get through life while feeling overwhelmed? This is a critical issue that has to be addressed to have a life that you love. I assure you that any and all work that you do in this area will be richly rewarding. I want more than anything for you to be happy and have a great life. What can I do to support you in having that? Please let me know!

LISA A. LUNDY

## How to Be Happy When You Are Suffering or Life is Bad

November 15, 2019

We are not so good in our society and culture in dealing with loss and suffering, which is something I have decades of experience with. I am 58 years old and my retirement money has been taken as well as most of my assets. I am starting over with pretty much nothing. Let that sink in. And I am still happy. I am happy despite my circumstances and I know what it takes to live a happy and healthy life during dark times. Nearly 25 years ago my first child died in utero when I was six months pregnant and then I had to deliver her and decide whether to bury her body or to have her cremated. I have her ashes with me and she will be buried with me when I pass away because I was going to be moving and I didn't want her to be alone in a cemetery that I would not be able to visit (and the Monsignor at my parish said that as long as I kept her ashes together that was approved in the Catholic faith).

The death of my daughter, Christina, was followed by the fact that I was told that I would have to have a hysterectomy and that I would never be able to bear any children, which was a crushing blow on top of losing my daughter. While I did end up having 3 children naturally and clearly didn't have a hysterectomy, those were difficult months following her death. I know a lot more about hardship and suffering that I can't write about because there are other problems I have endured that would not be appropriate to share – here and now or perhaps ever. I know that I have the skills and abilities to generate happiness and joy in my life even when times are excruciatingly painful. I also know that anyone can learn what it takes to be happy and have joy even in the most difficult of circumstances. That is what this post is about.

Human suffering can be caused by a multitude of situations like the death of a spouse, child, family member or friend, the loss of a job, a relationship breakup, a marriage ending, moving, abuse of any kind including emotional, psychological, economic, physical or sexual, health problems, being a care giver, financial problems, legal problems, never having children if you had wanted them, never getting married if you had wanted to, housing problems, not having good friends or enough of them, toxic relationships of any kind, and feeling isolated, alone, or lonely to name common ones. There are plenty of people suffering. The question is what do you do when you are suffering or feeling like life is too hard or bad?

We mostly don't talk about these things. We avoid them. We dismiss them. We skip over them. That's just not helpful to the people weathering these kinds of hardships. Before I dive into this topic I want to mention if you are feeling suicidal, please call your local suicide hotline or crisis center immediately. There is help available and there is no shame in asking for help. I must also repeat the fact that I am not a licensed therapist or medical professional of any kind and what I am presenting here is simply my views and experience on how to be happy in the face of painful or difficult circumstances that causes you to suffer or make life really hard.

Where do most people turn in very dark times regardless of their background? More often than not, in times of deep trouble, people turn to God and prayer. God offers hope eternal and even those individuals who have no belief in God often turn to the Heavens for help in desperate situations. In 2013, I happened to begin reading a book titled "Holy Abandonment" written in 1934 by Rt. Reverend Dom Vitalis Lehodey, O.C.R. A Goodreads.com summary states: "…that all whatsoever happens to us in this life either has been allowed to happen by Almighty God, or He has sent to us directly as some kind of special cross or lesson or chastisement." Little did I know the Divine Providence of this book coming into my life that year as a string of really horrific things came to light in the following year, which prompted, quite reasonably, a torrent of suffering and pain. While the "Holy Abandonment" book is not a book I would recommend to the average reader, there is one aspect that I want to share from this book, which categorizes the 3 levels of suffering.

## The 3 Levels of Suffering

I am totally paraphrasing here since I no longer have the book and it has been around 4 or 5 years since I read it. Off the top of my head, here is my recollection of how the author lays out the 3 levels of suffering.

1. You get through it. You get through the suffering basically.
2. You get through it with some joy and happiness. You still suffer but you are able to find some happiness and joy during the suffering.
3. You intentionally ask God for more suffering.

Now, ahem. Really? Who would ever ask for more suffering? Yeah. I have no idea because it is definitely not me. The balance of this post is about putting suffering in an empowering context and the process of how to get some level of happiness or joy while you are going through it- all from the vantage point of my personal experience having made it through 3 concurrent traumas in the past 20 plus years, not including the death of my daughter.

## An Empowering Context for Suffering

My takeaway from reading the "Holy Abandonment" book was a very empowering context for suffering, which inspired and empowered me. One purpose for suffering is for the purification and sanctification of our souls. What does that mean? Sanctification of a soul means the Holy Spirit's work of making us holy or creating faith in us so that through his power we produce good works. To think of the horrible pain that I was going through as something that would purify and sanctify my soul made me feel infinitely better. It gave a purpose to the suffering. And guess what? I am for sure a better person because of what I have been through. I would never ever wish it on anyone else. Nor do I talk about it for the most part. And at the same time, I am clearly a better person because of it.

Another way to look at the empowering context of suffering is that it is the opportunity to increase our virtues namely that of humility, kindness, patience, diligence, charity, temperance, and chastity. In March 2015, while still in the throes of deep suffering, our local parish priest gave a talk about the Book of Job from the Bible, which was also deeply empowering with respect to suffering. For those of you who are unfamiliar with Job from the Bible – basically he suffered a lot. The priest introduced us to the concept of redemptive suffering, and what follows are my exact notes from the priest's lecture, which I am sharing here because this has been very powerful for the many people with whom I have shared it with over the past years.

## Redemptive Suffering

*Redemptive Suffering: is when a person is uniting their suffering (spiritually) to the suffering, passion and death of our Lord, Jesus Christ. GRACE is available when you use this process – the process of joining our suffering with the suffering of Jesus for _____ (fill in who you are offering your suffering for). It is also a process by which you are co-creating with God for the betterment of the world.*

*You would say it like this: "Lord, I am suffering, and I unite my suffering with the suffering of your son, Jesus Christ and I offer my suffering for _____ (fill in the blank)."*

*Who do you offer your suffering for? Here are some examples of what could go in the blank:*

- *Yourself*
- *The salvation of the world*
- *The souls in purgatory*
- *The healing of someone*
- *The benefit of someone – you pick the person*
- *Or you can leave it up to God and say – I am offering this up for whomever or whatever you, God, sees fit.*

*Other notes on this subject: We have a choice when faced with suffering. Do we offer it up and unite our suffering with the suffering of Jesus for the benefit of (whomever) OR for yourself. Or do we become bitter? It is not selfish to pick yourself as the person to benefit from the act of redemptive suffering so don't be afraid to say for the benefit of myself!*

*The priest concluded with: Life is hard. Very hard.*

## The PROCESS of how to be Happy when you are suffering:

This is my abbreviated take on the process – the process of how to move from suffering at any level to being able to be happy even while things are difficult and you are suffering. I will refer to some of my past blog posts so as not to repeat myself because I have already laid out some of the practices and habits that will help you move from where you are to a happier place in the Dealing with Overwhelm post.

1. Acknowledge whatever it is that is the source of your hardship or suffering. There is great power in acknowledging what you are dealing with. It is the place to start.
2. Speak it/Own it/Claim it. To be able to say "I am having difficulties or hardship because of X, Y, or Z" is part of you claiming the situation. It is the beginning of transforming it and doing the work to get to a better place. The more you can authentically speak and claim what you are dealing with, the more help and support you will find sometimes in unexpected ways and through unexpected people.
3. FEEL your feelings. Denying your feelings does not make them go away. Neither does minimizing them or diminishing your feelings. The most powerful place to start after acknowledging and claiming the situation is to feel your feelings – whatever they are – and most likely there are several feelings that need to be processed.

4. GRIEVE the loss or hardship. While grief and grieving a loss is worthy of an entire post alone, for the purposes here, let me just say that to learn how to grieve a loss is a powerful life lesson. Life is hard. There are plenty of things that will leave you grieving over time. To learn how to deal with that is powerful. Now is the perfect time to start if you are up against it.
5. Have a Pity Party, if needed, but for a limited duration. Pity parties are sometimes appropriate. Do that, if needed or as needed, but make sure that you are not excessively engaging in feeling sorry for yourself because that is never going to get you to a happy life.
6. DECIDE what you COULD be grateful for and make a list of that. Gratitude is a powerful emotion that is very positive for health and wellbeing. Gratitude is also the subject for a coming post, but for now, do what you can to be grateful because regardless of what you are experiencing there are always things to be grateful for.
7. Look at your attitudes and beliefs. What are your attitudes and beliefs about life? Do you have the "I can't win" belief or the "life sucks" mentality? Contrast that with the philosophy of "Good things happen to me" or "everything is happening for my good" concept. If you believe that things are never going to get better then they probably won't. If you believe that things are going to get better, then they will. What if you asked the question: what am I to learn from this experience? Or how can I grow and develop from this situation? A close examination of your attitudes and beliefs can be very helpful here and there is a lot more to come on this topic.
8. Examine what practices or habits you can put in place to move forward. On this note, I would strongly urge you to read my post on dealing with Overwhelm, which contains 29 tips to help you with overwhelm because the same 29 tips will help you when you are suffering or dealing with hardship. I would suggest that you read through the

overwhelm post and pick a few of the 29 tips and start implementing them. They are not overly difficult and they will help you feel better.

9. MAKE A LIST. Oh, here I go again with making a list! Yep. Here I go again. I'm very excited about an upcoming post about the major benefits from making a list and I would venture a guess that you will be surprised at the substantial benefits making a list provides. I would make a list of what habits and practices you need to implement to move forward and begin to start doing those things.

10. MAKE A LIST of what makes you HAPPY. When you are suffering or in difficult times, you need to get really, really clear about what makes you happy. What are the things you can do that bring you joy and happiness? Who are the people you can be around that make you laugh and bring a smile to your face? Make a list of everything that makes you happy and start intentionally putting that into your life. I have written about doing this in past blog posts, so you can find more in previous posts.

11. Create a TEAM to help you. I wrote a little about this in my previous blog post on dealing with Overwhelm, so you can look at that. I will be putting up a whole post dedicated to the formation and creation of a TEAM, so that's coming. People will help you. I promise you that there are people in your life, or perhaps people you have yet to meet who would be very happy to help you if they knew you needed help.

12. Pay attention to your feelings, attitudes and beliefs as you might need to corral them every now and then. This touches on the subject of training your mind and your brain, which I will not get into here because it is also a future post coming as soon as I can get to it. Given what we know about the neuroplasticity of the brain, it is very possible to train your brain. For now, pay attention to how you are feeling and what you are thinking. If you are not

feeling happy then take an action to counter-balance that feeling and move you into a happier state.
13. Make up your mind that NO ONE and NOTHING has the power to take ALL of your happiness and joy away. One of the reasons that I was able to deal with 3 concurrent traumas, lasting more than 2 decades, was this very statement. I made up my mind a long time ago that no one and nothing had the power to take away all my happiness and joy in life. Then, given that philosophy, I took actions to put happiness and joy in my life. It's all about being intentional and counter-balancing negativity and suffering, which can be done.
14. Go into therapy if you need to.
15. Get a coach if you need to.
16. Start helping other people who could really use a hand – if that is possible. Sometimes when you have extenuating circumstances and an overwhelming situation, this is just not humanly possible. Yet, some people have the circumstances that they could help others if they wanted to. Consider whether this is possible for you, and if so, start right away.
17. Pray like crazy. Pray while you are walking, driving, pumping gas. Pray like it matters. If you don't believe in prayer then this suggestion is not for you. However, if you are really suffering or experiencing really difficult times, you might find prayer helpful. If not try meditating.
18. Create a vision for your future that inspires you. While this is not the easiest thing to do when you are suffering or having great difficulties or hardships, almost everyone can create a future event, trip, or get together that they can look forward to. So, do that. In the meantime, the most powerful thing you can do is start to look to the future and create a vision of what your life will look like – and then begin to do the work to get there.
19. Do the work. It takes something to be happy when times are tough. It's not something that magically happens in

difficult times. And yet, there is no question that you can be happy and feel love and joy when you are suffering or up against it. It does take something though. You have to be intentional. You have to do the work. You have to have the habits and practices that give you happiness. When you establish the practices and habits as ingrained habits and practices then it won't be work anymore because it will be a natural expression of you living life.

## Concluding Thoughts

Napoleon Hill, Author of *Think and Grow Rich*, a classic written in 1937, is quoted as saying: *"Every adversity, every failure and every heartache carries with it the seed of an equivalent or greater benefit."* Life is hard. That's not in question here. What is in question is what are you going to do when you are having difficult times or hardship? You can slink away quietly into the night, or you can dig in and start planning to pull yourself out of it. I know it's not easy. I know how brutally tough life can be. What I know for a fact is that the more work you do on yourself, the more you grow and develop, the easier it is to deal with life's difficulties and hardships.

The skills and habits that you develop by doing the work on yourself will serve you well. Fortunately for me, I just happened to have developed these practices and habits early in life. Thank God. I mean, you have no idea how much I mean Thank God. At the present moment I am dealing with some things in life that are really painful and I can't write about that because they involve other people. Yet, due to the work I have done on myself, I have mostly happy days despite the hardships that I am experiencing. So, I know first-hand that this can be done.

The question is are you willing to do what it takes to have a happy life? Are you willing? If you are willing, then it can be done. Let me know how I can support you on your journey. You can do this. I know that you can. Let me help you.

*Love.Life.*

## Dealing with Depression – 43 Tips to Help You Stave Off Depression

January 20, 2020

Depression is an unpleasant and very real medical condition that affects approximately one in 15 adults in any given year, with one in six people experiencing depression at some point in their life. Depression negatively affects how you feel, how you think and how you behave and is characterized by feelings of sadness and/or a loss of interest in things you once enjoyed. There are different types of depression notably major depression, persistent depression, situational depression – depression related to an event like the death of a loved one, a divorce, loss of a job and so on – as well as postpartum depression (after the birth of a baby), as well as a few other types. The good news is that depression is treatable with 80 to 90 percent of people responding well to treatment. The even better news is that there are a lot of things you can do to stave off depression in your everyday activities.

The symptoms of depression include but are not limited to: feeling sad or down; loss of interest or pleasure in activities you once enjoyed; changes in appetite unrelated to dieting -either weight loss or weight gain; trouble sleeping or sleeping too much; loss of energy or fatigue; feeling worthless or guilty; difficulty thinking, making decisions or concentrating; thoughts of suicide or death. If you are having thoughts of suicide or death please contact your local suicide hotline or the national suicide hotline at 1-800-273-8255, which is open 24 hours a day. While you might not be feeling it right now – your life does make a difference and you would be missed if you were not here.

As per my usual disclaimer, I am not a therapist or medical professional in any capacity and hence, my blog post does not constitute medical advice. See a licensed medical professional if you are depressed. What is interesting to note with respect to depression is the fact that people with low self-esteem, those who are easily overwhelmed by stress, and those who are generally pessimistic appear more likely to experience depression. It's important to take note of those factors that predispose you to depression because you can learn habits, techniques and practices that will help you increase your self-esteem, and deal with stress – two of the factors.

Being a pessimist is more of a belief system or attitude, which can also be changed. In the past, when I have met people who were pessimists, I would always recommend the book titled *"The Power of Positive Thinking"* by Norman Vincent Peale – a book that I, myself, have NEVER read. First published in 1952, *"The Power of Positive Thinking"* was then and continues to be a popular book, which I only recommend to pessimists or "realists" as some pessimists call themselves. For what it is worth, the people to whom I have recommended that book to, who actually got it and read it, found it very worthwhile – and pretty much had a much more positive outlook on life after reading it. Since I have never read it, I can't say that I endorse the book because I don't know what it says. However, I do totally support the concept of positive thinking.

Pretty much everything I blog about are the practices and habits that will help you avoid feeling depressed. While you might have a situation or circumstances that are depressing – oh, I know about that – your situation or circumstances do not have to dictate your feelings. What will help you to avoid feeling depressed on an ongoing basis is to have a plan for your life and be in action in executing that plan. You get to decide how your life will go. Even if you are in a situation that you can't control or change, you can still do things to have a powerful and happy life. By that I mean that you could be in a reasonably difficult or horrible situation and still find a way to be happy. That I can say with absolute conviction from experience.

I would suggest that you consider all the reasons why you are depressed and write them down. What plan could you formulate to address those reasons? Who could be on your team to help you? Additionally, you should also write down all the things that you have to be grateful for. Gratitude is a very powerful emotion. It's hard to feel depressed when you are feeling grateful. I'm not saying you can't be feeling both of those emotions at the same time, but if you are really feeling grateful it's a very positive and powerful feeling.

I have written about tips and techniques to deal with overwhelm, time management, and how to be happy when you are suffering. This is my thing. How to deal with life when it is very difficult. Much of what I write about deals with actions you can take, new habits or practices to learn, and the process for how to create a life that you LOVE. I write about you taking control of your life instead of letting life just happen to you. This is a process that is foreign to many people. We are not born into this world with a manual on all the habits and practices that you could employ to handle stress, hardship, or very difficult times. There is a great deal to life that we have to learn by doing or through the school of hard knocks. It is one reason why we have so many unhappy people in this world. We don't even know how to be happy.

If you are a regular reader of my blog, then some of this list is going to sound very familiar because there are standard practices, in my humble opinion of course, that go along with having a powerful and happy life. The more that you do these practices, take on new habits, and do the work of personal growth and development – the happier you will be, in my humble opinion.

**Top 43 Ways to Stave Off Depression:**

1. Improve your diet – more fresh, whole foods – less junk food and sugar. Recent research shows that eating a diet of fresh fruits and vegetables, fish and lean meat helped young adults reduce their depression (https://doi.org/10.1371/journal.pone.0222768). One medical fact I found in my research was that magnesium deficiency is well known to produce neuropathologies (Med Hypotheses. 2006;67(2):362-70. Epub 2006 Mar 20). NOTE: Up to 50% of Americans are deficient in magnesium! This was a very interesting medical article, whose title "Rapid Recovery from Major Depression Using Magnesium Treatment (PubMed-NCBI) caught my eye, so I am including a little more from this abstract:

*"Case histories are presented showing rapid recovery (less than 7 days) from major depression using 125-300 mg of magnesium (as glycinate and taurinate) with each meal and at bedtime. Magnesium was found usually effective for treatment of depression in general use. Related and accompanying mental illnesses in these case histories including traumatic brain injury, headache, suicidal ideation, anxiety, irritability, insomnia, postpartum depression, cocaine, alcohol and tobacco abuse, hypersensitivity to calcium, short-term memory loss and IQ loss were also benefited."*

Equally fascinating from the same paper: *"The possibility that magnesium deficiency is the cause of most major depression and related mental health problems including IQ loss and addiction is enormously important to public health and is recommended for immediate further study."*

This is from a 2008 study found in the US National Library of Medicine – National Institutes of Health (U.S. medical database):

*On the basis of accumulating scientific evidence, an effective therapeutic intervention is emerging, namely nutritional supplement/treatment. These may be appropriate for controlling and to some extent, preventing depression, bipolar disorder, schizophrenia, eating disorders and anxiety disorders, attention deficit disorder/attention deficit hyperactivity disorder (ADD/ADHD), autism, and addiction.[4] (*Indian J Psychiatry. 2008 Apr-Jun; 50(2): 77–82.) This sentence comes from this journal reference: 4. Shaheen Lakhan SE, Vieira KF. Nutritional therapies for mental disorders. Nutr Jr. 2008;7:2.

The bottom line is that if you are dealing with depression, then improving your diet could really help you! Also, talk to your physician about taking magnesium.

2. Exercise of any kind has been shown to improve mood and do great things for your body even if it is just walking. According to Harvard Medical School (Harvard Health Publishing), exercise is an all-natural treatment to fight depression (although it might not be enough for some types of depression). Get out there and move!

3. Get a mission/vision/purpose for your life – one that inspires you. There's no doubt in my mind to stave off depression nothing

works like having a vision, mission or purpose for your life that you are inspired by. If you don't have one, then get going because there is no time like the present to create your future.

4. Get outside in nature – go for a walk or a drive. The research shows that simply being in nature has physical health and wellbeing benefits for people. This is a simple way to elevate your mood and get some health benefits as well.

5. Organize or clean anything. I am not saying if you are depressed that you will feel like cleaning or organizing anything, I am however saying that you will feel better if you do.

6. Do things that make you happy. If you don't have a list of things that make you happy, then get busy and start making a list of things that make you happy. Then sprinkle your life with items from your list. This actually works.

7. Get together with friends. As I have written in the past, there are major health benefits for socializing that might surprise you, so get together with friends for a definite way to stave off depression. Unless you have bad friends, in which case then it is time to make new friends.

8. Plan a reunion or other event. Planning a reunion or event will help you have something to look forward to, which is always helpful. It will also give you something to keep you busy, which can also be effective for staving off depression. I have done this and I can say with clarity that it works.

9. Do or start a hobby. I have an entire blog post dedicated to hobbies (December 11, 2019: How Hobbies Can Help You Love Your Life and the Top 23 Reasons You Should Hobby Up), so I am definitely a fan of hobbies. Hobbies can help you in many ways. If you don't have one or more hobbies that you really enjoy, yes, hobbies are something that you should enjoy – then it's high time you hobby up!

10. Call a friend or family member for a pick me up call. While this can be very hard if you are feeling depressed, letting people know that you need a pick me up can be so helpful.

11. Keep a gratitude journal or list. As I mentioned earlier, it is really important to keep things in perspective. Keeping a gratitude journal or a list of things you are grateful for can really help alter your mood and help you stave off depression.

12. Set attainable goals for yourself that will make you happy. Setting attainable goals and working towards them can help you boost your mood. You set the goal(s) that would make you happy and then get to work.

13. Groom yourself. Take a shower. Do your hair. We all know that we will feel better after a hot shower or a good soak in the tub. Get cleaned up and do your hair or other grooming. You will look and feel better.

14. Dress up. Yes, even if you are not going anywhere, putting on a decent outfit will help you feel better. I'm not talking about your Sunday best, but something that you would wear out in public if you were meeting a friend.

15. Find someone worse off than you and help them. Study poverty in third world countries. There are literally so many people who are much worse off than you. I am not saying this to minimize your feelings or minimize your situation. I am saying this because if you got yourself together you could really make a difference in the world. The world needs you! Yes, we do. So, pull yourself together because there is a place for you and your gifts are needed.

16. Volunteer at an animal rescue shelter or any place for that matter. If volunteering at an animal rescue shelter does not appeal to you, then there are lots of other places that need you! Find an organization that calls to you and then pitch in. You will not only be doing the world a great service, but you will also meet new people, make new friends, and how is that ever bad?

17. Self-care: Make a list of what you can do to take better care of yourself and start doing it. Too many of us are not so great when it comes to self-care. So, make a list of all the things you could do in the area of self-care and start doing it.

18. Read inspiring material – books, articles, or stories or watch inspiring movies or shows.

19. Get your attitude adjusted – try thinking positively. While this might be more difficult for some, it's important. A positive thought will make you feel way better than a negative thought.

20. Understand the concept of the self-fulfilling prophecy. You are or will become what you think you are or will become. The self-fulfilling prophecy is a psychology concept that basically says, in essence, we have a belief that comes true because we were behaving in a manner for it to come true.

21. Start training your brain with affirmations. Affirmations can help you change your attitudes, rewire your brain, and help you in many ways to stave off depression.

22. What are your coping skills? Work on boosting them or getting better ones. What are your top coping mechanisms? Go to work on either improving the ones you have or by getting better coping mechanisms.

23. Write the story of your future and then live into that future. Write a story about how you would like your life to go and then start living into that. Start taking the actions you would need to take in order for the story you have written to come true.

24. Make a list of things you can do today (anything) and go do one thing. Something this simple can improve your mood a lot. Go do something. You will feel accomplished unless you are very good at beating yourself up, in which case you might still feel defeated. If that is the case then it is time for self-love and self-care.

25. Listen to music you love. This is an easy way to improve your mood and help stave off depression.

26. Even better – dance to a song that makes you happy. If you have the ability to, dance to your favorite music. You will definitely be boosting your mood and the little bit of movement won't hurt your body.

27. Start using a reward system to spur you onto getting things done. I have been using a reward system for decades and I know that if you set one up that it can really motivate you. Having a system set up for things that need to be done and the corresponding rewards can help you stave off depression because, hopefully you actually want the rewards that you have put into your system.

28. See a doctor to rule out any medical conditions that could cause depression like thyroid problems, a brain tumor, or vitamin deficiencies. While the research indicates that a magnesium deficiency could be at the core of depression for many, it is always a good thing to rule out any other possible medical causes for depression.

29. Own your feelings instead of resisting them. Claim them. Sometimes claiming your own feelings can be very liberating. The acknowledgement of your feelings can free you up to create a plan to deal with things. Pretending you are not depressed if you are is not helpful. Owning it and creating a plan is where the power is.

30. Pray or meditate. Prayer or meditation can be very helpful in staving off depression. I am one who prays and finds it very comforting, uplifting, and freeing. Some people get great benefits from meditation.

31. Get a coach or accountability partner. An accountability partner or a coach can help you move through tough times and stave off depression because you will feel empowered and that someone is on your side. You can work with a friend or family member so it doesn't have to cost you money. It can be really helpful to have someone else to hold your proverbial feet to the fire, which is especially good if you are still working on being self-disciplined.

32. Deal with the source of your depression or feeling depressed. If you are grieving a loss including unfulfilled dreams or broken

*Love.Life.*

promises then go through the grieving process and then create a bright new future for yourself after you have gone through the process of dealing with your feelings.

33. Put up empowering or inspiring signs. This might seem ridiculous to some of you, however I can say with clarity that it works very well. I would recommend graphically appealing signs that you like to look at.

34. Reframe your view of your life and your future. Sometimes all you need to do is reframe your view of your life, a particular situation, or an event to become empowered by it. I know this can be a powerful tool in staving off depression.

35. If you can't find a mission/vision/purpose for your life then MAKE IT UP! It's okay to make up a purpose, a vision or a mission. You simply have to find something that lights you up and pulls you forward. If you can't find it, then just make it up. Do yourself a favor though and make up something great! You deserve that.

36. Ask for help. I know that asking for help can be hard. Here's what I know about asking for help – the worst case is you ask for it and you don't get it. So, what. You will never know if you don't ask. Making your needs known allows other people to help you where and when or if they can. I love helping other people. Most people do. Let your needs be known and see what happens.

37. Create a team. Ask people to be on your team in life. Ask, ask, ask. Create a team to help you moving forward. Life is so much more fun when done in a team.

38. Be present. In the NOW. Being present in your life is one big way to stave off depression. If you are worried about the future or spending time regretting the past, that is not living in the present. We only have now. Right now.

39. Find ways to laugh – it's so good for you. Spend as much time as you can laughing. And I hope you can laugh at yourself. Life is so much better spent laughing. If it's either laughing or crying then I'll take laughing any day.

40. Get into therapy. Therapy can be helpful. Get into therapy and learn what your issues are and then get to work on them.

41. Draw a line in the sand and make a commitment to be happy, be joyful, and live a life that you love. Seriously, throw down the gauntlet. Make a declaration. Decide. Choose. And don't look back.

42. Work on yourself – growth and development. Okay, I do love personal growth and development because the more you know yourself the easier your life can be. If you want to stave off depression, then start doing the "work".

43. Try tapping or EFT- According to a recent research article, the Emotional Freedom Technique is an evidence-based, self-help therapeutic method and over 100 studies demonstrate its efficacy (Bach D, Groesbeck G, Stapleton P, Sims R, Blickheuser K, Church D. Clinical EFT (Emotional Freedom Techniques) Improves Multiple Physiological Markers of Health. *J Evid Based Integr Med.* 2019;24:2515690X18823691. doi:10.1177/2515690X18823691.

**Concluding Thoughts:**

I was in a very depressing situation for an extended period of time and I was able to be mostly happy because I did the things that I blog about. I still do these things. You can be in an extremely difficult or horrible situation or circumstance and it doesn't have to define you. You don't have to be miserable. There ARE things you can do. The better you get at having certain habits and practices then the better off you are in life. Period. Regardless of what happens – good or bad.

What makes you happy? What do you love? Sprinkle that into your life! Do the work. How can I help you live a better life? It's all I want for you! Please let me know how I can support you in your journey!

## Worry & Fear Hurt Your Health: 15 Tips to Overpower Fear & Worry & Start Taking Risks

March 4, 2020

---

*"Let our advance worrying become advance thinking and planning."*

— WINSTON CHURCHILL

---

In looking at what it takes to LOVE your LIFE, the essence of my blog, it makes sense to me to look at some of the things that stop you from having a life that you LOVE, and I have grouped worry, risk and fear into this one post because I believe worry and fear overlap a great deal and directly impact one's willingness to take a risk. Failure is a huge topic in and of itself and I am going to hold the topic of failure for another day because while it is inherent in taking risks dealing with the subjects of fear, worry and taking risks is enough. The negative health impact on the human body for on-going or chronic worrying and fears is extensive. Worry and fear are two things that will stop you from having a live that you love so I am hopeful that I can help you start to deal with these things.

In general, we have a long list of things that we worry about or have fears about – and I will get to that shortly. Let's start by getting on the same page with the definitions of fear, risk and worry even if that seems totally unnecessary to you.

**Fear:** an unpleasant emotion caused by the belief that someone or something is dangerous, likely to cause pain or a threat.

**Risk:** noun: a situation involving exposure to danger (the possibility of suffering harm or injury); verb: to expose someone or something valued to danger, harm or loss.

**Worry**: noun: state of anxiety and uncertainty over actual or potential problems; verb: to give way to anxiety or unease; allow one's mind to dwell on difficulty or troubles.

According to a Time.com article from May 8, 2018, almost 40% of Americans were more anxious than in the previous year and about 18% of the population suffers from an anxiety disorder, which equates to about 40 million Americans. This is a topic that I have been discussing with close friends for more than 15 years, and as such I have great compassion for people who worry. I mean I understand that some people are just wired that way. I am grateful that I am not a worrier. I also believe that there are several things that you can do to deal with both worry and fear that will forward your life in a very powerful and meaningful way.

I wrote up a list of the more common things that people have worries or fears about. Look over the list and make a mental note on how many of the things you fear or worry over. Breathe this in. Seriously how many of these 31 things do you worry about or are you afraid of and how often? Just go through the list and pause and reflect.

**Worries/Fears:**

1. Not having enough money (financial security)
2. Health issues
3. Job security
4. Relationships: keeping one; finding one; losing one; repairing one
5. Housing issues
6. Retirement
7. Children: want/don't want/have/don't have/problems with/etc.
8. Parents/siblings: problems with; taking care of; etc.
9. World issues: all kinds of World issues and problems
10. Politics

*Love.Life.*

11. Health Insurance
12. Transportation: have it/don't have it/repairing it/replacing it/etc.
13. Worried/Fear of what people think of you
14. Worried/Fear of what people are saying about you
15. Worried/Fear are you good enough (inadequacy concerns)
16. The meaning or purpose of your life or lack thereof
17. Are you loved
18. About failure
19. Making friends or making new friends
20. Of being rejected
21. Of getting hurt
22. Of being betrayed
23. Of Divorce
24. Of Marriage
25. Of Death or dying
26. Of being judged negatively
27. Of change
28. Of losing control
29. Of uncertainty
30. Of the other shoe dropping (something bad happening)
31. FOMO (Fear of Missing Out)

Worry and fear take a huge toll on the human body. The health impacts are extensive enough that I am hopeful that you will consider the steps I cover later to help yourself deal with your worrying and fears. The following list is a compilation of all that I could find online about how worrying and fear negatively impact health from many different sources.

**Negative Health Impacts of Long-term worrying or fear:**

1. Raises blood pressure increasing your risk of heart disease
2. Depresses the immune system making you more susceptible to diseases including cancer

3. Stress (worrying/fear) changes your blood chemistry, which if chronic or on-going, can increase your risk of diabetes
4. Increases your risk for clinical depression
5. Impairs the formation of new fast-growing cells like bone and hair, which over a long period of time can contribute to baldness
6. Reduces your ability to form new memories and recall other memories
7. Depresses fertility
8. Muscle aches and pains
9. Extreme fatigue
10. Loss of libido
11. Upset stomach, ulcers and acid reflux
12. Breathing problems
13. Irritability
14. Headaches or migraines
15. Panic attacks
16. Irritable bowel problems
17. Sleep problems
18. Worsening of skin conditions like eczema
19. Backaches
20. Anxiety
21. Difficulty concentrating or making decisions

The negative impact of worrying and fear on your body is obviously significant to say the least. The above list is a comprehensive list and you might only get one or two of the impacts. Is it worth it? I don't know. I do think some people are addicted to worrying. Either that or they are unwilling to do the work necessary to break free of it. I share the Bob Newhart "Stop It" video from YouTube in an effort to bring some humor to this subject.

*Love.Life.*

## Bob Newhart "Stop It" Video on YouTube:

https://www.google.com/search?q=bob+newhart+stop+it+youtube+video&oq=Bob&aqs=chrome.0.69i59j69i57j0l5j69i61.1291j0j7&sourceid=chrome&ie=UTF-8

My children and I roared about this years ago. It is obviously poking fun at therapy – after all it is from a sitcom. If you watch it I do hope that you think it is funny. However, there is some validity to at times just telling yourself to stop it. I have some other ideas to help you deal with fear and worry if you keep reading.

One of the commodities that I do trade in is happiness! I am really skilled at generating my own happiness, which I wrote about recently in my blog post titled How to Generate Your Own Happiness & Why It's the Skill to Learn, February 13, 2020. The more your mind is filled with fears and worries the less room there is to be happy in my humble opinion.

## Dealing with Fears

I don't happen to believe that we have too much facility in the area of fear and dealing with our fears. That's an opinion not a fact but I do believe that there's enough evidence to support that statement. I am a firm believer that fear is a powerful emotion that stops us dead in our tracks unless or until we deal with whatever the fear is. So how do you deal with fear?

My reaction to fear is to identify what I am afraid of and get a solid mental picture in my mind. Then I go through the possible outcomes if the worst-case scenario happened. Could I live with and deal with the worst case happening? The answer is most always yes. It takes a conscious mind to deal with fear. Often times fear lurks around unidentified and unnamed. It's just there in the unspoken. That's not helpful.

While I have not counted it myself, I understand that the sources on the internet state that the Bible says some form of "be not afraid" about 365 times. So, if you happen to be religious then you can take the stance that God does not want you to worry or be afraid. God wants you to trust in HIM. And for some people that is not enough. I understand.

What is it that you are afraid of? What do you fear? Getting a handle on what you fear would be enormously helpful because then you can pull your fears apart like taffy and discover what is at the base of your fear. I assert that dealing with fear is a completely mental process that can be done. It might mean that you have to have a few conversations with friends, family or a good therapist. It might mean that you have to confront some belief system or attitude. It could mean a lot of things. Fear is what holds us back from many things. It holds us back from applying for a job you would love, from asking someone to join you for coffee, from moving, from ending a bad relationship, from starting a new relationship, from being your best self. Fear stops all of us from so many things.

It just doesn't have to be that way if you are willing to do the work to distinguish what you are afraid of and deal with the fear. Although I have not read it in over a decade or more, I recall that Napoleon Hill's book *Think and Grow Rich*, first published in 1937 and still in print today, had an entire chapter devoted to fear. If you have never read that book and are struggling with fear(s) I would suggest that might be a great book. It's an excellent book in general.

Sometimes fears are just not rationale. It would be powerful to determine if you had a fear that was not rationale. Having conversations about your fears could be a complete game changer in helping you sort it all out. It could be. It depends. While I wouldn't say that I am fearless, I tend to go do whatever I want in spite of my fears or in the face of my fears. Why? Because I want what I want. I have always had goals and a vision for my life even if some of those goals and visions were thwarted by circumstances. I believe that the more you take on creating your life the way that you want it to go and take the actions that align with that created life – the less fear will stop you. But that's just my opinion. Often fears show up when it comes to taking risks in life so let's briefly look at taking risks.

**Taking Risks**

*"Do one thing that scares you every day."*

— Eleanor Roosevelt

I just love that quote by Eleanor Roosevelt. What would life look like if you did that? It's hard to imagine! Some people are more wired to take risks. In thinking about this post, I thought of how businesses are wired to categorize and deal with risk of all kinds. While there are many, many types of risk, here are 4 types of general risk management:

- Avoidance (eliminate, withdraw from or not become involved)
- Reduction (optimize -mitigate)
- Sharing (transfer – outsource or insure)
- Retention (accept and budget)

In the business categories you can find strategic risk, compliance risk, operational risk, financial risk, and reputational risk. There are even scholarly articles about calculating risks. And in the financial investment world there are even more categories for risk.

Here's the question for you: how bad do you want X, Y, or Z? What would happen if you failed? Do you really care that much about what people think of you? What is holding you back? What is the benefit if you succeed? Which matters more – taking a risk or staying right where you are?

In college an amazing group of women and I started working to get a chapter of an International sorority on our campus. In the process the campus newspaper wanted to interview some of the girls who were planning on being in the sorority - if the sorority was ever approved by the Panhellenic Council. None of the women I was working with were willing to be interviewed by the newspaper, so I did the interview. As a result of my name being in the paper as associated with the group trying to start this new sorority, people started talking and laughing about me little did I know. Oh, no. I found out rather quickly when a waitress that I worked with at the Deli started talking to me while we were sweeping the floors – ABOUT ME! She started talking to me – about me!

I stopped her right away and told her that my last name was Lundy, to which she laughed and said no way. I insisted and she thought I was joking. Ultimately, she followed me to the time card machine where I pulled out my time card, which clearly read "Lisa Lundy". No, I don't know what she was about to say, but I am pretty clear it was not good. I later heard from a man on campus that everybody was laughing at me (okay my name was the only one in the paper so who else would they be laughing at) – until he said – you were successful then we stopped laughing.

Back in the day when I was a sales representative for Bausch & Lomb I had gotten a new sales manager and we had a travel day scheduled. On the appointed travel day I took him to my largest customer whose business I had grown enormously. The customer raved to my manager about how much more business they were transitioning over to Bausch & Lomb and how much she loved me. I mean this customer raved about me and the work I had done to win them over from the competition. My manager and I went to lunch with me pretty pleased with the sales call. My manager, however, proceeded to tear me to pieces. He was extremely unhappy, which was a mismatch for the sales call we had just experienced. Then it dawned on me – he didn't like me OR he just didn't want me in my job.

So, I took a risk – a reasonably big risk – and point blank asked him if he wanted me in my job. He said no that I was not well suited for the position and I would be better off somewhere else. Wow! Just wow! I had watched a former manager at Xerox Corporation get bruised and bloodied by a manager who didn't want him in the position he had – even though he was a superior manager so I knew how things would progress. When I got home that evening I put in a few phone calls to headhunters and got my resignation letter ready. I had a new job very shortly after my two weeks notice was up.

After the word got around to my teammates that I had resigned I received a phone call from a co-worker who asked what had happened because he knew that I was doing very well in the company and he was shocked. I told him what had happened and that I was unwilling to work for a sales manager who didn't want me in the job. Then this sales representative told me that this particular sales manager picked one sales rep per year to get rid of and that they had all lived in fear year after year about who was going to get it this year. Wow. I was shocked because I didn't know that about this manager. Can you imagine year after year being worried about whether your neck will be on the chopping block by such a manager? No. I just don't do life like that.

Sometime later I found out that my actions had a ripple effect and other sales reps working for this manager left the company as well. You have to be prepared for the consequences if you take a risk. In this case I was well aware of the consequences of asking a direct question just as much as I was aware of the consequences of being in a political battle with a manager who didn't want me in the job. No thanks. I like to go where I am wanted.

I like to think about taking risk as taking *calculated* risks. I like to look at the pros and cons of all of the different outcomes of a risk I am taking. I am taking a risk doing what I am doing right now. It might work out or it might not. Believer as I am in the self-fulfilling prophecy, I am confident that it will work out very well for me. And I have a plan B. I am not throwing all caution to the wind and risking everything. You can't get huge rewards without taking some risks.

There is power and freedom in being able to be able to live your life without being held back by what other people think of you. I remember Dr. Phil saying on one of his shows to a guest – if you knew how little time other people spent thinking about you – you wouldn't really care what they thought of you. There's a fine line or a boundary. I am not talking about disregarding people who really love you and care about you expressing a concern. I am talking about not giving up on actions that support the life you are creating. Calculating the risk versus return on investment (ROI).

It's just my belief that anything worthwhile – anything of value has inherent risk involved. That is clearly true in the business world. I say it is also true in the area of love and friendships. You can get burned in a friendship or in a love relationship. That's a fact. You can also experience deep connectedness, love, companionship, laughter, and beautiful moments. I just happen to believe that LOVE is worth it. Love is worth the risk. I say that having been burned in a pretty huge way actually more than one time. Huge is not enough to cover it. But I believe LOVE always wins. It is the emotion that lights me up and calls me to be. It is what life is about in the world according to me.

It seems to me that to be able to take some level of risk you have to be able to calm your fears and worries. Here are some ideas to get you moving out of the world of fear and worry and into the world of taking risks and moving your life forward.

## 15 Ways to Overpower Fear & Worry & Start Taking Risks

1. Name and own any worries or fears that you have. Be specific. Have no shame in having them. Just own up to them.
2. Have a plan you are actively executing to move your life forward.
3. Be present! Live in the NOW.
4. What action(s) can be taken to address the worry or fear? Make a list. Take the action(s) appropriate to deal with the situation.
5. Employ the habits and practices to use your time very well

so you are doing what you love and want to be doing and don't have time to worry or be afraid.
6. Make yourself signs or reminders if you need to. They can be very effective.
7. Discuss your worry and fears with close friends or family. Get supported.
8. Remember the self-fulfilling prophecy: Write out your beautiful outcome and story – on paper. Be specific and think big. After all, it's your story.
9. Read success stories to inspire yourself.
10. See your success in your mind – visualize it like professional athletes do. See yourself crossing the finish line of your story.
11. If you catch yourself having a worrisome or fearful thought then take an immediate action to counterbalance the worrisome or fearful thought. That could be an action that moves your life powerfully forward. It could be a phone call to a friend for support. Counterbalance any negative thoughts immediately.
12. Make sure you are getting the proper amount of sleep and good quality sleep as that is helpful to the body, mind and spirit.
13. Boost your nutrition while you are working to stomp out worry and fear as that can be confronting like most change is. Any positive change in your nutrition will be helpful.
14. When you are working on personal growth and development, which can be confronting, try going for a walk or getting some exercise as that will help relieve any stress. While exercise is very good for the body at any given time, it's especially helpful when you are working on mental challenges.
15. Growth and development! Of course, this makes the list because the rewards are so extensive. See my past post titled: Top 45 Ways that Personal Growth & Development Will Help You Have a Life You Love, November 29, 2019.

Work on yourself because that will help you in so many ways!

## Concluding Thoughts

> *"Happy is the man who has broken the chains which hurt the mind, and has given up worry once and for all."*
>
> — Ovid

Worrying and having fears can have an extremely negative impact on your health. Some people are more prone to worrying and being fearful than others. Regardless if you have a propensity to worry or not, there are habits and practices that will help you stop worrying and being afraid. One of the best practices it to have a plan for your life and be actively engaged in forwarding your life. That puts you in the driver's seat and you won't be sitting around worrying or having doubts and fears because you are actively engaged in creating your life.

If you are not used to actively creating your life then it might feel a bit foreign or awkward but those feelings will pass as you start doing what it takes to have a life that you love. How can I help you have a life that you LOVE? How can I help you have a life that you wake up to every day and say – really? I get to live THIS Life? I want you to be happy and healthy and enjoying every day. How can I support you in your journey? Let me know!

## Is Low Self-Esteem Stealing Love, Joy & Happiness from Your Life? Top 29 Tips For Boosting Self-Esteem Like a Boss

March 6, 2020

Self-esteem is all the rage these days and has been for some time now. How do you know if you have high or low self-esteem? What does it really mean and why is it important? Well, according to the research, self-esteem has a strong relationship to happiness! Happiness and loving your life are my thing so it is important to understand those things that can undermine happiness, love and joy. Low self-esteem, I assert strongly, is one of those things that sucks love, joy and happiness from your life. I will give you the really, really great news up front. Self-esteem is something that you can impact so if you have low self-esteem you are by no means stuck with it! Keep reading!

Many years ago, a friend and I were discussing self-esteem and whether or not either one of us had low self-esteem. She knew that I had occasions now and then to talk to a therapist and she asked me to ask the therapist, if I got the chance, about low self-esteem. One day I got the chance and I asked about low self-esteem. The therapist roared with laughter and said immediately: "Who are you asking for?" I was taken aback and not prepared for this response. I casually said that I was asking for myself because I didn't want to admit that I was asking for a friend. The therapist laughed even harder saying again, "Who are you really asking for?"

So, I copped to the fact that I was asking for a friend. Then he stopped laughing and said, that it was clear that I didn't have low self-esteem so it had to be for someone else that I was asking the question for. He went onto explain by giving me an example that went like this:

*A husband comes home from work and is in an angry huff. The wife seeing her husband's behavior upon arriving home immediately thinks to herself that she should have worn a different outfit or she should have cooked something else for dinner or perhaps cleaned up the house a bit more.*

Upon hearing the above example, it was my turn to laugh hard. No! That's definitely not me. I would never think like that. It would never occur to me to think like that. That exchange was so shocking to me that it lives as something that I will possibly never forget. That is a completely foreign way of thinking for me, yet it is commonplace for many people in our society.

Before I get into low self-esteem, let me provide you with a compiled list of the characteristics or traits of someone with high self-esteem, which should give you a good basis for comparison as you read further. Here I am talking about high self-esteem, which is different than someone who is self-actualized – that is an entirely different subject (for another day).

## **Characteristics and Traits of People with High Self-Esteem:**

1. Love meeting people
2. Have the courage to express themselves
3. Have lives full of adventures
4. Don't care about other people think of them
5. Are nicer to be around
6. Have a belief in themselves and their abilities
7. Willing to accept failures
8. Respect the differences in other people
9. Have healthy relationships
10. Look for people who respect them and that they respect in return
11. Self-confident
12. Have an internal peace
13. Seek continuous self-improvement
14. Accept themselves unconditionally (self-love; self-acceptance)
15. Take responsibility for their own lives
16. Tolerate frustrations well
17. Willing to take calculated risks

18. Loving and Loveable
19. Self-directed
20. Assertive
21. Natural curiosity
22. Love challenges
23. Eager to learn new things
24. Able to express emotions
25. Spontaneous
26. Competitive with themselves not with other people
27. Can handle both positive and negative emotions
28. They are always willing to help other people
29. Less susceptible to social pressures
30. Capable of forming satisfying love relationships
31. Happier with life

Low self-esteem can be found in all types of people including very successful professionals across all employment fields. It is not limited to one socioeconomic category. Some years ago, when I was working with my children, I did extensive research to find all of the signs and symptoms of low self-esteem. What surprised me was that low self-esteem was not like depression where there is an agreed upon list of criteria for what constitutes depression. Low self-esteem was all over the board. Because of that I compiled every sign and symptom that I could find into one massive list.

As we all know I am not a therapist or medical professional in any capacity, this list is simply that – a list of what is said to be a sign or a symptom of low self-esteem. It seems from my research one of the more noticeable signs or symptoms is being sensitive to criticism, or perceived criticism, and being hypervigilant to signs of rejection or perceived signs of rejection. Individuals with low self-esteem can perceive criticism, rejection, rebuff, or disapproval when there isn't any.

Before I get into the signs and symptoms, let me share with you the negative impact that low self-esteem can have on you. This is a compiled list with everything I could find online about the negative effects it has on people.

**Negative Impact of Low Self-Esteem:**

1. Interpret non-critical comments as critical
2. Increased anxiety
3. Increased stress
4. Loneliness
5. Increases chance of depression
6. Causes problems in platonic friendships
7. Causes problems in romantic relationships
8. Can impair academic success
9. Can hinder job performance
10. Negative feelings
11. Self-loathing
12. Obsessed with being perfect
13. Lowered resilience (harder to recover from setbacks)
14. Feeling powerless
15. Leads to increased vulnerability to drug and alcohol abuse

The above list is not going to give you a happy life. The above impacts of low self-esteem are not going to help you have a LIFE that you LOVE. The negative impacts of low self-esteem are counter to what you want going on in your life. Here's two tools to help you determine where you are with self-esteem.

In the 1960's sociologist Morris Rosenberg developed a self-esteem scale, which can be found online in the form of a simple test that can even be scored electronically. Here is a link to one such test: https://wwnorton.com/college/psych/psychsci/media/rosenberg.htm. This is an online test you can take and score in a few seconds. Just make sure you read each question fully before answering.

Alternatively, you could look over this list and see how many of these signs and symptoms you have.

## Signs and Symptoms of Low Self-Esteem:

1. Sensitive to criticism or perceived criticism
2. Social withdrawal
3. Hostility
4. Excessive preoccupation with personal problems
5. Negative thoughts and/or self-critical thoughts
6. Inability to handle praise
7. Condescending or puts other people down
8. Controlling personality (instead of empowering others)
9. Can't say no
10. Being indecisive
11. Blames others (instead of taking responsibility for one's actions)
12. Overly apologetic
13. Doesn't stand up for him or herself
14. Gives up too easily
15. Aiming too low or avoiding challenges
16. Chronically comparing yourself to others
17. Easily depressed
18. Ruin your own fun or good times
19. Claim everything is luck
20. You buy things you don't like
21. You tell really dumb lies (and then wonder why)
22. Pessimism
23. Exaggeration
24. Lack of boundaries
25. Overly concerned about others opinions of you
26. Timid behavior
27. Absence of assertiveness
28. Pretend to be someone that you are not (Pretense)
29. Non-conformist/Anti-social behaviors

30. Rebellious behaviors
31. Lack of generosity
32. Material outlook (judging others by what material goods they have or don't have)
33. Doubting yourself
34. Thinking that other people treat you badly because you somehow deserve it
35. Competitiveness
36. Perfectionism
37. Alienation (alienating others)
38. Procrastination
39. Anxiety and emotional turmoil
40. Eating disorders
41. Overthinking
42. Workaholic
43. Over or Under achieving
44. Disliking people in general
45. You have self-limiting beliefs
46. Difficulty being in the present moment
47. Shame

**Phrases used by people with low self-esteem:**

1. I can't
2. It's impossible
3. I hate the way I look
4. I'm not good enough
5. I'm not worth it
6. I can't say no
7. I'm not as good as...
8. I don't deserve...
9. I'm sorry
10. I can't decide

If you compare the characteristics and traits of someone with high self-esteem to the signs and symptoms of someone with low self-esteem, it should be pretty clear which of the two most people would prefer. The good news as I mentioned in the beginning is that low self-esteem is something that you can change – over time with some effort on your part. You want to have a happy life that you LOVE living! At least that is my intention here. Why not? What are you waiting for? I have listed some of the best ways to start your journey on moving up the scale of self-esteem. You can get there. I know that you can. I am positive you can do this.

**Top 29 Tips for Boosting Self-Esteem Like a Boss:**

1. Practice loving yourself AND your imperfections.
2. Make a plan for your future that makes you happy and inspired. See my post titled: Road Map for Creating a Life that YOU LOVE. September 2019.
3. Start using your time to forward the plan you have for your life. See my post titled: LOVE the TIME of YOUR LIFE – September 12, 2019.
4. Engage in personal growth and development like it matters. See my post titled: Top 45 Ways that Personal Growth & Development Will Help You Have a Life You Love, November 29, 2019.
5. Make signs and place them around your living space. For example: "I am good enough." Or "I don't have to be perfect." Or "I am loved and valued." Signs really work.
6. Volunteer someplace. Hopefully somewhere that would make you feel happy.
7. Practice gratitude.
8. Hobbies. I have written extensively on this. See my post titled: How Hobbies Can Help You Love Your Life and the Top 23 Reasons You Should Hobby Up, December 11, 2019.
9. Figure out what makes you happy and sprinkle your life with that. No kidding. Bring intentionality to your daily living.

10. Practice Self-Care. This is important and I have written about this in my post titled: Self-Mastery, Self-Motivation, & Self-Care: The Holy Grail of Happiness & Joy, January 30, 2020.
11. Recognize that this is a process. Rome was not built in a day nor will you go from having low self-esteem to high self-esteem overnight. Have compassion for yourself that you even recognize that you do or might have low self-esteem. That's a good starting point.
12. Learn to manage your thoughts. Replace any negative self-talk with life-affirming positive thoughts.
13. Manage your integrity like it matters because it does. Integrity is a muscle that will help you feel better and make progress in every area of your life. See my post titled: The Sheer Joy and Magic of Integrity, October 9, 2019.
14. Don't skimp on your sleep. It's very important to your overall well-being, which is critical as you work on raising your self-esteem.
15. Increase your nutrition any way that you can. Every little bit helps. See my post titled: The Ultimate Consumer Guide to Nutrition, Why It Matters and How It Could Save or Change your Life, October 29, 2019.
16. Try doing affirmations. They can work wonders.
17. Take a page from professional and Olympic athletes and visualize you living your dream life. See it in your mind. If you can see it and believe it – you can achieve it or so the saying goes. I firmly believe that is true.
18. As for help, support or coaching or a mentor!
19. Really get to work on being present! You can't be in your head if you are really being present in the moment.
20. Make it a point to play and have fun. Laugh as much as you can.
21. Exercise is good for the body and it will definitely help you if you have low self-esteem. Remember that walking is a very effective form of exercise.

22. Read or watch inspiring materials. Stay away from negative, depressing or dark material.
23. Make up your mind about how your life is going to go moving forward – and be rigorous and relentless in your pursuit of happiness and joy. Don't let anything stop you from having a happy and beautiful life.
24. Determine if you need therapy. If so, get going.
25. Get out there and socialize because that is a great way to boost your feelings. Read my post for more detailed benefits about socializing: 21 Reasons Why Making Friends Will Help You LOVE Your Life & 17 Ways to Make New Friends, December 3, 2019.
26. Spend 15 minutes a day doing something to improve your life. Go for a walk – preferably outside. Clean up your living space or car. Get rid of stuff you don't use or need. Find something to do for 15 minutes a day to improve your life and that will equal over 91 hours in a year. That's a lot of time!!
27. Pray or meditate.
28. Dress and groom yourself every day! You will look and feel so much better!
29. Get a partner who wants to work on their self-esteem or their life and support each other. It will be a lot more fun than doing it alone!

**Concluding Thoughts:**

On the road to having a life that you LOVE, low self-esteem is one of the show stoppers that can rob you of love, joy and happiness. Yet, even if you have low self-esteem right now, it is not something that you are stuck with. There are plenty of things that you can do on a daily basis that over time will completely transform your life. If you spent 15 minutes a day working on your life or yourself then in a year you will have spent 91 hours forwarding or improving your life. That is significant. That is so doable! Everyone has 15 minutes that they can spare. The question is are you willing to have a life that you LOVE?

We are all works in progress. While some people are stuck in the past or have no traction to move forward, it is possible for anyone to create a life that they love over time. Helping people live their best life with LOVE, Joy and Happiness is one of my passions. What is holding you back in life? What support do you need? How can I help you? There is no time like the present to take command of your life and start doing the things that are necessary for you to be happy and have a powerful life you LOVE. That is what I want for all of you – sheer love, joy and happiness. Let me know how I can help you get there.

## Deep Dive into Emotional Pain and How to Use It to Your Advantage

September 8, 2020

Being alive and being human involves emotional pain because that is simply a part of life. There are so many reasons and causes for emotional pain. What seems clear to me is that we are just not that good at dealing with emotional pain. Emotional pain has skyrocketed with the pandemic as it often does when there is a natural disaster or some other catastrophic event. What is powerful for us as people is to be able to identify when we are feeling emotional pain and then developing the skills, habits and practices that allow us to successfully get through the emotional pain in a healthy way. By far the best thing to do with emotional pain is to use it to your advantage to grow, develop and become a better person because of it. In the meantime, while you are gaining skills in how to do that it is really important that you bump up your self-care.

Learning how to deal with emotional pain is a skill you can learn that is a priceless gift you give not only yourself but also to those who are in your life. Emotional pain can be intertwined with depression, anxiety, low self-esteem, overwhelm and many other states or conditions. When you are in emotional pain it can be exceptionally difficult to get motivated, which is why I recommend a personal reward system and working on self-mastery. Speaking of reward, I am giving away FREE stuff for the next 11 months in my Year of Freedom Giveaway so please be sure to enter to win a prize! I promise that I won't be bombarding you with emails because I don't have time for that.

While we are talking about emotional pain it is worth mentioning that being angry, resentful, hating someone or something takes a lot more energy than love, forgiveness and compassion, which underscores the significance and importance of doing the emotional work – processing your feelings – so you can be freed up and live life with your whole heart.

What is immensely helpful during periods of emotional pain is if you have a belief in God. When times are hard it is not unusual for people to turn to God. Faith in God can be very comforting for people when times are tough even non-believers have found comfort in prayer and having faith.

**Possible Causes or Sources of Emotional Pain:**

1. Death of a loved one
2. Loss of a job, relationship, house, money, etc.
3. Watching someone endure a difficult situation
4. Pandemics
5. Catastrophes of any kind (weather, accidents, etc.)
6. Loss of purpose
7. Divorce or relationship break-ups
8. Health problems
9. Friendships that end
10. Being betrayed, lied to or cheated on
11. High stress situations
12. Thinking you have inadequacies
13. Failing at something important
14. Loss of a pet

15. Feeling powerless
16. Not having friends or enough friends (or good friends)
17. Knowing you hurt someone or caused another pain
18. Feeling guilty for your actions
19. Feeling rejected
20. Feeling like you don't have control over your life
21. Not feeling connected to people or life
22. Loss of hope
23. Feeling wounded by someone or some event
24. Having a high amount of negative thoughts
25. Certain depressive conditions or anxiety disorders
26. Unfulfilled expectations
27. The death of a dream
28. Not allowing yourself to experience the good things life has to offer you

**Special Kinds of Emotional Pain:**

It is worth pointing out or distinguishing that there are a few situations that are life changing and typically cause a special kind of emotional pain that can be different from the normal emotional pain. These situations will most often require extra effort to process the pain and move through the emotions.

1. Death of a child
2. Suicide of a family member, friend or someone significant
3. Death of a sibling
4. Death of a parent

## Feelings Associated with Emotional Pain:

I am providing this list because some people have not gotten cued into when they are in emotional pain. This list gives you some indicators that you are likely dealing with some level of emotional pain.

1. Loss
2. Sadness
3. Isolation
4. Rejection
5. Failure
6. Anger
7. Betrayal
8. Grief
9. Feeling wounded
10. Despair
11. Loneliness
12. Depressed
13. Hopelessness
14. Helplessness
15. Despondent
16. Worried
17. Terrified
18. Bitter/Resentful
19. Abandoned
20. Left out
21. Destroyed
22. Crushed
23. Humiliated
24. Confused
25. Nervous
26. Exposed
27. Shamed
28. Neglected
29. Abused
30. Anguished
31. Horrified

32. Paralyzed
33. Wrecked
34. Reeling
35. Shocked
36. Tortured
37. Crippled
38. Inferior
39. Washed up
40. Desperate
41. Disgraced
42. Judged
43. Seething
44. Devalued
45. Crestfallen
46. Downhearted
47. Miserable
48. Tearful
49. Upset
50. Anxiety

## Some of the Ways People Often Cope with Emotional Pain:

1. Substance abuse (alcohol or drugs)
2. Self-harm
3. Denial
4. Shopping (retail therapy)
5. Overeating
6. Not taking care of themselves
7. Crying
8. Complaining
9. Blaming
10. Justifying

11. Abuse others: bullying, shaming, emotional, psychological or physical abuse
12. Hoarding
13. Self-medicating
14. Anger/Rage and however that manifests
15. Being mean or rude to other people
16. Addictions of any kind, which covers a lot of territory

## Physical Manifestations that COULD mean Emotional Pain:

These things *do not* automatically mean that someone is in emotional pain by any means. That being said, it is not entirely unusual for a person to do these things when they are in emotional pain.

1. Cutting your hair or growing your hair
2. Growing a beard or facial hair
3. Getting a tattoo or piercing
4. Gaining or losing weight
5. Coloring your hair
6. Not taking care of yourself
7. Making sudden or drastic changes, which can include a lot of things

## The Relationship Between Emotional Pain and Physical Pain

According to Susanne Babbel, MFT, Ph.D., a psychologist specializing in trauma induced depression, studies have shown that chronic pain might not only be caused by physical injury but also by stress and emotions, which was first published April 8, 2010 on PsychologyToday.com. Case Western Reserve University has research demonstrating that heartbreak can take a toll on your IQ with a drop by 30% in reasoning and a 25% decrease in IQ after exposure to rejection. And there is more evidence that your emotional pain be causing physical pain in your body.

Dr. John Sarno, Jr. was a Professor of Rehabilitation Medicine, New York University School of Medicine, and attending physician at the Howard A. Rusk Institute of Rehabilitation Medicine, New York University Medical Center, who wrote and spoke about pain being in your head. Dr. Sarno developed methods for treating patients with pain to alleviate their pain without surgery or other interventions, which you can read a good summary about here. Dr. Sarno also wrote several books before he passed away one day shy of his 94th birthday. There is even a film documentary about Dr. Sarno titled *All the Rage: Saved by Sarno*, which will give you insights about how and why his patients felt like they were saved by Dr. Sarno. It is quite fascinating to see the growing body of research and evidence that physical pain in the body can be caused by emotions and trauma.

The mind-body connection is not just a theory anymore as you can read about in this research piece. If you simply do an internet search on "books on the mind body connection" you will find a rich plethora of books on the subject available. I personally am a firm believer that pain will show up in the body due to emotional pain, unresolved feelings or trauma. It's my personal experience and one of the reasons that I don't have any pain in my body, usually, because I do the emotional work necessary to make sure that I am pain free. In my humble opinion, if you have chronic or intermittent pain in your physical body, it would be worth exploring the relationship between emotional pain and pain in the body or the mind body connection. Or you don't have to. No one is going to make you. It's your choice.

## How You Can Use Your Emotional Pain to Your Advantage

I am an absolute believer and fan of using emotional pain to learn, to grow and to become a better person otherwise known as using emotional pain to your advantage. Pain can leave you bitter, angry, resentful, sorrowful and so much more on the negative side, which really adds nothing to your quality of life. Pain can be a great teacher. The question is what is the lesson to be learned.

Some people focus on the question *why* did this happen to me. From my vantage point the better question is how can I grow from this? What can I learn from this? How can I use this to become a better person? And the lessons might not always be what you think they should be. Let me give a few examples of painful events and the growth and development that happened as a result.

## Example 1: Deep Betrayal & Exploitation

Without giving specifics (Haha, although I would love to) I experienced a situation that involved deep betrayal and exploitation over a long period of time. Of course, it was very painful. Because of this experience:

- My virtues were polished.
- My understanding of narcissism grew from nothing to a good understanding.
- I learned a lot about psychopaths and the Psychopath Check List (PCL-R & SV).
- I learned more about myself and the ways that I could be exploited, used or betrayed
- I became more educated about mental health issues that some people have.
- My prayer life expanded.
- I came to see who I really am and who I have been for my entire life.
- It increased my resilience, fortitude, and Grace.
- I chose to love, trust, be vulnerable and not let that experience taint me or change the person I was and have always been.

**Example 2: Death of My Firstborn Child**

My daughter passed in utero when I was six months pregnant. I was stunned to hear that I would have to deliver her and then later either bury her or have her cremated. That was the law at the time. I have her ashes that will be buried with me when I pass because I refused to bury her in a cemetery that I would not be able to visit since I was likely to be moving. Her DNA, chromosomes and placenta were are free of any abnormalities – just as normal and perfect as could be so they could not provide me with a reason for her death. Yes, that was so very painful. Having pictures of your baby that you can't show people because she is discolored not to mention deceased. Here is how I grew from this:

- My appreciation for life increased (in part because they said I would not make it through the delivery and to call my parents to come to the town I lived in to say goodbye in case I didn't make it).
- My understanding of the grief process grew.
- My ability to function in the midst of great sadness and still be happy and find some joy in life grew a lot.
- My compassion for people turning away from me because I was experiencing a painful event grew. Some people just can't deal with other peoples' pain.
- My research in to health and wellness grew.
- My coping mechanisms and resilience grew a great deal.

**Example 3: Workplace Bullying of My Boss**

Very early in my professional career in sales working for a fortune 500 company, my immediate boss came under political attack for no good reason as happens in all kinds of organizations from time to time. I stood up for him not just because he was a good man, but also because he was an extraordinary leader, consummate professional and amazing sales manager. I knew that there would be consequences for openly standing up for my boss at work. I knew that. And I did it anyway. He ended up getting a two-level promotion over the individual who was doing the political bashing at the end of the debacle. My boss offered to create a job for me so I would not have to endure the backlash that we both knew was coming however I chose to stay and learn what there was to learn. Here's how I used that to my advantage:

- Grew in my abilities to recognize workplace bullying and political games, which would be extremely valuable later on in my career.
- Grew in my abilities to be resilient and resourceful.
- Learned a lot about how some people will sit by and allow terrible, awful things – unjust things- happen and do nothing about that. That was a shock to my young self.
- I learned that even if you are right and completely justified sometimes you just have to walk away from bad people doing bad things.
- My coping mechanisms grew and developed.

**Example 4: Workplace Sexual Harassment**

Later in my sales career I was sexually harassed and physically threatened by my immediate supervisor while on the job. After I filed a complaint with the company, also a fortune 500 company, I was given the choice to get back in a car with the man who had been sexually harassing me and had physically threatened me or resign. Humm. What do you think I did? I resigned. Of note, after I filed an EEOC complaint I learned through the process that the company had received the exact same complaint about my supervisor from another female sales representative SIX months before I had filed my complaint. Here's how I used this to my advantage:

- I took a further deep dive into the nasty world of corporate politics, which was educational and a bit shocking.
- I further grew my coping mechanisms and ability to function during difficult times.
- I saw again the number of people who would cower and shake and lie rather than do the right thing and tell the truth because they were afraid of losing their jobs. It was very sad to see people who didn't have the backbone to do the right thing.
- I grew in my self-awareness and emotional skills.

If you are willing to use your emotional pain to your advantage then you are entering into the world of growth and development, which has significant benefits outlined here. It's all too common that people don't deal with their emotional pain or they are left disempowered, damaged, or somehow wounded by their pain. Don't get me wrong here, emotional pain is hard. Emotional pain is painful. Yet it doesn't have to ruin or wreck your life if you are willing to do the work and learn from your experiences.

It's my personal belief system that every difficult or painful event can teach us, help us grow, help us become better versions of ourselves if we are willing. It's a choice. What can you learn from your emotional pain that furthers your life instead of setting you back, closing you down, or leaving you otherwise disempowered? I don't know what that is for you. I assert that if you started talking to people you could discover what life is trying to teach you.

**How to Process Emotional Pain:**

1. Identify – Identify that you are in emotional pain.
2. Pinpoint the causes or sources of your emotional pain because there can be multiple sources or causes at any given point in time.

3. Feel the feelings – in your body and heart. Allow yourself to feel instead of covering it up, denying it, self-medicating or any other strategy that numbs the pain.
4. Give words or language to how you are feeling – the feeling words in this post should help you pinpoint how you might be feeling.
5. Don't make yourself feel bad or guilty for having the feelings that you are having.
6. Assess: Is your reaction reasonable? Would most people feel the way that you do? Look for reactions that are more significant or magnified that might point to some underlying feelings or causes missed in the previous step. Sometimes the cause of emotional pain is hidden or masked by something. If the magnitude of your feelings is out of range of what most people would likely feel then stop and examine the situation looking for other reasons why your feelings might be exacerbated.
7. Bump up your self-care immediately the moment that you recognize that you are feeling emotional pain.
8. Take the actions dictated or necessary based on whatever is happening.
9. Recognize that this is a process and it takes time.
10. Ask for help.
11. Seek counseling if needed.
12. Do things that bring happiness and joy to your life while you are moving through the emotional pain.
13. Socialize, which can be done with the current constraints, because it is good for your heart and dealing with emotional pain.
14. Hobby up.
15. Volunteer if you have time on your hands.
16. Get a life plan or vision for your life and start taking actions to have the life that you love.

## Actions You Can Take While You Are Processing Your Emotions:

1. Journal – write down your feelings and thoughts.
2. Listen to music appropriate to your mood.
3. Call a friend and tell them you need a pick me up call.
4. Clean out your sock drawer, closet, cabinets – clean out anything.
5. Do something nice for someone you know.
6. Go for a walk.
7. Take a nap.
8. Start planning something that you can look forward to.
9. Set some attainable goals and start taking the actions to meet those goals.
10. Reward yourself for every good thing you do to help yourself get through it.
11. Create a vision for your life (this may be counter-intuitive, but it works).
12. Make a list of things that make you happy and start doing them.
13. Make self-care part of your daily routine.
14. Practice Gratitude.
15. Live in the present – in the now!
16. Don't take it personally.
17. Have compassion for yourself – after all, you are dealing with emotional pain.
18. Pray or meditate.

## Call to Action:

We live in a world where emotional pain is inescapable unless you wall yourself off and become void of emotions. What is valuable, powerful and healthy is to acknowledge when you are feeling emotional pain and learn to process, deal with and manage your emotional pain in a healthy and productive way. Yes, emotional pain is terrible. There's no disputing that. No one likes emotional pain. Yet, there is it. What can you do today to begin dealing with any emotional pain you have? Are you using your emotional pain to your advantage? Do you need help in figuring out how to use your pain to your advantage or what the lesson is? Who do you know who is dealing with emotional pain? Would this post be helpful to them? If so, would you share it with them? How can I help you deal with your emotional pain? Please let me know in the comment section because I care deeply about you having a happy and healthy life!

**Here's How to Ditch Loneliness and Isolation for Good**

September 16, 2020

## The Common Nature of Loneliness and Isolation

Feeling lonely or isolated has been an issue that has plagued mankind since the beginning of time according to the research. Feelings of loneliness or isolation fall under the umbrella of dealing with emotional pain and can lead to or be sourced by depression, low self-esteem, feeling overwhelmed with life or a number of physical or environmental changes taking place in your life. It's one of many topics that we simply don't talk about. Not talking about loneliness or feeling isolated doesn't help or change things. One of my personal goals is to help you boost your happiness and ability to function well in life, therefore it's critical that you understand the ins and outs of loneliness and isolation, the impact on health, and the tips that will help you decrease the amount of time you spend feeling lonely or isolated – meaning the actions that you can take to minimize feeling lonely or isolated. Shameless plug – don't forget to enter my FREE giveaway in the Year of Freedom to win some cool stuff – why not?

Let's get on the same page with the definition of lonely: sadness because one has no friends or company. Isolated is defined as: having minimal contact or little in common with others. Interestingly the definition of isolated lists words like lonely, lonesome, unreachable and cutoff. Feeling lonely or isolated is not fun, cool, or good in anyway, yet it is extremely common. You can definitely feel alone even when you are with a group of people, which means that you can feel lonely even if you are with a person or group of people. Being alone – all by yourself – doesn't necessarily mean that you are feeling lonely. These are two different concepts and people can be alone without feeling lonely or conversely you could be with people yet feel very alone or lonely.

> *"The most terrible poverty is loneliness, and the feeling of being unloved."*
>
> — MOTHER TERESA

Of all of the populations, Generation Z (meaning young people from ages 18 to 22) comes out as the loneliest and claim to be in worse health than older generations. Forty-six percent of Americans report either sometimes or always feeling alone or left out. Only roughly half of Americans are reported to have meaningful in-person social interactions. Is it any wonder why suicide is the 10th leading cause of death? Suicide increased by 33% in America from 1999 to 2017. This increase in suicide point to the increasing unhappiness, loneliness and isolation people feel.

First off, every human being experiences feelings of loneliness or isolation from time to time. It's just part of being human. There is nothing wrong with you if you feel lonely or isolated or both. You are NOT a failure if you feel lonely or isolated. There is absolutely NO reason for you to feel embarrassed or ashamed if you feel lonely or isolated. As I just listed, you are in very good company. I am having this conversation or blog post so that you can have a breakthrough in this area. Loneliness and feelings of isolation don't feel good and aren't good for your health at all, which is a good reason to soak in the content of this post and then take the actions required to put an end to those feelings. Feelings of loneliness or isolation

*Love.Life.*

could mean is that it's time to make some changes in your life. You can use these feelings as a springboard for change. So why are we feeling so lonely and isolated?

## Why Are We So Lonely and Disconnected?

1. **Changes in the nuclear family** – it's no longer like the *Walton's* on TV with a whole family living together including the grandparents all loving and supporting each other. No, family members are scattered across the country or sometimes not even in the same country. This change in and of itself leads to loneliness and isolation because you are separated from your family members.
2. **Social Media** – There is no question that instead of gathering around someone's dining room table for laughter, fun and food that people of all ages are glued to their social media feed. Some of the research indicates that this is not helpful when people compare themselves to others and end up feeling like their life doesn't measure up to what they see on their friend's social media.
3. **On-line gaming** – Gone are the days of meeting at the corner gaming place to play pinball or other electronic games. Now people can play on-line without ever leaving their home. While there are sandbox games and ways that people can game with others in an online community, it is not the same as being in the physical presence of other people.
4. **Cell phones and apps** – Look around at people out in public and instead of talking to strangers and having pleasant conversations people are glued to their cell phones whether they are talking, playing games or doing some app or another. Clearly cell phone technology has amazing benefits, yet it disconnects people that could meet and become friends.
5. **Lack of Knowing How to Make Friends or Get**

**Connected:** We have a generation of young people who were never exposed to the social graces of how to make friends, talk to strangers and develop deep, meaningful friendships.

6. **Independence valued over Dependence:** We live in a culture where independence is highly valued over the interconnectedness of being in a nuclear family, a.k.a. the Walton's, where there was always someone there to help, cheer you on and provide support. People are reluctant to ask for help, share their feelings or be vulnerable.
7. **On-line shopping** – How much interaction is necessary for on-line shopping? The convenience is fantastic yet it cuts us off from social interactions and developing relationships with retailers. Back in the day people actually had relationships with the shop keepers, bankers, butcher and other business owners.
8. **Experiencing a broken heart:** divorce, death, breakups can be a big cause for loneliness and feeling isolated. There is nothing that ramps up feelings of loneliness or isolation like a broken heart. This is more common now with the breakdown of the nuclear family unit.
9. **Geographic move to a new area** – Moving and having to make new friends in a new town is a big cause for loneliness and isolation. Frequent moves can have an impact on a person's willingness to make the effort.
10. **Job changes** – Changing jobs can also be a source of losing connections and longtime co-workers causing feelings of loneliness and isolation until new relationships are established.
11. **Changes in the relationship status/family status of your friends or family**. If your friends get married, start a family, or experience some other change, which impacts their ability to spend time with you that could leave you feeling lonely and isolated.
12. **Lack of a spouse, intimate partner, companion or roommate** – Not having a roommate, spouse, partner or

companion can be a big source of loneliness and isolation especially since more people are living alone than in previous decades.
13. **The Over Scheduling of Kids** – Some parents over schedule their children with so many activities that there is simply little room for playing with their friends cutting them off from learning the valued skills of how to have and maintain friendships.

## Negative Health Consequences of Loneliness & Social Isolation:

1. It heightens health risks as much as smoking 15 cigarettes a day or having an alcohol disorder according to the research.
2. It is twice as harmful to both physical health and mental health as obesity.
3. It increases a person's risk of premature death from all causes for every race.
4. It is associated with a 50% increased risk of dementia.
5. Poor social relationships, meaning loneliness or social isolation, is associated with a 29% increased risk of heart disease and a 32% increased risk of stroke.
6. Loneliness is associated with higher rates of depression, anxiety and suicide.
7. Loneliness in heart failure patients was associated with a nearly 4 fold increased risk of death, 68% increased risk of hospitalization, and a 57% increased risk of emergency room visits.
8. It increases depression.
9. It causes poor sleep quality.
10. It impairs the executive functioning of the brain, which can impact the working memory, flexible thinking and self-control.

11. It speeds up cognitive decline.
12. It causes poor cardiovascular function.
13. It impairs the immune system at every stage of life.
14. It contributes to child abuse when the abuser is lonely.
15. It contributes to personality disorders.

## Signs that Could Point to Loneliness

These items do not automatically indicate loneliness but they could be a sign of potential loneliness.

1. They spend a lot of time alone.

2. They are unproductive.

3. They dwell on the negatives.

4. They seem to get sick often.

5. They seem overly attached to their possessions or hobbies.

6. They seem to do a lot of binge-watching of shows.

7. They seem tired a lot.

8. They spend a lot of time on social media.

9. They have gained weight.

10. They shop a great deal.

11. They take very long hot showers or baths.

12. They talk about themselves a lot – redirecting the conversation back to themselves.

13. They engage in mindless talk – they are talking without really saying anything.

14. They engage in attention seeking behaviors or are manipulative.

15. They have poor social skills.

16. They have low self-esteem.

17. They constantly interrupt others.

18. They are living in the extreme.

---

*"The eternal quest of the human being is to shatter his loneliness."*

— NORMAN COUSINS

---

## Some of the Top Benefits to Dealing with Loneliness & Isolation:

1. You will be happier.
2. You will reap all of the benefits of happiness.
3. You will have more fun.
4. Your life will be more rewarding and fulfilling.
5. You will find that time goes by faster.
6. You will avoid the negative health impacts listed above.
7. You will likely learn new things because you are spending time with people.
8. You will have gained new life-sustaining skills.
9. You will be contributing to the wellbeing of another human being outside of yourself.
10. You won't dread getting up in the morning.
11. You will have things and people to look forward to.

**Tips for Putting Loneliness and Isolation to Bed:**

1. Recognize it. Name it. Claim it.
2. Don't judge or condemn yourself for having these feelings. It is normal. It is common.
3. Understand the significant benefits that come from addressing this issue. Don't you want to be happy and grab all of the benefits that come with happiness and feeling good? Of course you do!
4. Make a commitment to address this area. Make it a priority.
5. Create a plan of actions and steps that you can take to alleviate the loneliness and isolation.
6. Start talking to people about this. Open up. Trust me other people are lonely and feel isolated – even people in marriages and intimate relationships have these feelings at times or in some relationships loneliness and isolation are the name of the game.
7. Give up the shame and any embarrassment. I mean it!
8. Ask for help! People will help you more often than not.
9. Be brave. Be courageous. Live a life with no regrets (video).
10. Make new friends. Say to people: I need new (or more) friends! Who do you know? See my post about making new friends. Just do it!
11. Volunteering is a fantastic way to meet new people, make potential friends, contribute to a worthwhile organization, and not be isolated. Volunteering is a fast way to jump start dealing with these issues. You can use this as a stopgap measure while you are going through the process of making new friends or more friends.
12. Work on your own growth and development. Sometimes, it's low self-esteem, anxiety issues or some attitudes or beliefs that keep you lonely and isolated. Growth and development can help you in so many ways to address the underlying issues that could be contributing to your feelings of loneliness or feeling isolated. Trust me, it's amazing!

13. Bump up your self-care right now! Do not wait! It will help you feel better and help you get motivated. Yes. It is THAT important!
14. Get a pet or become a volunteer at a pet shelter. If you don't want to commit to getting a pet many shelters need temporary foster homes for pets.

**Call to Action:**

Isn't it time for you to have a wonderful, rich, fun and amazing life? Isn't it time to end those awful feelings of loneliness and isolation? Why wouldn't you want to do that? What are you willing to do to end these feelings? How can I help you? Who else do you know who is struggling with this? Right now, it's most people! Consider sharing this to give your people a boost. Please let me know how I can help you tackle this issue or other things that are preventing you from having a happy and healthy life.

## How Anger Can Help You Heal

October 5, 2020

### Why Anger is So Important

Anger is one of those emotions that we don't talk about openly or frequently. Anger is often looked at as a "bad" emotion and many times people have shame or embarrassment about feeling angry so it gets a bad rap more or less. As a society or culture, we are simply poorly equipped to deal with anger and most emotions to be frank. More people are unhappy because they just don't know how to be happy or how to generate their own happiness and given that, it is no surprise that we don't deal with anger. Anger can be healthy and healing and is definitely a component of healing your heart.

Anger can also be an underlying factor of low self-esteem, anxiety, depression and several mental health conditions including antisocial personality disorder, ADHD, bipolar disorder, borderline personality disorder, intermittent explosive disorder, narcissistic personality disorder, obsessive-compulsive disorder (OCD) and more. From this list of mental health conditions that it is clear that getting ahead of anger and learning how to process and deal with anger in a healthy way is extremely critical to your mental health. Later on in this post you can read the list of physical health problems that anger can cause people, which is extensive and very negative.

Unidentified anger can be directed either inwards towards yourself or outward at other people. When anger is directed inwards it can cause shame, self-blame, self-attacks, self-loathing (when you don't like yourself), self-harm and addictions to name some of the consequences of not dealing with anger. When anger is directed outwards, it can be put upon the people in your life – spouses, significant others, children, coworkers and even strangers. This is another reason to learn to deal with anger because it is an emotion that doesn't disappear when not dealt with – it goes inward or outward.

You want to be able to identify, process and manage anger and use it to your advantage and make sure that you heal your heart from any anger that lingers from the past. Anger can fall under the umbrella category of emotional pain so it's helpful to understand emotional pain. If you are alive and living life you will from time to time have to deal with things that are painful or that make you angry. It is just part of life. Getting skills, habits, practices, attitudes and beliefs that empower you will help you stay mentally healthy and avoid the negative health impacts on your physical body.

Interested in winning free prizes while you are on the growth and development journey? Don't forget to enter to win free prizes in my Year of Freedom Giveaway going on until July 2021! You can see the people who have won prizes already! Yes, this is fun…giving away stuff. You know what is even better? Having people be able to be empowered to live a happy life. That's the best!

## Types of Anger

Anger is defined as an intense feeling of tension and hostility in response to being hurt, frustrated, disappointed or threatened with respect to one's self, property, rights or values. It can vary from mild irritation to intense anger or rage. It's helpful to distinguish a few different types of anger and some emotions often associated with anger as you build your knowledge base and grow skills in managing and dealing with anger.

**Denial of anger:** It is important to note that some people go into denial when it comes to anger because they just can't face their anger or there is some inconsistency with the anger that they can't acknowledge or deal with. If you grew up in a family where you were not allowed to be angry then you would not be highly skilled or possibly not even be able to realize when you are or should be angry. Denial is one of the stages of grief that precedes anger and it is part of the grief process, which is normal.

**Displaced anger:** When you don't feel safe directing your anger at the person, organization or individuals with whom you are angry you instead place your anger on a "safe" target. This is a coping mechanism or strategy that is unconsciously done where or when it is either unsafe or somehow unacceptable to be angry with the actual person involved. It is extremely valuable to understand this concept because you can then determine when someone is being angry with you whether you might be the target of their anger inappropriately or unnecessarily. The more self-aware you become the easier this will be. To give you an example: you are mad at a family member yet you don't feel like you can express your anger with them so instead you take your anger out on someone else. It's like the phrase – who kicked the dog.

**Projected anger:** Projection in the field of psychology is where you attribute feelings that you actually have onto others. In projected anger, you are angry with someone or some entity and since you don't feel or believe that this is acceptable you then in turn begin thinking that the other person/people/entity are actually angry with you.

**Suppressed anger:** this is where anger is set aside to be dealt with at a later point in time. For example, something happens while you are out with your friends, which causes you to be angry with one of your friends and rather than hashing it out in the group, you make a mental note to talk to your friend privately about it later.

**Repressed anger:** This is anger that has been placed or pushed into your unconscious mind so that it is out of your awareness. This can happen when something is so traumatic or unexpected or is otherwise something that your mind simply cannot deal with. It is extremely important that you get to the bottom of any repressed anger because it can completely destroy your life and your future.

**Acting out:** This involves engaging in extreme behavior in order to express thoughts or feelings that the person feels that they can't otherwise express. Acting out is an expression of unconscious impulses or desires that takes the form of action when the person acting out is not aware that there is an emotion driving their actions. Instead of using words and expressing feelings the person takes an action. Self-harm can be a form of acting out. Acting out can provide a pressure release to help the person feel calmer or more peaceful. An example would be an individual who goes shopping instead of telling his or her spouse that they are angry with them for X, Y, or Z.

**Aggression:** This is intentional behavior that aims to hurt another person. It reflects the desire to control and/or dominate another individual.

**Rage:** this is violent, uncontrollable anger or an explosion of emotion that is out of control.

## Special Considerations with Anger

**Emotional reasoning:** A person who reasons emotionally misinterprets normal events and things as direct threats against their goals and needs. Aaron Beck, the founder of Cognitive Therapy (now Cognitive Behavior Therapy) defined emotional reasoning as whenever someone concludes that their emotional reaction to something thereby defines its reality. In other words, someone who uses emotional reasoning does not have a reality based in facts, rather their reality is based on their emotions. It is a false reality. It is a cognitive distortion. It is the opposite of living a true reality. This is important to understand because some people get angry because they are engaging in emotional reasoning. If you are dealing with a person who is angry it's helpful to understand this concept because it could be the source of their anger.

## Betrayal

Betrayal is frequently a source or cause for anger so it is worth mentioning. Betrayal is the sense that you have been harmed by the intentional actions or omissions of a trusted person, which could come in the form of infidelity, dishonesty, disloyalty, or disclosing information of a confidential nature that could be harmful. Betrayal can leave individuals with a huge loss of self-esteem and can have long-lasting effects, so it is worth understanding and serious attention. While betrayal is extremely painful, you don't have to be wounded for a lifetime from a betrayal no matter how big or small. Growth and development is the path to healing from the pain that betrayals cause you.

## Resentment

Betrayal is often accompanied by a handmaiden called resentment so it is helpful to understand this frequent companion to betrayal. Resentment is a feeling of bitter indignation at having been treated unfairly. Individuals prone to resentment are unwilling or unable to deal with emotional pain of betrayal, dishonesty, sadness, abandonment and other emotions. Instead of processing and managing their emotions they lock them away – doing the opposite of what I recommend – and the emotions fester and can lead to hatred among other things. This is not healthy for you in any capacity.

## Revenge

While we are in the discussion of anger it is worth mentioning revenge. Revenge is taking actions to inflict harm or hurt someone because they hurt you or somehow wronged you. The research shows that the individuals who engage in revenge behavior are motivated by power, by authority and by the desire for status. Interestingly enough, the research also indicates that people usually don't feel better after taking revenge on someone else. Revenge is the attempt to change shame into pride, and usually leaves people stuck in the wound as opposed to healing and moving on.

## Posttraumatic Stress Disorder (PTSD)

This is definitely worth a mention in the discussion on anger because anger can be a sign or a symptom of posttraumatic stress disorder. PTSD affects between 7-8 % of the population at any given time and can be triggered by witnessing or experiencing a terrifying or horrific event. There is a fairly long list of the types of events or situations that can cause someone to develop PTSD, and a list of conditions that make some people more prone to it than others. Any work you do on growing and developing skills to make you highly functional in life – growth and development – will help you build resilience to make it less likely that you will develop PTSD.


## What Causes Anger?

1. Betrayal
2. Perceived or actual mistreatment
3. Injury
4. Problems
5. Obstacles to getting what we want
6. Past experiences

7. Learned behavior
8. Genetic predispositions
9. Lack of problem-solving ability
10. Internal cause: emotional reasoning
11. Internal cause: low frustration tolerance
12. Internal cause: unreasonable expectations
13. Internal cause: people-rating (derogatory labeling on others, which dehumanizes them and makes it easier to be angry at other people)
14. External cause: personal attacks (verbal abuse)
15. External causes: attacking someone else's ideas or opinions (cutting them down)
16. External cause: threatening someone's basic needs (work, life, family, etc.)

**Negative Health Impacts of Anger and Chronic Anger**

This comprehensive list was compiled by looking at both medical literature in PubMed as well as other reliable health websites online. It is interesting to note that most of the information I looked at on the negative health impacts of anger or chronic anger only listed between 5 to 7 negative consequences with not a lot of overlap.

1. Heart disease or heart attack
2. Eating disorders
3. Diabetes
4. Increased risk of car accidents
5. Adoption of unhealthy behaviors like alcohol, cigarettes, caffeine
6. Obesity
7. Low self-esteem
8. Migraines or headaches
9. Addictions – drug, alcohol, and others
10. Depression
11. Lower quality relationships

12. Increased chance of abusing others emotionally, physically or both
13. Stroke
14. Increased anxiety
15. Insomnia
16. Fatigue
17. Decreased immune system functioning
18. Possible increased risk of cancer
19. Shortened life expectancy
20. OCD
21. Phobias
22. Loneliness
23. Exhaustion
24. Skin disorders
25. Digestive problems
26. Psoriasis
27. Hives
28. Asthma
29. Lower back pain
30. Glaucoma
31. Brain fog
32. Feelings of isolation

**Benefits of Anger**

1. Builds confidence (affirms self-worth)
2. Preserves dignity
3. Upholds principles
4. Catalyst for communication
5. Can help clarify relationships
6. Can increase sense of self-control
7. Can help provide clearer thinking and a clearer mind
8. Can help increase creativity
9. Can lead to self-insight and self-awareness

10. Can help reduce violence
11. Often gets results
12. Can make you feel powerful
13. Can give people a sense of purpose
14. Can help you overcome fear
15. Can help you be more optimistic
16. Can motivate change (personal, family, societal)

**Signs of Possible Hidden Anger**

This list is a list very widely circulated on the internet, which interestingly has no known author or citation of the source. I am sharing it because it has value although I am not happy that the author or source is unknown. If you know the original source for this list, which I believe was before the year 2000, please let me know!

1. Procrastination in the completion of imposed tasks.

2. Perpetual or habitual lateness.

3. A liking for sadistic or ironic humor.

4. Sarcasm, cynicism or flippancy in conversation.

5. Over-politeness, constant cheerfulness, attitude of "grin and bear it."

6. Frequent sighing.

7. Smiling while hurting or feeling angry.

8. Frequent disturbing or frightening dreams.

9. Over-controlled monotone speaking voice.

10. Difficulty in getting to sleep or sleeping through the night.

11. Boredom, apathy, loss of interest in things you are usually enthusiastic about. 12.Slowing down of movement; feeling lethargic.

13. Getting tired more easily than usual.

14. Excessive irritability.

15. Getting drowsy at inappropriate times.

16. Sleeping more than usual.

17. Waking up tired rather than rested and refreshed.

18. Clenched jaws - especially while sleeping.

19. Facial tics, fist clenching and similar repeated physical acts done unintentionally or unaware.

20. Grinding of the teeth - especially while sleeping.

21. Chronically stiff or sore neck.

22. Chronic depression - extended periods of feeling down for no reason.

## 12 Tips for Dealing with Anger

1. **Make a commitment to grow your skills and abilities in the area of anger.** Everything worthwhile in life starts with a commitment. Committing yourself to learn about anger, to learn how to recognize anger and then deal with it in a healthy manner might make some people uncomfortable because we do not live in a world where healthy expression of anger is the norm. Do it anyway because it is not only good for your physical and mental health, but also because it will help you live a happy, functional and powerful life.
2. **Ask yourself: Are you frequently or chronically angry**? If so, this could be a sign of low self-esteem. It is a sign that something needs to change in your life or in your relationships with people who are in your life. If this is the case, then pause and look at what is going on. It's time to take actions to get the source of your anger dealt with. It's

*Love.Life.*

also time to work on growth and development, which will help you build the skills you will need to create a powerful life and move forward. Even if you are in a toxic family or relationship that you don't have to power to change right now, you can still go to work on yourself and there is actually a lot you can do to improve your life and feel better.

3. **Ask yourself: Are you never angry?** If so, you may either have low self-esteem, were raised that this is an unacceptable emotion to have OR you could be an anger denier and that's not healthy or helpful. Denial of anger is a way to protect yourself from feelings or from acknowledging a situation or person for what it is or who they are. Denial of anger can come from being brought up in a family where anger was not allowed or tolerated and thus it was not an acceptable emotion. Denying anger can fuel depression, anxiety and addictions. If you never get angry, it is time to pause and see if that is actually a true reality or a false reality.

4. **Ditch any shame or embarrassment.** Anger is nothing to be ashamed of or embarrassed about. There is power in being able to claim your emotions whatever they are even though we as a society or culture don't do it.

5. **Start pinpointing the moments that you get angry**. You will have to be awake and aware of yourself and your life to pinpoint the times where you feel angry. If you are new to anger this is a whole new experience so be patient with yourself.

6. **Start expressing your anger in a healthy and assertive way**. That means you are not shaming, demeaning, bullying or being mean as you express your thoughts and feelings. This is a skill that you build and learning how to be assertive will help you communicate your feelings in a healthy way.

7. **Prepare for difficult conversations** by making notes on the behaviors or statements of those involved. This will

help you get clear about what happened and your reaction to whatever happened. It will provide an outline for having a healthy and assertive conversation.

8. **Practice difficult conversations** with a friend, roommate, family member or someone before you actually have the conversation. Being able to have a difficult conversation with a good outcome is a skill that you build over time. While no one likes having difficult conversations, the more prepared you are and the more you practice – the better they will go.

9. **Learn the skills of identifying, managing and processing your emotions**. This is a skill set not just for anger but for all of your emotions. You want to learn how to manage your emotions so that you are not at the whim of your emotions. You want to be in the driver's seat of your emotions – all of them not just anger.

10. **Identify the healthy coping mechanisms or strategies** that you can use while you are processing and dealing with anger. Examples of healthy coping mechanisms include going for a walk to clear your head, talking to a friend to sort it out, writing in a journal. You want to put in place healthy strategies for how you are going to deal with anger.

11. **Start talking to the people in your life about anger.** One of the best ways to build your skill set in any area is to incorporate the people in your life on the journey. Start having conversations with the people in your life about anger. What do they think about anger? How do they handle, process and manage anger? Don't be surprised if they lack skills in the area of anger because it is sadly lacking in the majority of the population. That's not a reason to stop talking about it. It is the very reason TO start talking about it. You are on the road of growth and development – why not take the people in your life with you? I mean, why not?

12. **If expressing your anger doesn't go well** – shake it

off and try again. Any skill, habit or practice worth having is worth failing at. You could celebrate that you failed. Get back in the game and try again. You can do this.

**Call to Action**

Learning to identify, process and manage your emotions is one of the most critical skills to learn and build if you want to have a happy life. It takes practice. It takes an open mind. Anger can be a helpful tool in life if you learn how to deal with it. Clearly, not dealing with anger can make you sick and unhealthy in a long list of ways as mentioned earlier. How do you deal with anger? Are you awake and aware when you become angry? How can I help you more effectively deal with anger? Who do you know that could benefit from this information? Will you consider sharing it with them? Please let me know with a comment below how I can help you with anger. I want you to have the best life possible.

**Healing from Dysfunctional & Toxic Families and People**

November 1, 2020

## What Does it Mean to Have a Dysfunctional or Toxic Family?

Families are supposed to be about love, caring, compassion and taking care of each other. In an ideal world yes, that is what a family is about. However, research shows that between 70% to 96% of people are growing up in dysfunctional families and 45% have been exposed to some form of alcoholism or alcoholic behavior. Let those numbers sink in. Is it any wonder we have such an alarming suicide rate in our young people? Is it any wonder that people are so unhappy? What that means is that most people have grown up in some type or level of dysfunction. Growing up or living in a dysfunctional family is painful and causes emotional pain for the family members that can sometimes leave them feeling lonely and isolated or angry and some filled with rage.

Growing up in a dysfunctional family can leave people with depression, anxiety, low self-esteem, chronically feeling overwhelmed with life, drug and alcohol addictions, obesity or eating problems, and a host of extremely negative impacts. People who grow up in a dysfunctional family often don't learn how to take care of themselves or self-care and often have a harsh inner critic so they lack self-compassion. Another core issue is that the net result of a dysfunctional family can leave a person lacking the emotional abilities to identify, process and manage their emotions, which falls under the category of emotional intelligence.

What is the answer to healing from dysfunctional or toxic families and people? The answer lies with healing yourself, which can be done through growth and development. This is what all of my blog posts and YouTube videos are about. It is also the theme of my Year of Freedom campaign – freedom from depression, anxiety, low self-esteem and all of the negativity that comes from being wounded or hurt by dysfunctional or toxic people in your life and stepping into love, happiness, joy, freedom, vitality and all of the good stuff. Speaking of good stuff, you can enter to win free stuff in my giveaway. The giveaway ends in July 2021 and you can see the rules here.

You didn't get to choose your family. You didn't get to choose the circumstances of your birth or events that happened in your dysfunctional or toxic family. It is predictable that you learned disempowering attitudes and beliefs growing up. It's predictable that you didn't learn assertiveness skills. It is extremely predictable that you did not learn how to identify, process and manage your emotions. It is likely that you didn't learn the skills to have difficult conversations. Regardless of whether your parent(s) played favorites or perhaps your siblings were not nice to you, or you just had a bad family, you probably feel like you were not well loved. Starting now, however, you have a choice. You can choose to learn new skills, take on new practices or habits, learn empowering attitudes and beliefs.

*Love.Life.*

You are not stuck with the past. You can create a brilliant future for yourself.

You can let go of the past, the hurts and the wounds and take on your own personal growth and development and heal. It is entirely possible for you. I am here to help you get there because I want you to have a happy, healthy life where you are well loved.

## What Causes a Family to be Dysfunctional?

1. Mental health issues in a parent or both parents
2. Addictions
3. Codependency
4. Lack of emotional abilities
5. Lack of personal awareness/healthy functioning abilities
6. Lack of boundaries
7. Low functioning of parents (GAF scale)
8. Repeating cycle from the past
9. Poverty or financial problems
10. Low self-esteem in one or more parent

## Signs of a Dysfunctional Family

1. Abuse of any kind: physical, emotional, sexual
2. Domestic abuse or domestic violence
3. Neglect: inactive harm; not meeting the needs of the child
4. Addictions
5. Secrets, lies, denial of problems
6. Lack of emotional abilities: don't deal with feelings; don't talk about our problems; don't trust outsiders
7. Lack of boundaries
8. Mixed messages; Criticism; Conflict; Ridicule
9. Lack of love, compassion and closeness
10. Rigid perfectionism

11. Denial of spiritual focus
12. Exploitation of children: having to cheer a parent up; having to protect a parent; having to take on parental responsibilities at a young age
13. Children who are forced to take sides between parents
14. False reality: pretending something bad was actually good
15. Overly intrusive, overly involved or protective parents
16. Distant or uninvolved parent(s)
17. Playing favorites or rejecting a child
18. Name calling
19. Gaslighting
20. Rudeness or contempt
21. Frequent lying
22. Manipulation
23. Lack of communication
24. Parental selfishness
25. Lack of empathy
26. Lack of trust
27. Use of guilt or shame
28. Gossip
29. Jealousy
30. Smear campaigns
31. Scapegoating
32. Blaming
33. Double bind situations

## Impacts of a Dysfunctional Family

This is compiled from a variety of sources. This represents the possible problems that someone growing up in a dysfunctional family *might* or *could* end up with. One of the resources I used to come up with this list is from Erik Bohlin, M.A., LMHC and he has a handout on this subject.

1. Lying
2. Harsh inner critic
3. Serious temperament or difficulty having fun
4. Overly sensitive
5. Difficulty with intimate relationships
6. Overreacts to changes they can't control
7. Constantly seeks approval and affirmation from others
8. Feels different from others (people don't understand me)
9. Very responsible OR very irresponsible – OR both
10. Very loyal even if it is not warranted
11. Strong independence (I can take care of myself)
12. Control issues
13. Trouble taking praise or compliments
14. Black and white thinking
15. Poor self-image
16. Poor self-worth
17. Compulsive need to be right
18. Denial
19. Depression – from repressed or unrecognized anger turned inwards
20. Sleeping problems
21. Overeating/Eating disorders
22. Fear of being authentic
23. Repeat the cycle in adult life with spouses/children
24. Personality disorders
25. Anger issues
26. Self-destructive behaviors or self-harm
27. Prone to addictions: alcohol, smoking, drugs

28. Mental health issues- like anxiety, suicidal thoughts, paranoia
29. Loss of childlike innocence

## Benefits to Healing

There are tremendous benefits to healing from dysfunctional or toxic families and people. These are the top benefits:

1. Improved immune system
2. Increased happiness
3. Increased sense of peace and contentment
4. Less aches and pains
5. Better sleep
6. Feeling more connected with people (less loneliness and isolation)
7. Feel more in control of your life
8. Less annoyed by other people
9. Improved self-esteem
10. Improved mental health
11. Increased satisfaction with life
12. Improved productivity
13. Increased energy and vitality
14. You will have more love available to you
15. It will lengthen your life span
16. You will feel better
17. It can help lower your healthcare costs
18. It will build resilience
19. You will have increased motivation
20. You will have more friends and social connections
21. You will be better able to deal with stress
22. You will have richer and more meaningful conversations
23. You will take better care of yourself
24. You will be more functional in life
25. You will have more fun in life

26. You will have healthier relationships with people in your life
27. You will feel more optimistic
28. You will have more self-control and self-mastery
29. You will have a clearer mind and thinking
30. You will have greater wisdom
31. You will have more curiosity about life

## Steps to Deal with Dysfunctional & Toxic Families and People

1. **Become Awake and Aware:** Because we are not talking about the commonality of family dysfunction or toxicity, people are hiding or masking the damage they have endured as a result. It can be painful to admit that your own family treated you badly. Becoming awake and aware to the nature of your dysfunctional family is the place to start. Own it and claim it even though it is painful. Truthfully, it has always been painful. Now you are giving language to it and acknowledging what it is. That is the beginning of freedom and power.
2. **Own the emotional pain and use it to your advantage:** Learning how to deal with, process and manage emotional pain is an extremely valuable skill set to have in life. Pain is simply a part of life because things happen. Begin to grow your skills in this area and you will never regret it.
3. **Commit yourself to healing:** With a firm commitment and the proper actions, you can heal from any wounds, trauma, or negative situations. You can heal from anything if you put your mind to it AND do the work.
4. **The umbrella for healing falls under growth and development:** Growth and development is a broad category containing all kinds of actions, materials, habits, practices, attitudes and beliefs. All of my blog posts and

YouTube videos are about growing and developing yourself so you can be happy, healthy and living an empowered life. If you are new to this concept, I believe that you will find it to be the best investment that you could ever make on yourself.

5. **Grow your emotional skills and abilities:** One of the best areas to work on in the growth and development genre is emotional intelligence. This is an absolute must for a happy and healthy life. Not being able to identify, manage and process your emotions leaves you bankrupt in life. I am not kidding. This is a must have skill for a great life.

6. **Look for, identify and process any anger, which can be hidden:** It is very reasonable to feel anger if you are among the majority of people who grew up in a dysfunctional or toxic family. Anger is an emotion that society is simply not good at. Most of people are extremely limited in dealing with anger. Anger can destroy your life if you don't deal with it. You will reap great rewards for learning this skill set.

7. **Set up a personal reward system:** I recommend a personal reward system because change is not easy for most people. If you are committed to healing yourself from your dysfunctional or toxic family or people then you are talking about change. Get a reward system and use it to stay motivated. It works.

8. **Self-Care:** This is what I call a foundational building block for life. It is a must. You want to take care of yourself and have fun doing it. Why not? The benefits are tremendous and you will definitely feel better by doing it.

9. **Assertiveness Skills:** Another skill set sadly lacking in society is assertiveness. This is a very helpful set of skills that anyone can learn. It will help you in every area of your life – for the rest of your life. I am grateful that I learned assertiveness skills in high school. Thanks Mom!

10. **Self-Compassion:** We don't talk about self-compassion but we most certainly should be talking about this. Put this

on your list as an area to grow and develop. It took me a good while to learn this skill, which I did with help from my children and friends.

11. **Be a person of character and integrity:** There is absolute joy and magic in integrity. The same goes for having character. Go to work to keep your promises and your commitments and you will start to feel better immediately.

12. **Make really great friends:** The research is compelling on the benefits of having great friends and social connections with respect to human health. Having really good friends is not optional for a healthy and happy life. I know that making friends is difficult for many if not most people, which is why I have written about it and made videos with tips. This is a must for you to heal and be well loved.

13. **Use affirmations to rewire your brain:** To properly heal it is necessary that you get ahead of negative thinking, catastrophizing, over-thinking, and anything negative. Affirmations use the concept of neuroplasticity of the brain to create new pathways in the brain. Negative thinking has to go simply based on the principle of the self-fulfilling prophecy.

14. **Learn the skills on generating your own happiness:** I have written a great deal about happiness because I know how to be happy when life is extremely bad. Happiness is one of my things. Being happy is a skill set that you can learn.

15. **Set goals and go to work on them:** To heal you are going to have to get into action. Healing is an active process. Set goals and then get to work on them. You will feel better as you see yourself making progress. I am a big fan of having a life plan, a purpose or a vision for your life, which hopefully will be your end goal because you want to be the one driving your life – not just letting life happen to you.

16. **Forgiveness is gift you give yourself:** Healing from a dysfunctional or toxic family or people will involve forgiving. Forgiveness is a gift that you give yourself. It has nothing to do with the other people. Put this on your list. Your family or whomever did the best that they could even if it was really awful or traumatic. Eventually, you will want to forgive them, which does not mean that you will continue to tolerate bad behaviors or maltreatment from them.
17. **Learn the skills to have difficult conversations:** It is always powerful to have skills for having difficult conversations because they are also a part of life. This is going to come in handy not just in the healing process but all through your life.
18. **Consider distancing yourself or removing yourself:** Often the dysfunction of childhood continues into adulthood meaning the dysfunctional behaviors are alive and well in the present time. At some point it might be valuable to consider either distancing yourself from family members or removing yourself altogether, which can be difficult and painful. You have to consider what is best for you and your wellbeing since it is unlikely that they are going to change.
19. **Be well loved:** The most painful part of growing up in or in having a dysfunctional or toxic family is that many people end up feeling not well loved. This is tragic and heartbreaking. At the same time, people can still grow and develop and be well loved in life. This is my wish for all of you – that you are well loved.
20. **Understand that this is a process and it takes time:** The more you understand that this is a process that takes time the better this will probably go. Realistic expectations are always helpful in life.

## Call to Action

With the majority of individuals growing up in dysfunctional or toxic families, we have a majority of our population walking around wounded in life and not fully functional. We have limited abilities in skill sets that are critical. To have a happy and healthy life healing needs to take place. Are you ready to heal from your dysfunctional family or toxic people? What do you need to get going on your journey? How can I help you? What do you need? Are you excited to create a happy and powerful life for yourself? Are you ready to be well loved? Please let me know how I can support you!

# CORONAVIRUS & PANDEMIC

**The Juicy Good Parts of the Coronavirus PLUS the Top 52 Things You Can Do to Make This a Good Thing In Your Life Now**

March 14, 2020

You are worried, fearful, anxious, depressed or maybe even panicked. That's understandable. However, you don't have to stay stuck in worry, fear, anxiety, depression or panic. You can stay there with those emotions including a whole host of other negative emotions if you choose, but that's not a powerful place to be. The juicy good parts of the Coronavirus are many, which I will be talking about along with the top 50 things you can do to make this a good thing in your life right now.

For those of you who are new to my blog, I write about what it takes to be happy and LOVE LIFE when things are really difficult, hard or even really horrific. As someone starting over in life at age 58 with basically nothing, I know all too well how extremely hard life can be. Yet my circumstances don't stop me from having a very happy, joyous and healthy life. In other words, my circumstances don't dictate my happiness. I have learned how to generate my own happiness, a skill that I highly recommend and wrote about in a post titled How to Generate Your Own Happiness & Why It's the Skill to Learn from February 13, 2020. Let me also state up front that my site DOES in fact have a security certificate through GoDaddy.com although we have not been able to get my site to show up as "secure", which is being worked on.

The other thing you should know before I dive into how the Coronavirus could be a really good thing in your life is that I am all about LOVE and living with an open heart. My first post was titled Love.Life.™ after the name of my blog and my second post was titled Living Life with Your Whole Heart (September 2019). I am one of those happy people who can find the silver lining to any problem. I believe in loving everything that you can about your life, the people in it, the places you go, and so much more. I am the embodiment of love. I love people – even you whom I do not know and will never meet. It's about loving humanity and the human condition. LOVE is the one thing that more people want and need in their lives but don't know how to get it. LOVE is the most powerful emotion on the planet and is Divine in every way. As such, you will find ways to bring LOVE and happiness into your life through my posts. Yeah, I have been called unorthodox, unconventional, weird and a whole lot of other names.

Right now, we have the highest percentage of people suffering over the impact of the Coronavirus. I hope in some way I can cast a positive light on this situation and cause a turnaround in how this is being viewed by the majority of people in the world.

Every single problem in your life also represents an opportunity. It's a matter of how you look at it. Granted the Coronavirus has disrupted our everyday life in excruciating ways. That is true. Yes, the Coronavirus has caused severe economic hardship to individuals, businesses and organizations. And yes, the Coronavirus has caused human beings to suffer greatly. While I will not be specifically addressing the suffering in this post, I wrote a post titled How to Be Happy When You Are Suffering or Life is Bad from

November 15, 2019, which may be helpful to you now depending on your ability to deal with suffering. I address the financial impacts later on in this post. We all understand the negative impact of the Coronavirus on our lives.

Yet the same disruption offers you a golden opportunity. The Coronavirus offers you a moment in time to completely change your life for the better because this situation offers you the gift of time. You now have time that you have longed for and yearned for. It just didn't come in the way that you expected it. Time is precious. Life is precious. You have the gift of unplanned time even though it has come in a somewhat shocking way and with some hefty consequences.

So many of you are filled with such worry, anxiety, depression or panic that you are not functioning or you are not functioning well right now. I understand. I have compassion for where you are. My request is that you read this post in full with an open mind and heart. Are you willing to have this Coronavirus be a golden opportunity for you and your life? Are you willing to do what it takes such that when you look back, all negatives aside, you can see that the Coronavirus was overall a very positive and life changing event – where your life changed for the better? Do you believe that is even possible? Or do you want to be a victim to all that you have lost? Do you want to be happy and productive during this unplanned interruption to your life? It's okay whatever you choose, just be clear that you are choosing your point of view.

I am talking about a shift in your thinking. I am talking about a shift in how you do life. A shift in how you live life - a positive earth-shattering gift to yourself. To help you make the shift I am going to address a few key areas, which deal with your emotions and perspective.

### Reality vs. Fiction/Rational vs Irrational fears and behaviors

Having spend two decades dealing with health issues with people that I love – I happen to know a lot more about health and wellness than the average person. Part of what is happening in society and the world is not based on fact, statistics or reality. You have a much, much higher chance of dying from a number of things you are exposed to in everyday life than you will ever have from the Coronavirus. At this stage, I hate to go into how much higher your chances of dying are from more common life events and situations because you are already in a heightened state of worry and fear and I believe that would be more harmful than helpful. I have all kinds of statistics about how people die in the U.S. at least and it's not pretty. Suffice to say, your chances of dying are significantly higher by umpteen percent from things other than the Coronavirus.

Given that the statistics and facts do not support the level of fear, panic and worry that is present in society then we have to look at the fact that what you are concerned about falls into the irrational category. With most things shut down and people practicing good handwashing hygiene, social distancing, etc. - things are under control. Having had a child with no immune system for too many years, I know about how germs are spread and how to avoid catching a cold or the flu. One of the reasons that colds and the flu spreads at all is because people walk around in life when they are sick and not always out of necessity.

It's clearly not necessary for someone to go to church when they are sneezing or coughing – yet they do. We have become cavalier about sending kids to school sick, about going to work sick, about doing everything sick. Hopefully that has changed. We would ALL be better off – all year round – IF people would just stay home when they are sick. Doctors and the medical community have been banging the drums for many years about the overuse of antibiotics for bacterial infections to the point that it is a severe problem because the bacteria have changed such that the bacteria have become resistant to many antibiotics. Meaning antibiotics don't have the same effectiveness. I won't address the severity of this issue in this post because it's too involved. TRUST ME – IF we can get the people of the U.S. and the World to STAY HOME when they are sick – WE will ALL benefit in ways that you can't imagine.

Bottom line: The panic, fears, worry and concern over the Coronavirus are irrational unless you have been traveling or exposed to someone who actually has the virus.

## Managing your emotions of panic, fear, anxiety, worry, depression, etc.

I understand you are feeling panic, fear, anxiety, worry, depression and so on. I want to help you deal with your emotions so that you can get unstuck and move to a more functional, productive and empowered position during this time and moving forward. Overall, speaking in general, we live in a world where happiness is an elusive concept and unhappiness, anxiety, worry and fear run the day. I don't work like that. As a result, I blog about how to be happy and have joy in your life. If you experience anxiety, depression and worries NORMALLY or typically, of course you would have increased anxiety, worry, depression and when life gets disrupted. Because what else could happen? It is your normal way of functioning in life so the Coronavirus would exacerbate that.

While I am not a psychotherapist or medical professional in any regard, what I am an expert in is how to function powerfully in life without many worries, little anxiety and low amounts of fear even under traumatic circumstances. I say that as full self-disclosure so you don't get the wrong idea and think that I am a therapist or medical professional. Apparently, I am an expert in dealing with trauma and the habits, practices, coping mechanisms, attitudes and beliefs to function well during a trauma.

I believe much of the unhappiness, depression, health problems and anxiety can be traced to the fact that people, in general, are not directing their own lives. We graduate from high school (hopefully), either go to college or trade school or get a job and life begins. We often then become like hamsters on a wheel going around and around and around again. Most people rarely stop and actively engage in directing and planning their future. We just go through life. Life just happens. Given the statistics on the lack of happiness in the world, which over the years is increasing, we are generally speaking not too happy in life.

What would happen if you used the Coronavirus as an opportunity to actively think about what YOU want your future to look like? If you could create your future to be anything imaginable, then what would it look like? What are your hopes and dreams for the future and your life? What would make you happy? What would inspire you? What would you create IF you believed that you could have any future that you can think of? This, in and of itself, is scary to some people because there's a certain level of resignation in society. There's a certain level of "this is just how it is for me" mentality. That's all fine and good. It's just not a powerful position to take. I am inviting you to stop and use this time to draw a line in the sand and alter the trajectory of your future.

When you take charge of your own life and you are intentionally taking actions to get you where you want to be, you will naturally have less anxiety and worry. When you are creating a life that you want, of course you would experience little or no depression because you would be creating a life that makes you happy! If you are creating your future – a future you have freely chosen – then you should experience a great deal of happiness, peace, satisfaction and joy. After all, you are doing what you have decided. We, as a society, are overrun with problems and issues and we lack (in my opinion) the skills, habits and practices to FUNCTION WELL in life. That is what my blog is all about – how to function well in life and be happy no matter what.

I recently blogged about worry and fear in a post titled: Worry & Fear Hurt Your Health: 15 Tips to Overpower Fear & Worry & Start Taking Risks, March 4, 2020. That will help you with taking steps to permanently reduce worry and fear. In my layperson opinion, having coached people for many years – once people have a plan for their future and start taking the actions to achieve their dream life – it is magical. It is so awesome I can hardly speak! It is miraculous. It brings me to tears. YOU might want to consider your future. You might want to consider your dream life. You might want to read ALL of my blog posts starting from the beginning because there are 30 FREE juicy posts packed with ideas and suggestions on how to get more LOVE in your life and be HAPPY. Right now, you have the unplanned gift of time so you have plenty of time to read posts designed to empower you and help you be happier!

For now, in the short term – just choose. Just choose to finish reading this post, look over the ideas on what you could be doing, and just start. If your mind is occupied doing a task you will have less mental ability to worry. You could choose to be happy about the gift of time you have been given. That is up to you. Keep reading.

**Financial Concerns**

With the stock market as far down as it is or has been, there are obvious financial concerns. I do not take financial concerns lightly – ever. And as someone starting over at 58 with pretty much nothing, I have more empathy and compassion for the financial hit you have taken with your retirement or investments. What I know from my limited knowledge of the stock market is that they periodically go down, think of the Great Depression, but the stock market ALWAYS comes back up. Or at least in all of history it always comes up. It just takes time and enough people to be reasonable and rational and not hit the panic button. Hitting the panic button almost always makes things worse. In the stock market and investment world – it always makes things worse in my opinion.

You may have lost 25% or more of your retirement or investments. Let the dust settle and let life get back to normal and then you can make a financial plan. Then you can plan for how to deal with your new financial situation. What is not going to help you is to panic and sell your investments at a loss. Then you really are at a loss. Talk to your financial advisor. Study the stock market to better understand what to do when it goes down. Do NOT panic. That's just not going to helpful!

When all of my money was taken fraudulently, once I recovered from the shock that neither law enforcement, the FBI nor the judicial system was going to get my money returned to me, I sucked it up and I planned. I have a bold and beautiful plan, which I am working on every day. Breathe. Do the mental processing of your emotions and then when the opportunity presents itself you can come up with a plan for the future. Just don't make hasty decisions. Have faith that things will work out.

If you are a pessimist, then that's a tall order. If you don't know about the self-fulfilling prophecy, then it's high time you understood that concept. What you believe will happen mostly does. What you believe will not happen – often doesn't happen. There's more psychology behind that – look it up. For now, just have faith that things will work out.

**52 Things You Can Do Right Now to Make Your Life Better**

1. Get your game on.
2. Plan your future.
3. File your taxes.
4. Call a friend – everyday.
5. Send a card to someone.
6. Go for a walk everyday if you are able.
7. Make a juicy bucket list.
8. Make a list of everything you would love to do in this period of time.
9. Clean up your emails in your inbox.
10. Learn how to make a new dish or learn to cook.
11. Organize your pictures or order copies of pictures online.
12. Figure out a reward system to motivate you during this time. Reward systems, personally designed self-reward systems, really do work well. See my post titled Self-Motivation: The Nuts & Bolts of Leveling Up with a Reward System, February 18, 2020.
13. Clean out or organize anything – your fridge, your living space, your sock drawer.
14. Take an online test of your emotional quotient. See what there is that you can do to improve in this area. Not sure what emotional quotient is? See my post titled Top 17

Benefits to High Emotional Intelligence and Why It's Important, October 25, 2019. This is important to your quality of life in my opinion.

15. Start purging any clothing or shoes you don't wear, don't fit, or really don't need. Someone would love to have the stuff you don't want.
16. Work on a hobby. I am a huge fan of hobbies because they are really good for people in a lot of ways. Don't have any hobbies? Read my post titled How Hobbies Can Help You Love Your Life and the Top 23 Reasons You Should Hobby Up, December 11, 2019.
17. Take a hot bath and relax. Add Epsom salts if you have some.
18. Plan a road trip for when life is back to normal.
19. Reconnect with high school or college friends, old co-workers, old neighbors, etc.
20. Get goals for the week, month or year. Get a buddy to join you in this new adventure of goal setting and goal attainment. Support each other in having beautiful new futures.
21. Write a letter to someone – a former teacher, professor, priest, Rabbi, coach, or someone else who made a difference in your life and thank them! Let them know that they had an impact on your life.
22. Organize your food supplies. What do you even have? Make an inventory and plan your meals.
23. Bake cookies to share or some other goodie.
24. Listen to music you love while you are doing other things from this list.
25. Make "well check" calls to people who live alone and see how they are doing and if they need anything.
26. Pray or meditate because that is very calming.
27. Read an inspirational book or story.
28. Tell the people in your life how much they mean to you.
29. Watch a funny movie or sitcom. Laugh as much as you can. That's a practice I recommend for daily living.

30. Delete old pictures and videos from your phone or computer or upload pictures and videos from your phone to your computer.
31. Clean your computer screen and keyboard.
32. Clean out your wallet or purse.
33. Go through crowdfunding sites and find a worthy cause to donate to. Donate to that cause.
34. Play a game called "Clean Out Every Drawer" and then systematically clean out every drawer you have. Best played with a friend or family member for fun – make it fun people! I highly recommend a reward for doing this – or even a small reward for each drawer. Why not?
35. Back up your computer and laptop files. No! Really – do this!
36. Play a "I Have IT WHO Wants It Game" on social media to find homes for the items you have amassed during your cleaning out. This is really fun! I did it in 2019 when I was cleaning out. I mean this was extremely fun and people were overjoyed to get some of my stuff.
37. Wash your bedspread or comforter.
38. Play a game with a friend called "First One to Fill Up a Black Trash Bag Wins" and race to fill up a black trash bag with stuff you just don't need. Obviously, you will have a prize for whoever wins.
39. Clean your coffee pot.
40. File your personal papers. I mean who doesn't have personal papers that need to be filed or dealt with?
41. Start doing affirmations if you are feeling anxious, worried or fearful or otherwise struggling. Affirmations could be very simple like: "It's all going to work out". I love this one from the *I Surrender* Novena – "Oh Jesus, I surrender myself to You, take care of everything." You can find lots of affirmations online. Find one that works for you.
42. Make a list of habits and practices that would help you have a better life and start doing them now. Hint: There's

plenty of habits and practices in my previous 30 blog posts to help you with that.

43. Practice gratitude. If you aren't feeling grateful, then write up a list of things that you can be grateful for. If you are really struggling with gratitude then I would suggest that you go online and study poverty in third world countries. Gratitude is such a powerful emotion. Start each day being grateful for what you have.

44. Do a health assessment. How is your health? What can you do to improve your health? Make a list of what you can do to be healthier and start doing that. It's much easier to be happy when you are healthy and feel good.

45. Mending fences: Take the actions necessary to mend any fences and repair broken relationships that are important to you.

46. Make a list of upcoming milestones in either your life or the lives of the people you love and decide how you will celebrate those milestones and accomplishments. There is no time like the present to plan fun stuff like that!

47. Get complete. There is absolute power in completion. Completing tasks. Completing projects. Completing relationships. Make a list of everything that is incomplete in your life and then get to work on that. To help you better understand what I am talking about you can read my post titled The LOVE and POWER of Completion, September 16, 2019.

48. Increase your nutrition in anyway possible. To understand the significance of how important nutrition is to your health you can read my post titled The Ultimate Consumer Guide to Nutrition, Why It Matters and How It Could Save or Change your Life, October 29, 2019.

49. If you are feeling overwhelmed then it's high time to deal with that. I have written all about overwhelm and how to put overwhelm to an end in my post titled Dealing with Overwhelm: How to Put an End to Feeling Overwhelmed

with Life Once and For All Plus 29 Tips to help you in the Meantime, November 6, 2019.

50. Do a self-assessment of where you stand with integrity in your life. Do you live a life that is full of integrity? Do you almost always keep your promises to other people? Once you have done an assessment of your integrity then make a plan to bring yourself into full integrity. I am beyond a fan of integrity. I blogged about it in a post titled The Sheer Joy and Magic of Integrity, October 9, 2019.

51. Assess your time management and list making skills. Not a fan of time management or making lists? To be fully empowered and engaged in creating your life you will want to have rock solid time management and list making skills. I have written about this in two posts: LOVE the TIME of YOUR LIFE – September 12, 2019, and Top 35 Ways that Making a List Will Help You Have a Life You LOVE, November 18, 2019.

52. BE PRESENT. If you are being present – being in the NOW as in right now – you can't be worried about the past or what else is happening. The more present you can be the more freed up you will be.

**Concluding Thoughts**

While the Coronavirus poses problems and issues and has resulted in financial and other losses, this time doesn't have to be a complete negative time in your life. You could shift your mindset and take advantage of the opportunity the Coronavirus affords you. You could use this time and the gift of time it provides to better yourself and your life. You could even have fun and be happy during this time. If you can shift your view and probably change some of your behaviors then it is entirely possible that you could look back on this period as a life-changing event that altered your future for the better. That could happen. Will it happen? It's hard to say because the choice is yours. Here is what I can say with some certainty: The more you enjoy this "break" the quicker it will come to an end. The more you allow yourself to suffer – the longer it will go on. Humm. Which of those is more empowering?

The entire point of my blog is to help people LOVE their LIVES. You can learn to be happy despite your circumstances. When you learn to be able to generate your own happiness separate from your circumstances then you have the power to be happy regardless of what is going on around you or in your life. That is a powerful way to live life. How can I help you get through this time? What do you need to be able to start feeling better and being productive? I care deeply about you having a great life. Now. Not tomorrow. Let me know what I can provide to help you get there.

If you liked what you just read then subscribe to my blog. What I can promise you with all integrity is that I will not sell my subscriber list and your email address to anyone – ever. I can also promise you that you will not be bombarded by emails from me. You will only get the new future blog posts by email because quite frankly I am way too busy to be sending you emails. Now, go live your happy life!

## Disaster Relief: How to "Flip the Switch" on Your Emotions and Feel Better Now!

March 22, 2020

Right now, you may be in shock or disbelief, feeling anxious, worried, fearful, out of control, depressed, helpless, panicked, irritable, restless, angry, lonely and isolated – and a whole host of other negative emotions that you may not be used to feeling. Clearly the entire world has been upended or disrupted. It is like the rug has been pulled out from under you and you had no warning or little warning that this was going to happen, which adds to the feelings of shock or disbelief. You are in pain and you are suffering – or at least the majority of people are.

You may also be experiencing physical symptoms as a reaction to the stress of what is happening like trouble sleeping, aches and pains like headaches, stomach aches or back aches, diarrhea or constipation, and a host of other physical manifestations of a trauma. What has happened in the world of late would fall under the definition of a trauma: something that infringes on a person's sense of control and can affect your ability to process a situation or circumstances into your current reality. A trauma is a deeply distressing or disturbing experience. And many of you have little expertise in dealing with the emotions that come with a trauma. That's what I am addressing today – how to deal with and manage your emotions in a way that you can move more quickly to being functional and productive and to hopefully give you the concept of how you "Flip the Switch" with respect to your emotions.

As someone who has overcome many life traumas including 3 concurrent traumas that lasted for much longer than a decade, I know a lot about trauma. I am 58 years old (almost 59) and starting over in life with pretty much nothing and not because I was irresponsible or the cause of my situation. I know firsthand what you are feeling now having your life upended in a sudden way without warning. I know the vast host of emotions you are likely to have. I know just how painful and difficult life might be for you at this moment. I wish that you did not have to go through this – ever.

I also, by the sheer Grace of God, have the skills, practices, habits, attitudes and beliefs that carried me through what other people describe as a deeply horrific situation among other things. It pains me greatly that much of the world is now having to experience this situation. It pains me more than you can know because I feel your pain in my heart. I want to help you not only get through this, but become better, happier, stronger and more resilient. That's what I see as possible for you and the world if you are willing to read what I have written and do what I call "the work".

Let me first address the fact that everyone is not in the same space or place emotionally right now. If I drew it out on a continuum, we would have people at one end who are not too worried and at the other end we would have people who are beyond fearful and panicked. Two polar opposites of the emotional continuum. Neither one of them is wrong. Then we have the middle of the road people and everything in between. You are wherever you are emotionally. Just have it be okay whatever state you are in. The power in all of this is being able to learn the habits and practices on how to deal with your emotions. No one needs help dealing or managing their emotions when life is good or great. That's easy. What we are typically NOT good at is dealing with loss, pain, suffering, hardship, and trauma – the negative emotions so to speak. When you have the life skills, habits and practices for dealing with the negative emotions including anger, then you have a much higher level of power in your life, more resilience and the ability to recover more quickly when life knocks you down.

What this - the upending and disruption of the world - offers the majority of the population is the time for a pause. A time to reflect on how we have been living life or not living life. What is interesting is the number of people who are now turning to prayer and to God for Mercy. As a fan of God, obviously I support this move. It's often what happens for people when bad things happen to people. What would happen if you took the time that you now have, unexpected and painful as it is for most people, and used your unexpected time to make your life better? What would happen if you used the "pause" that is happening to evaluate your life? Would you be willing to do that? Are you living your life in a way that is pleasing to yourself? Are you living a life that makes you happy?

Given the statistics on happiness in the World, the answer for too many people is a clear and resounding no. Happiness for too many people is an elusive concept that never fully arrives. You might be experiencing the emotions of the "Flight or Fight" response, also known as the acute stress response, given the state of the world. That would not be unreasonable. The "Flight or Fight" response refers to the choices our ancestors had in response to danger – flee or fight. With what is going on now, the flight choice has left the station. Given that we are pretty much hunkering down in place – that removes the fight choice. What are you to do? I offer you the third choice of growing and developing while you are self-quarantined. I am offering you the alternative of learning new ways of thinking, new habits and practices that will give you extraordinary power in your life moving forward.

Why am I able to be extremely happy at age 58 starting over in life with pretty much nothing? How is that possible? That is the question I get from people who hear my backstory, which unfortunately I can't share in this forum because that would be dangerous and definitely not prudent. I am happy because I have learned how to generate my own happiness as a life skill separate from my circumstances. I am happy because although I weathered a really horrific situation, I have come out on the other side as a BETTER PERSON. Hardships can either make you or break you or somewhere in between. Please don't let the hardships you are experiencing break you. Please let these difficulties MAKE you – into a better person. Let this world event mold and shape you in a way that you have a richer and more fulfilling life than before.

How would that be for you to be able to be happy distinct and separate from your life circumstances? It might be pretty amazing.

You could learn how to open your heart (see my post titled Living Life with Your Whole Heart from September 2019), which I believe is critical. You could heal past hurts. You could grow and develop such that you are not recognizable. Or you could stay the same wounded by the current events in the world. Anything is possible.

You could spend your precious time wondering why this has happened. You could spend your time worrying about your future. You could spend your time doing nothing productive to forward your life. You could spend your time being stuck feeling sad, angry, worried, anxious, fearful, depressed and unmotivated or any of the other negative emotions. You could do that. Or you could consider one of the gifts of this world event to be understanding how precious your life is. You could look at this horrible, awful event as a gift to assess and evaluate how you want your life to go moving forward. You could do lots of things to make your life better if you were not stuck feeling the way that you feel now. I understand that it can be hard to learn new things. I understand that this is foreign territory talking about how to deal with your emotions let alone the fact that you could learn to manage and control your emotions. I am well aware that this might sound like something that you can't buy into. I get it. Yet, this is my assertion. You can learn to process, manage and change your emotions.

This situation has created catastrophic financial losses for so many individuals, families, small businesses to large businesses. I have a lot to say about financial loss given that my own money was fraudulently taken from me and I have some ideas that might be helpful. I do think that subject of dealing with catastrophic financial loss is worthy of an entire post and as such I am not going to address it here other than to say I understand the significance of the loss. I have more to say about that and will in the near future. Right now, the power for you by beloved, is in getting a grip on your emotional state and learning how to process and deal with your emotions.

**The Power of Emotions**

Emotions are extremely powerful. Emotions drive our lives in ways that we don't understand or at least most of us don't understand. Emotions are what allow us to get connected to other human beings. Emotions are what motivate us to do certain things or NOT do certain things. If you want to have a really happy, joyous and powerful life then, in my humble opinion, this is the power source of life. To be able to have abilities and skills in the area of dealing with and managing your emotions.

It goes without saying that no one needs help when it comes to the positive emotions like love, joy, happiness, peace and contentment. You get a raise or a bonus, you get a job or promotion, you get into a new relationship, you make a new friend and you don't need any help feeling happy. It is the negative emotions that are the ticking time bomb from where I stand. We don't know how to grieve a loss. We don't know how to deal with anger in a healthy respectful way so we are passive-aggressive or act out. We don't know how to let go of resentments or forgive fully. The ability to handle your negative emotions will give you untold power and peace in your life because you can express yourself in a healthy, assertive, non-threatening way. It will go a very long way to increasing your happiness in life. I am all about happiness. It's one of the commodities that I trade in – how to be happy in life regardless of your circumstances.

This is a shitstorm for sure. What I have learned about life is that every painful problem or issue I have been forced to deal with has given me precious gifts. Not that I would ever want to go back and relive some of the traumas and ordeals, but I have found a way to grow and develop out of the trials, tribulations and traumas. You can too. It's a matter of perspective. It's a matter of how you want your life to go. This awful mess that the World is in right now could be a moment in time where you change your life for the better moving forward. It could be. It has that potential. The whole point to my blog is to help you LOVE your LIFE. What I promise you is that if you took processing your emotions to heart, IF you took on the practices that would allow you to manage and deal with your emotions like a champ that your life would never be the same. Your life would be infinitely richer. Your life would be so much better. You will never regret learning how to process, manage and deal with your emotions. I PROMISE YOU THAT. Or your money back! Haha. This is a free blog so this costs you nothing! Trying to lighten the mood here.

We are borne into the world and most of us don't get a lesson on how to deal with and manage our emotions. We just start living life and figure it out as we go. Some people believe that emotions are NOT something that they can control. For some, emotions just come and go and they have little or no ability to change how they are feeling. So, there are two parts that I want to address for you: (1) Processing your emotions, and (2) Changing your emotional state. If you never heard or learned that you can, in fact, learn to "Flip the Switch" on your emotions, of course, you would believe or think that. I believe that it is extremely important to know HOW to process your emotions so I will start there before moving onto what I call "Flipping the Switch".

## Steps to Deal with and Manage your Emotions

1. Identify how you are feeling, name it, own it. When you start learning how to process your emotions it is very helpful to have a list of emotions that you can find online to help you with this. When I was working with my children years ago, we got a two-page document that listed feeling words for both positive and negative emotions. I highly recommend that. Regardless, the ability to identify and name how you are feeling is the first step.
2. Acknowledge and Accept your feelings. It is powerful to acknowledge and accept your feelings. Trying to suppress or deny your feelings is the opposite of powerful. Suppressing or denying your feelings can, in my humble opinion, lead to greater and potentially larger problems including both health and psychological problems.
3. Share your feelings and emotions with someone else. While that would mean being vulnerable, I believe having the ability to be vulnerable is magical – my post on being vulnerable might help you with that. It is titled The Power & Magic of Vulnerability: Top 10 Ways You Can Start Increasing Your Ability to be Vulnerable, March 10, 2020.
4. Breathe and understand that no emotional state is permanent or at least is doesn't have to be. Breathe. You are going to be okay. Tell yourself that. Believe it.
5. Take on a self-soothing or self-care practice that nourishes your heart and soul instead of an addictive practice or habit that does not forward your life.
6. Consider your emotional quotient or emotional intelligence level – in general. The situation we are in magnifies worry, anxiety, fear and depression for people who typically experience worry, fear, anxiety and depression. Where are you on the emotional quotient or emotional intelligence scale? I wrote a post about emotional intelligence/emotional quotient titled Top 17 Benefits to High Emotional Intelligence and Why It's Important,

October 25, 2019. There is never going to be a better time – right now while you are sitting at home with LOADS of time on your hands – to get a handle on this subject of emotional intelligence. How emotionally intelligent are you? This is great stuff. At least in my eyes it is.
7. Take back your power and sense of control by making a plan for your life OR taking actions that will give you a sense of accomplishment or satisfaction.
8. Learn how to Flip the Switch on your emotions.

**Flip the Switch on your Emotions**

The process of what I call "Flipping the Switch", which you could call shaking it off after the Taylor Swift song involves you taking a definite action to change your emotional state. Obviously, you would need to recognize that you are feeling some negative emotions and then you take a purposeful action to make yourself feel better. Once you start this process – noticing you are angry, or depressed or feeling unhappy – and then you take an action that allows you to feel energized and better – this will then become a habit that you will want to continue.

Having been in 3 concurrent really awful traumas for an extended period of time, and being of a personality type that I LIKE to be HAPPY, I learned a long time ago how to "Flip the Switch" and manage my emotions because I believe you simply can't allow someone else or some circumstance dictate how you feel. You can learn to "Flip the Switch" or shake it off. It's not that hard.

**Examples of Activities to Help You FLIP the SWITCH:**

1. Go for a walk if you are able, which you can easily do with social distancing in place.
2. Pick something to be grateful for and experience the feeling of gratitude for that thing or person.
3. Pray or meditate. I find that a few minutes of prayer will change my mood every single time. I have heard that about meditation, but since I don't meditate I can't speak to that.

4. Call a friend or family member and SAY out loud: I need a pick me up call. Are you available? Keep making calls until you get someone who is available. If you don't have many or enough friends, then go on social media and say that same thing. Trust me, people will rise up to support you sometimes in unexpected ways.
5. Take a 15-minute cat nap to get centered and relaxed. I have even done this in my car while waiting for someone. It can be refreshing and help you flip the switch on your emotional state.
6. Go do one small chore as in a 10-15 minute task, which should be helpful.
7. Make a list! If you are not a list maker, then it's high time to start. If you want to have a life that you love and get through difficult times, lists can be your guide, your support and extremely helpful. I have blogged about this in two posts titled Top 35 Ways that Making a List Will Help You Have a Life You LOVE, November 18, 2019 and LOVE the TIME of YOUR LIFE – September 12, 2019.
8. Engage in one of your self-care practices as you learn self-soothing skills. I wrote about self-care in my post titled Self-Mastery, Self-Motivation, & Self-Care: The Holy Grail of Happiness & Joy, January 30, 2020.
9. Spend some time doing a hobby that you love. If you don't have any hobbies, then I might gently suggest that you look at my post on hobbies because I am beyond a fan of hobbies. My hobby post is titled How Hobbies Can Help You Love Your Life and the Top 23 Reasons You Should Hobby Up, December 11, 2019.
10. Listen to music that you love.
11. Think of someone you could be of assistance to and provide what you can, which can be done with social distancing in most cases.
12. Read an inspiring book or short story or watch some inspiring show.

13. Do something that is likely to make you laugh. Laugh as much as you can and as often as you can.

**Concluding Thoughts:**

Your life as you know it has been upended almost overnight or in a very short time period and as a result you are feeling a host of emotions most of them negative. I have deep, deep compassion for your pain and suffering because it pains me greatly that this has happened for all of us. Yet, this is a chance for you to learn an extremely powerful skill – how to manage and deal with your emotions. If you have the ability to process, manage and deal with your emotions then you are functioning at the highest level possible. Your emotions won't run your life. You will be running your life. You will be able to "Flip the Switch" when you are feeling angry, sad, depressed or otherwise unhappy.

Happiness is an elusive concept to many in the world. Yet, I assert with all the conviction that I have that when you learn to process, manage and deal with your emotions you are well on your way to learning to generate your own happiness – a topic that I blogged about in a post titled How to Generate Your Own Happiness & Why It's the Skill to Learn, February 13, 2020. This World event offers you the time to work on yourself. This horrible, awful, upending event gives you the gift of time. Time to work on your life. Time to learn new skills. Time to take on new habits and practices. It's really up to you whether you want to learn how to manage your emotions or just let your emotions run your life. It's a choice. It wasn't a choice up to now – but now I have laid out the steps to go through. Now, you know that your emotions don't have to RULE or RUIN your life. For some of you, this is the gift of recent events. Take it. Run with it.

Let me know how I can help you! Start now! Life is precious. Your time is valuable. Your life is valuable. What are you waiting for? Get going. I love you. I want you to be happy and succeed in life. If this post was valuable in any way, please share it. You probably know several people who need to hear this conversation to help them get unstuck and move forward or at the very least see a way out. We have a world of people who are in pain and who are suffering who need help finding the way out. Give them that gift.

## The ONE Coronavirus Article That Could Change Your Life for the Better FOREVER

March 25, 2020

When I say that this is the ONE Coronavirus article that could change your life for the better forever I am not fooling or kidding around. The entire purpose of my blog is to help people have a life that they LOVE and provide the tools to help them get there. Right now, you have had your world turned upside down and you have a host of new emotions, which are not so positive. You are likely feeling afraid, anxious, worried, panicked, lonely, depressed, frustrated, angry, resentful and bored to name some of the top emotions that come to mind. How you deal with *yourself* and your emotions RIGHT NOW could forever alter your future outcome of this current situation. Before I give you the 3 key ways this article could change your life for the better forever let me address some key elements that should be of value. One element is that all of live involves loss and grief at some stage or point in time. You can't avoid loss or grief if you are a human being living life.

There is loss and grief when someone you love dies, when you lose a friend, a relationship or a marriage, when you lose your assets or your home, when you lose a beloved pet, and in betrayals of all kinds. There is no avoiding loss and grief at some time in your life. Yet, a large majority of people simply don't have many skills when it comes to dealing with loss and grief. No one needs to help you when life is great or even good. It's easy to be happy when life goes your way. Yet, life throws us curve balls and hardships as often as it does and then what happens? It's difficult to function in life when you have your world turned upside down unless you have the coping skills and habits and practices to still function. To be able to move through loss, grief and hardship without having it disable you − that is true power.

Here's how this article could change your life for the better forever − assuming you actually read it and I do mean read it − not skim over it. Read it like it matters to get these 3 significant benefits:

1. FOREVER: Learn the skills, habits and practices to deal with great loss, grief and suffering and you will have those skills forever! That is the ultimate power in life to be able to have skills and to function well when life is hard.
2. Get OVER the trauma & shock more quickly − which means that you can heal faster and get on with life.
3. Give you a BETTER chance of recovery without deep, permanent wounds − the chance for a full recovery.

First and foremost, this Coronavirus pandemic is a world event and for a large percentage of the population it is a trauma. While it is not a trauma for everyone, it is a trauma for a huge number of people. IF you don't deal with a trauma it can absolutely affect your future life and health, which you can read all about in various medical and scholarly sites on the web and in many books as well. I want to help you develop the skills, abilities, habits and practices to not be damaged by this trauma. I can help you to get through it and come out the other side as a fully functioning individual IF YOU are willing to do what I call the work. The more you understand how a trauma can impact you and what it takes to offset a trauma, the faster and better you will recover and the more chance you have of no long-lasting side effects.

My last post was all about dealing with your emotions: Disaster Relief: How to "Flip the Switch" on Your Emotions and Feel Better Now! Flipping the Switch is, in my humble opinion, an extremely valuable concept of how to deal with negative emotions and turn things around quicklly that everyone should know and be able to use when needed. In this post, I am going to drill down specifically on the process of dealing with a loss, grief and suffering because that is exactly what a lot of people are feeling right now.

Before I get into the process of loss and grief, I want to mention as someone who has experienced a complete and total upending of my life without warning that there can be significant good that can come out of hardship and really horrible events. I speak from experience. I would give you more details but that could actually be dangerous to me on multiple fronts. I say this because I want to give you HOPE. Hope can be the most glorious thing when you are in dark and difficult times. Having HOPE gives you something to hold onto when you feel crushed by life. I have observed a huge uptake in the amount of prayer going on in the world – or so it seems to me. Maybe people are just being more vocal about asking for prayers and asking people to pray for the world. Regardless, a belief in God and Eternal life offers believers HOPE for life after death in the spiritual realm.

God is synonymous with the word love. God is love. Love equals kindness, compassion and charity among other things. Believing in a religion provides the guidelines for good and moral living. Where is LOVE in your life? This might be the time to open your heart to love. This might be the time to heal some of your old wounds. This might be the time to grow and develop on purpose. This might be the time to have more love, joy and happiness in your life. Change is inevitable in life. It rarely stays the same. How you deal with change is entirely up to you. You can resist change or you can embrace change or dip your toe in and see what happens. Our world is changing that is for sure.

We don't know what the future holds, which is the scary part for so many. When you have lived through very long periods of uncertainty like I have then you grow your capacity and your ability to live in uncertainty. Don't get me wrong – we all love certainty. We all love knowing how things are going to go. We all love to know what we can count on. Who wouldn't love that? It is just not our reality now. Our reality is filled with unknowns and uncertainty. It's probably hard for you to imagine that your life could be better or that you could be a better person because of a hardship or a trauma. Yet, for me that is almost always the case. Because I am constantly choosing an empowering view of my life and my circumstances. Because I know what it takes to be able to function well during great hardship and trauma. This is what I want for you – for you to be able to make it through this and come out as a stronger, better, happier and healthier you. And I am convinced that is possible – IF YOU are willing.

Don't ask me why, but in college I took a course on death and dying, which included a book by the premier expert at the time, Elisabeth Kübler-Ross, titled *"On Death and Dying"*. It was an amazing course that I probably took because I was a Resident Assistant, or because my boss asked me to, or because I needed a one credit class. Who knows. Dr. Kübler-Ross (1926-2004) was the co-founder of the hospice movement around the world, a Swiss-born psychiatrist and humanitarian. Her book, *"On Death and Dying"* was first published in 1969 and included The Five States of Grief. For much of the time between 1969 to now, Dr. Kübler-Ross's the Five Stages of Grief was accepted as the gospel. While it is still well accepted newer research has broadened and expanded upon the research base that Dr. Kübler-Ross started decades ago. The Five Stages of Grief are:

1. Denial: This can't be happening.
2. Anger: Why is this happening to me/us?
3. Bargaining: I will do anything to change this.
4. Depression: What's the point?
5. Acceptance: It's going to be alright.

Another classic book on dealing with grief and loss is *Good Grief: A Constructive Approach to the Problem of Loss* by Granger E. Westberg, published in 1962. Granger Westberg expands on the Kubler-Ross stages of grief broadening her work. Granger's overview of grief includes 10 phases:

1. We are in a state of shock.
2. We express emotion.

3. We feel depressed and very lonely.
4. We may experience physical symptoms of distress.
5. We may become panicky.
6. We feel a sense of guilt about the loss.
7. We are filled with hostility and resentment.
8. We are unable to return to usual activities.
9. Gradually hope comes through.
10. We struggle to readjust to reality.

**Grief/Loss/Suffering Affects:**

1. Your emotions – how you feel
2. Your physical body – sleeping and with other physical issues
3. Your thinking -confusion (inability to concentrate; difficulty making simple decisions; memory problems; feeling confused); dreams; memories
4. Your behavior – social (isolating from others; easily irritated by others; loss of interest in normal activities and hobbies); habits – increased use of alcohol and cigarettes or other drugs; either loss of appetite or increased eating; loss of interest in enjoyable activities; work (not wanting to go to work; poor motivation; poor concentration or attention; sense of lost purpose in your work)

**How Grief/Loss/Suffering affects your ability to Function**

When my life was totally turned upside down – the rug ripped out from under me – I was surprised when people asked me the question: "How are you functioning?" What does that even mean I asked? I am not a therapist or medical professional and I just literally did not know what they were asking. Over time I got the gist of the question. Are you eating? Are you sleeping okay? Are you taking care of yourself? Are you doing normal activities? How are you feeling? Are you able to do what needs to be done in your life? And so on. In the medical field there is actually a scale for how well you are functioning called "The Global Assessment of Functioning (GAF)

Scale", which if I understand has somewhat recently been replaced by the WHODAS scale.

Regardless of the functioning scale that you use, going through a trauma, a loss or grieving can impact your ability to function in life, which is why I have a sense of urgency to help you get a grip on how this can affect you so that you can deal with it. If you were functioning at the highest level, a GAF scale of 91 to 100, reads like this – superior functioning in a wide range of activities, life's problems never seem to get out of hand, is sought out by others because of his or her many positive qualities. No symptoms. Does that describe you prior to the Coronavirus pandemic? The next level down on the GAF scale (scoring 81-90) is described as: Absent or minimal symptom (e.g. mild anxiety before an exam), good functioning in all areas, interested and involved in a wide range of activities, socially effective, generally satisfied with life, no more than everyday problems or concerns (e.g. an occasional argument with family members). Does that describe you prior to this pandemic?

The lower the level that you were functioning prior to the pandemic – the harder or potentially harder hit you could be by the trauma, loss and grief that the present situation presents. In other words, someone who experienced a great deal of anxiety, worry, and fear normally would have a heightened sense of worry, fear and anxiety due to the current circumstances. People who were functioning at a lower level can easily be pushed over the edge. This is why I am stating for the record that this article could change your life forever. IF you learn how to deal with loss, grief or suffering in a positive way then you are in a powerful position moving forward. IF you were not highly functioning before the pandemic – this is your chance! If you were not all that happy or life was not so great for you before the pandemic then this is an opportunity for you.

Suicide or intentional self-harm is the 10th leading cause of death in the U.S. as of 2017 statistics. Suicidal behaviors relate to a low GAF score. Therefore, I say that the more you can increase your ability to function in life – the lower your likelihood to die by suicide. We simply have people who don't know how to feel their feelings. We don't have a society that validates loss and grief. We shy away from someone who has lost a loved one. We don't know what to say when a parent loses a child, when there is a death of a sibling or loved one, or some other catastrophic loss. It's easier to be silent and not risk saying the wrong thing. Or so it seems.

Now, we are in the midst of a group trauma – or a trauma for the largest number of people clearly not everyone. Now, I assert is the time to grow and develop your ability to deal with loss, grief and suffering because that is the only powerful way out. It's not the only way out, but it's the way out that will empower you forever moving forward.

Grief and loss are not the same for every person. It's a personal process. What matters is that dealing with the grief or loss is going to benefit you in huge and tremendous ways. Denying or suppressing your feelings – the feelings of loss, grief, loneliness, fear, panic, anxiety and depression - could come back to haunt you in the future. It is in fact predictable that if you ignore your feelings that it will in fact come back to haunt you down the road. Research it yourself if you don't believe me.

Everything that I write about is how to have a LIFE that you LOVE. Being able to feel your feelings is part of that. Being able to feel and deal with negative feelings is a part of that. If you can only love life when it is good – that's a problem. The power is in being able to LOVE ALL of LIFE – the good, the bad and the ugly.

What's to love about the bad parts you ask? The bad parts or the painful parts of life can help you grow and develop. The bad or hard parts of life can help you become a better person. The awful or horrible parts of life can help you develop virtues like humility or help refine your character, which is always beneficial. To be able to say, "I am hurting" is powerful. Of course, to be able to say that you would have to be able to be vulnerable, which I just recently blogged about. Regardless, I want you to be able to function WELL in life. I want you to be happy. This is the subject of all that I write about – how to help you get from where you are to where you want to be.

*Love.Life.*

There is so much more I can say about this. Yet, for now, I think this is the place to leave you with the top ideas I have for getting you through the <u>next week</u>. When times are hard – you live moment to moment or as I say – problem to problem. When life is extremely tough you get through it minute to minute – one problem at a time. I know a lot about that. Here are some thoughts for the coming week to help you.

**Things to Get You Through the Next Week:**

1. Understand you are not alone. Group trauma or massive trauma is going on now.
2. Trust that you will get through this and be better off for it. More on that in a future post.
3. Identify how you are feeling. This is really important. Then FEEL your feelings. Let them in. Don't try to resist them. Cry. Feel lonely. Feel sad. Feel your feelings. Crying is really good for the body and soul – so have a good cry if you need to.
4. Talk to people about how you are feeling. If you can't do that for any reason, write in a journal.
5. Commiserate with your social media friends or call a friend. Misery loves company and it will be good for both of you or all of you. You can do group chats on a variety of platforms.
6. Recognize and understand that when you develop the skills to be able to grieve a loss of any kind – you will have a powerful skill that no one can take away from you.
7. Self-care: What can you do each day in the area of self-care? I know...what is self-care? I blogged about this in a post titled Self-Mastery, Self-Motivation, & Self-Care: The Holy Grail of Happiness & Joy, January 30, 2020.
8. Take a shower every day and get dressed. Do your grooming. You will feel better. Trust me.
9. TURN OFF the news! Oh my goodness people! The news is not helping you!! It is NOT helping you at all. It is ramping up your fears and anxiety. I NEVER watch the

news. It's not helpful. It doesn't leave people feeling good. Trust me – if something major happens you will either hear about it on social media or someone will tell you.
10. Make up your mind that you will not only survive this – but you will FLOURISH! Why not? It's a much more empowering point of view.
11. Listen to music that you love.
12. Do you have a list of things you can do at home that makes you happy? If so, do that stuff. If not, it's time to create that list. Your handy-dandy, go-to list for things that make you happy.
13. Read up on emotional intelligence or emotional quotient. This is extremely important in my humble opinion. I blogged about this in a post titled Top 17 Benefits to High Emotional Intelligence and Why It's Important, October 25, 2019.
14. Start planning events for the future – this really works people! I have done it so many times when life is hard. Plan parties, reunions, potlucks, post-graduation graduation parties, dinners, etc. Why not? What else are you doing your time? This gives you something to look forward to and that is important!
15. Play a made-up game with your real friends or those you know through social media! Make it up! For example: The last one to do X, Y, or Z has to host a party when this blows over. Or the first one to do _____ has to _____. Get creative! Have fun with this! Play!
16. What kind of life do you want moving forward? You can use this to "reset" or "restart" your life or start all over like I did last year! You get to decide. You can use this time for that.
17. Hobby up! Spend some time on hobbies. I am a big, super-huge fan of hobbies. You can read about that in detail in my post titled How Hobbies Can Help You Love Your Life and the Top 23 Reasons You Should Hobby Up, December 11, 2019.

18. Write a letter to someone who has had a positive impact on your life and let them know that they made a difference in your life. Mail that letter. Now.
19. Be present. The more you practice the skill of being in the moment, being in the NOW, the less worry and anxiety you will have. The more connected you will be able to get with people. Being present is a wonderful gift.
20. Forgive someone. Forgiveness is actually for you. I intend to blog about this soon. But in the meantime, just do it.
21. Write up your bucket list.
22. Pray or meditate. These have proven benefits.
23. Inventory your food and supplies. Then make a meal planning list based on the food that you have. This should ease your mind when you see how many meals you actually already have on hand.
24. Reward yourself for anything and everything you can! I am a huge advocate of a reward system because I have been using one for decades and I know it works. To read more about how to do this in your own life read my post titled Self-Motivation: The Nuts & Bolts of Leveling Up with a Reward System, February 18, 2020.
25. Go for a walk because that will put you outside in nature and has proven health benefits.
26. Growth and development: I am a die-hard fan of growth and development. It is the path to higher functioning in life. It is the path to more happiness, joy and peace. I mean I totally LOVE growth and development. I blogged about it in a post titled Top 45 Ways that Personal Growth & Development Will Help You Have a Life You Love, November 29, 2019.
27. Laugh as much as you can and as often as you can! Watch funny movies or sitcoms, tell jokes or whatever it is that makes you laugh.

**Concluding Thoughts:**

There are several life skills, if you will, that will help you have superior functioning to use the language from the GAF scale. Given the suicide rates in the U.S. and the world, we are missing the boat on some dramatic level. Life offers us many opportunities to experience loss unless we are living under a rock or in a cave. Learning how to process loss, feel grief and deal with suffering provides an extremely powerful skill that no one can take away from you once you learn it.

We are living through a period of chaos, deep disruption and trauma. The majority of people simply do not have the skills to cope with this this kind of loss and grief. We need to urgently get the message out that there is hope. You will get through this. We will get through this. There are skills to learn and new habits to embrace – AND your life will be better and richer as a result. As someone who has weathered many traumas, I know what it takes to reach that highly functioning level no matter what happens. I want to help you get there. This can be a gift or a curse. It's really up to you how it all ends up. We will absolutely get through this. You get to decide if it is a gift to you or a curse.

Think about this. Print this out for later. Bookmark it. Above all, share it with your people. They are struggling. We need to work together like never before. Please let me know how I can support you. I am deeply pained by what is going on. I know how hard it is. I wish you didn't have to go through this at all. Let me support you in developing new habits, practices and skills to get through it and have a better life moving forward.

**19 Potential GIFTS of the Pandemic & the Top 29 Tips to Help You Get Through It**

March 29, 2020

If you have been through enough hardship in your life up to now then you know that hardship and problems offer you potential gifts depending on how you deal with the hardship or problems. I can just imagine some of you rolling your eyes, scoffing, or otherwise reacting in disbelief. Yet, as someone who has weathered a ton of hardship in life, I can assure you that this pandemic offers you 19 potential gifts. While you are welcome to skip to that list, I hope that you will consider reading what I am providing in between here and there – because some of that is absolutely for YOU! Nobody likes this pandemic. Nobody likes dealing with hardship. It's not fun.

You might be feeling helpless and out of control. You might be filled with worry, fear, panic, anger, resentment, depression and anxiety. I completely understand and quite frankly that is reasonable given the circumstances. Most people simply were not prepared for what has happened. What I know from dealing with tremendous hardship, which I would say more about if it was not dangerous for me to do so, is that hardship has the potential to either break us and make us bitter or it has the potential to help us be more resilient, more focused and energized, and better people all around. At least that is my take on hardship with all the experience I have with it. My desire is to help you get through this and come out the other side with a better life. I believe with all of my heart that is possible for you – if you are willing to entertain that possibility.

If you are new to my blog, I picked the title, Love.Life.™, because I am a fan of LOVE and all things related to LOVE. I am also a firm believer that if you are going to LOVE LIFE then that means being able to LOVE and appreciate all aspects of life including hardship, troubles and problems. I don't mean that I love it when I have a problem or a hardship. But I have the skills and abilities to deal with the troubles, problems and hardships that life brings to me. I chose my title because to be powerful and effective in LIFE – you have to be able to deal with all of it. The content of my blog posts are all about the habits, practices, skills and attitudes necessary to have a LIFE that you LOVE – even during horrible times. This pandemic brings a whole host of new issues and problems to the forefront of life. We are in a position that we have never had to deal with before on this level. It is an opportunity for us to bring LOVE to the center of LIFE and grow and develop.

How you deal with hardship or big problems depends on a variety of things including the coping mechanisms or strategies that you use in daily living, how you deal with your emotions, your emotional quotient or emotional intelligence, your beliefs and attitudes in and about life, your religious beliefs, and the choices that you make. If you didn't have great coping mechanisms or strategies in life prior to the pandemic, then it is extremely likely that you might be hard hit by the pandemic. Not to worry – it's never too late to start to develop strong and healthy coping mechanisms or strategies for life. Hint: Most of my blog posts deal with either directly or indirectly having strong coping mechanisms and strategies so there is over 150 pages of free help on that.

How are you dealing with your emotions? How high is your emotional intelligence (EI) or emotional quotient (EQ)? The higher your emotional intelligence or quotient was prior to the pandemic, the easier this will be for you. Don't worry if you don't know what emotional intelligence or emotional quotient is – I have written a blog post devoted to EI/EQ because it is so important. It is titled Top 17 Benefits to High Emotional Intelligence and Why It's Important, October 25, 2019. If I can be frank, we are not living in a society or a world where people are really great in dealing with their emotions. We mostly are not trained in how to manage, process and deal with our emotions. The better you are at this – the easier life will be for you now during the pandemic and afterward. My last blog post titled The ONE Coronavirus Article That Could Change Your Life for the Better Forever, March 24, 2020, was all about dealing with this topic.

Let's talk about the choices you can make as a result of the pandemic. This is my view on choices:

1. You get to choose how this will impact you.
2. You get to choose how you will use this to benefit you.
3. You get to choose how you will use your unexpected gift of time assuming you are in the category of not working during this time.

4. You get to choose how you will deal with or not deal with your emotions.
5. You get to choose if you will practice learning how to manage, process and deal with your emotions.
6. You get to choose how you will move forward from this.

Before I get into the 19 potential gifts from the pandemic, let me address the issue of money and the financial impact of the pandemic, which is beyond belief. While it remains to be seen at this moment in time how things will play out, there is no doubt that the pandemic will have a crushing impact on the economy and the financial stability of individuals, families, businesses and organizations and entire countries. We will get through it. History has shown that when there is a tragedy, a catastrophic loss, a war, a terrorist attack, or mass genocide – we always get through it. The current pandemic might mean that you will have to go into debt to survive it financially. You might have to borrow money. You might have to change how and what you spend money on. You might have to change your financial plan moving forward. If you have food, shelter and the basic necessities – you could be grateful. Not everyone has that. If you have an abundance of money or assets – this could be your time to be compassionately generous with people you love or strangers. Miracles happen frequently out of the worst of times. Just hang in there because things have a way of working out. And you play a big role in how that goes.

**The 19 Potential Gifts of the Pandemic**

1. It can help you appreciate the fragility of life.
2. It can help you appreciate the little things in life like a warm smile from a stranger, like having food and toilet paper, like nice weather, like help given or help received.
3. It can help you gain the gift of humility.
4. It can help you re-evaluate *what your life is for* and what *you want out of life*.
5. It can help you get clear about what is important to you and what is not – the gift of clarity and introspection.

6. It can help you become a better person – more compassionate, more loving, more kind, less righteous, less judgmental, less arrogant, and so on.
7. It can help you gain a sense of humanity – we are all in this together.
8. It can help you re-evaluate the people and relationships you have in your life.
9. It can help you make changes in your life in the areas of health and wellness, emotional quotient, relationships, how you use your time and so on.
10. It provides you with the gift of learning new skills, habits and practices.
11. It provides you with the potential to have more LOVE in your life – more love, joy, happiness – can become a priority instead of an evasive illusion that might happen one day.
12. It can help you make new friends – either who help you or whom you help.
13. It can help you to value your time and how you use it – the more you value your life and life in general – then valuing time is a natural progression or evolution.
14. It can help you take charge of your life in a new way, perhaps for the first time ever, which can be both exciting and scary.
15. It can help you learn to "Flip the Switch" and manage and control your emotions. See my post titled Disaster Relief: How to "Flip the Switch" on Your Emotions and Feel Better Now! From March 22, 2020.
16. It can help you learn how to generate your own happiness instead of letting the circumstances dictate how you feel and how happy you are. This is so important and I have a blog post on this titled How to Generate Your Own Happiness & Why It's the Skill to Learn, February 13, 2020.
17. It could help you get connected or reconnected with God.
18. It could help you grow and develop in so many rich and

compelling ways – it's growth and development. This is such a deep and amazing topic that I am a strong fan of, which you can read more about in my post titled Top 45 Ways that Personal Growth & Development Will Help You Have a Life You Love, November 29, 2019.

19. It could help you deal with your feelings of depression, overwhelm, anxiety, fear and low self-esteem once and for all. I have blogged about these emotions in several posts, which I highly recommend: Dealing with Overwhelm: How to Put an End to Feeling Overwhelmed with Life Once and For All Plus 29 Tips to help you in the Meantime, November 6, 2019; Dealing with Depression – 43 Tips to Help You Stave Off Depression, January 20, 2020; Worry & Fear Hurt Your Health: 15 Tips to Overpower Fear & Worry & Start Taking Risks, March 4, 2020; Is Low Self-Esteem Stealing Love, Joy & Happiness from Your Life? Top 29 Tips for Boosting Self-Esteem Like a Boss, March 6, 2020.

Life is changing. How things will end up remains to be answered. What is clear is that we are up against it. We are in a group trauma. Not everyone is experiencing a trauma, but a very large percentage of the world is in a trauma right now. It is hard. It is going to be hard – for a while. And in the midst of this time of difficulty – there are plenty of things that can be done to help you get through each day.

**Top 29 Tips to Help You Get Through It**

1. Be all about integrity. Be your word. Keep your promises. It will help you feel better.
2. No gossiping. There is no integrity in gossip.
3. Laugh as often as possible. Watch comedies. Tell jokes. Make funny videos to share.
4. Give LOVE.
5. Remember YOU ARE ENOUGH.

6. Work on healing yourself – through growth and development. After all, most of you have time right now.
7. Give generously to others if you can.
8. Don't take yourself too seriously.
9. Believe in a higher power like God or something good.
10. Take care of your body.
11. Take care of your mind and spirit.
12. Socialize by calling people, getting on Zoom or some other platform or other communications tool.
13. FORGIVE – Forgiveness is for you not the other person. Forgiveness does not mean forget.
14. Distance yourself from negativity.
15. Don't watch the news! Turn off the news because it is NOT helping you. If anything major happens, someone will call you or you will find out about it on social media.
16. Let life FLOW – don't force things.
17. Don't give away your power -ever.
18. Figure out what you can do to make the world a better place – and start making plans to do that.
19. Clean up or organize your living space, or anything.
20. Be authentic and vulnerable. More about that in a post titled The Power & Magic of Vulnerability: Top 10 Ways You Can Start Increasing Your Ability to be Vulnerable, March 10, 2020.
21. Be PRESENT. Live in the now.
22. Do anything that is creative – art, hobbies, etc.
23. Keep a journal. If you have never done that – it's a great time to start.
24. Boost your coping skills and mechanisms. Why not?
25. Set up a reward system to get yourself motivated! I am a fan of this and do it all the time. I have this covered in a post titled Self-Motivation: The Nuts & Bolts of Leveling Up with a Reward System, February 18, 2020. It's effective and quite fun!
26. Listen to music that you love.
27. Go for a walk, which is allowed with social distancing. You

can even walk around your living space and get lots of steps. Trust me I have done that in bad weather when outdoor walking didn't work.
28. Set up events for the future to give yourself something to look forward to – reunions, potluck dinners, parties, road trips – this can really elevate your mood!
29. Spend time working on your hobbies! If you don't have any hobbies – now is the perfect time to start one. I am an absolute believer in hobbies. You can read more about this in my post titled How Hobbies Can Help You Love Your Life and the Top 23 Reasons You Should Hobby Up, December 11, 2019.

**Concluding Thoughts:**

With a few rare exceptions, most hardship or difficulties in life offer you potential gifts if you are open to them. How you react to hardship or difficulties can make you a better person and your life much richer and more powerful. That might not be how you are used to handling or dealing with hardship. I promise you as a trauma expert and someone who learned a long time ago how to have strong coping skills, habits and practices – you can not only get through this pandemic, but you can flourish. That might not seem possible to you now. I am asking you to trust me and have some faith.

How can I help you get through this pandemic with a more powerful and happy life? What do you need? The whole point of my blog is to help my beloved readers to live a LIFE that they LOVE. It is about developing the skills, habits, practices, attitudes and beliefs that provide you with a powerful life full of love. I know how hard life can be as someone who is starting over in life at age 58 with pretty much nothing – unrelated to the pandemic. Trust me I know how painful this is for you right now. It breaks my heart that you and the world is experiencing this right now. I wish it was not so. But it is our new reality and how you deal with it will impact your life moving forward. Please let me know how I can support you during this time of hardship.

## The Coronavirus Tipping Point: Which Way Will You Tip?

April 2, 2020

The largest percentage of the world's population is in the vice grips of a host of negative emotions including fear, anxiety, depression, worry, anger, resentment, and a sense of helplessness among others. Many people are unmotivated, bored, unhappy, struggling to get through the day and just unsure of what to do. That is completely reasonable. Life as we knew it has disappeared and has been replaced by uncertainty. We have never been in this position before or at least most of us have not.

This is familiar territory for me. This is the commodity that I trade in: how to deal with horrific hardship and be happy and well in the face of severe adversity. My life has been anything but easy for the last 25 years dealing with 3 concurrent traumas for much of that time - all out of my control. I know what it is to be forced to home school three children for much of 15 years. I know what it is like to start over at age 58 with pretty much nothing. I know what it is like to be forced to borrow money to pay 72% of the marital debt while you are unemployed in a state where marital debt is split 50/50 and the other party is making significant money. Trust me, I know the meaning of having the rug pulled out from under you and having your entire world upended. I totally get it.

It is extremely humbling. And humility is a gift. Sometimes you have to have your world turned upside down to get the Grace of humility. Humility is gift often arriving after some disaster or catastrophic loss. I am lucky because I had the coping skills, habits and practices to deal with multiple concurrent traumas and not be disabled or ruined by it. I had the attitudes and beliefs as well as emotional skills to not be crushed by what I went through. I am extremely fortunate in that regard. I am also a better person for having been through it although I would never wish it on anyone.

I have a tremendous sense of urgency to help people because I understand the things that people need to do to come out of this and be okay or flourish. I have an unwavering commitment to help people get through this because I see that as possible for people. This Coronavirus pandemic provides a tipping point for individuals, families, businesses and organizations as well as entire nations. The question is which way will you tip?

The tipping point is defined as the point at which a series of small changes or incidents becomes significant enough to cause a larger, more important change. A tipping point is the critical point in an evolving situation that leads to a new and irreversible development. Another way to explain a tipping point is that it is a turning point. This coronavirus pandemic offers you a turning point in your life and which way you tip is largely dependent upon what you do today, tomorrow, in the next week and in the coming months.

Regardless of how functional you were before the pandemic – this situation offers you a turning point or a chance to make your life better. This offers you the time to reflect upon what you want in your life or don't want in your life. It is a rare pause that you can take advantage of if you choose. Several things will help you tip this situation in your favor.

Psychological resilience is the ability to mentally or emotionally cope with a crisis or to return to pre-crisis status quickly. The condition of resilience happens or exists when a person uses mental processes and behaviors in taking care of oneself and protecting oneself from the possible negative impact or effects of the crisis or stressors. This is exactly what my last 6 blog posts have been devoted to. What do you need to do to not only survive the Coronavirus pandemic but to flourish? What are the things you need to be doing? How are you going to take care of yourself emotionally, mentally, physically and spiritually?

According to Courtney E. Ackerman, MSc. In her 9/26/2019 article titled *"How to Measure Resilience with These 8 Scales"*, there are 10 components of Resilience. You can find her full article here: https://positivepsychology.com/3-resilience-scales/. Here is her list of the components:

## Components of Resilience

1. Optimism
2. Altruism
3. Moral Compass
4. Faith & Spirituality
5. Humor
6. Having a role model
7. Social supports
8. Facing fear
9. Meaning or purpose in life
10. Training

Wow. That's great some of you are thinking. I know that most of you are not feeling optimistic at the moment. I understand. You might not be able to find much humor in life right now. And it is painfully obvious that too many people are feeling fearful and panicked. The issue is not how you are feeling right now, the issue is that you are probably not dealing with your feelings. The issue is that most people don't know how to deal with, process and manage their emotions. This is a definite skill that you can learn.

I would assert that learning how to deal with, process and manage your emotions is the most powerful or one of the most powerful gifts you could ever give yourself because once you have that skill – you have it for life. Your emotions control much of your life. Do you know how to manage or control your emotions? You can learn to change your emotions on a dime, in what I call "Flipping the Switch". I am a huge fan of what is called high emotional intelligence or high emotional quotient and have blogged about that too. If you want to learn how to master your emotions, I would start with these posts on that subject:

1. Disaster Relief: How to Flip the Switch on Your Emotions and Feel Better Now!, March 22, 2020
2. The Juicy Good Parts of the Coronavirus PLUS the Top 52

Things You Can Do to Make This a Good Thing in Your Life Now, March 15, 2020
3. The ONE Coronavirus Article That Could Change Your Life for the Better Forever, March 24, 2020
4. 17 Potential GIFTS of the Pandemic & the Top 29 Tips to Help You Get Through It, March 29, 2020

The feelings associated with a lack of resilience include anger, sadness or depression, guilt, anxiety or fear and embarrassment say authors of the book *The Resilience Factor*, Karen Reivich and Andrew Shatte (2002). Guess what a lot of people are feeling right now? Yes. Anger, sadness, depression, anxiety, fear, and so on. To be able to get back on track, even with things in a state of uncertainty, you need to be able to shift your emotional state. Otherwise you are simply stuck feeling bad. Unmotivated. Unhappy.

I call being able to change your emotional state "Flipping the Switch". And I refer to the actions necessary to offset a negative situation counterbalancing. You need to counterbalance the negativity in the world or in your life right now. Counterbalancing negativity works extremely well. So you have the Coronavirus pandemic at the moment, which you can't control and is obviously negative. You can counterbalance the negativity of the Coronavirus pandemic by engaging in self-care, making phone calls to family and friends, spending time working on a hobby, or any number of things. In fact, in my March 15th, 2020 post I listed 52 things you could do to make your life better – all of which fall under the counterbalancing category. Put things into your day that make you happy. While that is not going to change the external world and what is happening it will change your mood, your feelings and what you are able to accomplish.

Life is hard. There is no doubt about that. Life is also beautiful, fun, sweet, memorable. Life is what you make it. You can sit around and do nothing just waiting for things to go back to "normal" or the "new normal" or you can grab life by the hand and rush headlong into planning your delicious and fabulous future. For me it's always about carpe diem – seize the day. Make hay while the sun shines. Live. Laugh. Love. Especially the love part. Why the heck not? It feels better and is way more fun than being the victim to the circumstances. We are all in this together and together we can do anything.

**Concluding Thoughts**

Two questions come to mind here. How resilient are you? And, how happy were you really before the Coronavirus pandemic? We know that a very significant percentage of the world was unhappy prior to the pandemic. We know this because of the volume of researchers who research happiness and how to be happy and as a subset the amount of unhappiness people experience. If you were not that happy prior to the Coronavirus, then this is a chance for you to re-evaluate, reassess, reconsider how you live your life. This could be a tipping point for your life to change for the better.

Which way will the Coronavirus pandemic tip you? Will you be able to find the silver lining for yourself? Will you be able to grow and develop new skills and abilities that make your life so much better? Will you grow your coping skills? Will you work on self-care? Can you find your way to seeing that you have control over how this pandemic affects you in the future? How can I help you? What do you need to be well supported? I want you to make it through this with flying colors looking back at the awful mess and be able to say that you learned from it, you grew from it and your life is better as a result. I believe that can happen. Let me help you!

## The Do's and Don'ts of Handling Challenging Times

May 21, 2020

When times are challenging or difficult often times negative emotions come to the surface like fear, anxiety, depression, anger, and worry to name a few and occupy way too much of your time. This is what I blog about how to be happy or how you can be happy when times are hard. If you have never experienced prolonged hardship then you might not be trained in the Do's and Don'ts of handling challenging times. There are just things that you should NOT do when life is hard. If you are experiencing depression you will also find help in my post titled "Dealing with Depression – 43 Tips to Help You Stave off Depression from January 8, 2020 (https://lisaalundy.com/empowerment/dealing-with-depression/), or if you feel stuck you might need a stopgap measure to help you get turned around, which I offer in a blog titled "Disaster Relief: How to Flip the Switch on Your Emotions and Feel Better Now from March 22, 2020 (https://lisaalundy.com/empowerment/disaster-relief-how-to-flip-the-switch-on-your-emotions-and-feel-better-now/). A stopgap measure or technique will help you in the short term. The long term solution is learning how to powerfully cope with life and to develop the habits and practices that will see you through challenging times.

Even without a pandemic, life is often very, very hard or challenging. My Love.Life.™ Blog is devoted to helping you get through life and find happiness and joy or at the very least peace when life is hard. There are practices, habits, attitudes and coping strategies that can help you be very functional when life goes south. Another post that might help you is "How to be Happy When You Are Suffering or Life is Bad" from November 15, 2019 (https://lisaalundy.com/empowerment/how-to-be-happy-when-suffering/). Obviously, pandemics and lockdowns are extremely hard. There is no dispute about that. And there is the fact that life offers many situations that are so painful during normal times.

## Examples of Hardship & Challenges Found in Normal Life

1. Death of a loved one or friend
2. Loss of a job
3. Financial problems and bankruptcy
4. Divorce
5. Abusive or toxic relationships
6. Lack of the basics: food, housing, security
7. Health problems
8. Being a caregiver of any kind
9. Losing people to suicide (an added impact to just death)
10. Having your money stolen
11. Being exploited or betrayed
12. Traumatic accidents of any kind
13. Loss of a pet
14. Dealing with a special needs child or adult (and the special challenges that brings)
15. Never getting married if you desired that
16. Never having children if you wanted that
17. Other broken dreams or unfulfilled desires that can be crushing
18. Dealing with someone who is addicted to drugs or is an alcoholic

I just happen to be someone who is highly skilled in dealing with hardship and life's challenges. To tell the truth, I am actually a trauma expert who knows what it takes to have happiness even when life is excruciatingly difficult or challenging. Says someone who is starting over in life at age 58 with basically nothing. Yes, I am well aware of how hard life can be. At the same token I know how to be happy regardless of the circumstances, which you can find out more about in this post titled "How to Generate Your Own Happiness & Why It's the Skill to Learn This Year" from February 13, 2020 (https://lisaalundy.com/empowerment/how-to-generate-your-own-happiness/). I have compiled my top Do's and Don'ts

Love.Life.

from years of experience. I know, I am so lucky! Haha. Not kidding though. Like everything else, this is my opinion based on lots of practice.

## The Do's and Don'ts of Handling Challenging Times

The Do's and Don'ts of Handling Challenging Times
© Lisa A. Lundy www.LisaALundy.com
Love.Life.™ Blog

| DO's | DON'TS |
|---|---|
| 1. Watch or listen to anything inspirational, entertaining or uplifting – books, videos, movies | Turn off the news of any kind! If something happens, trust me someone will let you know. It doesn't serve your emotional state or wellbeing to watch the news. |
| 2. Take a shower or hot bath – every day. | Don't skip bathing as tempting as it might be. You will feel better, smell better, and have an improved mood by taking a shower or bath. |
| 3. Get dressed up or put on your outside clothing on. | Just say no to PJ's all day or slopping sweats and old t-shirts. You will absolutely feel better when you put on your outside clothes. |
| 4. Pull yourself together by doing your normal grooming – hair, makeup, shaving, jewelry – whatever you normally do. | Skipping your normal grooming routine is not going to help you feel better. Even if you are not going to see anyone it will help you feel better and help you with motivation. |
| 5. Limit your TV/Netflix to X hours in the day or evening. You can even use your TV/Netflix as a reward for doing chores or other projects on your list. | Binging on TV or Netflix all day or night is not going to leave you feeling empowered. It is not going to forward your life. Putting a limit on it or use it as a reward will go a long way to productivity and feeling good. |
| 6. Minimize contact and interactions with negative people or situations that will bring you down. | Spending time with negative people or in negative situations can be very draining. Just say no. Do what you have to do to avoid anything negative. |
| 7. Limit alcohol or just say no. Same thing for other addictions. | Day drinking should be reserved for tailgates, parties and special events. You will feel better by skipping or reducing your addictions. |
| 8. Increase your nutrition in any way that you can. | Eating junk food all day long will not help your health or help you feel better. Trust me any improvements you make in your diet will yield big results. |
| 9. Limit your feeling sorry for yourself or pity parties to a specified and short period of time like maybe 10 minutes a day or something reasonable. | Prolonged pity parties that go on all day or for days on end are not going to help you. Grieve the loss/losses you are experiencing and then start moving forward with positive things. |
| 10. Work on building your emotional intelligence and empowering attitudes. | Skip the negative or defeatist emotions and attitudes. If you have a tendency towards being a pessimist, I would suggest "The Power of Positive Thinking" a decades old book that has helped so many people get out of dark places. |
| 11. Learn to look on the bright side or find the silver lining of situations. It can be done. | It is time to stop catastrophizing and thinking and believing the worst of things. It is simply not an empowering way to live life. You can learn to change the way you think. |
| 12. Focus on building and creating your life to be what you want it to be. By doing that you | Worrying is not a good use of time and energy. It is draining to spend time worrying. You can learn to |

**The Do's and Don'ts of Handling Challenging Times**
© Lisa A. Lundy www.LisaALundy.com
Love.Life.™ Blog

| | |
|---|---|
| will be focused on things that bring you happiness and joy. | do productive things with your life and to stop worrying. |
| 13. DO SOMETHING – walk, clean, organize anything. You will have a better sense of wellbeing by being productive. | No one feels great about wasting time and lazing around. To truly feel better get busy and do something you will not only feel better but you will get something done! |
| 14. Spend time doing a hobby or start a new one if you need to. | Being bored is not empowering. Boredom doesn't have a positive feeling associated with it. Get busy doing a hobby to feel better. |
| 15. Pray or Meditate to improve your emotional state. | Feeling anxious, fearful or afraid does not contribute to wellness or wellbeing. There are several things you can do to reduce feelings of anxiety, worry and fear covered in my blog beyond prayer and meditation. |
| 16. Make a plan for your life and your future. | To reduce or end feelings of helplessness and feeling out-of-control, make a plan for your life and start to execute your plan. |
| 17. Deal with any anger or feelings of resentment because that is important to your wellbeing both emotionally and physically. | If you don't deal with your feelings of anger or resentment, it is likely that you will either turn those feelings inward on yourself or outward towards others. |
| 18. Get your head in the game and skip the blame game because that is not helpful. | Whatever happened is water under the dam. Get over it. Move on. Focus on the future and creating the life you love. |
| 19. No one is ever happy in the divisive, bad-mouthing, corrupt world of politics. Let other people deal with that. Learn what you need to in order to be able to vote, but it's not going to help you to get involved in political fighting. | Stay out of political discussions and fighting. Focus on things that empower your life and move you towards your future – the future you are creating. |
| 20. Design your life. Create your future. Live the life you have always wanted. | Don't stay stuck. Get in action to pull yourself forward into a future of your design. You can do it! |
| 21. Deal with your problems instead of being in denial about them. What problems do you have and how can you solve them. Ask for help if needed! | Being in denial can be helpful at times. Yet what is even better is dealing with your problems head on. What needs to be done to take care of your problems. |
| 22. Make a list of what you could be doing instead of complaining or whining. List goals or projects – anything! Just make a list and get to it! | Complaining or whining is not going to get you anywhere. Limit the time you spend complaining and whining if you want to feel better sooner than later. |

Now the question, do I really do the things listed in the table above? You bet your bottom dollar I most certainly do. Why? Because this really works. Of course I do because I practice what I preach. I have been doing the things that I blog about since college or you could say for a very long time as in decades. From the above table of 22 Do's and Don'ts, I will give you my top 10 habits to start working on if you don't already have them in your arsenal of daily habits.

*Love.Life.*

. . .

**Top 10 Habits to Have in Challenging Times:**

1. **Self-care on a daily basis.** See my post titled "Self-Mastery, Self-Motivation, & Self-Care: The Holy Grail of Happiness & Joy" from January 30, 2020 (https://lisaalundy.com/empowerment/self-motivation/).
2. **Walk.** Unless you have mobility issues walking is a low-impact, easy, free activity that will benefit you emotionally, psychologically and physically. Even if you simply shoot for 10-15 minutes a day. Make this a habit.
3. **Deal with your emotions.** Here is the really, really great news – dealing with your emotions is a skill set that will provide a lifetime of benefits. It's never too late to learn how to deal with, process and manage your emotions. You can find some help for this in the post titled "Top 17 Benefits of High Emotional Intelligence and the 29 Traits of People Who Have It" from October 25, 2019 (https://lisaalundy.com/empowerment/benefits-of-emotional-intelligence/).
4. **Start directing your life.** You will feel ten or twenty times better on a daily basis when you are directing your life. It's one of the things that most people just don't do. I talk about directing your own life in most of my blog posts and the place I would start is early on in the post titled "Road Map for Creating a Life that YOU LOVE" from September 2019( https://lisaalundy.com/empowerment/road-map-for-creating-a-life-that-you-love/).
5. **Improve your nutrition.** Any little thing that you can do to improve your nutrition is going to help your emotional, psychological and physical health. Simple little things like substituting one healthy food for one junk food, or drinking more water, or reducing your sugar intake. There are so many things you can do here or there. You will find out what I have to say about nutrition in this post

titled "The Ultimate Consumer Guide to Nutrition, Why It Matters and How It Could Save or Change Your Life" from October 29, 2019 (https://lisaalundy.com/empowerment/the-ultimate-consumer-guide-to-nutrition/).

6. **Do things that make you happy.** I am well aware that most people that I have coached over the years do not have a list of things that make them happy. And that is one of the things that clients end up making in the coaching process. How are you ever going to be happy if you don't even know what makes you happy. Once you understand what makes you happy you can then sprinkle your day and life with those things. My post titled "Level Up Your Happiness" from September 25, 2019 might help you with that (https://lisaalundy.com/empowerment/level-up-your-happiness/).
7. **Use a Reward System to Motivate Yourself.** It's frequently hard to establish new habits especially if they are habits that are foreign to you. Using a personally designed reward system that you design for yourself will absolutely help you get and stay motivated. I have been doing this for decades because it not only works but it is FUN! For more on how to set up your own personal reward system, look at my post titled "Self-Motivation: The Nuts & Bolts of Leveling Up With a Reward System" from February 18, 2020 (https://lisaalundy.com/empowerment/self-motivation-with-a-reward-system/).
8. **Pray or Meditate.** I personally pray daily because I find it calming, it lines up with my religious and spiritual beliefs, and it is grounding for me. If praying doesn't light you up maybe meditation would be of value. This falls under the heading of being mindful. Clearing your mind and getting centered, grounded, or whatever you want to call it.
9. **Ask for help**. While asking for help is never on anyone's list of "oh yeah, I want to do that" kind of thing, asking for help is sometimes the thing that is called for. There are people who WOULD help you if they knew that you

needed help. There are people who would be extremely happy to help because it would give them JOY and Happiness to contribute to you. I am actually terrible at this, and yet I do it when I have to. I am not saying that you have to like it. Just be open to asking for help as the situation calls for.

10. **Pick an affirmation that is healing or appropriate for you.** If are struggling in life, prone to negative thinking, have feelings of anxiety, depression, etc. then affirmations are a great way to start to change the wiring of your brain. It can be a very simple affirmation or statement. Here are a few examples: I am absolutely good enough. Happiness is a choice and I choose to be happy. I don't have to be perfect. God loves me. One of my new 2020 favorites is actually a refrain from the "I Surrender Novena" which is: "Oh Jesus, I surrender myself to you, take care of everything." An affirmation, simple statement or short prayer can help you in several ways.

**Call to Action**

More people in the world are struggling now than ever before. If you found some value in this blog post please help others by sharing it on social media. What are the specific areas that you are struggling with? How can I help you? Please leave me a comment with what I can do to support you to thrive and flourish in challenging times. I feel a deep sense of urgency to help people. How can I do that for you?

**Getting Unstuck – Pandemic Style**

June 3, 2020

Long before we had a pandemic it was not unusual for people to arrive at a space or time in their lives when they felt stuck. Now, with the current pandemic we have more people than before who are out of sorts and who are feeling stuck. The pandemic has caused catastrophic financial losses for many people around the world. There are businesses that will never reopen. You might be in a financial crisis personally and feel stuck about that. Millions and millions of people are in a position that they have never been in before and as a result they are at a loss for what to do. Then there is the emotional and psychological impact of being in a lockdown or sheltering in place for months. Many people are feeling frightened, anxious, worried, fearful, angry, resentful, and so much more.

Many people don't know how to deal with the emotions that they are feeling because most of us don't get any training in how to deal with our emotions among other things. Feeling stuck or being stuck is separate and distinct from other emotions that I have written about thus far. It has its own unique cast. I wrote about dealing with your emotions in my post titled: "Disaster Relief: How to Flip the Switch on Your Emotions and Feel Better Now here from my March 22, 2020 post. If emotions are weighing on you then you might find other help in my post titled "Worry and Fear Hurt Your Health: 15 Tips to Overpower Fear & Worry & Start Taking Risks here from my March 4, 2020 post.

A huge number of people are now dealing with depression and my post titled "Dealing with Depression – 43 Tips to Help You Stave Off Depression" from my January 20, 2020 post can be found here. It's easy to see that many people might feel stuck right now. We had a fair number of people who felt stuck prior to the pandemic.

If you have never been in a position before where you felt stuck then this is brand new territory for you. However, for as long as human beings have been alive there have been situations and circumstances or events that propel people into feeling stuck. Let's define being stuck as: in a difficult situation or unable to change or get away from a situation; unable to move, or set in a particular position, place or way of thinking; and caught or held in a position so that you cannot move. When people are feeling stuck it can be caused by circumstances or an event, like a pandemic. It can also be caused by less than empowering points of views or ways of thinking, attitudes or beliefs. It can be caused by a number of things to be frank.

Totally separate from the pandemic, I want to give you some of the events or circumstances that can cause people to feel stuck, which should give you a good idea that it's just common. It just happens sometimes for different reasons. This is my own list from years of coaching and working with people.

## Reasons Why People Get Stuck in Life

1. They suffered a loss or a trauma.
2. They had a bad childhood.
3. They suffered some abuse.
4. They were exploited or betrayed.
5. They experienced a divorce or a relationship breakup.
6. They lost a baby or a child.
7. They are a caregiver of any kind.
8. They feel trapped by their circumstances regardless of what the circumstances are.
9. They never learned the habits and practices for living life in a highly functional way.
10. They lack emotional skills and abilities.
11. They live in fear, anxiety, depression normally.
12. They had an accident or experienced a significant health problem.
13. They live life as a pessimist or have some other negative belief system.
14. They blame others for their plight in life.
15. They have anger, resentment or rage issues.
16. They live in a false reality or are in denial.
17. They don't understand themselves and what makes them tick.
18. They have experienced broken promises or shattered dreams.
19. Life did not go the way that they had planned.

20. They lack motivation, support or the knowledge on how to get unstuck.

Here is the bottom line. It doesn't matter what led you to be feeling stuck or how you got there. What matters is that you recognize that you are feeling stuck. Acknowledging that you are feeling stuck is the place to start. Just being able to say that you are feeling stuck can be very freeing especially if you don't hold that as a bad thing. Being stuck is neither good nor bad. It's just how some people feel. It's not an empowering feeling to be sure. But it's not bad or wrong to feel stuck. Feeling stuck week after week or month after month is not good for your emotional state or your health. So, while feeling stuck is neither good or bad – it is a state that you want to move out of by taking specific actions simply because it is not an empowering state to stay in.

What I have to offer you is the components for getting unstuck. I base this on years of helping people get unstuck because one of the primary reasons that people seek coaching is that of feeling stuck or unhappy with their lives. It's not the only reason that people seek coaching, but it's up there as a reason.

## Components of Getting Unstuck:

1. **Commitment to getting unstuck** – There is no way around this so I will be direct. To get unstuck you have to have a firm, unwavering commitment that you are simply unwilling to tolerate being stuck any longer. There's no room for half-heartedness. You have to be of the mindset that you are sick of it and ready for a change. Sometimes people will say that they are committed or that they are ready to make a change but they are really not ready, willing or committed. Having a steadfast resolute attitude to do whatever it takes is critical to getting unstuck.
2. **Openness to ask for help/Get coaching/Find support** – The reality is that if you are open to change

and willing to do the work, you can find lots of valuable support for yourself. If you are open to getting unstuck you will find 39 separate blog posts on this site to help you create a happy and fulfilling life regardless of how you are feeling even though they do not specifically deal with being stuck. One of the ways that I personally use my own blog is to help clients that I coach by assigning them to read my blog. It's really quite handy for me. I wish I had thought of that back in 2005! It is likely that you have people in your life who would be happy to support you in getting unstuck if they knew that you wanted their help. While some people can get unstuck all by themselves, more often than not people need a little support to do what is necessary.

3. **Do the work/Take the coaching** – If you are open to getting unstuck then this won't be so hard. Changing your life can be invigorating and fun. It simply doesn't have to be hard or difficult. I believe in making life fun whenever and wherever I can. Why not? You could take on getting unstuck as a fun journey into growth and development. I mean you could do that. Or you could have it be some kind of chore. It's your choice.

4. **Do a reality check** – Are you living a true reality or a false reality? Get grounded in a true reality. By the way, the whole concept of psychotherapy is talking with a licensed therapist to do a reality check and see if your map of life matches up with your real life. You don't have to go into therapy to do a reality check. You can talk to your close friends or family, coworkers, neighbors, etc. and see what unfolds in the conversation.

5. **Make a list of things that make you happy or bring you joy** – Most people don't have a handy list of the things that make them happy. Moreover, most people I coach really have to think about what makes them happy. So, if you don't know what makes you happy then you are in good company. Think about it. Happiness doesn't have to be an elusive concept. It's available to everyone. Make a

list of all the things that make you happy or bring you job. Then your job is to sprinkle your day with those things – here or there. This activity will not only help you get unstuck but is a lifelong habit that will help to give you a life that you love.

6. **List and triage your problems or issues** – Getting unstuck involves being able to be frank about what you are dealing with and beginning to deal with those issues or problems. Make a list of all that needs to be dealt with and then prioritize them. I like to call it triaging my tasks. Yes, that is a valid use of the word in case you are wondering. This can be confronting if you have a lot of problems or issues. I have great compassion if that is the case for you. I also know that being honest about your life and all that involves is the only way to create a powerful, happy and joyful life. This is also why I recommend that you have support as you move through the process of getting unstuck.

7. **Begin to deal with your problems** – Some people like to avoid problems and/or pretend they are not that bad. We call that minimizing your problems. That works in some cases for a little while however it is never a long-term solution and can lead to much bigger problems down the road. The best way to deal with problems is head on. Figure out what needs to be done. If you don't know what to do then you could always research your problem. There are a multitude of resources available to you if you are open to it. Most people, even when faced with multiple, large-scale problems begin to feel better when they start making a plan for how to deal with their problems – even when they have huge problems.

8. **What areas do you need to grow and develop to move forward powerfully** – Understanding what areas of yourself or your life you need to grow and develop is extremely powerful not just for getting unstuck but for life in general. I am personally a huge fan of personal growth

and development. That is the substance of what I write about. If you are new to the concept of personal growth and development, I would love for you to look at my post titled "Top 45 Ways That Personal Growth & Development Will Help You Have a Life You Love" from November 29, 2019 here. Sometimes the reason a person feels stuck is because they have a life issue that they have never dealt with like low self-esteem, which is a very common life issue and you can read my post about that here. Growth and development will definitely help you not only get unstuck but it will also help you from getting stuck in the future! Now, that is what I am talking about!

9. **Weekly support and accountability** – In my humble experience, most people need regular support when they are embarking upon making a change to their life. So, if you want to be successful, then it's always a good idea to have support. Who is going to hold you accountable for your commitments during the process of getting unstuck? You could subscribe to my blog and get my new posts by email. You could enlist a friend to go on a fun journey of changing your lives together. In a few weeks I will be announcing a special campaign with great giveaway items to help support people on their journey to a better life. An easier life. So, watch for that because I am committed to helping people not only get unstuck but having amazing and beautiful lives that the love.

10. **Celebrate every single accomplishment** – I mean: Every. Single. One. No kidding. When you take on making a change to your life it's extremely important to celebrate every single thing you do to improve your life. Why not? There's no reason not to acknowledge yourself and celebrate. It always feels good to celebrate so that's just one more reason to do it.

11. **Get a personal reward system** – As soon as it is feasible, implement a personal reward system to help keep your motivation levels up. If you are like most people, this

is a new concept to you! Not to worry, I have an entire blog post titled "Self-Motivation: The Nuts & Bolts of Leveling Up with a Reward System" from my February 18, 2020 post here. This is something that I have all of my coaching clients do early on. Why? Because it is effective. It supports you with motivation and gives you good feelings. I simply love this idea and use it myself as I have for many decades.

12. **Rewire your brain** – It can be extremely powerful to start rewiring your brain for success, which you can do with affirmations, tapping, prayer, meditation, and so on. Because of neuroplasticity of the brain, we now know that your brain can be rewired. It's pretty exciting stuff. Sometimes people get stuck because they have disempowering thoughts about themselves like "I'm not good enough" or "No one cares about me" or "Nothing good ever happens to me" or anything else along those lines. Often those thoughts can be laying around in your subconscious mind. You will want to rewire your brain with more empowering, loving and positive messages.

13. **Self-care is critical** – Getting extra sleep, unless you are oversleeping because of depression or feeling stuck, increasing your nutrition and engaging in self-care is very important to helping you get unstuck. If you are not sure what I mean by self-care, I cover it in my post from January 30, 2020 titled "Self-Mastery, Self-Motivation, & Self-Care: The Holy Grail of Happiness & Joy here. I am a huge fan of doing whatever it takes to be healthy and well, and you can read more about health and wellness in my post on nutrition here or my post on 8 ways to improve your health and look younger here. The more you take care of yourself and your body, the healthier you will be.

14. **Go easy on yourself** – It's all too common that people are extremely hard on themselves expecting perfection or beating themselves up when they don't get things right. Self-compassion not only feels better but is better for you. This is not an overnight process. Do your best to appreciate

that you are doing what few people in the world will actually do – improve yourself and your life. Life is not about being perfect. Enjoy the journey.

15. **Know that you CAN DO IT** – Even if you don't have the self-confidence or belief that you can do it – I know that you can! I am absolutely positive that you can do this. You can get unstuck. You can have a better and happier life. Trust me. And you are going to have to take specific actions to get unstuck. There is nothing magical to it. I am giving you the formula for getting unstuck knowing that you can do it. I am sure of it.

16. **Learn to deal with, manage and process your emotions** – Part of getting unstuck is learning to deal with how you are feeling. Learning to identify, deal with, manage and process your emotions is an extremely valuable skill set. Extremely valuable. You will find support in this in the previously mentioned post from March 22, 2020 here and also from my post titled "Top 17 Benefits to High Emotional Intelligence and the 29 Traits of the People Who Have It" from my October 25, 2019 post here.

17. **There's no room for negative thinking or being a pessimist** – It's the old is the glass half full or half empty question. Which feels better to people? I still have half left? Or it's halfway gone? It's the same amount in the glass but clearly thinking you have half left is a more positive view. Negative thinking is never going to get you a powerful life. It's just not. If you have a tendency towards negative thinking or being a pessimist, then I would recommend that you start working on changing that right away. The book titled "The Power of Positive Thinking" by Norman Vincent Peale, which was written in 1952 is a classic that has helped millions of people.

Well, I could just stop there. Or could I? No. I am so committed to helping you get unstuck that I want to take a minute and give you the contrast of what I call the keys to a powerful, happy and contented life. This is just my list boiled down into the fewest points that I can and still feel like it is a complete list. In my humble opinion it gives you a glimpse of what you are striving for in the long term. Yes, this is completely doable. Yes, I actually live this way. And yes, I may be starting over at 58 years of age with basically nothing but I am happy. I have a rich life. I feel great and I am well loved.

**Keys to a Powerful, Happy & Contented Life:**

1. **Know yourself.** Or start getting to know yourself. The more you understand yourself the easier life is. The better you know yourself the more you can set your life up to make you happy and give you joy.
2. **LOVE More.** Focus on putting more love in your life. Love your friends. Love your family (if you can). Do things that you love or bring you happiness or joy. Be intentional to bring love and joy into your life.
3. **Have guiding principles or a moral code to live by.** To live a healthy and powerful life you need to either have religion or some moral code to live by. It has been written that people who either subscribe to a religion or believe in a higher universal power that dictates morality and behavior are psychologically healthier on average than those who do not (M. Scott Peck, M.D., *People of The Lie*).
4. **Run your life with high integrity.** Keep your promises. Do what you say you will do. If you can't keep a promise then get in communication and say that. See my post on this titled "The Sheer Joy and Magic of Integrity" from October 9, 2019 here.
5. **Be intentional and design your life.** Take back your power by being intentional and designing your life how you would like it to go. You only get one beautiful life. How you live it is up to you.
6. **Increase your emotional intelligence.** Learn how to

process, manage and deal with your emotions. I have mentioned two posts on that: here and here.
7. **Practice daily self-care.**
8. **Take care of your body.** I promise you this – the better you take care of your body, the better it will work for you. I mean getting enough sleep, the right nutrition, walking several times a week or some other form of exercise and of course socializing as much as you can or want to.
9. **Have boundaries.** If you either don't have or understand boundaries, it's time to start.
10. **Deal with your issues**. If you have trust issues then deal with them. If you can't be vulnerable, then deal with that. Whatever your issues are just deal with them.
11. **Change how you view failure**. If you viewed failure like Albert Einstein or Henry Ford you would probably try lots of new things and not particularly care if you failed or were successful. You could celebrate every failure because you took a chance.
12. **Learn the habits and practices that will give you the life you want and deserve**. What do you need to learn? What habits do you need to take on? Self-discipline? Self-motivation? Time management? Organization? Whatever it is – do it.

**Call to Action**

If you want to get unstuck you will need to take actions to move yourself forward. There are over 38 other blog posts filled with information, habits, practices and more to help you create a powerful life. You really can get unstuck. You really can be happy. You can do this. I am here to help you. If this has been helpful in any way, please hit the share button to share this with your friends. And please let me know how I can support you in getting unstuck.

# MISCELLANEOUS

## Why It IS Okay to be Mad at God and What to Do If You Are Mad at HIM

February 11, 2020

It was 1995 when someone first suggested that I was probably mad at God and that it was absolutely okay to be mad at God. I had lost my first daughter, Christina, when I was six months pregnant and had been told that I would have to have a hysterectomy compounding my grief over the loss of my daughter with the broken dream of never being a mother. Yes, I was mad. Probably more like furious. I remember going to pick up her ashes from that place – looking at this plastic brown box, sans any marking but a piece of paper with her name on it – and thinking that this was just cruel. How could a loving God allow such hardship and suffering? It was unthinkable to me at the time.

In the past 25 years, I have had plenty more opportunities to be mad at God, get over it, and get mad again like when I found out that over 2 decades of my life had been a total lie, or that I was starting over at age 58 with basically nothing. Yes, I have had plenty to be mad at God about over the years.

I have had many memorable conversations with priests, nuns and laypeople on this topic starting in 1995. This is not some blasphemy or heresy. I have spent 25 years discussing this subject with anyone who had an interest. Of note, I spent a decade helping some Catholic cloistered nuns and that provided some exceptionally sweet and very rich opportunities for religious discussions. Being mad at God is not something that we often discuss, yet I believe it is so worthwhile. And I can only speak about this from the Catholic perspective. Perhaps in other Christian religions or other religious denominations being mad at God is not okay. I am completely confident that it is absolutely okay in the Catholic religion.

If we are fortunate to live long enough we all get the chance to experience disappointments, broken promises, shattered dreams, losses of all kinds, the death of loved ones, deep betrayal, and pain. When we have a relationship with God, HE – our Heavenly Father – expects us to have these human feelings and HE understands. In order to be mad at God, you have to have some sort of relationship with HIM. Let's face it, we can all get mad at strangers, however unless you have really low self-esteem, or other issues like holding grudges, etc. most of us don't hold onto anger with a stranger. It comes and goes quickly and is forgotten. So being mad at God is reasonable if you have a relationship with Him. Or even if you don't, you could start a relationship with God by being mad at Him. Before I talk about how you might deal with being angry at God I want to pause and talk about why this is so important AKA the benefits to a belief in God.

**Benefits to Believing in God:**

Since we could also call this blog, "The World According to Lisa" (Haha), I am going to give you my rendition of why believing in God is so powerful. I never knew until recently that believing in God and religion was a coping mechanism or strategy. Wow! I just never,

ever knew that. Not a surprise given that I had also never thought about my own coping mechanisms or strategies. So, this is my take on the benefits to believing in God – from the Catholic perspective.

1. God is LOVE. Belief in God is belief in Love and all things good.
2. Provides guidelines for moral living.
3. According to M. Scott Peck, M.D., people who believe in God or a 'higher power' were psychologically healthier than people who did not. (from *People of the Lie* by M. Scott Peck, M.D.)
4. Provides eternal hope – for eternal life and Heaven.
5. Provides a powerful context for suffering (Jesus on the cross for example).
6. Provides a powerful context for evil.
7. It's a good coping mechanism or strategy.
8. You are NEVER alone when you have God, Jesus, and the Holy Spirit (The Trinity).
9. Provides a community.
10. Provides a purpose – you are working your way to Heaven.
11. Provides the space the miracles to occur – with God ALL things are possible.
12. Significant comfort when loved ones pay away to have the belief in Heaven and eternal life.
13. Provides a "super hero" mentality that GOD has your back – the Most Powerful Entity in the Universe cares for you! HE has a better plan for you.
14. Provides the Corporal Works of Mercy
15. Provides the Spiritual Works of Mercy
16. Prayer provides comfort, peace, healing, strength, and more.
17. Confession – teaches self-forgiveness, self-compassion, forgiveness of others, humanity.

To me, that is an amazing list of benefits! To me, the above list is exceptionally powerful. And this is why, in my humble opinion, it is important to understand that is it okay to be mad at God and have an idea of what to do about that because you would never want to give up that list of benefits permanently or at least I hope not.

The first step in dealing with any situation or problem is to acknowledge it. Acknowledge that you are angry with God and have that be okay. It doesn't matter what you are angry with God about, big or small, just own that you are mad at God. Acknowledge the loss, the pain, the disappointment, the broken promises or shattered dreams. Give words to your situation. Then I would suggest that you start the grieving process and feel your feelings. There is a progression to grieving anything, which humm…not sure I want to get into that right now, but at any rate – start grieving. Feel your feelings.

While you might not feel like it, it can be very therapeutic to pray to God while you are angry and furious. Let's face it, don't you want your children, if you have them, to express their anger at you when they are angry? I sure hope so. God, as our Heavenly Father, expects us to have the full range of emotions that HE designed us to have. HE, as our Father, can take us being angry with HIM. Trust me, HE can take it. So, when you are furious, angry or mad, it's the perfect time to tell God how HE let you down. Vent. Express. Rage if that is your style. Get it all out of your system. And then do it again if you have to.

Keep the Faith.

Eventually, your anger will subside. Then you can look at what there is to grow and develop in your spiritual life. A few years ago, when I found myself in a rather unpleasant and frankly shocking situation, of course I was angry with God. Once I cooled off, I did an inventory of what I could grow and develop in my spiritual life and set some goals to grow my spiritual side. One of the goals that I set back then was to increase my prayer life. While I had always been a fan of prayer and praying, especially praying for others, it just seemed to me that I could increase my prayer life. And so, my children and I embarked on memorizing new prayers at part of the process. In hindsight, this was a rich gift to me. I can't say that I was thinking that at the time when I was in the throes of such extreme difficulty and hardship. But then that's how life goes. We can look back and see how God has used hardship and difficulties to make us be better people.

Hardship either makes you better or bitter. You get to choose.

Talking to a priest or other religious person can help. So, can books, DVD's, and other materials. The most important thing is to understand that it is okay to be mad at God. And you will eventually get past it with time, prayer, and sometimes some support from your peeps. I have found it very freeing to be able to own when I am mad at God. It's an opportunity. Having the faith that HE has a better plan for me than I could ever have for myself – now that is powerful. That's the kind of power that I would never give up. I would only temporarily get mad and then get over it.

**Concluding Thoughts:**

I wish for your this beautiful life that you LOVE. I want you to LOVE your LIFE. And we all know that life is hard. Sometimes so, so hard. Having a belief in God can be overwhelmingly positive and helpful. So, if you happen to be out of sorts with God, perhaps you are mad at HIM. And that would be a powerful place to start.

How can I help you LOVE your LIFE? What do you think about being mad at God? What can you grow and develop in your spiritual life? What is on your heart and mind today?

**FORCED Home Schooling: Short Cuts to Better Results**

April 1, 2020

I spent about 15 years of my life home schooling three children, about 12 or so of those years being forced to home school against my wishes. So, I completely understand the position so many of you are in now being forced or feeling forced to home school. My three children are all in college now with two of the three in the honors programs at their respective universities and the third one having had very close to a perfect score on the SAT without any major studying or preparation. While I was home schooling against my will I did the best job I could because my children deserved that much. Clearly, I didn't do too badly.

My degree was in marketing so I did not have an education background. I learned the hard way what worked and how to do things. Today I want to offer you some short cuts for better results. By the way, the easy way for one parent to force another parent to home school their children is to refuse to sign the matriculation paperwork to register a child into the school district. Most states require both parents' signatures to register a child into a school district unless there is a protection from abuse order or a custody agreement allowing one parent that authority. So that is a little-known fact that is true in New York State and Pennsylvania or at least the 2 districts I was in at the time.

Let me address your emotional state right up front. You might be a little upset to very upset, worried, panicked, anxious, depressed, angry and so much more. The more you can deal with your emotions the better you will be able to deal with home schooling – an added burden for you or very likely so. I have put up several blog posts on how to deal with your emotions. So, if you go through the last 4 posts you should find ample support. The reason that I mention this is because your children are most likely going through some emotional struggles right now too. Now is the time to train yourself on how to manage, process and deal with your emotions because then you can role model that for your child or children. The other reason I mention this is because high stress impacts a child's ability to learn. So there is an extremely high amount of value for YOU to learn to deal with, process and be able to "Flip the Switch" on your emotions so you can help your children learn that too.

Before I get into the short cuts it is worth mentioning that there are different ways of learning – something that I was late to the party on. If you look online you will find that some educational sites say that there are 4 ways of learning while others say that there are 7 or more ways of learning. What is important here is that some children learn better in one format and the more you can gear your educational efforts in the format that your child learns best in – the better results you will get.

One common list of methods of learning is the VARK list, which stands for V-visual (seeing or watching); A-auditory (hearing); R-Reading/writing; and K-kinesthetic (doing, touching and interacting). Out of doing the home schooling for 15 years I learned that I am a visual learner – I learn better when I can see something. I also learn well with reading and writing. My children varied in how they learned best. Once I caught onto that I could better tailor the structure of the curriculum to their individual learning styles. It's wonderful if you can have a course or a class that incorporates more than one method of learning.

Here is one other **GOLD NUGGET**: When your child has some autonomy in selecting the specific area of focus for his or her school project, paper or school work – you will get SIGNIFICANTLY better results. Why? Because they are working on a subject or topic that THEY are interested in. For example, one of my kids had to write a paper on a current event, which might have been in the 7th grade. In any case, I gave my child the newspaper and said, pick a current event that interests you. He did. Then he proceeded to dive into the topic, that HE picked, and he wrote a 12-page paper on it! Twelve pages! That far exceeded the minimum. He did that because he was engrossed in a subject that he selected.

### Write Reports

I figured this out relatively early on, thankfully. If you have your child write reports, hopefully on a subject they have selected, they will learn how to research a topic. They will practice their language arts skills of writing. I firmly believe that writing a report is a much better way to get the subject matter to "stick" and be remembered because (1) they are learning while doing the research, and they are (2) covering the same material when they are writing the paper. To really boost this to the next level – have your child give oral presentations on their report. Yes, we did that. Often.

Having your child give an oral report to me is the double whammy of report writing. If you want the triple win then ask your child to give the oral report with "pizzazz", which means something special like a visual display to accompany the report. When the Korean news station (MBC) came to our house in 2007 to do a news story on us because they viewed me as an allergy expert in the U.S., one of the pieces they were interested in covering was the home schooling aspect of our life. So, one of the kids gave an oral report with their visual display – and the producer's mouth fell open. She could not believe it. She had lots of questions. You could tell she was amazed.

My children wrote reports in science and history. They wrote lots of reports, which means that I corrected and coached them on how to write a better introduction and conclusion as well as how to organize their papers. And they learned how to write pretty well. And I have no doubt that they were better able to recall materials from reports than from other learning structures like on-line courses or simple reading and take a test. Just my two cents.

### Make Maps & Timelines & Notebooks

One of the best things I discovered although late in the game was the high value of making both maps and timelines. The kids and I made world maps for high school and it was extremely valuable. In a do-over situation I would start having the kids make maps in early grade school. Number one it is far more interesting than most geography course work and number two there is a lot you can do with the map. You can even do historical maps for battles and specific time periods. Along with maps I would highly recommend timelines. You can tape 8 ½" x 11" paper together end to end to get a long piece of paper. It is a visual way to put history in perspective and there is a lot you can do with a timeline.

I happened to have a roll of brown craft paper for our world maps, but any paper will do. The other thing that worked well was having the kids make notebooks on specific subjects like the Presidents of the United States, and they also had a book of the states. These made learning much more interesting because they were working on a project while learning.

## Hands on learning (kinesthetic)

Whatever you can do to incorporate hands on learning will really help you get better results in my humble opinion. One year I did a horticulture and agriculture class for the three kids and as part of that we planted a cover crop over a 5-acre piece of land BY HAND. Basically, we had buckets of seeds that we hand cast over the 5 acres. Do you want to know what they all said? This will never work. These seeds will never grow. Of course, it was an opportunity to teach how many people in other countries cast seeds by hand over their land. Of course, you know that the cover crop grew. It was a very memorable experience.

Hobbies can offer a huge potential for learning and can be incorporated into your learning program. Building things, cooking foods, doing experiments are all great ways to provide valuable learning experiences for your children.

## Arts & Crafts

For very young children, doing arts and crafts is an excellent way to build fine motor skills, which is something that I did not know early on. Art for any age child or adult provides for an emotional release or at least it can – if not it at least provides a distraction for daily life. It counts for school. Because art is so important and can really be valuable to students, I am going to give you a few ideas of things you can do – while you are sheltering in place with the items you already have laying around.

You don't have to have an arsenal of arts and crafts supplies if you know about the term ephemera. Ephemera is various items, often printed or written ones, that were originally expected to have only a short-term use. You can use ephemera to make beautiful artwork. Examples of ephemera include:

- New or used gift wrapping paper
- Old tea boxes, cereal boxes, or boxes from whatever
- Clippings of pictures or whatnot from magazines
- Words cut out of old magazines
- Stamps from the mail that you get
- Labels from canned goods
- Pages from a old book that is no longer useful
- Junk mail often has some good useful parts to it
- Old ticket stubs or movie stubs
- Play money from an old Monopoly game
- Old candy wrappers

I think you get the idea. You have items where you live that could be used for art that falls into the ephemera category. Kids usually pick this up very quickly and can see and find ephemera fast. So what would you do with the ephemera you are asking yourself! Perfect question. I will introduce you to what is called Artist Trading Cards or ATC's.

Artist Trading Cards are 2.5" x 3.5" sized pieces of art. You can cut out 2.5" x 3.5" sized pieces of paper or cardstock if you have it. Then you can draw on the ATC. You could paint on it if you had paints, but a very fun thing you can do is to use ephemera to collage onto the ATC. I will include some pictures to give you a visual. This is a very easy project and kids of all ages love it. Trust me I have done it with very, very young children through teen agers to adults. You can find books and lots of materials about artist trading cards online. You are never supposed to sell them though. You can trade them with people, but you are not to sell them.

The other thing that you can do with ephemera is make journals with them using the ephemera to cover note books. I love making blank journals covering inexpensive composition books. I will include a picture or two. The other thing you can do that is fun is use the ephemera to cover an old shoe box. The possibilities are many!

Another thing that my Mom, who happens to be an artist, introduced us to is what is called a 30 Days of Drawing Challenge. Get some paper and each day, every day, you draw. Just start drawing. You can look at pictures from a magazine or a book. You can find something online that you want to draw. Just keep drawing. If you do this with your children you will be amazed at how much better you become at drawing in 30 days. We loved this challenge and did it several times. You have paper and pencils or pens. This can be very fun. When we did the 30 Days of Drawing Challenge we did not show each other our drawings and instead did a reveal at the end of the 30 days over a special dinner. I can't tell you what a fan I am of this. It's fantastic. I can absolutely say that I learned to draw by doing that challenge – a few times.

**Adventure Novel**

One of the products that I happened upon later in the game was a product called "Adventure Novel" by Daniel Schwabauer, M.A., which is a DVD series with workbooks. It is absolutely amazing! While we started this late in the game, I still remember components of the "Adventure Novel" DVD all these years later! That should tell you something. If you are in home schooling for the long haul or you just want to help your child write really compelling novels, then I would recommend this product. I don't remember the cost of it but it was well worth it – whatever I paid for it.

*Love.Life.*

## Concluding Thoughts

Home schooling has been around since the beginning of time. It was the way of the day before the one room school house. We have had U.S. Presidents who were home schooled – two I believe but don't quote me on that. You can do this. It is not as hard as it seems although you may be feeling overwhelmed. There is a tremendous amount of online support materials available for free. Let people know what you need. Ask for help. Don't be embarrassed or afraid to say – what is the best way to do this or that?

I hope that you found this somewhat helpful! That was at least my goal. If so, please share this on social media We are all in this together. The more we can help each other the better things will be. How can I support you in this? What questions do you have? I hope you can find some joy in the process. Even though I was forced to home school, I found happiness and joy in much of it because that is what I do. I wish you the best! Please let me know what I can do for you!

# A GLIMPSE INTO MY OBSERVATIONS OF THE WORLD AT AGE 22

The writings that follow were written when I was about 22-years old. It will give you a good glimpse into how and what I was thinking at that age. This is what survived decades of moves. Each of these was untitled and paired with a picture that was glued to colored paper and given to women in the sorority that I was in. I'm going to number them although they were not numbered back in 1982-83 and give you the subject for each. Each one with L.A.L. at the end (my initials).

## #1. Being Alone

At one point or another, everyone feels alone in this seemingly over populous world;
Whether it is a lone walk on a snowy trail,
Or an evening spent by yourself;
This is a time to think, evaluate, and grow.
But out of this feeling, comes a deep appreciation for others and the friendships that grace your life.

Always remember that, and your times alone will have so much more value.

© 1982-1983, Lisa A. Lundy

## #2. Being Caring

The quality of caring is so intangible; and yet, it is so distinguishable.
It is being there for someone in need.
It is a feeling of empathetic compassion; it is the utmost sign of friendship.
The quality of caring is so often not commended; and yet, it is never unappreciated.

© 1982-1983, Lisa A. Lundy

## #3. Being Unique

Nothing can match the feeling of independence felt when soaring through the air unencumbered by anyone or anything.
Nothing can match the feeling of independence felt when you act only to suit yourself, and not those around you.
Nothing can match the unique personality and fine characteristics that you possess.
Nothing can match the radiance that you give off by just being you; so be that and nothing more, and the world will be a wealthier place because of it.

© 1982-1983, Lisa A. Lundy

## #4. Friendship

Friendship is the unbelievably comforting warmth of having a companion;
A special individual caring for you and about you,
Whether it be in the moments that the sun graces your life with sunshine and the beautiful moments, or whether it be in those moments that the sky clouds over and darkens your life.
And never can you offer anyone more than the warmth of a shoulder in their times of need.
Open your heart to those around you; offer that special gift of friendship, and your life will never be the same.

© 1982-1983, Lisa A. Lundy


## #5. Being Individual

Doing your own "thing" however isolating it may seem, never fails in giving you a strong sense of identity.
Whether it be skiing down a snowy white slope, taking a long walk, or joining a group separate from your mainstream –
Doing your own "thing" is vital to your own sense of well-being.
Remember this always and you will be uninhibited in doing your own "thing" – whatever it may be.

© 1982-1983, Lisa A. Lundy


## #6. Going for It

The world is a revolving mass, just waiting for you to conquer it. You may not realize it at present, but you do possess all the character and strength necessary for you to make your mark upon it. Strike out and forge your very own path.

And the reward you feel for doing so will be unmatched in your lifetime.

© 1982-1983, Lisa A. Lundy

## #7. Inner Peace

Being true to yourself brings with it an inner serenity unequaled by anything else; it is knowing that no matter which way the wind blows or the tide flows, you will continue to sail peacefully.
Let not others guide what you say or do, or you will feel an anchor holding you still.
Rather, sail alone following your own feelings and instincts; for it is then that you really will feel strong and capable; and live in inner harmony.

© 1982-1983, Lisa A. Lundy

## #8. Friendship

Friendship is one of the most beautiful aspects of life; it adds sunshine to a dark and rainy day, and sparkle to an already glorious afternoon.
In and of itself, friendship is comforting like a light shining through a snowy storm.
The friendships you acquire throughout your lifetime, will vary in magnitude and duration; but never in the comfort that they bring to your life.

© 1982-1983, Lisa A. Lundy

## #9. Learning from Hardship

Each and every life event has truly good and beautiful points to it.
Some, like the glowing sunset or a warm friendship, are more obvious than others.
Some, like a raging thunderstorm or a bad experience are less obvious than others.
Search for the good and the beautiful in each and every person and every event, and you shall find it.
And your life will be so much richer as a result.

© 1982-1983, Lisa A. Lundy


## #10. Being Responsible for Your Life

Sailing your own boat is akin to doing your own thing.
You follow the breeze to some degree, but for the most part are responsible for the direction your boat takes.
Life is so much like sailing.
There are those around you that function like a breeze; but in the end, you alone are responsible for your actions and the direction of your life.
Sail your boat with strength and determination and you will never falter, even if there is no breeze for guidance.

© 1982-1983, Lisa A. Lundy


## #11. Love

Love, it is the essence of life, the essence of all meaningful relationships.
Love, it is warm, caring, sharing, supportive, enduring, and trusting; it is given from the heart.

Love, in its most powerful form develops over time; with years of careful nurture and patience.
Love, and you will most certainly be loved.

© 1982-1983, Lisa A. Lundy


## #12. Friendship

Opening your heart and soul to others in friendship means taking a risk; the risk that they will not accept you for what you are or for the value you place on their companionship.
But this risk is not at all much different from the risk you take when you hand glide, move, or accept a new job.
Be not afraid to open yourself to those surrounding you so that you can soar to new heights, and have a richer life because of it.

© 1982-1983, Lisa A. Lundy


## #13. Being Unique

There are many landmarks in this world that mark eras in time. They signify a variety of different peoples, ideas, dreams, thoughts, and efforts; but there are two things that they all share – they have survived centuries of time, and they are unique in and of themselves.
Individual so to speak.
So hold your head high and be your very own landmark and all around you will be richer for it.

© 1982-1983, Lisa A. Lundy

## #14. Gratitude

Standing for a moment on a coastline, mountain top, or ridge serves to increase one's appreciation for the surrounding scene.
And so it is with life.
Stop and take a moment to take in all that surrounds you; and your appreciation for life, for those who truly care about you, and all that you are fortunate enough to have will multiply tenfold.

© 1982-1983, Lisa A. Lundy

## #15. Peace

Peace is a state of mind that comes from being in a familiar setting, being around people who care about you, or even just knowing that you are in a warm, safe environment.
When you are at peace, everything else in your life seems to flow so much more smoothly and the colors of the world seem so much brighter.
I wish you peace now and in all of your life adventures – that your life will flow smoothly and the world is the brightest possible colors.

© 1982-1983, Lisa A. Lundy

## #16. Gratitude

Being out in natures is one of the most calming things in life.
When you are outside you cannot help but marvel at the colors and complexity of all of God's creations.
People are unique just as all of the living growing plants and animals in a serene forest.
Remember this and appreciate each individual that you come into contact with in your life; and you will find the world so much more pleasant.

© 1982-1983, Lisa A. Lundy

**#17. Friendship**

Friendship is one of those things that money just can't buy; it is available to all people at all times no matter what their occupation, race, religion, or socio-economic status.
Friendship is lending an ear to someone who wants to talk, casting a knowing smile to someone who cares, doing a thoughtful deed for no particular reason.
All you need to have friendship is an open mind and a giving heart – all of which you have in abundance.
May your life always be graced with rich friendships.

© 1982-1983, Lisa A. Lundy

**#18. Being Unique**

Being unique is something that brings a very special beauty to this often cluttered and busy world.
It means stating your opinion, and doing what you feel is right. And all the time knowing that you are serving to accentuate the beauty of being an individual.
Like the rock formations in an ancient canyon that radiate their splendor through the diverse colors and shapes that compose it so too, can you radiate splendor in the groups to which you do and will belong to in your life by…being unique.

© 1982-1983, Lisa A. Lundy

## #19. Be Yourself

Strike out on your own, and discover your own inner strength and beauty.
Like rowing your own boat, you will find that in individualism there is a serenity unparalleled in any other form.
You will find that standing out on your own does not necessarily mean being alone.
Be yourself, for no one can do that with such unequivocal success.

© 1982-1983, Lisa A. Lundy

## #20. Gratitude for Difficulties

A brilliant sunset's beauty is intensified by the contrasting dark clouds interspersed within it.
Life is somehow just like that picturesque sunset.
The truly great and wonderful days, the brilliant colors are intertwined with the not so wonderful gloomy days, the dark luminous clouds only to emphasize the really good things in life.
Appreciate those glorious colors in your sunset and remember the purpose of the darker, ominous colors and your life will be that much richer.

© 1982-1983, Lisa A. Lundy

## #21. Patience

Patience…is one of those qualities that everybody thinks everybody else should have more of.
Patience… is best exemplified by waiting, whether it be a young puppy waiting for its master's return, or a young woman checking the mail daily for that special letter.

Patience…is knowing when to hold your tongue and when to turn the other cheek.
Patience…generally comes with maturity, and is demonstrated through acts of love.
May the patience you so often show to others spread to those around you, that the world might be a better place.

© 1982-1983, Lisa A. Lundy


**#22. Being Unique**

Being unique is like being a windmill, a rare wildflower or an endangered species.
It is not something that everything or everyone can be no matter how hard they try.
Being unique is believing in yourself and the worth of your ideas and actions.
It is not something that comes easy for most people in this world.
Being unique is one of the most valuable things you can bring to the world around you; so be unique and relish in knowing that you are that special.

© 1982-1983, Lisa A. Lundy


**#23. Being All In**

There is nothing in this world that compares to the exhilaration of putting your all into a project or task.
It is not so much the final outcome of the effort; but rather knowing that you put most into it that you could.
Rejoice in not the end happenings in your life…whether you win or lose, but rather in all that went into it.

© 1982-1983, Lisa A. Lundy

## #24. Generosity

Giving to others is so often overlooked in this fast paced and hectic world.
Giving to others is something done from the heart and never motivated by anything but the warm glowing feeling that results.
Giving to others is what makes you the very special person that you are.
Remember that in the quietest, darkest moments your giving to others does not go unnoticed – so give to others and you will receive back in triplicate what you give.

© 1982-1983, Lisa A. Lundy


## #25. Dealing with Difficult Days

Fishing out on a sea is calm and peaceful.
Yet not always.
The waters of the sea can be rough and risky.
Such it is with life.
Mostly there will be days when you sail through life happy and content with life.
Yet not always.
There will be days when life seems dark and gloomy and when you will question life and your position in it.
It is then that your inner strength will surface to make the sailing safe so that you will indeed make it back to the shoreline.

© 1982-1983, Lisa A. Lundy


## #26. Being an Individual

Sometimes you may fear that you will lose your identity when you belong to a group.

*Love.Life.*

Just as a building in a city may seem insignificant compared to the whole.
In the city, it is the variety of the buildings, ages, purposes, and architectural structures that give the city its character.
And so it is in a group.
The individual personalities come together to give the group character and strength.
Never be afraid to be yourself, to speak your own mind, and be your own person
For that is what the group values most of all.

© 1982-1983, Lisa A. Lundy

## #27. Goodness

A light shining through darkness serves to emphasize the intensity of the darkness and also the intensity of the light.
And so, being a caring individual serves to emphasize both the good and bad in the world.
But the contrast really only helps to point out and reinforce those really good things in life making them seem all the stronger.
Let your personality shine so that it will intensify the good in this world to those surrounding you.

© 1982-1983, Lisa A. Lundy

## #28. Love

Nothing compares to having people care for and about you.
It's like being out in the chill of winter and coming home to find a light on and someone waiting up for you.
It comes not so much out of obligation, but rather from love given from the heart.

LISA A. LUNDY

May you always experience a light waiting your arrival, and the heartfelt love that accompanies it.

© 1982-1983, Lisa A. Lundy

# CALL TO ACTION

Life has always been difficult. Long before we had a pandemic, life was hard for many people because they grew up in mildly to highly dysfunctional families, or because they grew up in poverty, or because of many other circumstances beyond their control. Life was hard because people didn't learn the life skills, habits and practices, attitudes and beliefs that allowed them to be happy, healthy and very functional in life. Throwing a pandemic in the mix is just piling on. It is adding a burden to people already barely getting through life. Or getting through life on the surface but not happy inside. More people than ever are suffering deeply and need help but don't know where to get help or what kind of help would be beneficial to them. They just don't know what to do or where to turn.

My ***first call to action*** to you is that you start to learn how to be happy and healthy. That you create a happy life for yourself where you are well loved and you have the skills, habits and practices, attitudes and beliefs that will give you a happy and powerful life even when times are hard. By you taking on the changes that are needed or healing as applicable, you will create a ripple effect in your life. People will observe changes in you and how you are dealing with life and what you are doing in your life. Trust me, people will notice. Some people will follow your lead. I am asking you to be a leader in your own life and to set an example for others. Happiness is highly contagious. People will notice when you get to work on your life and have a newfound sense of peace, happiness and wellbeing. People will notice that.

My **second call to action** to you is that you share what you are doing and learning with your circle of people – those people who are in your life. My blog posts and YouTube videos (numbering over 118 at the moment) are all FREE. Nobody has to spend a dime to have access to my information. It was requested last year by one of my blog readers that I put my content into a book for ease of use, which I have now done. Yet, people can access all of my content for free. Let your people know what you are doing and where they can find support.

My **third call to action** is that you share my website (www.LisaALundy.com) and my YouTube channel (https://www.youtube.com/channel/UCN35joBFA9gQzPg1lQaAUTg) on social media to help people. By doing this, you can make a difference for others who are suffering. Yes, I am asking for you to be a leader in helping others, which you can do by simply sharing my content. We need everyone pulling together to help each other get through the toughest times we have known in a very long time. You sharing my content is a way to help others even though you might never know if or how you helped someone else.

My **fourth call to action** (I know, I'm so demanding- Haha) is that you let me know what other support you need to heal, to become happier, to get on with your life. What else do you need? I have a whole list of other topics to blog about so there are plenty of subjects that I have on my schedule. But what do you need? What is missing for you? You can let me know by posting a comment on my blog or YouTube videos. I am here to support you so please let me know what it is that you need.

# ABOUT LISA LUNDY: B.S., D.T.M.

The author of the best-selling gluten-free and allergen-free cookbook *The Super Allergy Girl™ Allergy & Celiac Cookbook*, Lisa A. Lundy, is the former Executive Director of the Integrative Medicine Consortium and a seasoned sales executive who previously worked with Xerox Corporation, Bausch & Lomb, and Rhone-Poulenc Rorer pharmaceuticals (Dermik Labs). On top of it all, she is a mother to three young adults whose goal in life is to help others master ways to be happier with their life via her Love.Life.™ blog, her YouTube video channel, this book, and her public speaking events and soon her Podcast of the same name Love.Life. ™.

Due to her daughter's premature birth, failure to thrive diagnosis, severe allergies, malnutrition, malabsorption, and other health issues, she was not predicted to survive or have a high quality of life if she did survive. Due to many factors, including expert integrative physicians, advanced medical treatments, and other interventions, Lisa's daughter not only survived but has broken all medical milestones and is a thriving young woman in the honors program at her college a year ahead of schedule.

Her daughter is not brain-damaged, has no cognitive or functioning impairments, and has avoided the heartbreaking medical prognosis given at age one. There are few success stories like this in the world, which has given Lisa the medical research and training to speak to laypeople in everyday language about a variety of health-related topics, in addition to the self-improvement topics covered in her content.

While Lisa was the first Executive Director of the newly formed Integrative Medicine Consortium (IMC), she also homeschooled her three children, marketed her Allergy & Celiac Cookbook, and participated in getting credentialed by Toastmasters International to the highest level of Distinguished Toastmaster (DTM) of which only 1% of Toastmasters ever achieve. All of these demonstrate her extraordinary time management skills. Lisa received her B.S. degree in Marketing from Penn State University where she participated in many extracurricular activities that provided leadership and growth opportunities.

Fully engaged in life, Lisa's hobbies include watercolor painting, paper crafting, sewing, soap making, walking and outdoor activities, teaching her dog new tricks and of course socializing with her peeps. She loves helping people have happier lives full of love, which inspired the theme of her blog: Love.Life.™

# BLOG POSTS – TITLE – DATE – CONTENT

1. Love.Life. – September , 2019

2. Living Life with Your Whole Heart September 2019

3. Road Map for Creating a Life that YOU LOVE. September. , 2019

4. LOVE the TIME of YOUR LIFE – September 12, 2019

5. The LOVE and POWER of Completion, September 16, 2019

6. Level up Your Happiness, September 25, 2019

7. 8 Ways to Improve Your Health & Look Younger, October 2, 2019

8. What Tripping Over the Truth Looks Like in Real Life- Ker splat, October 8, 2019

9. The Sheer Joy and Magic of Integrity, October 9, 2019

10. 10 Ways to Get Yourself Motivated for a Happier Life, October 15, 2019

Blog Posts – Title – Date – Content

11. Top 17 Benefits to High Emotional Intelligence and Why It's Important, October 25, 2019

12. The Ultimate Consumer Guide to Nutrition, Why It Matters and How It Could Save or Change your Life, October 29, 2019

13. Dealing with Overwhelm: How to Put an End to Feeling Overwhelmed with Life Once and For All Plus 29 Tips to help you in the Meantime, November 6, 2019

14. How to Be Happy When You Are Suffering or Life is Bad, November 15, 2019

15. Top 35 Ways that Making a List Will Help You Have a Life You LOVE, November 18, 2019

16. Top 45 Ways that Personal Growth & Development Will Help You Have a Life You Love, November 29, 2019

17. 21 Reasons Why Making Friends Will Help You LOVE Your Life & 17 Ways to Make New Friends, December 3, 2019

18. Here's How to Have the Best New Year of Your Life, December 5, 2019

19. How Hobbies Can Help You Love Your Life and the Top 23 Reasons You Should Hobby Up, December 11, 2019

20. Stress Kills Your Brain Cells – Here's 19 Strategies to Prevent that and help you To Be Happy & Healthy, January 2, 2020

21. Love & Miracles – How to Get More Love & Miracles in Your Life, January 8, 2020

22. Dealing with Depression – 43 Tips to Help You Stave Off Depression, January 20, 2020

23. Self-Mastery, Self-Motivation, & Self-Care: The Holy Grail of Happiness & Joy, January 30, 2020

24. Why It IS Okay to be Mad at God and What to Do If You Are Mad at HIM, February 11, 2020

25. How to Generate Your Own Happiness & Why It's the Skill to Learn, February 13, 2020

26. Self-Motivation: The Nuts & Bolts of Leveling Up with a Reward System, February 18, 2020

27. LOVE Involves Trust: Why It's Time to Deal with Your Trust Issues, February 28, 2020

28. Worry & Fear Hurt Your Health: 15 Tips to Overpower Fear & Worry & Start Taking Risks, March 4, 2020

29. Is Low Self-Esteem Stealing Love, Joy & Happiness from Your Life? Top 29 Tips for Boosting Self-Esteem Like a Boss, March 6, 2020

30. The Power & Magic of Vulnerability: Top 10 Ways You Can Start Increasing Your Ability to be Vulnerable, March 10, 2020

31. The Juicy Good Parts of the Coronavirus PLUS the Top 52 Things You Can Do to Make This a Good Thing in Your Life Now, March 15, 2020

31. Disaster Relief: How to Flip the Switch on Your Emotions and Feel Better Now!, March 22, 2020

32. The ONE Coronavirus Article That Could Change Your Life for the Better Forever, March 24, 2020

33. 17 Potential GIFTS of the Pandemic & the Top 29 Tips to Help You Get Through It, March 29, 2020

34. LOVE in the Midst of Chaos – And, Yes, I love you! March 31, 2020

35. FORCED Home Schooling: Short Cuts to Better Results, April 1, 2020

36. The Coronavirus Tipping Point: Which Way Will You Tip?, April 2, 2020

*Blog Posts – Title – Date – Content*

37. Do You Have these 8 Things That Will Help You Flourish in Life Regardless of What Happens? Hint: It's Not Too Late!, April 28, 2020

38. The Do's and Don'ts of Handling Challenging Times, May 21, 2020

39. Getting Unstuck – Pandemic Style, June 1, 2020

40. The Miracles of Gratitude, June 30, 2020

41. August: Awake & Aware, August 1, 2020

42. Feel Better Now with Self Care, August 4, 2020

43. Pandemic Sleeping Tips, August 14, 2020

44. The Road to Happiness Starts Here, August 20, 2020 (September Theme)

45. Deep Dive into Emotional Pain and How to Use It to Your Advantage, Sept. 8, 2020

46. Here's How to Ditch Loneliness and Isolation for Good, September 16, 2020

47. Healing Your Heart, October 1, 2020 (October Theme)

48. How Anger Can Help You Heal, October 7, 2020

49. The Healing Nature of Self-Compassion, October 15, 2020

50. Healing from Dysfunctional or Toxic Families and People, November 1, 2020 (Theme)

51. The Healing Nature of Assertiveness, November 9, 2020

# NOTES

## Nutrition, Health & General Wellness

1. Bozzetti F, Mariani L, Lo Vullo S, et al.: The nutritional risk in oncology: a study of 1,453 cancer outpatients. Support Care Cancer 20 (8): 1919-28, 2012. [PUBMED Abstract]
2. Hébuterne X, Lemarié E, Michallet M, et al.: Prevalence of malnutrition and current use of nutrition support in patients with cancer. JPEN J Parenter Enteral Nutr 38 (2): 196-204, 2014. [PUBMED Abstract]

www.ingramcontent.com/pod-product-compliance
Lightning Source LLC
Chambersburg PA
CBHW071223290426
44108CB00013B/1268